THE
BASEBALL STADIUM
INSIDER

THE BASEBALL STADIUM

INSIDER

A DISSECTION OF ALL THIRTY BALLPARKS, LEGENDARY PLAYERS, AND MEMORABLE MOMENTS

MATT LUPICA

FOREWORD BY STEVE BLASS

Black Squirrel Books™ 🐿️ ™
Kent, Ohio

BLACK SQUIRREL BOOKS™ 🐿️ ™

Frisky, industrious black squirrels are a familiar sight on the Kent State University campus and the inspiration for Black Squirrel Books™, a trade imprint of The Kent State University Press. www.KentStateUniversityPress.com

Every effort has been made to obtain permission from persons interviewed by the author to be quoted in this book.

ISBN 978-1-60635-250-2
Manufactured in the United States of America

Cataloging information for this title is available at the Library of Congress.

19 18 17 16 15   5 4 3 2 1

My dad, when he took me to the first game in Detroit, we were poor farmers and did not have good seats—we sat in the bleachers—but driving in from the farm, into Detroit and all the concrete and all that the metropolitan area represents, and as we got to the ballpark, the inside, we got our tickets and were about to enter, he stopped me and he said, "Now I want you to remember this experience," and I was eleven or twelve years old and it was after the war, and he said, "We are going into a ballpark. It is a park where they play baseball. Don't ever forget that—you are going to see a beautiful park" . . . and every time I go into a baseball stadium, I don't even want to say the word; it's a baseball park.

—Legendary sports broadcaster Dick Enberg

Dick Enberg is seen here with author Matt Lupica in a photo taken inside the visiting television broadcast booth at PNC Park in Pittsburgh on September 17, 2013.

CONTENTS

West Region

FOREWORD
STEVE BLASS

Like millions of other baseball fans, I remember every detail about the first time I walked into a Major League ballpark. It is, in every sense, a rite of passage in America.

For me, it was truly a momentous day. When I was a ten-year-old from the small town of Falls Village, Connecticut, my father drove us to Brewster, New York, and then we took a commuter train the rest of the way to Yankee Stadium.

While walking through the dark tunnel, underneath the stands, for a 1952 game between the Yankees and my beloved Cleveland Indians, my father took a quick glimpse at our tickets to confirm that we had arrived at our section. We suddenly entered the grandstand, and I got my first glimpse inside Yankee Stadium. The site was *breathtaking.* My first impression was how the perfectly manicured green grass looked like a bed of emeralds under the massive light towers. I then looked up to see the famous white façade stretch across the top of the upper deck. I glanced quickly at the small scoreboard in right field that—in just four years—would be the backdrop of the iconic photo of Don Larsen's last pitch of his World Series perfect game against the Brooklyn Dodgers. I had seen it all on television before, but now it was *live.* Now it was in *color.* And it all seemed so *massive.*

There is nothing like being in a ballpark in person. The sights. The sounds. And as a former Major Leaguer, I could certainly appreciate the memorable line given in the movie, *Field of Dreams,* when Shoeless Joe Jackson, played by Ray Liotta, said, "I'd wake up at night with the smell of the ballpark in my nose, the cool of the grass on my feet. The *thrill* of the grass."

The thrill of the grass, indeed!

Throughout baseball history, its ballparks have become a vital part of their communities. Ask an old Brooklyn fan what it felt like when the city took a wrecking ball to Ebbets Field after their beloved "bums" were moved to Los Angeles following the 1957 season. For so many, it was like a death in the family.

And as for Dodgers owner Walter O'Malley? Around the Flatbush Avenue part of the borough, it's been said that "If you asked a Brooklyn Dodgers fan,

'If you had a gun with only two bullets in it and were in a room with Hitler, Stalin, and O'Malley, who would you shoot?' The answer: 'O'Malley, twice!'"

The great Frank Sinatra even recorded a heartbreaking song based on the Dodgers' move entitled "There Used to Be a Ballpark." Can it hardly be a coincidence that Brooklyn struggled economically, and crime rose from almost the exact year Ebbets Field was torn down and continued for decades?

And spare me the argument that the Dodgers needed a bigger and newer ballpark than the jewel that was Ebbets Field. Fenway Park opened a year *before* Ebbets Field and seems to be doing quite well in its old age. And that other treasure, the one up on Chicago's north side, Wrigley Field, was opened just a year after Ebbets and continues to be as much a part of that city's soul as any other landmark.

As a Pirates pitcher in the 1960s and 1970s, my career was split between Forbes Field, an older park that opened in 1909, and Three Rivers Stadium, which had a design similar at that time to Veterans Stadium, Riverfront Stadium, and Busch Stadium. The modern Three Rivers Stadium was, naturally, more comfortable to play in, but I missed some of the grit of old Forbes Field. My only regret is that I miss the "ballpark smell" of Forbes Field. I know it was mostly a result of stale beer and cigar/cigarette smoke, but I miss it just the same.

My first experience at Forbes Field was for my tryout with the Pirates in 1960. To show how times have changed, following my workout, my father and I sat up in the stands to watch the Buccos play a doubleheader. By the fifth inning of the second game, there were streams of beer cascading down the aisles throughout the ballpark. Because the Pirates didn't sell beer at Forbes Field at the time, fans were allowed to bring coolers into the stadium, provided they bought an extra ticket for it. What a hoot!

Can you imagine any club passing on beer revenues today?

Dodger Stadium is another one of my favorite ballparks. The backdrop of Chavez Ravine and the pine and palm trees beyond the bleachers make it a beautiful place to play. But there is one reason why Dodger Stadium will always be close to my heart. It was the venue of my first big league win against none other than Hall of Famer Don Drysdale in his prime back in 1964. So one could conclude that some ballplayers have favorite ballparks in part because of the success or big moments they may have enjoyed in them.

Today, as a color analyst for the Pirates, I have the luxury of working the broadcast booth at PNC Park and looking out at one of baseball's most beautiful backdrops. Beyond the outfield bleachers, the Steel City skyline glistens behind the Roberto Clemente Bridge. And now that the Pirates' performance on the field has matched the stadium's brilliance, it's like a carnival atmosphere at every home game.

Enjoy this book about baseball's ballparks, where lifelong memories are made at every game.

Steve Blass pitched for the Pittsburgh Pirates in 1964 and again from 1966 to 1974, compiling an overall record of 103–76 to go along with a career ERA of 3.63. The pinnacle of his career came in 1971, when he helped lead the Pirates to their fourth World Series championship. In that series, Blass turned in two complete game wins, allowing seven hits and two runs over the course of 18 innings.

ACKNOWLEDGMENTS

I would like to thank the Major League Baseball teams and the individuals who assisted me in preparing the revised edition of *The Baseball Stadium Insider*. Whether it was getting me vital information regarding a specific attribute of the ballpark, or sending me a media guide to help assist in the research, it was greatly appreciated.

To the players, broadcasters, or managers who contributed quotes for this book, I want to express my gratitude that you took the time out of your schedule to speak with me. I know you are asked thousands of questions throughout a baseball career, but I hope that answering questions about the ballparks provided a change of pace and something different. Your insight contributed greatly, and I know that readers will be enlightened by your perspective.

I'd also like to give a special thanks to the following:

The Pittsburgh Pirates Baseball Club for all of their assistance along the way. From allowing me—with no hesitation—to conduct interviews with the players for this revision, to providing me with pictures, media guides, and anything else I needed, this team truly came through for me. I want to personally thank Dave Arrigo, Steve Blass, Buzz Gradek, Dan Hart, Neal Huntington, "Jimmy T," and the entire Pirates organization for their incredible willingness to do whatever was necessary to help me. The Pittsburgh Pirates organization is a class act, and I am forever grateful for their kindness to me when I was revising *The Baseball Stadium Insider*.

Baseball-Reference.com: If you are seeking in-depth information on the history of a franchise, players' statistics over the years, and past box scores, www.Baseball-Reference.com is truly an impressive compilation of statistics, all in one place. Thank you to Neil for letting me utilize the Web site as a reference for some of my material.

Baseball Pilgrimages (www.baseballpilgrimages.com): Many photos and coverage on both Major and Minor League ballparks can be found at this site. Graham Knight, the creator, has done an outstanding job in compiling the data. If you haven't checked this site, I highly recommend it, and there's even a baseball storefront to boot!

Most of the exceptional photos are from fellow baseball fans, who used Flickr to showcase their fine pictures, and who graciously allowed me to include them in *The Baseball Stadium Insider.* I want to personally thank Alicia Barnhart (be sure to visit her Web site, www.ballparksonabudget. mlblogs.com), Matthew D. Britt, Carol Ohler, Brian Skversky, Russel Tiffin, and Mark Whitt. I encourage you to visit Flickr and search for more of their outstanding work.

A special appreciation to the following individuals who have supported me from the start, and along the way have helped in some way: Bob Burton, Lanny Frattare, Steve Grande, Dan Hampu, John Kerezy, Rich Kipp, Jim McIntyre, John Patti of WBAL radio, *Wheel of Fortune* host Pat Sajak, Jake Schwartzstein, Gary Spring, and Steve Testa.

I also want to thank the people most important to me—my family. Thanks a million to my parents Pat and Jerry, my brother and fellow baseball fan Mike, and sisters Melissa and Michele. I appreciate your support and willingness to be there and keep me in check whenever necessary. I love you all very much. I also want to thank Emily; your encouragement and kindness in listening to me rant whenever I came across a rough patch while preparing this book assisted tremendously in getting me through it. I love you very much and am forever grateful that you are in my life.

Lastly, I once again would also like to thank you, the reader, for picking up a copy of the revised edition of *The Baseball Stadium Insider.* Please note that I have made a very conscious effort to include every detail from each ballpark, but it seems that every year, new things are added and others are taken away. For a more detailed look at retired numbers, pick up a copy of the first edition of *The Baseball Stadium Insider,* published in 2012. Rest assured, though, that this book is not only a great reference guide, but I believe the quotes from the players will help shed even more light on each Major League ballpark for years to come.

So go ahead, take yourself out to the ballgame!

A NOTE ABOUT THE QUOTES

Over the course of many years, I collected the over three hundred quotes in this book. My original goal was to include the players' quotes as part of the first edition, released in 2012. However, with the inception of new ballparks, coupled with the fact that I did not reach my goal of getting 10 quotes per Major League ballpark, I had decided to hold off and make it one of the focal points of this revised edition.

The interviews were made possible thanks to the Pittsburgh Pirates, Tampa Bay Rays, and Cleveland Indians organizations. As I am from nearby Cleveland, I was able to use PNC Park as my National League base and Progressive Field as my American League base. In essence, I was able to get all of the National League teams in Pittsburgh, and the American League teams in Cleveland. The Rays allowed me access during a trip to Tropicana Field in 2012. These organizations graciously provided me with a press credential, which allowed access to the home and visiting clubhouses, dugouts, press box, and field before the game.

In all, I interviewed over 130 baseball personalities, including broadcasters and managers, and the host of *Wheel of Fortune,* Pat Sajak. Sajak, who once hosted a show on Major League Baseball radio and a program about the ballparks in the past, kindly had a 40-minute conversation with me on the phone and gave me his thoughts about the ballparks and great moments in baseball, for which I am forever grateful.

Every effort was made to work with each public relations department to garner representation from each team. I know you will find the comments of those who are represented in the book both intriguing and interesting.

For the record, an attempt was made to conduct interviews with players from the Boston Red Sox and Chicago Cubs, but they were unable to accommodate my requests.

EAST
REGION

CITI FIELD
HOME OF THE NEW YORK METS

Citi Field, New York Mets (*Photographed by Mark Whitt/Flickr*)

When the doors to Shea Stadium closed following the 2008 season, the Mets left behind a ballpark filled with plenty of great moments. From the Amazin' Mets and their magical, astonishing World Series championship run in 1969, to images of Jesse Orosco throwing his glove in the air following a 1986 World Series come-from-behind victory over Boston, plenty of history had made its mark on the old ballpark over the course of 44 seasons.

The introduction of Citi Field was not without some indifference, with many fans voicing their discontent over obstructed sight lines and what they thought was too much emphasis on the Brooklyn Dodgers and their rich history over that of the National League's Mets. Despite it all, the opening of Citi Field represented a new era in New York Mets history, and it has fast become known for its reputation as a pitcher's park.

Plans to replace Shea Stadium officially got underway in the 1990s, when management unveiled their first ideas in 1998 of having a retractable roof and removable grass field—that is, one that would slide out into the parking lot and allow for other events to be hosted at the facility. The price tag for that proposal was exceptionally high, and the team scrapped it in favor of a far more conservative approach. Relocation was also on top of the list, and other potential spots included Mitchell Field and Belmont Park in Nassau County, Long Island, Sunnyside Yard in Queens, and West Side Yard in Manhattan.

New York City mayor and avid baseball fan Rudy Giuliani had a hand in the stadium situation and shortly before leaving office, he had a tentative agreement in place for both the Yankees and Mets to construct new facilities. With $1.6 billion on the table, an arrangement was proposed in which city and state taxpayers would pay for half of the construction costs while each team would be allowed to keep all of the parking revenue. When Michael Bloomberg assumed mayoral responsibilities, he triggered an escape clause, citing the fact that it cost too much money for the city to construct two brand-new ballparks.

The Mets finally got their wish for a new Major League ballpark when plans for Citi Field were part of a bid for the 2012 Summer Olympics. Although the city failed in its efforts to host the world's best, it helped kick-start the project Mets management had long been hoping for. The official model of Citi Field was unveiled on March 18, 2006, and construction began four months later in July.

The ballpark was finished well ahead of opening day in 2009, and fans attending games at Shea Stadium in its final year had the opportunity to see Citi Field take shape right from the comfort of their own seats. That's because the construction of the Mets' new digs was taking place just beyond the outfield walls. Another noteworthy accomplishment in getting a new home: The overall agreement included a 40-year lease that prevents the team from leaving New York through the year 2049.

SPECIAL FEATURES OF CITI FIELD

AUDITORIUM

The Auditorium and Business Center at Citi Field can impress potential clients and create an experience like no other. With a capacity of 150 theater-style seats, state-of-the-art amenities, and a stage, this spot can be rented on non-game days. Other services include Wi-Fi, printers, copiers, fax machines, and ports to charge electronic devices.

BOB MURPHY RADIO BOOTH

Dedicated on August 17, 2002, at Shea Stadium, the radio booth at Citi Field is named in honor of the Hall of Fame announcer who broadcasted Mets games from the team's inception in 1962 until he retired in 2003. From 1962 to 1978, Murphy teamed with Ralph Kiner and Lindsey Nelson to handle both radio and television broadcasting before Murphy assumed his role in the radio booth on a permanent basis in 1981. Prior to coming to the Mets, Murphy was a broadcaster with the Boston Red Sox from 1954 to 1959 and the Baltimore Orioles from 1960 to 1961.

CAESARS CLUB

Searching for incredible views? Want to kick back and enjoy a relaxing drink? Maybe you are hoping to recreate a taste of home and relax on a couch. All of that can be accomplished at the Caesars Club, which is behind the home plate area. Its sweeping views of the New York City skyline will make for great pictures, and a 50-foot-long full-service bar is available to the public. Comfortable couches complement 28 flat-screen televisions for your viewing pleasure.

CHAMPIONS CLUB

In the long-standing tradition of Mets baseball in New York, two teams have stood out above the rest: 1969 and 1986. Those legendary teams are appropriately honored at Citi Field in the Champions Club. Memorabilia, pictures, and other artifacts from those championship-winning clubs are on display, so fans can reminisce about the days when the Mets were truly amazing.

DIMENSIONS ALTERED

Prior to the 2012 season, Mets management took a good hard look at the outfield dimensions and decided, due to a lack of home runs and offensive numbers, that it was time to take action and alter the look slightly. The outfield walls were moved closer by as much as 12 feet, and were shortened to eight feet. A new wall, painted blue for the team's fiftieth anniversary, was built in left field and was moved four feet closer to home plate. In all, the biggest changes made include the left-center wall, which went from 371 feet to 358 and right-center, which went from 415 to 398.

FANFEST

Positioned on the concourse level, just behind the center-field scoreboard, is a fully interactive area that combines fun and excitement for fans of all ages. Among the highlights: A miniature Wiffle-ball field modeled after Citi Field, a batting cage, video games, and other baseball attractions that are sure to get the blood flowing.

HOME PLATE CLUB

Positioned directly behind home plate and featuring 1,600 premium seats spanning from dugout to dugout, this 22,500-square-foot restaurant, café, and lounge are certainly worth checking out for the fine dining and two full-service bars, which have the finest selection of liquor.

INFLUENCES

When Citi Field was constructed, it borrowed many ideas for features from existing ballparks. One of the major influences was PNC Park in Pittsburgh, a personal favorite of Mets COO Jeff Wilpon. In fact, the interior layout of Citi Field is based upon the home of the Pirates and mimics the Steel City structure. The stadium also incorporated snippets from Great American Ball Park in Cincinnati, Coors Field in Denver, and Citizens Bank Park in Philadelphia.

JACKIE ROBINSON

It makes perfect sense that the club would honor the late Jackie Robinson and his contributions to the game of baseball, and the Mets have made every effort to remember the legacy he left. Inspired by Ebbets Field, the Jackie Robinson Rotunda reminds fans of his accomplishments both on and off the field. For starters, the rotunda's 160-foot diameter is engraved with larger-than-life images that helped to define his values: *Citizenship, Commitment, Courage, Determination, Excellence, Persistence, Integrity, Justice, Teamwork,* and *Integrity.*

His famous line, "A life is not important except in the impact it has on other lives," is inscribed on the upper section of the rotunda. An eight-foot sculpture of Robinson's jersey number 42 is a popular spot for pictures and honors a man who broke down the walls of baseball's color barrier with the Brooklyn Dodgers in 1947.

The Jackie Robinson rotunda is a grand entranceway for fans. (*Photographed by Alicia Barnhart*)

METS HALL OF FAME

Each team celebrates their baseball history in different ways, but the Mets really went all out with the building of the Mets Hall of Fame and Museum, adjacent to the Jackie Robinson Rotunda. Introduced in 2010, the museum features plaques for Mets players who were inducted into Baseball's Hall of Fame, along with the World Series Championship trophies won by the 1969 and 1986 teams. Interactive touch screens were installed to take fans on an illustrated journey through the team's history, and selected memorabilia from previous players and managers are also on display.

METS, METS, METS!

There are constant reminders of great Mets players of the past, along with historic moments in the team's history, notably on the field and promenade walls. Championship banners, which were once just behind the left-field wall during the 2009 season, were moved to a new location on the Excelsior Level façade in 2012 and bring back memories of the glory days when the New York Metropolitans reached the pinnacle of success.

NAMING RIGHTS

On November 13, 2006, it was announced that the home of the Mets would be known as Citi Field, and that Citigroup, Inc. would be forking out $20 million a year for the next 20 years in order to have the sole rights to the name. It became the second Major League sports venue to be named after a corporate sponsor, following the then-Continental Airlines Arena in the Meadowlands, the former home of the New Jersey Nets.

ORANGE FOUL POLES

Historically, baseball has seen many ballparks rise and fall, and and although each has different dimensions and quirks, one factor has been a constant—yellow foul poles. That all changed when, while at Shea Stadium, management decided to paint the foul poles orange. Citi Field did the same, and continued a trend for using a color other than the standard yellow for the foul poles.

OUT-OF-TOWN SCOREBOARD

One of the largest out-of-town scoreboards in the league is on the front of the roof canopy in left-center field, and serves as a one-stop shop for all the latest and updated scores from around baseball. Two displays—American League on the right, National League on the left—feature a baseball diamond, which displays the runners and the score of each game. In addition, seats beneath the structure afford relief from the hot sun during the warm summer months.

RETIRED NUMBERS

The Mets have retired the numbers of five individuals who have made their mark on the history of the franchise, and are located in left field just behind the wall. They include: Gil Hodges (14), Casey Stengel (37), Tom Seaver (41), former owner William A. Shea (SHEA), and Jackie Robinson (42), whose number is retired league-wide.

RIGHT-FIELD PORCH

The right-field porch, one of the more nostalgic parts of Citi Field, evokes memories of legendary Tiger Stadium in Detroit and offers left-handed batters the opportunity to take aim and deposit a ball into the upper deck. This 1,284-seat section extends eight feet into fair territory and gives fans the sense that they are closer than ever to the action. A Pepsi sign pays homage to the vintage sign on the East River.

SCOREBOARDS

Everything might be bigger in Texas, according to an old adage, but Citi Field takes a page from the Lone Star State with a massive scoreboard situated in center field and other video boards scattered throughout. Measuring 51 feet high by 70 feet wide, the main video board, which provides 1,200 lines of resolution, is front and center for fans to view high-quality replays and other pertinent in-game information displayed throughout the contest.

The colossal high-definition board in right field measures 40 feet high by 90 feet wide and garners plenty of attention from fans, who are quickly entertained and informed by it. It provides lineups, in-game information, box scores and statistics, and other pertinent details pertaining to the game.

SHEA BRIDGE

When one thinks of Major League ballparks with bridges, one of the first to come to mind is the Clemente Bridge at PNC Park in Pittsburgh. At Citi Field, a replica bridge serves as a connection point for the right and center-field walkways. Nearby is a dedication plaque for the bridge. The idea of incorporating this was to emphasize the Mets' link with New York's five boroughs, serving as a symbolic tribute to its surroundings.

TASTE OF THE CITY

Sampling fine cuisine and enjoying New York favorites is one of the popular aspects of Citi Field at the Taste of the City food court, situated in the center-field section of the stadium. There is a plethora of good eats, including Blue Smoke Barbecue, Catch of the Day, and the Shake Shack, which has the standard ballpark burgers, fries, and shakes. Pay close attention to the Shake Shack sign—it replicates the skyline graphic from the scoreboard at Shea Stadium.

THE BIG APPLE

The giant apple from Shea Stadium, another fan favorite, was recreated at Citi Field, and this version is now better than ever. An oversized apple in center field rises above its base whenever a Mets player goes deep or New York registers a victory. The apple, which is illuminated at night and features the Mets logo prominently on the front, is a shell weighing 4,800 pounds and a frame that officially tips the scales at 9,000 pounds; that's roughly more than four sizes larger than the previous model at Shea Stadium. The original was spared from the demolition and relocated to the Jackie Robinson Rotunda.

WORLD'S FAIR MARKET

Variety is the name of the game at this popular eatery anchored in the right-field corner of the Field Level. From sushi to sandwiches to ice cream, the wide selection offers something for everyone.

MEMORABLE GAMES AT CITI FIELD

APRIL 13, 2009: FIRST GAME AT CITI FIELD

The San Diego Padres rode into town and stole the spotlight, spoiling the debut of Citi Field in front of a packed house with a 6–5 squeaker over the hometown Mets. Jody Gerut led off the game for the Padres and promptly became the first visiting player in Major League history to lead off with a home run for a stadium's first hit, with the long ball coming on the third pitch of the game. For New York, fan-favorite David Wright collected the first Mets hit and home run—a three-run shot in the fifth, tying the game at five—but San Diego came back with the eventual winning run in the sixth. That's when Luis Rodriguez scored after a balk from Mets reliever Pedro Feliciano.

APRIL 17, 2009: SHEFFIELD CRACKS 500TH HOME RUN

Making a pinch-hitting appearance against the Milwaukee Brewers, the team he began his Major League career with, Gary Sheffield became the twenty-fifth member of the 500-home run club with a seventh-inning shot to left field off Brewers reliever Mitch Stetter. Not only did he join elite company, but he also became the first player in baseball history to have his first home run with a new team go for the historic milestone. The hoopla also helped the Mets come from behind and win in the bottom of the ninth, 5–4, on Luis Castillo's walk-off single.

JUNE 28, 2009: RIVERA ENTERS ELITE CLUB

In a Subway Series showdown, Yankees closer Mariano Rivera furthered his Hall of Fame credentials by registering his 500th save, joining Trevor Hoffman as the only two players to reach that hallowed mark during a 4–2 Yankees victory. To honor the achievement, the Mets presented Rivera with the pitching rubber from the mound. A three-run first, punctuated by an RBI double from Mark Teixeria, got the Yankees going on the offensive end. The game also saw Rivera collect career RBI number one when he drew a walk with the bases loaded in the eighth inning. Rivera entered the record books when he induced Alex Cora into a groundout to second, finishing off the four-out save.

AUGUST 23, 2009: AN UNASSISTED TRIPLE PLAY FOR THE AGES

Phillies second baseman Eric Bruntlett proved that nothing is impossible in the game of baseball during a 9–7 Philadelphia victory over New York. With Mets Daniel Murphy and Luis Castillo on first and second in the bottom of the ninth with nobody out, Jeff Francoeur stepped in, not realizing history was about to be made. Francoeur laced a shot to center that was snagged by Bruntlett, who then stepped on second to double up Castillo and tagged out Murphy moments later, dramatically ending the game. With that, it was the first time in the long history of America's pastime that a National League contest ended on an unassisted triple play and went down as the first time the Mets had ever experienced the misfortune of hitting into one.

JUNE 10, 2010: A CLOSE ENCOUNTER WITH HISTORY

With the Padres in town, Jonathon Niese authored one of the greatest pitching performances in Mets history, falling one batter short of perfection during the Mets win over San Diego, 3–0. In the third inning, Chris Denorfia slapped a double for the only hit, and Niese responded by retiring the final 21 batters of the contest consecutively. Offensively, Jose Reyes, who finished 3-for-4 and Jeff Francoeur, who went 1-for-2 with an RBI in the bottom of the second to get the offense rolling, led the Mets. With the one-hitter, Niese joined Tom Seaver as the only members of the New York Mets to finish a contest one batter from a perfect game and became the first New Yorker to toss a one-hit shutout since Aaron Heilman did so on April 15, 2005.

JUNE 1, 2012: SANTANA THROWS FIRST METS NO-NO

It took 8,019 games in their history before the Mets could lay claim to a no-hitter, but Johan Santana made it worth the wait. Needing 134 pitches, Santana crafted his ply against the St. Louis Cardinals and turned in a seven-strikeout, five-walk performance during a historic 8–0 victory. Santana seemed to benefit from a missed call when former Mets outfielder Carlos Beltran laced a hot shot down the third-base line that appeared fair via instant replay but was called foul. In the seventh, Mets outfielder Mike Baxter crashed into the wall simultaneously as he made a catch of a long fly ball, helping preserve the gem. The New York offense made things easy, highlighted by a three-run homer off the bat of Lucas Duda in the fifth, extending the lead to 5–0 and ultimately putting the game out of reach.

JUNE 18, 2012: DICKEY HURLS SECOND STRAIGHT ONE-HITTER

Mets knuckleballer R. A. Dickey tossed his second consecutive one-hitter, this time victimizing the Baltimore Orioles during a 13 strikeout, 5–0 victory. Coming off a previous outing in which he dominated the Tampa Bay Rays at Tropicana Field and nearly pitched a no-hitter, the knuckleballer was sharp right from the get-go, striking out five in the first three innings—including the side during the third—in becoming the first pitcher since Dave Steib in 1988 to throw two consecutive one-hitters. With the score deadlocked at 0, Ike Davis provided the fireworks offensively by launching a grand slam in the sixth, helping to give Dickey some breathing room on the mound. He sealed things in the ninth, freezing both J. J. Hardy and Chris Davis in succession for strikeouts numbers 12 and 13, respectively.

SEPTEMBER 26, 2012: WRIGHT BECOMES METS ALL-TIME HITS LEADER

With an RBI single in the third inning against the Pittsburgh Pirates, David Wright collected the 1,419th hit in his Mets career, surpassing Ed Kranepool as the New York Mets all-time hits leader during a 6–0 New York victory. Wright, who took 1,260 games to accomplish the feat as compared to Kranepool's 1,853, finished the night with two hits and added to his franchise dominance after already being number one in total bases, runs scored, extra-base hits, walks, and runs batted in. A four-run third, highlighted by RBI singles from David Murphy and Kelly Shoppach, along with an RBI double by Scott Hairston, gave the Mets a lead they would never relinquish in the quick two-hour, 35-minute contest.

MAY 7, 2013: NEAR PERFECTION FOR NEW YORK'S HARVEY

All that kept Mets starter Matt Harvey from history was an infield single with two outs by Chicago's Alex Rios in the seventh, but that didn't stop

New York from picking up the 1–0 win in 10 innings. Pitching with masterful dominance, Harvey retired the first 20 in succession before giving up the clean single, ultimately finishing the contest with 12 strikeouts. After New York reliever Nate Jones came on to pitch a scoreless top of the tenth, pinch hitter Mike Baxter singled into the right-field corner, scoring Ike Davis for the walk-off win. This was the first Interleague meeting between the two teams since 2002, and the first time the White Sox visited the Mets in Queens.

JUNE 8, 2013: MARLINS OUTLAST METS IN 20 INNINGS

In the longest Mets home game since a 25-inning, 4–3 loss against the St. Louis Cardinals on September 11, 1974, at Shea Stadium, Miami outlasted New York after Adeiny Hechavarria singled in Placido Polanco with the winning run, helping to give the Marlins a hard-fought 2–1 win. The Mets took an early 1–0 lead, when a double by Juan Lagares plated Ike Davis, but the Marlins answered in the top of the fourth after Chris Coghlan's sacrifice fly scored Derek Dietrich, tying the game at one. The two teams would play scoreless baseball for 15 innings before Miami struck for gold in the twentieth, and Steve Cishek slammed the door on the Mets in the bottom half. In all, New York finished 0-for-19 with runners in scoring position, subsequently stranding 22 runners on base. Interestingly enough, over on the American League side on this day, the Toronto Blue Jays outlasted the Texas Rangers 4–3, marking only the second date in Major League Baseball history that two games went 18 innings or later.

WHAT THEY'RE SAYING ABOUT CITI FIELD

CARLOS BELTRAN: "It was big [and] now they really shortened the fences in a little bit. . . . The facilities are unbelievable and from a fan's standpoint, they are amazing the way they built the stadium."

BOB CARPENTER, BROADCASTER: "I liked the changes they made. They really needed to bring that whole left-field behemoth not only in, but down a little bit. . . . They also took a bite out of that cut-in out in right field, which was really, in my opinion, too quirky and unfair."

R. A. DICKEY: "I think Citi Field is one of my top five fields that I have ever played on. I love the stadium, the architecture, the surface, [and] the dimensions are fair and it has . . . a lot of great amenities."

JOSH LEWIN, BROADCASTER: "I think it is architecturally really impressive and certainly more well organized and aesthetically pleasing than Shea [Stadium] . . . on a decent enough night when the wind is not blowing and the rain is not pelting you, it is a beautiful place to watch a game."

STEVE LYONS, BROADCASTER: "I know they brought the walls in there because everyone was having such a hard time hitting the ball out of the ballpark. . . . It is an odd broadcast booth too—you have to go through the press dining room to get to our booth. It is sort of strange [that] out the door, there is someone eating a salad right there."

BRANDON PHILLIPS: "I missed the old Shea [Stadium], but it is nice what they did with bringing a new stadium there and it is a beautiful stadium. . . . I am glad they moved the fences in a little bit, but [overall] it is a very nice atmosphere."

JOSE REYES: "When I was in New York, Citi Field was big and that helped me a lot because the kind of game I play [is] with a lot of speed."

CHARLEY STEINER, BROADCASTER: "I grew up in New York and Shea Stadium, about 20 minutes after it was built, was a dump. . . . Citi Field is certainly an improvement, [but overall] I do not think it is great. I think it is [just] okay."

JOEY VOTTO: "I love hitting [at Citi Field]. . . . It is similar to Houston. If I hit it good, it is going to be a home run, [but] if not, I have a chance to hit a double or triple."

DAVID WRIGHT: "It is beautiful, coming over from Shea [Stadium]. Obviously it has all the newest amenities and simple things that make our preparation a lot easier. . . . You look at the stadium as a whole and it [has] already got a personality [that] is unlike a lot of new ballparks, and it provides a tremendous home field advantage."

CITI FIELD FACTS AND FIGURES

CITI FIELD ADDRESS
126th Street and Roosevelt Avenue, Flushing, NY 11368

NEW YORK METS TEAM WEB SITE
www.mets.com

FIELD DIMENSIONS (in feet)
Left Field: 335', Left-Center: 358', Center: 40',
Right-Center: 375', Right Field: 330'

SEATING CAPACITY (as of 2015)

41,922

ALL-STAR GAMES AT CITI FIELD

July 16, 2013: American League 3, National League 0
MVP: Mariano Rivera, New York Yankees (AL)

CITI FIELD FIRSTS

Game: April 13, 2009—San Diego 6, New York 5
Single: David Eckstein, San Diego (April 13, 2009)
Double: David Wright, New York (April 13, 2009)
Triple: Jose Reyes, New York (April 19, 2009)
Home Run: Jody Gerut, San Diego (April 13, 2009)*

Denotes first hit in the stadium.

CITIZENS BANK PARK
HOME OF THE PHILADELPHIA PHILLIES

Citizens Bank Park, Philadelphia Phillies (*Photographed by Brian Skversky/Flickr*)

Much like every other team that had left their cookie-cutter stadium from the 1970s, the Phillies organization was happy to say good-bye to the cereal bowl–like Veterans Stadium and move to Citizens Bank Park in 2004. After all, "The Vet" had offered little in the way of intimacy, and the spacious setting was more often than not the home of many unoccupied blue seats as the Phillies played their home games throughout the baseball season.

As part of the South Philadelphia Sports Complex, which also includes the home of the NFL's Eagles and the home of the NBA's 76ers, the baseball-only Citizens Bank Park is a stark contrast from its predecessor as it offers great sight lines, is not enclosed, and the players don't resemble ants from the vantage point of the upper deck. Citizens Bank Park is a cozy ballpark that is not only an outstanding home field for the Phillies, but is a place fans have flocked to since its inception in 2004.

Talks began brewing in 2000 for a new ballpark when the city of Philadelphia, along with the Phillies organization, unveiled plans for Citizens Bank Park to be constructed just east of Veterans Stadium and on the north side of Patterson Avenue. The Phillies were hoping to duplicate the likes of Baltimore, Detroit, and San Francisco with a downtown setup, but those plans were later scrapped in favor of its current location.

The presentation of the ballpark and groundbreaking ceremonies commenced on June 28, 2001, and following the Phillies game that night (an 8–7 victory over the Marlins), the location of the left-field foul pole was ceremonially determined. Construction officially began in November 2001, and the project was completed just in time for the first pitch on April 12, 2004.

SPECIAL FEATURES OF CITIZENS BANK PARK

ALL-STAR WALK

Located at Ashburn Alley, black-granite medallions honor Philadelphia Phillies All-Stars since 1933. As current Phillies players receive All-Star honors each year, they, too, will most likely be added to the walkway and take their place among the other legends in the long history of the franchise, which began play in the National League in 1883.

ASHBURN ALLEY

This outfield establishment is named for the slightly overgrown grass that surrounded the third-base line at Shibe Park and enabled former Phillies great Richie Ashburn to lay down bunts with ease. Positioned along the third-base line, Ashburn Alley has many baseball entertainment options with fun and games for the whole family to enjoy. Much like Eutaw Street at Oriole Park at Camden Yards in Baltimore, Ashburn Alley opens to the public two-and-a-half hours before the first pitch.

BROADCAST BOOTH DEDICATIONS

The Philadelphia Phillies have dedicated two broadcast booths to men who made a significant impact on not only the game of baseball, but the organization as well. The Rich "Whitey" Ashburn radio broadcast booth honors Hall of Famer Richie Ashburn, who spent 47 seasons with the organization—12 of which he starred on the field—before heading upstairs to become a broadcaster. A plaque outside the booth displays a picture of Ashburn, along with the inscription, "This game's easy, Harry."

The Harry Kalas television broadcast booth honors a legend behind the microphone, a man whose voice was as recognizable as any in the game. The booth was renamed following his death in 2009 and pays tribute to Kalas, who was the lead play-by-play broadcaster from 1971 to 2009. A plaque outside the booth displays a photo of Kalas and features his famous home run call, "That ball's outta here."

BULLS BARBEQUE

Named for one of Philadelphia's most likable players, Greg "The Bull" Luzinski, the barbeque located at the eastern quadrant of Ashburn Alley is a popular destination for fans seeking to enjoy a taste of Southern cuisine. Ribs, turkey legs, and pork give off an irresistible aroma that permeates the ballpark and lures fans to stop by for a bite to eat. Luzinski, who played for the Phillies from 1970 to 1980, is best known for the cannon shots he deposited into the seats.

CITIZENS BANK NAMING RIGHTS

A historic moment took place on June 2003, when Citizens Bank, located in the Philadelphia area, pledged a total of $95 million over the course of 25 years to have the new ballpark officially named after it. The breakdown: $57.5 million for the naming rights and $37.5 million for the Phillies broadcast media package. The overall deal also alleviated some of the costs of constructing Citizens Bank Park.

COOPERSTOWN GALLERY

The Cooperstown Gallery, located on the Hall of Fame Club level, exhibits oil paintings and artifacts from players who not only starred in a Phillies uniform, but also have been enshrined in the National Baseball Hall of Fame. Identification banners at both ends of the exhibit serve as a history lesson and a blast from the past. Display cases provide fans with a firsthand account of some of the more unique items from Philadelphia's past.

EXECUTIVE DINING ROOM

Available for use on non-game days for hosting events, meetings, or other important dealings, the upscale dining room is another top-notch option at Citizens Bank Park. Reminiscent of old country clubs in Philadelphia, black-padded wooden seats encircle tables in this spacious indoor setting. Outside, umbrella-equipped seating offers a sweeping view of Citizens Bank Park and the chance to catch some fresh air.

GAMES OF BASEBALL

This fully interactive part of Ashburn Alley is one area that kids of all ages are sure to enjoy. Games include Run the Bases, Ballpark Pinball, and other fun athletic competitions. One thing's for sure: it'll keep the little ones—and adults who are kids at heart—occupied and out of trouble.

HALL OF FAME CLUB

One of the premier spots at Citizens Bank Park, the Hall of Fame Club is a 2,500-seat lounge on the Club Level. Access to a secluded, full-service bar, along with top-notch amenities, makes this destination a world-class facility. Oversized televisions and fine dining options enhance one of baseball's most luxurious settings. Nearby, the Cooperstown Gallery gives fans a quick history lesson on the franchise.

HARRY KALAS MEMORIAL STATUE

Unveiled on August 16, 2011, a seven-and-a-half-foot bronze likeness of the Hall of Fame broadcaster graces the Main Concourse behind section 141, strategically positioned near the restaurant named in his honor, Harry the K's. The statue displays a smiling Kalas—complete with a 2008 World Series ring on his finger—holding a microphone and leaning on a baseball bat. A plaque at the base reads: "Harry Kalas, Phillies Hall of Fame broadcaster 1971–2009. Presented by his fans and friends August 14, 2011." In case you're wondering, the date is not a mistake. The ceremonies were planned to take place that day, but were rescheduled due to rain.

HARRY THE K'S

In honor of Harry Kalas, the longtime broadcaster for the Phillies, Harry the K's is a restaurant located right below the left-field scoreboard, boasting made-to-order, created-from-scratch dishes. The food selection, combined with exceptional sight lines, make the Bar and Grille one of the top destinations for fans at Citizens Bank Park.

HIGH-DEFINITION VIDEO BOARD

Completed just in time for the 2011 season, the Phillies pumped $10 million into a new scoreboard positioned under the Phillies insignia in left field. It combines the latest technology with crystal-clear imaging, providing unprecedented clarity. One of the largest scoreboards of its kind in the National League, the structure measures 76 feet high by 97 feet wide and weighs an unbelievable 84,420 pounds.

HOME PLATE CLUB

Upscale concessions, a pregame buffet, and two full-service bars are just a few of the amenities in the exclusive Diamond Club. Positioned behind home plate, it offers second-to-none sight lines along with 1,281 extra-wide padded seats. Memorabilia dating back to the 1880s are displayed, and members have full access to the Clubhouse Lounge, which provides exclusive views of the batting cages used by both the Phillies and their opponent.

LIBERTY BELL

Supplied by Capitol Manufacturing, and perhaps the most distinctive part of Citizens Bank Park, the makeshift 35-foot by 50-foot Liberty Bell is situated in right-center field and soars 100 feet above street level. Whenever a Phillies player hits a home run, the bell and clapper sway from side-to-side and the neon edges light up and pulse, setting off a bell ring that echoes throughout the entire ballpark.

MCFADDEN'S BAR AND GRILLE

A year-round attraction, this lively bar and grille is conveniently positioned down the third-base line and combines the best of McFadden's menu along with another Philadelphia favorite, Zanzibar Blues. This is one of the more popular destinations for fans following the conclusion of Phillies games and for those wishing to grab a drink or bite to eat. It is also accessible from the outside and accommodates the crowds that attend 76ers or Eagles games.

MEMORY LANE

In Ashburn Alley, fans can stir up old memories and learn about the Phillies franchise when they take a trip down memory lane. On the back of the batter's eye wall is a pictorial account of Philadelphia baseball that includes the Phillies, the Negro League Baseball, and the defunct Philadelphia Athletics franchise. A platform nearby enables fans to see the bi-level bullpens as players warm up before entering the game.

OVERSIZED BASEBALL CARDS

As fans enter the left-field gate at Citizens Bank Park, they can view the starting lineup in a one-of-a-kind way. Baseball cards, much like the ones collected by fans young and old, measure 10 feet tall by 5 feet wide and display the starting nine for the upcoming game, offering a glimpse of the players taking to the field that day.

PHANATIC "PHUN" ZONE

Located within the first-base Gate Plaza, this area gives kids ages eight and under the opportunity to play games and participate in numerous other activities that are sure to provide a great workout. Nearby, a toned-down version of this attraction is available for kids under the age of two.

PHILADELPHIA BASEBALL WALL OF FAME

Another part of Ashburn Alley and a carryover from Veterans Stadium is one of the most comprehensive outfield entertainment sections in the Major Leagues. The Wall of Fame, a collection of plaques mounted on a brick wall, highlights the exceptional players who have come through the organization. As a yearly tradition, the Phillies have inducted one player every season from 1978 to 2003 who best exemplified what Phillies baseball was all about with their hard play on the field. A larger plaque honors the 1983 centennial team.

Ivy grows on the center-field wall, and fans have a bird's-eye view of the game. (*Photographed by Brian Skversky/Tiffin/Flickr*)

RETIRED NUMBERS

The retired Philadelphia Phillies numbers and letters are on top of the Ashburn Alley ivy-covered concession buildings in center field. They include: Chuck Klein (old English *P*), Grover Cleveland Alexander (old English *P*), Richie Ashburn (1), Jim Bunning (14), Mike Schmidt (20), Steve Carlton (32), and Robin Roberts (36).

ROOFTOP BLEACHER SEATS

At Shibe Park in the 1920s, once Philadelphia's previous home, the residents of 20th Street constructed bleacher seats on top of their buildings. Now, many years later, fans are once again given the opportunity to enjoy the breathtaking views of the ballpark and action by perching on top of buildings scattered along Ashburn Alley.

STATUES

Sculptor Zenos Frudakis has designed four statues that measure 10 feet high and overlook the crowds. The players honored with these larger-than-life bronze figures are Richie Ashburn, whose likeness is appropriately in Ashburn Alley; Steve Carlton's statue is at the left-field gate; Mike Schmidt's, appropriately, is placed at the third-base gate; and Robin Roberts's is set at the first-base gate.

THE ANGLE

The Angle, which is part of the outfield wall and strategically positioned between the left-center field power alley and dead center field, like The Notch at PNC Park in Pittsburgh, has dimensions that start at 19 feet and decrease to 12 feet, 8 inches. This quirk may create headaches for outfielders with the unpredictable bounces of the ball, much like the one in the center-field area at Fenway Park in Boston.

TRIBUTE TO THE PAST

To evoke nostalgia from ballparks of days gone by, the seating bowl was inspired by the likes of two former homes of the Phillies, the Baker Bowl and the Connie Mack Stadium/Shibe Park. The playing field at Citizens Bank Park, one of the more obvious tributes, is positioned 23 feet below street level, mimicking that of Connie Mack Stadium. In addition, a 360-degree open view on the main concourse affords fans the opportunity to meander around while not missing any of the action on the field.

VETERANS TRIBUTE

To honor Veterans Stadium, the Phillies former home, a monument to veterans was installed in Citizens Bank Park. This is on Pattison Avenue and includes bronze plaques commemorating the Air Force, Army, Coast Guard, Marine Corps, Navy, and POW/MIA. Flags, including one of the United States, fly year-round and honor those who have served the greatest country in the world.

MEMORABLE GAMES AT CITIZENS BANK PARK

APRIL 12, 2004: FIRST GAME AT CITIZENS BANK PARK

The Cincinnati Reds came into Citizens Bank Park and spoiled the fun, winning 4–1 behind the strength of a solid pitching outing by Paul Wilson, who went 7⅓ innings, allowing one run on seven hits. The Reds wasted no time scoring the first run to be recorded at the new stadium, when a wild pitch by Randy Wolf allowed D'Angelo Jimenez to trot home, giving Cincinnati the early 1–0 lead. Philadelphia answered in the bottom half, when Bobby Abreu launched a line drive home run over the fence, tying the contest at one. The Reds answered in the second with an RBI single by Ryan Freel, and in the fifth, an RBI double by Ken Griffey Jr. and a sacrifice fly by Sean Casey ended the scoring and gave the Reds the win. Although the Phillies' bats went silent, Jim Thome finished 2-for-4 with a single and double.

JULY 15, 2007: FRANCHISE LOSS NUMBER 10,000

Just before the Philadelphia Phillies turned into a perennial powerhouse, they added a dubious distinction to their history. As part of a 10–2 loss to the Cardinals, they became the first Major League Baseball franchise to eclipse the 10,000-loss plateau, and did so without putting up much of a fight. It was 10–0 heading into the bottom of the ninth before Michael Bourn hit a solo shot to lead off the frame, and four batters later, Chase Utley smacked an RBI double. The taste of 10,000 defeats for a franchise that began play in 1883 didn't linger very long. Philadelphia captured the National League Eastern Division crown later in the season before bowing out in three straight games to the Colorado Rockies, who would go on to win the NL pennant.

OCTOBER 25, 2008: FIRST WORLD SERIES AT CITIZENS BANK

The Fall Classic returned to the City of Brotherly Love for the first time since 1993, and the Phillies captured Game 3 in dramatic fashion, winning 5–4 in the bottom of the ninth. Both Tampa Bay and Philadelphia traded runs throughout the contest, with the Phillies getting home runs from Chase Utley, Ryan Howard, and Carlos Ruiz. It was 4–4 heading into the bottom half of the ninth when a pitch from J. P. Howell hit Eric Bruntlett to start the inning. Reliever Grant Balfour replaced Howell and proceeded to uncork a wild pitch that moved Bruntlett to third. He then intentionally walked both Shane Victorino and pinch hitter Greg Dobbs to load the bases, hoping to set up the double-play ball. Ruiz then returned to the scene and chopped a tapper to third that was hit just right, allowing Bruntlett to score on an infield single and marking the first time a World Series game ended on such a hit.

OCTOBER 27 AND 29, 2008: PHILLIES WIN WORLD SERIES

In a strange sequence of events, the Phillies captured their second World Series title in franchise history with a 4–3 series-clinching victory that took a few days to accomplish. Shane Victorino got the festivities under way in the bottom of the first by lacing a two-run single to left that plated Jayson Werth and Chase Utley, giving Philadelphia an early 2–0 lead. Tampa Bay answered with an RBI single by Evan Longoria in the fourth, and in the sixth, an RBI single by Carlos Pena tied the score at two, which is where things got interesting. Due to heavy rains, the players were ordered off the field, and they wouldn't return until two days later, when Mother Nature decided to go wreak havoc elsewhere.

When the game resumed in the bottom of the sixth, Geoff Jenkins hit a double, and Werth promptly drove him in, giving the Phillies a 3–2 lead. The Rays tied it in the seventh on a home run by Rocco Baldelli, only to be answered by Philadelphia in the bottom half, thanks to an RBI single by

Pedro Feliz, which helped regain the lead for the Phillies at 4–3. The combination of J. C. Romero and Brad Lidge would go on to shut out Tampa Bay, and a strikeout of Eric Hinske made it worth the wait for fans at Citizens Bank Park.

OCTOBER 6, 2010: HALLADAY NO-HITS REDS IN PLAYOFFS

Having already thrown a perfect game on May 29 at Florida earlier in the year, Roy Halladay made his postseason debut one for the record books. Mixing pitches that the Cincinnati Reds could only dream of hitting, Halladay hurled the second no-hitter in postseason history, striking out eight and walking only one during a 4–0 victory. The only thing that kept him from matching Don Larsen's perfect game in the playoffs was a two-out walk he issued to Jay Bruce in the fifth inning. The Phillies struck in the bottom of the first, when Chase Utley's sacrifice fly scored Shane Victorino for a 1–0 lead. Halladay helped out his own cause at the plate, connecting for an RBI single, and Victorino added a two-run single, giving the Phillies all the runs they would require in taking a 4–0 lead. But the storyline belonged to Halladay, who finished off the Reds in order during the bottom of the ninth, capped off by a ground ball out off the bat of Brandon Phillips.

MAY 25, 2011: LONGEST GAME EVER AT CITIZENS BANK PARK

In a game that lasted six hours and 11 minutes, the Phillies stood victorious at the end of the night, defeating visiting Cincinnati 5–4 in 19 innings. As if that wasn't impressive enough, it was second baseman Wilson Valdez who picked up the win, tossing the top of the nineteenth before Raul Ibanez's sacrifice fly in the bottom half scored Jimmy Rollins to end the game. It appeared as though it would be smooth sailing for Philadelphia, who jumped out to an early 3–0 lead after two frames. Cincinnati battled back on an RBI single by Joey Votto in the fifth, and a two-run single by Jay Bruce in the seventh tied it at three.

In the tenth, Bruce homered and gave the Reds a brief 4–3 advantage before Ryan Howard came up in the bottom half and hit a solo shot of his own, once again deadlocking the game. It stayed that way all the way until the nineteenth, when Ibanez gave Valdez the first win for a position player since Brent Mayne did so on August 22, 2000, as a member of the Colorado Rockies versus the Atlanta Braves.

MAY 25, 2014: BECKETT FIRES NO-HITTER

Josh Beckett fired the first no-hitter of his career, striking out six in a 128-pitch effort that helped guide the Los Angeles Dodgers to a 6–0 victory over Philadelphia. Retiring 23 straight batters during one stretch, Beckett became the first Dodgers pitcher since Hideo Nomo in 1996 to record a no-hitter and the first visiting player to hold the Phillies without a hit since Bill Stoneman of the Montreal Expos did so on April 17, 1969, at Connie Mack Stadium. Already ahead 4–0, the game was put out of reach in the seventh after three runs crossed the plate, highlighted by an RBI single off the bat of Adrian Gonzalez, who finished with three hits and two runs batted in.

WHAT THEY'RE SAYING ABOUT CITIZENS BANK PARK

R. A. DICKEY: "That is a nice field, but it is a very short field, so for pitchers, you are going in knowing that the dimensions are favorable for hitters, so that might play into your game plan a little bit . . . , [but] as far as the field and clubhouse, it is great."

RYAN HOWARD: "I love it—the fans provide so much energy there [and] it is just a beautiful ballpark the way it is put together . . . very scenic, very appealing to the eye, and you take a look around just the ballpark in general—including Ashburn Alley—there is just so much to do and see at the ballpark."

RAUL IBANEZ: "Great ballpark! [The] fans are right on top of you and [have a] lot of energy. . . . The atmosphere is just electric there every night [and it is just] a great ballpark."

JOSH LEWIN, BROADCASTER: "I love that one—obviously the fact that [it] is always packed and the energy there is so fantastic . . . really helps. . . . Traffic can be a little nightmarish, but if you are willing to come early and stay late, it just throbs with excitement and [also from a broadcaster's standpoint, it] is a great view from the press box."

JAMIE MOYER: "I think the Phillies have done a good job of creating an environment for the fan to enjoy. . . . There [are] different eating places in Ashburn Alley, and I think [Citizens Bank Park] is very tastefully done."

JIMMY ROLLINS: "It is a beautiful place. . . . Just the ballpark itself is brighter and cleaner, has a lot more activities, great food, and the symmetry of the ballpark . . . feels like a baseball ballpark and not just a bowl like in the 1970s."

DREW STUBBS: "Pretty wild atmosphere! It is some of the more intense baseball fans and they stay on you most of the game. . . . [It's] another good offensive ballpark that I would compare to Great American Ball Park, where you see some pretty good offensive numbers put up [on the scoreboard]."

JIM THOME: "Energy like no other. . . . Phillies fans are very into what they are doing. [They are] energetic and into every pitch and everything that is going on within the game; that is what stood out for me."

SHANE VICTORINO: "I love that place—it was a place I called home for seven to eight years and to me, [it has] arguably some of the best fans in baseball. They have a passion for the game and a love for the game, so I love that place very much."

DAVID WRIGHT: "It is a tremendous atmosphere and it is really cool because you have got Citizens Bank Park, the [NFL's Eagles stadium, and NBA's 76ers arena] all downtown. . . . It is a tremendous energy and atmosphere, especially with the Philadelphia fans."

CITIZENS BANK PARK FACTS AND FIGURES

CITIZENS BANK PARK ADDRESS
One Citizens Bank Way, Philadelphia, PA 19148

PHILADELPHIA PHILLIES TEAM WEB SITE
www.phillies.com

FIELD DIMENSIONS (in feet)
Left Field: 329', Left-Center: 374', Center: 401', Right-Center: 369', Right Field: 330'

SEATING CAPACITY (as of 2015)
43,651

ALL-STAR GAMES AT CITIZENS BANK PARK
None

CITIZENS BANK PARK FIRSTS
Game: April 12, 2004—Cincinnati 4, Philadelphia 1
Single: Ryan Freel, Cincinnati (April 12, 2004)
Double: D'Angelo Jimenez, Cincinnati (April 12, 2004)*
Triple: Austin Kearns, Cincinnati (April 12, 2004)
Home Run: Bobby Abreu, Philadelphia (April 12, 2004)

Denotes first hit in the stadium.

FENWAY PARK
HOME OF THE BOSTON RED SOX

Fenway Park, Boston Red Sox (*Photographed by Russel Tiffin/Flickr*)

A ll across baseball, new stadiums have been constructed over the last 20 years and, as a result, teams have said a big goodbye to their old ballparks. In Boston, Fenway Park has withstood the test of time and provided many great memories throughout its long history. Red Sox greats from Ted Williams to Carlton Fisk have called this palace home, and the moments have nearly been second to none.

The $650,000 Fenway Park replaced Huntington Avenue Baseball Grounds in 1912 and quickly became a fan favorite. In 1911, then-owner John Taylor purchased land and began to build the Red Sox a new home.

At one point, the fate of legendary Fenway Park hung in the balance, with a push to construct a brand-new ballpark. On May 15, 1999, then-Red Sox CEO John Harrington announced his plan to have a new Fenway Park constructed near the existing one with more amenities to accommodate the fans.

The idea went over like a lead balloon with the public. A major show of support to save Fenway ensued, with many around Boston and all of baseball considering Fenway to be sacred ground. In 2005, a collective sigh of relief could be heard all around the New England area as the new owners—John Henry, Tom Werner, and Larry Lucchino—put everyone at ease by announcing that the existing Fenway would be preserved, and plans for a new facility would be scrapped.

In making the declaration, the owners also vowed to pump $285 million worth of renovations to make it a more functional and user-friendly facility. They succeeded and in 2012, the famous ballpark with an unbelievable history celebrated its 100th birthday.

SPECIAL FEATURES OF FENWAY PARK

BLEACHER BAR
The Bleacher Bar made its debut in 2008 and is a popular spot for fans seeking out a libation either before or after a game. What was once the center-field storage room has now been expertly transformed into a full-service bar and lounge where fans can enjoy their favorite drink. What will they think of next?

CENTER-FIELD SCOREBOARD
While the old-fashioned, manual scoreboard is an icon of Fenway Park, an electronic scoreboard—added in 1976—proudly sits atop the bleachers in right-center. In 2011, the Red Sox updated the technological capabilities of the board and the outcome was unprecedented clarity, while simultaneously refreshing the interior of Fenway Park. Most of the time, replays and in-game information are displayed on this partcular scoreboard.

CHAMPIONSHIP FLAGS
To tell the story of league titles and championships collected by the Red Sox over the years, miniature flags are displayed directly above the press box windows and showcase the long tradition of the franchise. Red flags symbolize World Series triumphs, while blue ones represent the years the Red Sox stood victorious as the American League pennant winner.

CITGO SIGN
In baseball, no sign is as famous as the one visible from the seats in Fenway Park. Located at 660 Beacon Street, the CITGO sign towers high above the Green Monster in left and instantly became a part of baseball lore when it was introduced in 1965. The 60-foot by 60-foot sign comes to life, thanks in part to the 5,878 glass tubes that illuminate it along with 250 high-voltage transformers that light the sign from dusk until midnight each evening. In July 2010, the sign received a facelift and had all of its lights replaced with more technologically advanced bulbs. On September 17, 2010, during the seventh inning stretch, the sign was ceremonially relit, and fans all over Fenway rejoiced at the brighter, updated version of the famous structure.

DUFFY'S CLIFF

A 10-foot-high incline in left field existed from 1912 to 1933 and was named for former Boston left fielder Duffy Lewis. While in the field, Lewis mastered the art of running up the hill, which extended from the left-field foul pole to the center-field flagpole. Following the 1933 season, Red Sox owner Tom Yawkey arranged to have the hill flattened, thus eliminating Duffy's Cliff, but not the memory of it.

EMC CLUB

With the city of Boston and Fenway Park serving as a beautiful backdrop, the EMC Club is a stylish restaurant with padded seating, a full-service bar, and top-of-the-line amenities. There's plenty of history surrounding this structure. It debuted in 1983 and evolved into the 600 Club before the 1988 season, when 610 seats were added above home plate, replacing the current press box, which was then rebuilt on top of the 600 Club. In 2002, the seats were renamed the .406 Club in honor of Ted Williams's batting average attained in 1941. Yet another change occurred in the 2005–06 off-season, when the .406 Club was reconfigured and now boasts two open-air levels, consisting of the EMC Club on the bottom and the State Street Pavilion on the top.

FISK FOUL POLE

Carlton Fisk became a permanent fixture of Fenway lore when the club dedicated the left-field foul pole in his name during the 2005 season. Appropriately dedicated during an interleague contest against Cincinnati, Fisk provided the inspiration for the name change 30 years earlier when he homered off Pat Darcy in the twelfth inning to win Game 6 of the 1975 World Series for the Red Sox. In one of the most lasting images in baseball history, Fisk jumped up and waved his arms to the right immediately after making contact, seemingly willing it off the foul pole for the home run. The Red Sox lost the game and the Series the next night, but the moment Fisk created lives on forever.

GREEN MONSTER

Arguably the most famous quirk in all of baseball, the 37-foot-high Green Monster is worth the price of admission alone and is the highest wall among the current Major League ballparks. The inception of the Monster came following the 1933 season when 30,000 pounds of iron were used to construct the green giant in left field. The wall, which has plenty of dents from batted balls and was completely painted green in 1947 to cover advertisements, is 240 feet long and has a foundation that sinks 22 feet below ground level.

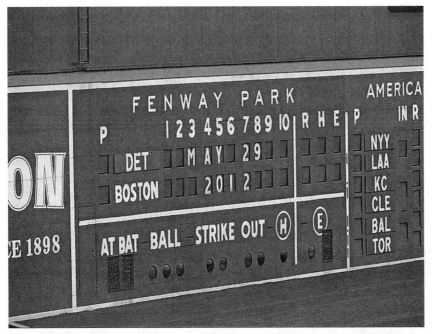

The manual scoreboard, installed in 1934, is a historic feature of Fenway Park. (*Photographed by Russel Tiffin/Flickr*)

MANUAL SCOREBOARD

Leaning coolly on the Green Monster and adding even more nostalgia to Fenway Park is the manual scoreboard. Installed in 1934 and moved 20 feet to the right in 1976, it features numbers for runs and hits that measure 16 inches by 16 inches and weigh three pounds each. Errors, innings, and pitcher's numbers measure 12 inches by 16 inches and weigh two pounds each. A door allows the scoreboard operator to slip inside and get to work on a job that takes plenty of patience.

NOT YOUR ORDINARY LADDER

Installed in 1936, a ladder sits to the left of the Green Monster and was once a groundskeeper's best friend when it was utilized to retrieve home run balls hit into the 23-foot by 7-foot screen during batting practice. The most famous incident involving it came in 1963, when Dick Stuart chugged around the bases for an inside-the-park home run, thanks to the wacky bounce created after he hit the ladder with a ball. Although seats were added following the 2002 season, and the ladder was no longer necessary, it was left in place for nostalgia and is a part of the landscape today.

PESKY'S POLE

Named for light-hitting shortstop Johnny Pesky, the right-field foul pole measures 302 feet from home plate, and holds the distinction of being the shortest home run distance in the Major Leagues. Pesky accumulated 17 home runs in his entire career—six of which he hit around the Fenway pole—but never off of it. On September 27, 2006, the Red Sox officially dedicated the foul pole to Pesky in his honor and placed a commemorative plaque at its base to mark the occasion. Although a placard attached to the pole states: "Out of respect please refrain from writing on Pesky's Pole," there are many signatures from fans.

RED SEAT

Fenway Park placed a red seat in right field to commemorate a blast by Boston's favorite son, Ted Williams. The crimson seat 21 in section 42, row 37 commemorates a 502-foot blast that Williams swatted on June 9, 1946. He hit the baseball so hard that it actually penetrated a straw hat that a spectator was wearing.

RED SOX HALL OF FAME

Created in 1995, the Red Sox Hall of Fame is located behind the EMC Club and offers a comprehensive look at the players who have made the most significant impacts on Boston's illustrious baseball history. A 15-member committee is responsible for nominating potential candidates, who must have played three seasons with the team and been out of uniform for three seasons. On the wall, plaques honor players already inducted and give a brief history of their career.

RETIRED NUMBERS

The seven numbers retired by the Red Sox organization are located along the right-field roof: Bobby Doerr (1), Joe Cronin (4), Johnny Pesky (6), Carl Yastrzemski (8), Ted Williams (9), Jim Rice (14), and Carlton Fisk (27).

ROYAL ROOTERS CLUB

In conjunction with Fenway Park's 100th anniversary in 2012, the Royal Rooters Club, located behind the right-field grandstand, was opened to season-ticket holders. It offers a unique food selection and displays memorabilia such as World Series trophies, Cy Young Awards, Most Valuable Player Awards, and various other Red Sox garb, including the second base from Game 4 of the 2004 ALCS, stolen by Dave Roberts, which propelled Boston to come back from being down 0–3 in the series against New York. The name is derived from a fan club that made its home at Fenway Park in the 1900s.

STATE STREET PAVILION

The second level of the EMC Club, the State Street Pavilion, is routinely sold out each game and features service accessible from the comfort of your seat. Club members can take advantage of this private lounge with its beautiful view of the Boston skyline both before and after games.

SWEET CAROLINE

Since 2002, Neil Diamond's hit song "Sweet Caroline" has been played over the loudspeakers in the middle of the eighth inning. Most of the time fans sing along to the tune, and even some players seem to get into the music and mumble along to the lyrics. Diamond performed the song in person prior to the 2010 season opener, a game won by the Red Sox over the rival Yankees, 9–7.

THE BOARDROOM

One of the premium hospitality options at Fenway Park, Gosling's Dark 'n' Stormy Boardroom, was once a secluded dining area before being transformed into a luxurious mini-suite that can accommodate between 8 and 12 guests. Upscale furnishings, combined with a picturesque view and tasty meals, are only the beginning. As an added bonus, an exclusive patio located on the EMC level offers fans the chance to take in the game from right behind the dish.

THE MONSTER SEATS

The screen atop the Green Monster was once a unique feature, but changes were made following the 2002 season that increased the seating capacity and created a buzz around baseball. That's when 269 seats, known as The Monster Seats, were added atop the famous wall. The swiveling green seats are a throwback from yesteryear and feature a baseball-drilled pattern in its bottom. These seats are tough to come by, so consider yourself lucky if you have the opportunity to view a game from one of the more unique vantage points in all of baseball.

TRIANGULAR TERROR

Center field, one of the toughest places in the Major Leagues from which to judge the wild ricochet of a batted ball, is home to The Triangle, where the walls come together to form a triangle whose furthest angle is an unbelievable 420 feet away from home plate. Often when a ball is struck and headed for this location, the fielder has only a split second to determine how he might field the ball created by a pinball-type bounce off the padding.

VIDEO BOARDS

In addition to the new center-field video board erected just before the 2011 season, other scoreboards were added as part of a 10-year, $285 million commitment to upgrade the interior and keep fans informed of any pertinent information throughout the course of a game. A 38-foot by 100-foot scoreboard in right-center field replaced the previous 23-foot by 30-foot version that was installed in 1976, and a 16- foot by 30-foot video board in right field updates fans in attendance on player statistics and other announcements.

WILLIAMSBURG

Appropriately named for arguably the greatest Red Sox player of all time, Ted Williams, this is a one-of-a-kind section invented by sportswriters that directly overlooks the bullpen area. It is built in front of the right-center field bleachers and was constructed to benefit Williams and other left-handed batters, who undoubtedly licked their chops when they saw it sitting 23 feet closer to home plate than the bleacher wall.

YAWKEY WAY

Yawkey Way, the main access to Fenway Park, is closed to vehicle traffic three hours prior to the first pitch in order to make room for live entertainment and other attractions that make game day exciting for everyone. The street was named for Tom Yawkey, the Red Sox president in 1933 and sole owner of the franchise for 44 years, the longest tenure of any owner in Major League history.

YASTRZEMSKI STATUE

This statue, dedicated by the Red Sox on September 22, 2013, and positioned outside the right-field entrance to Fenway Park, was in honor of Carl Yastrzemski, a Hall of Famer who won the Triple Crown in 1967 and accumulated over 3,000 hits in his Major League career. The statue recreates the scene of his final at-bat on October 2, 1983, with Boston against Cleveland, with Yastrzemski holding a bat in his left hand while tipping his cap to the fans. Yastrzemski would proceed to hit a fly ball to second base for the final out of the inning in a game eventually won by Boston, 3–1.

MEMORABLE GAMES AT FENWAY PARK

APRIL 20, 1912: FIRST GAME AT FENWAY PARK

The Boston Red Sox opened their new state-of-the-art ballpark while at the same time beginning what would become baseball's biggest rivalry, defeating the New York Highlanders (later known as the Yankees), 7–6 in 11 innings. The sinking of the *Titanic,* which occurred on April 14, 1912, overshadowed the first game at Fenway Park, but that didn't dampen the spirits of those who were at the game. After waiting out multiple rain delays, fans were treated to a classic contest that was decided in the eleventh, when Hall of Famer Tris Speaker struck for a game-winning RBI that gave Boston the win and began the Fenway Park era.

OCTOBER 16, 1912: RED SOX WRAP UP WORLD SERIES

In a tightly contested Fall Classic, the Boston Red Sox defeated the New York Giants in Game 8, 3–2 in 10 innings. With the location of this contest determined by a coin flip, a half-full Fenway Park crowd was treated to a classic when legendary pitcher Christy Mathewson squared off against Hugh Bedient. With the score tied at one in the tenth, New York's Red Murray stepped in and doubled ahead of an RBI single by Fred Merkle, swinging the pendulum back to the Giants in the form of a 2–1 advantage. In the bottom half, a routine fly ball to center turned into havoc when Giants center fielder Fred Snodgrass dropped it, which proved to be extremely costly. With two aboard, Tris Speaker hit a foul pop-up to first that no one called, ultimately dropping and giving the Red Sox another opportunity. Speaker took full advantage, wrapping an RBI single, and two batters later, Larry Gardner hit a sacrifice fly that enabled the winning run to score, putting an end to the World Series.

SEPTEMBER 11, 1918: ANOTHER TITLE FOR BEANTOWN

Featuring a Red Sox team with stars Babe Ruth, George Cochran, and Sam Jones, Boston captured another World Series championship by defeating the Chicago Cubs, 2–1, in Game 6. Carl Mays started for Boston and pitched a complete game, allowing one run on three hits. Meanwhile, the offense was helped out by the Chicago defense when, in the third inning, an error by right fielder Max Flack allowed two runs to score, giving the Red Sox a 2–0 lead. Chicago picked up one in the fourth, when Flack redeemed himself and singled, with Fred Merkle driving him in on an RBI single. Mays then buckled down and no-hit the Cubs the rest of the way, preserving the one-run lead and the championship.

OCTOBER 21, 1975: BEST WORLD SERIES GAME EVER?

Widely regarded as one of the single greatest baseball games in history, the Red Sox pulled off a dramatic 12-inning, 7–6 victory after Carlton Fisk willed his home run to stay fair. With Cincinnati leading 6–3 in the bottom of the eighth, Boston manager Darrell Johnson called upon Bernie Carbo—ironically a former first-round pick of the Reds—to pinch hit with two aboard. Carbo worked the count to 2–2 before striking for an improbable three-run shot off reliever Rawly Eastwick to left center, tying the score at six.

In the eleventh, it appeared as though Joe Morgan would put Cincinnati on top after he hit a deep drive to right, but it was Dwight Evans who snared the ball and doubled up Ken Griffey Sr. at first, snuffing out the threat. Finally in the twelfth, Fisk stepped in and on the second pitch of the at-bat, lofted it high down the left-field line. In what has become a classic piece of footage, Fisk wildly waved his arms to the right immediately after making contact, and the ball responded by staying fair, hitting the foul pole and subsequently winning the game for the Red Sox. Despite the victory, the Reds rebounded to win Game 7, taking the World Series hardware back to Cincinnati.

OCTOBER 2, 1978: YANKEES PUT "DENT" IN RED SOX POSTSEASON

In a battle between fierce rivals, Boston squared off against the New York Yankees in a one-game playoff. The tiebreaker was made possible due to the Red Sox winning their final eight games, catching the Yankees in the American League East standings on the very last day of the regular season. Boston held an early 2–0 lead when back-to-back singles sandwiched between two fly ball outs off Boston starter Mike Torrez set the scene for Bucky Dent. Dent, who had accumulated 40 home runs over the course of his career, quieted the Fenway Park crowd with a three-run shot just over the Green Monster, giving the Bronx Bombers a 3–2 lead and eventual win, propelling them to an American League pennant and, later down the road, a World Series title.

APRIL 29, 1986: CLEMENS STRIKES OUT 20

Roger Clemens became the first player in Major League history to strike out 20 batters in a nine-inning game, accomplishing the feat against the Seattle Mariners during a 3–1 victory. Providing baseball with a glimpse of what was to come over the course of his Major League career, "The Rocket" allowed three hits, walked none, and struck out the side three times, retiring eight in a row during the fourth, fifth, and sixth innings. Dwight Evans provided Clemens with all the run support he would require, blasting a three-run shot with two outs in the seventh. Clemens made quick work of Seattle in the ninth, striking out Spike Owen and Phil Bradley before Ken Phelps registered the final out by grounding out to short. Clemens broke the Red Sox record for most strikeouts in a game previously held by Bill Monbouquette, who in 1961, struck out 16.

SEPTEMBER 2, 2001: MUSSINA CLOSE AGAIN TO PERFECTION

On May 30, 1997, as a member of the Baltimore Orioles, pitcher Mike Mussina had cut down 25 consecutive Cleveland Indians batters at Oriole Park at Camden Yards before surrendering a single to Sandy Alomar, ending his bid for a perfect game. Four years later, as a member of the Yankees pitching staff at Fenway Park in a nationally televised game, he again came up short, allowing a two-out, two-strike solid single to Red Sox pinch hitter Carl Everett in the bottom of the ninth. Unfazed, Mussina retired Trot Nixon to finish off the one-hit, 13-strikeout performance and, more importantly, a 1–0 win for New York. The only run for the Yankees came in the top of the ninth, when Enrique Wilson laced an RBI double that brought home pinch runner Clay Bellinger.

JUNE 27, 2003: MARLINS EXPERIENCE BOSTON MASSACRE FIRSTHAND

Johnny Damon singled, doubled, and tripled as part of a 14-run first inning, and Boston scored 10 of those runs without recording an out to establish a Major League record as the Red Sox dismantled the Marlins during an Interleague matchup, 25–8. With the three hits in the first, Damon became only the second player ever to accomplish that feat, leading the incredible 28-hit attack. In summary: The bottom of the first lasted 50 minutes, 91 pitches were thrown by three separate Marlins hurlers, and the 14 runs in the first inning tied a record set by Cleveland against the Philadelphia Athletics in the second game of a doubleheader on June 18, 1950. This game didn't have any lasting effects on Florida as later on down the road they would eventually go on to win the World Series, taking out the favored New York Yankees in a stunning six-game series.

OCTOBER 17, 2004: THE COMEBACK BEGINS

The Red Sox, trailing the New York Yankees three games to none and knowing full well that no team in Major League history ever recovered from such a series deficit, began their quest to become the first with a 6–4 extra-inning comeback win in Game 4 of the American League Championship Series. The Yankees led 4–3 in the bottom of the ninth before Kevin Millar drew a walk-off, arguably the greatest closer in baseball history, Mariano Rivera. From there, Dave Roberts was inserted as a pinch hitter and in one of the most memorable plays in Red Sox history, stole second base just ahead of the tag, keeping the rally alive. Bill Mueller singled him home, tying the score at four while simultaneously changing the complexion of the series. In the twelfth, David Ortiz belted a two-run blast off Paul Quantrill, giving

Boston the walk-off win, ultimately propelling the club to four straight wins and a first 3–0 series comeback in baseball history.

OCTOBER 23, 2004: FALL CLASSIC RETURNS TO BOSTON

In the highest-scoring Game 1 in World Series history, the Red Sox outslugged the National League Champion St. Louis Cardinals, 11–9. In the bottom of the first, David Ortiz smashed a three-run home run that led to a four-run inning, but the Cardinals countered with two runs of their own over the next two innings, pulling to within 4–2. A three-run third pushed the lead to 7–2 for Boston, but St. Louis tallied three in the fourth and two in the sixth, when consecutive doubles by Edgar Renteria and Larry Walker tied the score at seven.

Undeterred, the Red Sox regained command in the home half of the seventh, when RBI singles by Manny Ramirez and Ortiz pushed the lead to 9–7, only to have the Redbirds answer once again, tying it at nine, thanks to multiple errors by Ramirez in left in the top of the eighth. The scoring finally drew to a conclusion in the bottom of the eighth, when Mark Bellhorn dinged a two-run blast off the right-field foul pole, which provided Boston with an 11–9 lead they would not relinquish. The Red Sox would go on to complete the sweep, capturing their first World Series crown in 86 years.

SEPTEMBER 1, 2007: ROOKIE NO-HITS ORIOLES

In just his second start in the Major Leagues, Red Sox right-hander Clay Buchholz was fearless on the mound, striking out nine and throwing a no-hitter against the overmatched Orioles during a 10–0 victory. He became the third pitcher since 1900 to toss a no-hitter in his first or second start, joining Bobo Holloman in 1953 and Wilson Alvarez in 1991. Run support was never an issue for Boston throughout the three-hour, two-minute contest. A three-run double by David Ortiz in the fourth got the offense rolling, and a three-run homer by Kevin Youkilis in the sixth ended any question about whether or not the Red Sox would score enough runs.

But the focal point remained Buchholz, who received a big boost from second baseman Dustin Pedroia in the field during the seventh after he made a no-hit saving play. Miguel Tejada led off for Baltimore and sent a rocket screaming up the middle, but Pedroia was ready and backhanded the ball, got to his feet, and fired a strike to first, retiring the speedy Tejada. In the ninth, Buchholz finished off the gem by striking out Brian Roberts, inducing Corey Patterson into a fly ball out, and saved his best for last, freezing Nick Markakis with a curveball right down Main Street to end the game.

AUGUST 23, 2012: ANGELS OUT-SLUG SOX, WIN SEESAW BATTLE

The Los Angeles Angels stormed into Fenway Park and did the same offensively in the late innings, tallying three runs in the ninth and two more in the tenth to secure a wild 14–13 victory. After Boston jumped out to a 6–0 lead after two, the Angels scored eight in the top of the third, giving fans a glimpse of what was to come. With the Red Sox firmly ahead 11–9 and headed to the top of the ninth, Vernon Wells connected for a solo home run, and Torii Hunter and Mark Trumbo followed with RBI singles, giving the Angels a 12–11 lead. Not to be outdone, Boston outfielder Cody Ross led off the bottom of the ninth with a home run of his own, tying the game at 12. Finally in the tenth, Kendrys Morales homered and two batters later, Wells doubled in a run to give the Angels a 14–12 lead and eventual 14–13 win. The four-hour, 32-minute contest saw a combined 15 pitchers take the mound, 38 total hits, and 410 total pitches.

SEPTEMBER 4, 2013: SOX SLAM EIGHT HOMERS, SCORE 20

The Red Sox tied a franchise record by slamming eight home runs, and David Ortiz notched his 2,000th career hit during a 20–4 pummeling of the playoff-bound Detroit Tigers. Boston led 5–4 heading to the bottom of the sixth before erupting for eight runs, highlighted by a grand slam off the bat of Will Middlebrooks and a two-run shot by Daniel Nava. Also adding home runs were Stephen Drew, Jacoby Ellsbury, Ryan Lavarnway, Mike Napoli, and David Ortiz, who accounted for two. Boston scored in every inning but the first, and in all totaled 19 hits during the offensive onslaught.

OCTOBER 12, 2013: A NEAR NO-HITTER FOR DETROIT

Tigers starting pitcher Anibal Sanchez was unhittable, striking out 12— including a record-tying four in the first inning—and pitching six no-hit innings before paving the way for the bullpen, which came within two outs of the first combined no-hitter in playoff history during a 1–0 win over Boston. In the seventh, Sanchez gave way to Al Alburquerque, who promptly retired the side in order, striking out two. A tag-team effort of Jose Veras (⅔) and Drew Smyly (⅓) took care of the Red Sox in the eighth before Joaquin Benoit came on in the ninth to try and complete only the third no-hitter ever in postseason play. After retiring Mike Napoli via strikeout, Daniel Nava smacked a solid single to center, ending the no-hitter and bringing the go-ahead run to the plate in Stephen Drew, who ended up flying out to right. Benoit then retired Xander Bogaerts, putting an end to any thought of a remarkable win by Boston. In all, Detroit pitching tallied 17 strikeouts, and the only offense—an RBI single by Jhonny Peralta in the top of the sixth—accounted for the final margin of victory.

OCTOBER 19, 2013: RED SOX CAPTURE PENNANT

Shane Victorino connected for a go-ahead grand slam in the seventh, which proved to be the difference, and the Red Sox punched their ticket to the World Series with a 5–2 Game 6 victory over the Detroit Tigers. After the Tigers took a 2–1 lead in the sixth, it appeared as though a Game 7 was becoming more of a reality with 21-game winner Max Scherzer on the mound into the seventh. That's when Boston loaded the bases and Victorino, signed in the off-season to help bolster the offense, stepped to the plate. After falling behind 0–2 to Jose Veras, Victorino hit the shot heard all around Massachusetts that put Boston ahead for good. With the win, it marked the thirteenth time the American League pennant belonged to the Red Sox and first time since 2007, when they defeated the Colorado Rockies in four straight to win the World Series for the second time in four seasons.

OCTOBER 26, 2013: BOSTON RECAPTURES WORLD CHAMPIONSHIP

For the first time in 95 seasons, the Boston Red Sox clinched a World Series at Fenway Park, this time doing so with a convincing 6–1 victory against the St. Louis Cardinals in Game 6. Led by Shane Victorino, who finished the game 2-for-3 with 4 RBI, and World Series MVP David Ortiz, who finished with a .688 batting average in the Fall Classic, the Red Sox tallied three runs in the third and fourth innings—more than enough for starter John Lackey—to put the finishing touches on the club's eighth championship. It was a stunning turnaround for Boston, who finished 2012 in last place before putting the pieces together in returning to championship form. With two outs in the ninth, Cardinals leadoff hitter Matt Carpenter struck out, setting off a wild celebration not seen at the Boston relic since September 11, 1918, when the Red Sox finished off the Chicago Cubs.

WHAT THEY'RE SAYING ABOUT FENWAY PARK

GEORGE BRETT: "[It's my] favorite place to play. The fans were so close and they are so knowledgeable about the game. It [was] always so fun to play in front of 35,000 fans when the stadium holds 35,000 fans. . . . They got a great tradition and when you go to the bathroom, you are pissing in the same urinal as Babe Ruth and all the other greats who have played there."

MARK BUEHRLE: "[It is] probably one of my favorite old places. I am not a fan of places like Wrigley [Field]. . . . [I was] not really crazy about the old Yankee Stadium, so of the older ones, [Fenway Park] is probably one of my favorites."

JOHNNY DAMON: "Great ballpark, great tradition. . . . It is definitely old and can use a few things, but I think they have done everything great to make it up-to-date, fan-friendly, and player-friendly."

JASON GIAMBI: "Nostalgic when you start to think of all the names that have played on that field, and you get to walk amongst them and see all the history and tradition. . . . Being on the field is pretty incredible."

JONNY GOMES: "I would have to say Fenway [Park] is my favorite, and the only thing that separates it from Wrigley [Field] is the visible dents in the wall [and] knowing those are [from] Babe Ruth, Ted Williams, and Wade Boggs."

JOSH HAMILTON: "It is hard to beat the history there [at Fenway Park]. It is probably the only stadium where the first time I played there I got nervous—walking out of the clubhouse, down the little hallway out to the field, and just knowing the history of the guys who [made the same trek], and the big wall in left, the legend of Ted Williams . . . it is pretty cool."

KEN "HAWK" HARRELSON, BROADCASTER: "I just hope and pray that when Fenway [Park] goes, it is empty. . . . I always walk by some of the places [inside Fenway Park that] I used to as a player and they are still crappy."

EVAN LONGORIA: "Fenway [Park] is fun, it is an experience in [and] of itself. Those fans are wild and they are all there for the Red Sox. You do not hear any other fans in there besides them. . . . I think it is more exciting to play there just because of the history of the ballpark more than anything else."

DON MATTINGLY: "Fenway [Park] I loved playing in. Just everything about [it] is cool looking. . . . [It's] really bad from a player's standpoint with the cages, locker rooms, dugout, and just listening to some of my family that were at games—the seats were too tight and all that stuff, so I heard a lot of negatives."

MARK MCGWIRE: "I enjoyed Fenway Park very much. I liked when they decided to tarp off center field. Back when they did not do it and you used to face Bruce Hurst, who had one of the biggest 12–6 curveballs around, it would come out of the stands and you would have to basically be in a squat stance so you could see the ball out of his hand."

FENWAY PARK FACTS AND FIGURES

FENWAY PARK ADDRESS
4 Yawkey Way, Boston, MA 02215

BOSTON RED SOX TEAM WEB SITE
www.redsox.com

FIELD DIMENSIONS (in feet)
Left Field: 310', Left-Center: 379', Center: 390',
Right-Center: 380', Right Field: 302'

SEATING CAPACITY (as of 2015)
37,499

ALL-STAR GAMES AT FENWAY PARK
July 9, 1946: American League 12, National 0
MVP: Not awarded until 1962
July 31, 1961: American League 1, National League 1 (9 innings)
MVP: Not awarded until 1962
July 13, 1999: American League 4, National League 1
MVP: Pedro Martinez, Boston Red Sox (AL)

FENWAY PARK FIRSTS
Game: April 20, 1912—Boston 7, New York 6
Single: Harry Wolter, New York (April 20, 1912)*
Double: Steve Yerkes, Boston (April 20, 1912)
Triple: Walter Johnson, Washington (April 24, 1912)
Home Run: Hugh Bradley, Boston (April 26, 1912)

*Denotes first hit in the stadium.

NATIONALS PARK
HOME OF THE WASHINGTON NATIONALS

Nationals Park, Washington Nationals (*Photographed by Russel Tiffin/Flickr*)

The well-traveled Washington Nationals could certainly boast of quite an itinerary prior to their arrival at the nation's capital in 2005. Once the Montreal Expos, they were forced to play at Olympic Stadium, a drab, cavernous ballpark that featured an atmosphere similar to that of your local library. And although they had great teams (including the 1994 team, which most likely would have challenged for the World Series had there not been a strike), on any given night plenty of seats were vacant, leaving the team to wonder if there was any hope of staying north of the border and receiving a new ballpark.

It had appeared as though the then-Expos would have a new stadium deal pending in 2000, when former owner Jeffrey Loria presented a plan for a new Expos ballpark in downtown Montreal. The overall cost was a bargain price tag of $200 million, significantly less than other ballparks going up around the Major League Baseball landscape.

Even before the new proposals were officially announced, the Expos and Labatt Brewing Company had teamed up to sign a sponsorship deal that would last 20 years, beginning in 2001, and pay the Montreal franchise $100 million over the course of the term. As part of the deal, the naming rights would go to the brewing giant and the ballpark would be known as Labatt

Park. The agreement was announced in 2000, but in the end, the Montreal Expos franchise was sold to the other 29 Major League teams, and on September 24, 2004, it was announced that the team would be leaving Quebec for Washington, DC.

When the team moved to Washington, they spent their first three seasons at RFK. Stadium before heading into Nationals Park. The ballpark, located along the Anacosta River in the Navy Yard neighborhood of Washington, DC, was a site chosen out of four possible sites by Washington Mayor Anthony Williams. Preliminary plans were released to the public on March 14, 2006, with the groundbreaking taking place shortly after. Thanks to an ambitious group of builders who helped construct Nationals Park, it opened right in time for Opening Day 2008, a quick turnaround considering that the bulldozers and cranes were first fired up in May 2006 and that many stadiums take between 36 to 48 months to complete.

An interesting discovery occurred during the early stages of construction when a layer of fill and bricks was found 12–14 feet below the surface. There was some speculation that it had been a roadway until the 1800s. The reason it wasn't found earlier? Garbage had been dumped on top of it.

HOK Sport, the architect of the ballpark, incorporated a unique feature from Griffith Stadium, the home of the former Washington franchise, the Senators. The odd, right-angled jag that is currently in the right-center-field fence is a subtle tribute to the ballpark that was once a mainstay before it was demolished in 1965.

The ballpark's name is a tribute to the past—to the original name of Griffith Stadium, utilized by the Washington Senators, before it was rebuilt in the early 1900s. Nationals Park was originally supposed to be only a temporary name until it was sold to a sponsor, but because a strong bid never materialized, the team elected to keep Nationals Park as its title.

When all was said and done, the $611 million Nationals Park became the newest landmark in the Washington, DC, area and provided a jolt to the Capitol Riverfront area. It also became the first major professional sports stadium in the United States to be LEED-certified (Leadership in Energy and Environmental Design), ultimately transforming into an environmentally friendly ballpark that uses methods to preserve the Earth's natural beauty.

SPECIAL FEATURES OF NATIONALS PARK

BEERPEN

The Beerpen, one of the popular spots within the ballpark, is a small part of the Scoreboard Walk, located in center field. It offers fans the opportunity to knock down a cold one while conversing with friends and family members. This high-energy, outdoor gathering spot comes to life during Nationals games and has three levels of standing room with bar-height drink rails. On select dates, pregame music and drink specials become the focal point and help make things even more exciting.

BUSINESS CENTER

The fourth level of the Stars and Stripes Club is where businesses can take advantage of top-notch technology. Tickets, credentials, or a pass are necessary for entry into the quiet work area, which has desks and various office supplies on hand for handling day-to-day operations.

CHERRY BLOSSOM TREES

There are 14 Kwanzan Japanese cherry blossom trees in the Center Field Plaza and Main Concourse areas, and in a spot beyond left field. Grown in southeastern Pennsylvania, the trees were transplanted on March 6, 2008, and an official dedication ceremony followed. In Japan and according to the Buddhist tradition, the cherry blossom tree symbolizes the transient nature of life. It is also associated with the samurai and is often depicted in art in samurai culture.

COMMEMORATIVE SEATS

Located inside the Diamond Club are two seats, accompanied by photos that commemorate mammoth blasts by two Washington players. A yellow seat, atop a brick base, pays tribute to a monster home run off the bat of Ryan Zimmerman that was eventually moved to the upper deck of RFK Stadium. To the right of it, a white seat, transported from RFK Stadium's upper deck, acknowledges a gigantic blast off the bat of former Washington slugger, Frank Howard.

CONFERENCE CENTER

For business clients, a conference center is available for rent with room for up to 300 in the main area and "break-out rooms" that can each accommodate 50 people. Located on the South Capitol Street side of the ballpark, it's a perfect place for winning over potential clients and stepping up to the plate when it comes to delivering game-winning presentations and speeches.

DIAMOND CLUB

The Diamond Club, situated between the dugouts, gives viewers another exceptional spot to take in Nationals Park and all its beauty. "Diamond Seats" in this ticketed area include access to the Diamond Club, which features an all-inclusive food menu and extensive draft beer selection. Nearby, a replica scoreboard hangs over the bar and displays the box score from Game 7 of the 1924 World Series (won by Washington, 4–3, in 12 innings over the New York Giants), paying tribute to the franchise's only title.

HALL OF PRESIDENTS

In the hallway of the Presidents Club, photos of former United States presidents who have participated in throwing out the first pitch line the wall. In all, 16 photos show the former commanders-in-chief tossing out the ceremonial first pitch, along with a brief description of the action underneath the photo. One of the more symbolic is of George W. Bush taking to the mound during the 2001 World Series—the year of the tragic September 11 attacks—and throwing a perfect strike right at Yankee Stadium in New York.

HISTORICAL TIMELINES

There is a timeline highlighting Washington's baseball history behind the home plate area on the concourse level. The display honors the 1901–60 club (known as the Senators before their move to Minnesota) and the 1961–71 team (before their relocation to Texas). All the key moments are noted, along with the greatest players who donned a Washington uniform and have made the biggest contributions in the history of the franchise.

LUXURY SUITES

Suites named for former presidents George Washington, Abraham Lincoln, and Thomas Jefferson provide sweeping views of Nationals Park, while offering fans an atmosphere similar to that of a condominium. Each suite includes leather-wrapped chairs, marble-topped tables, woven carpet, and tile flooring. Additionally, 42-inch televisions mounted above a wet bar enhance the overall experience. If you want to go outside to catch some of the game, sliding doors open to reveal stunning views of the field and three levels of seating.

OVERSIZED HAT

During the 2009 off-season, the Nationals installed an oversized baseball hat that stands near the center-field plaza above the entrance to the team shop. The hat, suitable for Big Bird or any other larger-than-life character, is entirely red with the signature Washington "W" in the middle. For the record, the Nationals wear a smaller version of the model for all home games.

PRESIDENTS CLUB

Fittingly named considering its location, the Presidents Club offers occupants the ultimate in luxury and satisfies those craving an experience that is "nothing but the best." With enough top-notch wood and marble to make you feel as though you are the president of the United States, exceptional comfort, combined with gourmet dining and multiple beer and wine options, highlight this members-only location. Inside, two walls of windows offer an inside look at the home batting cages and press conference room, where all the action occurs following a game.

RED PORCH RESTAURANT

The Red Porch, situated in center field, is one of the more popular destinations in Nationals Park, and was expanded and overhauled following the 2009 season. Tables were added to the concourse and field level, sliding glass doors opening onto a patio replaced stationary glass windows on the concourse side, and center-field lounge seats were replaced with an outdoor deck and patio. Just above, the Red Loft combines direct access to a full-service bar with great views of the baseball field. As an added touch, the seats at the Red Porch are red, a stark contrast to the dark-blue color scheme that dominates the rest of Nationals Park.

The right-field scoreboard serves as the primary information base for fans.
(*Photographed by Russel Tiffin/Flickr*)

RETIRED NUMBERS

Other than Jackie Robinson's number 42, which was retired by baseball universally on April 15, 1997, the Washington Nationals currently have no other retired uniform numbers.

SHIRLEY POVICH MEDIA CENTER

Named in honor of the late Hall of Fame writer, Shirley Povich, the Nationals press box, which is directly behind home plate in the upper deck, is chock-full of top-notch audio and video options for broadcasters and writers. Povich, a sports columnist and reporter for the *Washington Post* and sports editor for 41 years, was best known for entertaining fans with his daily articles on baseball entitled "This Morning with Shirley Povich." As an added touch, a typewriter once used by Povich is displayed inside the press box. He was inducted into the National Baseball Hall of Fame in 1975.

STADIUM TURF

Nationals Park has one of the finest fields, which consists of three varieties of grass—Midnight Star, Princeton 105, and Brilliant. The warning track trucked in from Culpepper, Virginia, features a blend of crushed stone. The infield dirt is from nearby Maryland and, for good measure, is topped off with a deep red shade, providing a distinctive look.

STARS AND STRIPES CLUB

A dining lounge and two full-service bars are part of a 33,000 square-foot space for fans to enjoy and relax in while taking in a Nationals game and conversing with friends. Truly a swanky locale, access to the Stars and Stripes Club and mezzanine levels requires a ticket. On non-game days, it can be rented out and utilized for parties or other festive occasions that require much pomp and circumstance.

STATUES AT NATIONALS PARK

The center-field plaza is the home to white-bronzed statues honoring Frank Howard, Walter Johnson, and Negro Leagues superstar Josh Gibson.

JOSH GIBSON: Starring for the Homestead Grays, who played most of their games in Washington, Gibson is considered to be the greatest Negro Leagues player of all time. It is said that he crushed over 800 home runs throughout the course of his career and was a double threat by being dominant behind the plate. In 1972, he received baseball's highest honor when the Negro League Committee voted to induct him into the Baseball Hall of Fame.

FRANK HOWARD: As a member of the Washington Senators from 1965 to 1971, Howard was a consistent power threat at the plate. He proved his mettle by connecting for 44 home runs in two separate seasons (1968 and 1970), and in 16 Major League seasons accumulated 382 career long balls.

WALTER JOHNSON: Arguably one of the greatest pitchers of all time, Johnson registered 417 wins and 3,509 strikeouts over the course of his 21-year big league career. Elected into the Hall of Fame in 1936, "The Big Train" was a two-time winner of the American League MVP (1913 and 1924) and pitched in two World Series (1924 and 1925), compiling a 3–3 record with five complete games, 35 strikeouts, and a 2.52 ERA.

MEMORABLE GAMES AT NATIONALS PARK

MARCH 30, 2008: FIRST GAME AT NATIONALS PARK

With President George W. Bush on hand to throw out the ceremonial first pitch, the Nationals couldn't have scripted it any better in their triumphant return to Washington with a 3–2 victory over the Atlanta Braves. Nationally televised, a sold-out crowd of 39,389 watched Ryan Zimmerman hit a walk-off home run with two outs in the bottom of the ninth to stun Atlanta. In the bottom of the first, Nationals shortstop Christian Guzman sliced a single to right for the first hit, and a batter later, Nick Johnson achieved the first extra base knock with a double. In the top of the fourth, Braves third baseman Chipper Jones cranked the first home run in the Nationals' new digs.

JUNE 4, 2009: JOHNSON REACHES ANOTHER MILESTONE

Considering throughout the course of his career he had thrown a no-hitter, perfect game, and struck out 20 in a game, it would make sense that intimidating lefty Randy Johnson would add to his Hall of Fame credentials by registering his 300th career win. It happened on his first attempt at the milestone as a member of the San Francisco Giants, as part of a dominating performance in which "The Big Unit" allowed two hits through six innings during a 5–1 win. With the W, he became the twenty-fourth pitcher and sixth left-handed tosser to accomplish the feat. A two-run double by Randy Winn in the top of the ninth put the Giants ahead, 4–1, at that point, sealing the deal for Johnson during a soggy night in the nation's capital.

JUNE 8, 2010: STRASBURG DEBUTS, CUTS DOWN PIRATES

In one of the most highly anticipated debuts for a pitcher in Major League history, Stephen Strasburg took to the mound and cut down the free-swinging Pirates, striking out 14 and dazzling the charged-up crowd of 40,315 at Nationals Park during a 5–2 win against Pittsburgh. Strasburg went seven innings, threw 94 pitches (65 for strikes), walked none, and set down the final 10 he faced, 7 by way of the strikeout. His 14-strikeout performance fell one short of the Major League record for most in a debut held by J. R. Richard of the Astros (September 5, 1971) and Karl Spooner of the Dodgers (September 22, 1954). The only blemish came when Delwyn Young connected for a two-run shot in the top of the fourth. Strasburg was aided by a Nationals offense that connected for three home runs, thanks to Ryan Zimmerman (solo shot in the first), Adam Dunn (two-run blast in the sixth), and Josh Willingham (solo shot in the sixth).

OCTOBER 10, 2012: PLAYOFFS RETURN TO WASHINGTON

For the first time in 79 years, playoff baseball returned to the nation's capital, but St. Louis flexed their muscles and shut out Washington, 8–0. Leading 1–0 in the second, Cardinals rookie Pete Kozma connected for a three-run home run off Nationals starter—and former St. Louis tosser—Edwin Jackson, and they never looked back. Chris Carpenter took the mound for the Redbirds and was as solid as one could be, throwing up scoreless frames into the sixth inning and helping out his cause by connecting for two hits. In the eighth, Matt Holliday lined a two-run single that pushed the score to 8–0 and sent the capacity crowd of 45,017 home disappointed. The last time the playoffs made a stop in Washington was on October 7, 1933, at Griffith Stadium during Game 5 of the World Series, a contest won in 10 innings by the New York Giants 4–3, who, with the win, clinched the championship.

OCTOBER 12, 2012: CARDINALS STUN NATIONALS FOR TRIP TO NLCS

St. Louis rallied from an early 6–0 deficit scoring four runs in the ninth to ultimately come out on top, 9–7 and staking claim to the largest comeback ever in a winner-take-all postseason contest. Things looked bleak for the defending champions after Washington jumped out to a 3–0 advantage after Ryan Zimmerman blasted a home run and rookie sensation Bryce Harper followed suit in the third with a long ball of his own. Undeterred, the Cardinals kept creeping back and finally took the lead in the ninth after two-out singles from Daniel Descalso and Pete Kozma made it 9–7. Closer Jason Motte came on and retired the Nationals in order, simultaneously ending Washington's dream season.

APRIL 1, 2013: HARPER YOUNGEST TO HIT MULTIPLE HOMERS ON OPENING DAY

Bryce Harper, at 20 years and 167 days old, connected for two home runs in his first two at-bats, becoming the youngest player to do so in a team's first game as the Nationals defeated the punchless Marlins, 2–0. Complicating matters for Miami was Washington starter Stephen Strasburg, who struck out three, walked none, and retired 19 batters in a row before Miami's Giancarlo Stanton connected for a double to left in the seventh. Harper wasted little time etching his name in the history books, hitting a 406-foot bomb to right in the first off Miami starter Ricky Nolasco and a 410-foot blast in almost the same location off Nolasco in the fourth.

APRIL 22, 2014: PUJOLS JOINS 500-HOME RUN CLUB

With two swings of the bat, Los Angeles Angels slugger Albert Pujols became the twenty-sixth member of the 500-home run club, also becoming the first in baseball history to slug number 499 and 500 in the same game during a 7–2 victory. Pujols, the most recent player to accomplish the feat since Gary Sheffield did so as a member of the Mets on April 17, 2009, wasted little time victimizing Nationals starter Taylor Jordan in the first with a three-run shot and again in the fifth with a two-run shot to left-center field for the history-maker. As a sign of respect, the Nationals faithful rose to their feet and gave Pujols a standing ovation and in return, he tipped his cap to the crowd.

SEPTEMBER 28, 2014: INCREDIBLE CATCH PRESERVES HISTORIC FEAT

Washington pitcher Jordan Zimmerman tossed the first no-hitter of his career and first in Nationals history, receiving major help in the process during a 1–0 victory on the final day of the regular season. With two outs in the ninth, Marlins leadoff hitter Christian Yelich drilled a Zimmerman offering to deep left-center, where rookie Steven Souza Jr., inserted as a defensive replacement in the ninth, made a tumbling catch to end the game and help rewrite the Nationals history book. From a historical standpoint, it became the first no-hitter in the nation's capital since Bobby Burke did so as a member of the Senators against Boston in 1931. Ian Desmond accounted for the only run of the game when he smacked a 393-foot home run to left-center off Marlins starter Henderson Alvarez, who ironically pitched a no-hitter on the final day of the 2013 season at Marlins Park against the Detroit Tigers.

OCTOBER 4, 2014: GIANTS WIN 18-INNING MARATHON

In a game that lasted 6 hours and 23 minutes by time and totaled 18 innings, San Francisco's Brandon Belt became the latest postseason hero after launching a solo home run in the top of the 18th off relief pitcher Tanner Roark, as the Giants outlasted Washington 2–1, tying the mark for most innings in the longest postseason game but setting a new time record. Trailing 1–0 heading into the top of the ninth, Pablo Sandoval came through in the clutch, slashing an RBI double that scored rookie Joe Panik but also saw Buster Posey thrown out at the plate, preventing the eventual go-ahead run. Both teams would play scoreless ball before Belt launched a no-doubter into the right-field seats and Hunter Strickland tossed an uneventful bottom of the 18th, giving the Giants a win for the ages on the road.

WHAT THEY'RE SAYING ABOUT NATIONALS PARK

BOB CARPENTER, BROADCASTER: "When people talk about [Nationals Park] from a baseball standpoint, the one thing they talk about most is that it plays fair [and] the dimensions are pretty standard; it is slightly asymmetrical in the outfield, you have to hit the ball over a 15-foot scoreboard if you go right-center.... [As a pitcher], you are not going to give up any cheap home runs."

J. J. HARDY: "Bigger, one of the ... fairer ballparks, and not necessarily a good hitter's ballpark or a good pitcher's ballpark, but one that is fair."

BRYCE HARPER: "Nationals Park is a beautiful ballpark right down in the city and it is a really fair park for pitchers and hitters.... It is big and just a beautiful ballpark."

ADAM JONES: It is nice, but it is different.... [They have] a big old scoreboard that I want to play Madden [video game for PlayStation] on."

MATT KEMP: "It is a pretty nice ballpark.... For me, I like to hit the ball to right-center and that right-center wall is pretty tall, so you definitely have to crush the ball to get it over right-center."

ADAM LAROCHE: "It starts out tough when it is colder out and the ball does not fly real well, but the further we get into [the] summer, it warms up a little bit and it plays pretty fair."

STEVE LYONS, BROADCASTER: "Worse vantage point to be a broadcaster. You are a nine iron away from home plate, so I have to watch the monitor more than I would like to.... Overall, it is a nice place if you are a fan, but I have never been a fan there."

NATE MCLOUTH: "They did a very good job with the clubhouse.... [Overall] it is great."

CHARLEY STEINER, BROADCASTER: "I like it a lot except for one thing. We are so high up [in the press box] that when it rains, we are above the clouds and it is difficult to track a fly ball there.... The other bad part, from a broadcaster's point of view, [is that] we are so high up [and] that is where they shoot the fireworks from, so when they hit a home run, it is like incoming!"

NEIL WALKER: "It is very, very nice.... It is player-friendly, [and] the amenities, clubhouse, field, and dugout [are nice]. They do a good job of maintaining it and keeping it a nice place for the players."

NATIONALS PARK FACTS AND FIGURES

NATIONALS PARK ADDRESS
1500 South Capitol Street SE, Washington, DC 20003

WASHINGTON NATIONALS TEAM WEB SITE
www.nationals.com

FIELD DIMENSIONS (in feet)
Left Field: 336', Left-Center: 377', Center: 402', Right-Center: 370', Right Field: 335'

SEATING CAPACITY (as of 2015)
41,418

ALL-STAR GAMES AT NATIONALS PARK
None

NATIONALS PARK FIRSTS
Game: March 30, 2008—Washington 3, Atlanta 2
Single: Cristian Guzman, Washington (March 30, 2008)*
Double: Nick Johnson, Washington (March 30, 2008)
Triple: Cristian Guzman, Washington (April 7, 2008)
Home Run: Chipper Jones, Atlanta (March 30, 2008)

Denotes first hit in the stadium.

ORIOLE PARK AT CAMDEN YARDS

HOME OF THE BALTIMORE ORIOLES

Oriole Park at Camden Yards, Baltimore Orioles (*Photographed by Russel Tiffin/Flickr*)

On the ballpark landscape, you can thank the Baltimore Orioles organization for going out on a limb. For nearly 30 years, multipurpose, cookie-cutter stadiums were being constructed everywhere and were all the rage. However, when the Orioles decided to authorize the construction of a baseball-only ballpark at 333 West Camden Street, little did they realize it would soon set the standard for all others to come.

Not only did Oriole Park at Camden Yards lift the spirits of baseball around the downtown area, but it kicked off a new period within the game of ballpark building that has seen the likes of Veterans Stadium and other massive, cement-laden structures crumble, while palaces such as PNC Park and Marlins Ballpark now rule the roost.

Positioned right on the inner harbor, Oriole Park at Camden Yards sits on an 85-acre parcel of land and rose to fame in just 33 months. The final price tag was $110 million, a bargain by today's standards. The actual construction began on June 28, 1989, or for all you ballpark historians out there, only 23 days after Toronto's Rogers Centre debuted.

An interesting note is that before the plans to scrap the multipurpose Memorial Stadium took place, the Maryland Stadium Authority actually drew up plans to model Oriole Park at Camden Yards after US Cellular Field, the new home of the White Sox. That idea was quickly tossed out the window when many favored the beginning of a trendy nostalgic look. Some time later, a design for a new baseball-only facility was sketched, and all those involved with the project soon fell in love with the prospect that their new ballpark could soon set the bar high for those to follow—and did it ever.

This was a publicly funded project financed through the creation of a new instant lottery game approved by the Maryland state government in 1987. All the proceeds from the sweepstakes went toward financial support for Oriole Park at Camden Yards. As you can imagine, there was some serious uproar regarding the way it was handled. What incensed many was that ultimately, the less-than-rich folks were the ones basically funding the stadium, since they had more reason to purchase lottery tickets in the hopes of striking it big, while most average and well-to-do people didn't really have much incentive to gamble.

Another complication was the refusal of Maryland's legislature a few years earlier to use the lottery as a way to fund schools in dire need of restructuring. When Camden Yards was brought to the table, it once again appeared as though sports took precedence over education.

The one-time railroad center is also home to arguably the greatest player in baseball history, Babe Ruth. And while there is no evidence that the "curse of the Bambino" exists at this location—what is now center field—it used to be the home of Ruth's Café, a coffee shop operated by Ruth's father. HOK Sport worked with many other firms to design what truly has become—and still is—one of the most eye-pleasing stadiums in the Majors.

Not only does Oriole Park at Camden Yards combine the feel of the downtown district, but it also takes a cue from the twentieth century and history of days gone by. Steel, rather than concrete, rules the landscape, while an arched brick façade, an asymmetrical playing field, and a natural grass field pay tribute to Ebbets Field, Fenway Park, and others that played home to Major League Baseball.

Sure, Memorial Stadium was the home to some of the greatest years in this franchise's history, but there's no denying that the city of Baltimore and the Orioles did it right by moving into a ballpark that truly captures the feeling a baseball park should possess. The days of the cavernous, rounded structures are gone forever, and you can thank Oriole Park at Camden Yards for putting an end to them.

SPECIAL FEATURES OF ORIOLE PARK AT CAMDEN YARDS

ALL-STAR CAFÉ

This café, which celebrates the two Major League Baseball All-Star Games hosted by the city of Baltimore in 1958 and 1993, is available to all club-level fans both before and during the game through the fifth inning. Great food and drinks are just the beginning, and orders from Boog's Barbecue can be made from this locale as well. Formerly known as the Diamond Bistro, the café is described as a "marketplace-style food court featuring a rotating menu of cooked to order entrees and an extensive dessert station," according to the Orioles.

BABE RUTH STATUE

He might not have played for the Baltimore Orioles, but that doesn't mean his legacy doesn't live on in his hometown. The four-foot-tall statue of a much younger Bambino, which greets fans who enter the ballpark through Gate H, depicts the baseball legend holding a bat over his shoulder, while his left hand holds a right-handed fielder's glove. While Ruth is historically known as a lefty and it might not make sense why he would be holding a right-handed glove, legend has it that when he was a youngster, the school he attended didn't have any left-handed gloves, so he settled for using a right-handed one and ultimately made the most of it.

BALTIMORE AND OHIO WAREHOUSE

If there ever were an instance of a building in desperate need of a miracle, it would have been the B&O Warehouse, which now has become a mainstay and icon within the ballpark's landscape. It took as long to build it as the actual ballpark (33 months). The building is the longest structure on the East Coast at 1,016 feet, but it went into major decline in 1988. Nearly every windowpane was broken, rats had taken over all eight floors of the building, and the bricks were beginning to crumble so badly that it posed a serious threat of becoming a major problem.

After many renovations and some serious work, the building now houses Orioles executives, ticket offices, and banquet facilities. A bar and lounge area called Bambino's is located on the bottom floor, and the eighth floor is home to the exclusive members-only Camden Club. The ballpark and warehouse are separated by a 60-foot-wide promenade, which is merely an extension of Eutaw Street. The building is 439 feet from the dish, and to prevent baseballs from breaking the windows, shatterproof glass was installed on the first three floors in case a left-handed slugger was to take aim at the building itself.

During the 1992 All-Star Game home run derby, Ken Griffey Jr. did just that, blasting a shot off the building and becoming the first player to ever do so.

BOOG'S BARBEQUE

When Boog Powell starred for the Orioles from 1961 to 1974, he was a force at the plate. Now that Powell is retired, he is a force to be reckoned with at the grill, cooking up some incredible food at his barbecue, located behind the center-field bleachers on Eutaw Street. Boog creates some of the best barbecue beef, pork, and turkey dishes available at Oriole Park at Camden Yards.

CAL RIPKEN JR. SEAT

To honor the new "Iron Man" and his 278th career home run, the Orioles marked, with a red seat, the spot where the ball landed. It is located in section 86, row FF, seat 10. Ripken Jr. hit the then-historic home run off of the Twins Scott Erickson on July 15, 1993, which surpassed the previous Major League record for shortstops held by Ernie Banks (but has since been broken).

CAL RIPKEN SR. PLAQUE

Inside the first-base dugout is a plaque that pays tribute to the late, great Cal Ripken Sr., a man whose guidance and nurturing of young players made him likable throughout the game. In a dedication ceremony before Cal Ripken Jr.'s final contest on October 6, 2001, the Orioles unveiled the tablet, which reads:

> CAL RIPKEN SR.
> Dedicated to a lifelong Oriole of thirty-six years, and one of the game's greatest teachers.
> Coach, manager and devoted mentor to countless young Orioles, "Senior" dedicated his life to baseball and passed on his respect of the game to everyone he coached. He preached "perfect practice, makes perfect" and stressed the importance of being prepared, learning the "right way" and playing to the best of one's ability every inning of every game.
>
> We will always remember his devotion to the Orioles, his love of the game, and his many lessons. . . .

Ripken Sr. was elected into the Orioles Hall of Fame in 1996 and sadly passed away on March 25, 1999, from cancer.

CAMDEN SEAT

Originally installed for the first time in this ballpark, this chair is designed for those who wish to recline their seat back a bit to take in the action more comfortably. It was one of the more innovative designs that made its world debut in 1992, and it paved the way for what now has become a permanent fixture in every Major League ballpark across the country.

CAMDEN STATION

Located on the north end of the warehouse is Camden Station, which first opened in 1856, was the departure point for travel from Baltimore to the rest of the country, and has become a significant part of the ballpark's landscape. The building, an expansion of the Babe Ruth Museum, measures 22,000 square feet and has been unused since 1980.

The inaugural Baltimore Orioles franchise arrived at Camden Station from Detroit to open the season in 1954 for the first game in Memorial Stadium history. Former United States President Abraham Lincoln passed through the station twice, once en route to his inauguration in 1861, and a second time on his way to deliver the Gettysburg Address. As part of renovations in 2004, the Gentleman's Waiting Room was restored to its Civil War magnificence.

CENTER-FIELD BAR

This bar and lounge, added during the twentieth season at Camden Yards in 2012, is situated behind the center-field wall and has quickly become a fan favorite. Its roof-deck vantage point features a rectangular open-air bar that comes complete with flat-screen televisions, "Orioles orange" couches, bar stools, and umbrellas. Unsurpassed views of the ballpark set the gold standard for Major League ballparks to follow upon its completion in 1992.

EDDIE MURRAY SEAT

Eddie Murray was one of the greatest baseball players and switch-hitters of all time. An orange seat was erected in the bleacher section to mark the location where his 500th career home run landed. The shot came on September 6, 1996—exactly one year to the day Cal Ripken Jr. reached baseball immortality by surpassing Lou Gehrig—off the Tigers Felipe Lira. It is located in section 96, row D, seat 23.

EUTAW STREET

This famous street forms a link between the B&O Warehouse and Oriole Park at Camden Yards. Fans congregate here before games, and have many options prior to the gates officially opening. If satisfying hunger is the goal,

This new area for fans was created before 2013 and offers a unique vantage point of the field. (*Photographed by John Patti*)

Boog Powell's Barbeque or a world-famous Baltimore crab cake is the answer. If quenching a thirst is the objective, grab a cold one before the first pitch.

Keep an eye out—you might even get lucky and have the chance to snag a home run ball during batting practice. To honor the players who have deposited balls on Eutaw Street during games via a home run, brass baseball plates are embedded into the sidewalk, marking the spots where baseballs landed. On each plate is the hitter's name, his team's logo, the distance the ball traveled, and the date on which it occurred.

FLAG COURT

For their twentieth season in 2012, the Orioles lowered the right-field scoreboard by four feet and incorporated waist-level iron railings, replacing a stone wall that once made views of the action tough for shorter fans. This change allowed for clearer views of the field for those who like to mingle in the area atop the scoreboard. In addition, 15 flagpoles each represent a team in the American League. Once games are completed for the day, members of the Orioles staff rearrange the flags to correspond with each team's standing in their respective division, à la Wrigley Field.

FOUL POLES

To pay homage to the previous residence of the ball club, Memorial Stadium, the Orioles transported the right-field foul pole from that stadium to Oriole Park at Camden Yards. It is now atop the tall wall in right field in the Flag Court. Additionally, before the 2001 season began, the Orioles replaced the original left-field foul pole with the one used at Memorial Stadium, and at 70 feet high, it was 20 feet shorter than the previous one. While it seems as though the winning ways of the 1970s and the World Series magic of yesteryear didn't exactly come with the poles, it was nice to see a relic of the now-defunct ballpark.

LEFT-FIELD PICNIC PERCH

Looking for a ticket to the game and an opportunity to load up on food before, during, and after? Search no further than these seats where, as part of the Left-Field Club Box seat purchase, you'll get unlimited hot dogs, nachos, sodas, and other select items whenever you want. That's a nice perk to an already-incredible bird's-eye view of Oriole Park at Camden Yards for a baseball game.

LEGENDS PARK

To commemorate 20 seasons of Orioles baseball at Camden Yards, in 2012 six statues were unveiled at Legends Park, which is just beyond the bullpens in center field. The six Orioles legends honored with statues included Eddie Murray, Jim Palmer, Cal Ripken Jr., Brooks Robinson, Frank Robinson, and former manager Earl Weaver. These bronze likenesses range in size from seven to eight feet, and weigh anywhere between 600 and 1,500 pounds each.

MAIN SCOREBOARD

A new LED video board, installed in 2008 courtesy of Mitsubishi, enlightens fans with stats, crystal-clear imaging, and plenty of information. A new DiamondVision LED video board now sits atop the LED scoreboard and delivers a brand-new experience to fans. It features each team's roster while at-bat, and the bottom portion of the upper half displays the in-game box score, complete with balls, strikes, and number of outs. The bottom half of the scoreboard displays player information flanked by two advertisements. At the very top is a retro clock, flanked by two Orioles bird weather vanes, which let fans know whether or not the ball will be flying out of the ballpark more so than usual.

MARYLAND ATHLETIC HALL OF FAME

With all the honors and Hall of Fames in Baltimore, perhaps Major League Baseball should consider moving the National Baseball Hall of Fame to Oriole Park at Camden Yards! The Maryland Athletic Hall of Fame is on the wall of sections 1 to 3 on Eutaw Street, and plaques scattered about the area honor native Maryland residents who represent more than 30 different sports.

MEMORIAL WALL

The south end of the B&O warehouse is dominated by a memorial wall for which ground was broken on Veteran's Day 2002 to honor residents of Maryland whose lives were taken in all of our nation's wars. At Baltimore's previous ballpark, Memorial Stadium, there was a similar wall. The 11-foot-tall, curving black granite partition features a quote: "Time Will Not Dim the Glory of Their Deeds."

ORIOLES HALL OF FAME

On the wall at the base of the scoreboard at the north end of the warehouse are many plaques that honor the men who have made significant contributions to the Baltimore Orioles organization while they played with the team. Members are inducted on a yearly basis, and the plaques are similar to the ones at the National Baseball Hall of Fame in Cooperstown. Each plaque features a picture and brief narrative of accomplishments that the recipient contributed to the organization while in uniform.

PLAQUES IN BULLPEN AND DUGOUT

There are more plaques to recognize men who have helped create history for the Baltimore Orioles. Relief pitcher Jesse Orosco, who passed Dennis Eckersley for the Major League record for most games pitched by recording his 1,072nd on August 17, 1999, is commemorated with a plaque with his uniform number (47) added to the Orioles bench above the bullpen. For former manager Earl Weaver's induction into the Hall of Fame, a silver plaque with his number (4), along with his years managing the club, was added to the Orioles' dugout wall in 1996, positioned where the manager normally stands during a game.

PLAQUES IN PRESS BOX

Three plaques spice up the press box and pay homage to three men who have made significant impacts within the organization. The late Rex Barney, who was the public address announcer for 25 years; the late Vernon Joiner, who was once the longtime head of the club's famed press box attendants' crew; and Bob Brown, who was the public relations director for more than 25 seasons and successfully assisted teams and the public with all of their needs are each commemorated with an inscription.

PLAYING FIELD

Situated 16 feet below street level, the natural grass turf—Prescription Athletic Turf (or PAT for short)—provides a refined irrigation and drainage system. It is designed to get the field ready for play despite a major rainfall by automatically removing as much as 75,000 gallons of rainwater from the field in an hour. This field was installed following the 2000 season, when the grassland was completely replaced. In the process, five tons of turf, sand, and dirt were removed to make way for the more modern and effective surface.

RETIRED NUMBERS

The retired numbers of six Orioles men are on the facing of the left-field upper deck and are denoted by orange circles. They include: Earl Weaver (4), Brooks Robinson (5), Cal Ripken Jr. (8), Frank Robinson (20), Jim Palmer (22), and Eddie Murray (33).

RIGHT-FIELD MINI-MONSTER

The wall in right field can be an imposing structure if you're a left-handed hitter who relies on having a short right-field porch like the one at Yankee Stadium. There are a few features that set this partition apart from the rest. An electronic scoreboard system embedded into the fence gives fans up-to-date scores (up to 16 games at once) from around the league via direct connection with SportsTicker, the automated service that tracks all of the contests, inning by inning. Following the 2008 season, a new high-definition video display and scoreboard were installed above the right-field bleachers, bolstering an already-impressive information center for fans in attendance.

SCULPTURES

The Orioles unveiled six statues, cast in bronze at the local New Arts Foundry, recognizing legends of Baltimore's past. In the area beyond the left-center-field fence are sculptures of Eddie Murray, Jim Palmer, Cal Ripken Jr., Brooks Robinson, Frank Robinson, and Earl Weaver that stand seven to eight feet tall and are sculpted in an iconic pose unique to each character.

THE NAME

In what turned out to be a political tug-of-war, the Maryland Sports Authority had originally favored "Oriole Park" as the stadium's primary name, noting that it would pay tribute to the baseball stadium that Baltimore once occupied in the 1890s. But on the other hand, there were others who wanted to use the name "Camden Yards" because of the stadium's location. To satisfy both sides, the name "Oriole Park at Camden Yards" was selected.

TWO-TIERED BULLPEN

The two-tiered bullpen gives fans a chance to see both teams whose pitchers are warming up at the same time. The Orioles' bullpen, located just in front of a standing room–only section in center field, dominates the foreground, while the visitors' bullpen sits elevated in the background.

MEMORABLE GAMES AT ORIOLE PARK AT CAMDEN YARDS

APRIL 6, 1992: FIRST GAME AT ORIOLE PARK AT CAMDEN YARDS

The Baltimore Orioles officially kicked off the Oriole Park at Camden Yards era by defeating the Cleveland Indians 2–0 in front of a sold-out crowd of 44,568. Baltimore starting pitcher Rick Sutcliffe overshadowed the festivities, pitching a complete game shutout and holding Cleveland to five hits. Chris Hoiles got the offense rolling in the fifth inning, connecting for a double to deep left field, which drove home Sam Horn, and Billy Ripken promptly followed by putting down a sacrifice bunt that scored Leo Gomez.

SEPTEMBER 6, 1995: RIPKEN JR. SETS IRON MAN MARK

With President Bill Clinton, Vice President Al Gore, and Cal Ripken Sr. all in attendance, along with a national television audience watching at home, Cal Ripken Jr. surpassed a mark many thought was unattainable by playing in his 2,131st consecutive baseball game. To top it off, the new "Iron Horse" cranked a home run off California Angels starter Shawn Boskie and celebrated with the fans when the mark became official. For the game, Ripken Jr. finished 2-for-4 with an RBI during the Orioles 4–2 victory.

SEPTEMBER 6, 1996: MURRAY JOINS 3,000–500 CLUB

It seemed very fitting that Eddie Murray, who began his career with the Orioles in 1977, would reach a major milestone in Baltimore by hitting career home run number 500. That's exactly what he did against Felipe Lira of the Detroit Tigers, and in doing so became only the third player in Major League history to collect both 3,000 hits and 500 home runs. The first to surpass the 500-home run mark since Mike Schmidt—who did so in 1987 at Three Rivers Stadium in Pittsburgh—Murray's blast landed over the right-field wall and was a no-doubter. Ironically, the record came exactly 365 days after Cal Ripken Jr. set off a celebration of his own when he overtook Lou

Gehrig's consecutive-games streak. The Tigers ended up taking the win in 12 innings after Bobby Higginson singled home Phil Nevin, notching the 5–4 victory for Detroit.

MAY 30, 1997: MUSSINA FALLS JUST SHORT OF PERFECTION

It seemed like a normal game to start, but the 47,759 in attendance that night were about to be treated to a special performance. Having retired the first 24 batters in a row without a hitch, Mike Mussina got Tony Fernandez to ground out to begin the top of the ninth inning. By this time, the crowd had recognized what was going on and stood in anticipation as Sandy Alomar Jr. stepped into the box. He soon became the town villain when he promptly smacked a clean single to left field, ending Mussina's bid for history. Like a true champion, he would strike out the next two batters—Brian Giles and Marquis Grissom—putting the final touches on one-hitter and 3–0 Orioles victory.

SEPTEMBER 20, 1998: RIPKEN JR. TAKES A SEAT

The old adage of "all good things must come to end" certainly applied this day when Cal Ripken Jr. decided it was time to take a seat for the first time in 2,632 games. It was a great run for Ripken, who, throughout the unimaginable streak, showed his toughness, grit, and willingness to play no matter what. The Orioles could have used his abilities on the field, with the New York Yankees taking advantage of the opportunity to tally a 5–4 victory, led by Derek Jeter, who notched a two-run triple in the eighth and finished 3-for-4.

SEPTEMBER 28, 2000: ORIOLES OFFENSE ERUPTS

While playing out the final days of the 2000 season, Baltimore took a quick 6–0 lead after two innings before striking for 10 in the fourth inning during a 23–1 shellacking over the visiting Toronto Blue Jays. Brady Anderson led off for the Orioles in the bottom of the first inning and immediately asserted himself, connecting for a solo home run to take Baltimore to a 1–0 lead. That seemed to set the tone for the rest of contest, and the 10-run fourth was punctuated by a three-run blast off the bat of Delino Deshields, which extended the lead to an insurmountable 16–0 advantage. Blue Jays designated hitter Darrin Fletcher responded with a blast of his own in the top half of the fifth, putting Toronto on the board, but that's all the scoring they would do this night, which saw them get outscored by 22 and out-hit by 21 (23–2). For good measure, five runs were tallied in the bottom of the fifth by the home team, fueled by run-scoring singles by Gene Kingsdale, Jerry Hairston, Deshields, and Albert Belle.

APRIL 4, 2001: NOMO TOSSES NO-HITTER FOR RED SOX

In his debut with the Red Sox, Hideo Nomo became the fourth pitcher in baseball history to toss a no-hitter in both the American and National Leagues, baffling Orioles batters with a brilliant mix of off-speed pitches during a 3–0 win. Credit should be given to Mike Lansing, who, in the ninth inning, made a backhanded, tumbling catch in center field of a sinking liner hit by Mike Bordick. Brian Daubach led the offensive charge for Boston, hitting two home runs in the game. With the win, Nomo became the first pitcher to throw a no-hitter in the history of Oriole Park at Camden Yards.

AUGUST 22, 2007: RANGERS SCORE 30 IN WIN

The Baltimore Orioles took a quick 3–0 lead over the Texas Rangers after three innings in Game 1 of a doubleheader. What followed was anything but ordinary as the Rangers reeled off a remarkable 30 unanswered runs on their way to becoming the first team in 110 years to reach that total as part of a 30–3 victory. It was the ninth time a Major League team scored 30 runs, and the first time since the Chicago Colts scored 36 in a rout over Louisville on June 28, 1897.

Texas scored 5 in the fourth, 9 in the sixth, 10 in the eighth, and 6 in the ninth in their march toward history. Along the way, plenty of records were established for Texas, including the most runs scored for a doubleheader *before* the second game even started. The 29 hits were the most since Milwaukee accumulated 31 as part of a 22–2 spanking of the Toronto Blue Jays on August 28, 1992. Ramon Vazquez put the Rangers at 30 with a three-run home run in the top of the ninth, much to the dismay of O's fans. David Murphy was the offensive star for Texas, finishing 5-for-7.

MAY 31, 2008: RAMIREZ REACHES HOME RUN MARK

When Manny Ramirez burst onto the Major League scene, right away he showed his home run potential by smacking two in his second game as a big leaguer with the Cleveland Indians. That was merely a sign of what was to come as Ramirez became the twenty-fourth member of the 500-home run club after hitting a 410-foot shot to right-center field off Chad Bradford in the seventh inning of an eventual 6–3 Red Sox victory. With the blast, Ramirez joined Eddie Murray as the only two players to hit their 500th in Oriole Park at Camden Yards. Dustin Pedroia and David Ortiz also homered for Boston, going back-to-back in the third inning.

JUNE 30, 2009: ORIOLES STAGE MAJOR COMEBACK

Although it appeared as though it would be an easy win for the first-place Red Sox against the last-place Orioles, Baltimore dug deep and showed a lot of heart, coming back from a 10–1 deficit in the seventh inning to ultimately defeat Boston, 11–10. The furious rally reached its apex in the eighth, when five runs crossed the plate, which put the Orioles up for good. Baltimore battled back and trailed 10–9 when Nick Markakis put Baltimore over the top. With Red Sox closer Jonathan Papelbon on the mound, he promptly stroked a two-run double to center, accounting for the final runs of the game and giving the Orioles the improbable victory. It marked the first time in baseball history that a comeback of that magnitude occurred by a last-place team over a first-place team.

SEPTEMBER 28, 2011: ORIOLES KEEP RED SOX FROM PLAYOFFS

The Baltimore Orioles rallied for a 4–3 ninth inning victory, simultaneously ending the season for the Boston Red Sox after they held the American League wild card lead by nine games on September 3. Needing a win and a Tampa Bay loss, the Red Sox couldn't shake a month-long slump that saw them finish September with a record of 7–20.

With Boston taking a 3–2 into the ninth, Jonathan Papelbon was summoned to the mound to close things out for a share of the wild card. After two quick strikeouts, Baltimore's Chris Davis doubled to deep right, and Nolan Reimold followed with an RBI ground rule, double-tying it at three. Robert Andino then broke the hearts of Red Sox fans everywhere, hitting a 1–1 pitch to left field, which enabled Reimold to score the winning run—a rally that occurred with two outs. Three minutes later at Tropicana Field, Evan Longoria capped a seven-run comeback with a solo home run in the twelfth, officially giving Boston the dubious distinction of missing the postseason after boasting a nine-game lead that late in the season.

MAY 8, 2012: HAMILTON BLASTS FOUR HOME RUNS

Playing in the shadow of where Babe Ruth grew up as a young boy, Rangers slugger Josh Hamilton put on a show that even the Bambino would be proud of. Hamilton blasted four two-run homers, added a double, and set the American League mark with 18 total bases as Texas downed Baltimore, 10–3. The sixteenth player in Major League history to connect four times in a game, his historic night began in the top of the first with a shot off Orioles starter Jake Arrieta with Elvis Andrus aboard via a walk. It was an instant replay in the third, connecting again off Arrieta with Andrus on base. After settling for a double in the fifth, Hamilton finished the night by pounding a blast to center field in the seventh off reliever Zach Phillips, and again in the eighth off another reliever, Darren O'Day—again with Andrus on base. The offensive display was witnessed by 11,263.

WHAT THEY'RE SAYING ABOUT ORIOLE PARK AT CAMDEN YARDS

SANDY ALOMAR JR.: "When we first played there [in 1992], we thought it was like playing in Disneyland and could not wait. . . . Playing in there, you could see the inspiration they had for looking to the future with the new ballparks here."

KEN GRIFFEY JR.: "The warehouse, the ivy—[Oriole Park at Camden Yards] was always one of my favorite ballparks . . . the people there, just the whole environment and the barbecue area, where people can do some other things other than watch a game is really cool."

JOSH HAMILTON: "With Baltimore, I think of my favorite player growing up, Cal Ripken Jr. . . . Just the history of the warehouse behind the outfield in right [and] knowing the history there with my favorite player—it is just cool to think about."

PAUL KONERKO: "Good place to hit . . . when it has a lot of people in it. It is a much better place to play in [and it has] a much better feel. As far as the right-field fence and the warehouse [are concerned], it is one place I would take a trip to if I were a fan."

DON MATTINGLY: "I liked playing in Camden Yards. I thought that was a great-looking ballpark and the fans felt like they were right on top of you. . . . In those days, they drew really well and they were good baseball fans, so that was a fun place to go."

MARK MCGWIRE: "I liked it. [It was] another good hitter's ballpark, but to me, it sounded like the ball was not as crisp off the bat and it seemed kind of dead, maybe because of the acoustics they had there. . . . Very picturesque—love the brick building behind the outfield and seeing some of the downtown."

ALEX RODRIGUEZ: "The best of the older-newer ballparks. . . . I thought it was a pioneer in many ways and set the golden standard for all the new stadiums, and that is probably the most impressive [thing] because they were ahead of the curve. They were the first ones to come out and do the first type of new ballparks, which, to this day, still plays really well."

PAT SAJAK, *WHEEL OF FORTUNE* HOST: "It is hard to overestimate what Camden Yards did for Baltimore and baseball. It became the gold standard for all the new stadiums that are built. . . . From the day it was built, when you walked in there, you felt that you were going back in time, yet it has an old-fashioned feel to it."

ROBIN VENTURA: "I think it is still kind of the model for everyone, [with] the warehouse outside, and Baltimore got to take things that we [US Cellular Field] did and improve on [them] and make it downtown, look older, and keep the warehouse in right field. . . . That is still the best one for me in regards to the newer ones."

MATT WILLIAMS: "You look back to Pittsburgh, Cincinnati, Philadelphia, and all the bowl ballparks that, when I first came into the league, played in. Camden [Yards] was the first to do something different. . . . It set the standard and is a wonderful place to play [at] and fun to hit in, too."

ORIOLE PARK AT CAMDEN YARDS FACTS AND FIGURES

ORIOLE PARK AT CAMDEN YARDS ADDRESS
333 West Camden Street, Baltimore, MD 21201

BALTIMORE ORIOLES TEAM WEB SITE
www.orioles.com

FIELD DIMENSIONS (in feet)
Left Field: 333', Left-Center: 364', Center: 400', Right-Center: 373', Right Field: 318'

SEATING CAPACITY (as of 2015)
45,971

ALL-STAR GAMES AT ORIOLE PARK AT CAMDEN YARDS
July 13, 1993: American League 9, National League 3
MVP: Kirby Puckett, Minnesota Twins (AL)

ORIOLE PARK AT CAMDEN YARDS FIRSTS
Game: April 6, 1992—Baltimore 2, Cleveland 0
Single: Paul Sorrento, Cleveland (April 6, 1992)*
Double: Chris Hoiles, Baltimore (April 6, 1992)
Triple: Cal Ripken, Jr., Baltimore (April 17, 1992)
Home Run: Paul Sorrento, Cleveland (April 8, 1992)

Denotes first hit in the stadium.

PNC PARK
HOME OF THE PITTSBURGH PIRATES

PNC Park, Pittsburgh Pirates (*Photographed by the Pittsburgh Pirates*)

When PNC Park opened its doors to the general public for an exhibition game on March 31, 2001, against the New York Mets, everyone expected it to be a major improvement over its predecessor, Three Rivers Stadium. It certainly was that. However, what many folks didn't realize was that it would quickly establish itself as one of the most eye-pleasing ballparks in all of baseball. Not only does the architecture of the ballpark incorporate the surrounding downtown cityscape with hints of its history and former homes, but it also reflects the blue-collar grittiness of the local citizens in Pittsburgh and its surrounding suburbs.

PNC Park tapped into baseball history by becoming the first ballpark since Milwaukee County Stadium in 1953 to feature a two-deck seating design, creating the most intimate setting for fans in all of baseball. The highest seat measures a mere 88 feet from the field—a far cry from the gigantic upper tank at Three Rivers Stadium, where players resembled ants and the highest seat rose 121 feet above the field of play.

Natural grass made its return for the first time since the Forbes Field era (1909–June 28, 1970), thus opening the door again to the true bounces that only the real stuff can provide. With most new ballparks built in this era utilizing brick for its main exterior material, PNC Park set a new standard by employing limestone both outside and on several interior façades of the stadium. The blue steel superstructure reminds visitors that they are indeed in the Steel City, ultimately reflecting the historical architecture of the region.

If you're searching for the most breathtaking part of PNC, it would be the sight lines, which is what dreams are made of. The park provides a dramatic sweeping view of downtown, and even a seat at the top of PNC Park is something to get excited about. Not only are the prominent landmarks such as the Clemente Bridge and glass castle PPG structure visible, but picturesque views of downtown, numerous other bridges, skyscrapers, and, of course, the famous Allegheny River can all be seen from your seat.

SPECIAL FEATURES OF PNC PARK

ALLEGHENY RIVER

Much like AT&T Park in San Francisco, which has a view of San Francisco Bay, the opportunity for a ball to make contact with the water is possible each and every game at PNC Park. With the Allegheny River sitting 443 feet, four inches from home plate down the right-field line, many players— mostly left-handed sluggers—take aim with each at-bat. The first official splashdown came on July 6, 2002, when Daryle Ward of the Houston Astros connected off Kip Wells during the fifth inning for a grand slam, sending it 479 feet on the fly and into the drink. On June 2, 2013, Pittsburgh's Garrett Jones became the first Pirate to accomplish the feat when he sent a ball flying 463 feet into the liquid.

BATTER'S EYE

The center-field batter's eye showcases some of the most beautiful foliage in Pennsylvania. Indiana County rhododendrons, Norway pines, and mountain laurels decorate the grassy knoll, and a shrub topiary that spells "PIRATES" completes the display. A hunter-green wall serves as the batter's eye, and was struck on the fly by a baseball when Pittsburgh's Kip Wells delivered a 457-foot blast on April 25, 2003.

BOWTIE BAR

Sponsored by Anheuser-Busch, a 5,000-square-foot bar and lounge available to all ticket holders was opened in 2012 and is in the right-field corner. With the beautiful skyline and Allegheny River as the backdrop, it holds

Boats float along the Allegheny River near right field, waiting for a home run to splash into the water. (*Photographed by the Pittsburgh Pirates*)

the distinction of being the only full-service bar located on the main concourse level. Half the space can be rented on a per-game basis for groups of up to 50, but in the event the space has not been reserved, it is available to the general public.

BUCCO BLASTS TICKER
Positioned on the right-field wall and just to the right of the foul pole, a manual sign tallies the number of home runs clubbed by the Pirates at PNC Park throughout the course of a season. The board features room for home runs hit from 1 to 99, and since there is no room for a third digit, it would be interesting to see what would happen if the Pirates happened to hit more than 99.

BUCCO BRICKS
During the construction of PNC Park, fans were offered the unique opportunity to purchase bricks with their own personalized messages on them. All of the money collected from that special promotion was donated to the Roberto Clemente Fund. The bricks are scattered in and around the outside of the ballpark.

CHAMPIONSHIP FLAGS

Just beyond the perimeter of the ballpark and in front of the walkway next to the Allegheny River, flags fly high and commemorate championships won in the history of Pittsburgh baseball. Black flags indicate the years Pittsburgh won the World Series, while yellow flags symbolize the seasons in which the Pirates captured the National League pennant.

CLEMENTE REMINDERS

One thing the Pirates didn't forget to do at PNC Park was pay tribute to one of the greatest right fielders to ever play the game, Roberto Clemente. For starters, the bridge—formerly known as the Sixth Street Bridge—was renamed the Roberto Clemente Bridge. On game days, the bridge is closed to automobile traffic and serves as a pedestrian walkway to PNC Park. Perhaps the most fitting acknowledgment can be found where Clemente once roamed, in right field, where the wall serves as a silent reminder and stands exactly 21 feet high (the height in honor of his jersey number).

CLOSED CAPTIONING BOARD

For those who are hearing-impaired, there is a closed-captioning board, which was installed directly beneath the main scoreboard in left field. This helpful feature is utilized whenever the announcer says anything, or if there are highlights being shown on the scoreboard featuring any kind of commentary.

CLUB 3000

Club 3000, a sports bar behind sections 207 and 208, includes memorabilia and photos of Pirates Hall of Famers Roberto Clemente, Honus Wagner, and Paul Waner, all of whom are members of baseball's famous 3,000th-hit club. Among the items you'll stumble upon here: a full bar, a pool table, a 16-foot shuffleboard table, and popular games, including Golden Tee, Chexx Bubble Hockey, and (surprise!) assorted baseball games.

CLUB-LEVEL AMENITIES

Three 7,500-square-foot restaurants on the club level allow premium-seat customers to relax and view the game in style. The eateries available are Gunner's, a sports bar on the first-base side that features memorabilia of Pirates broadcasting legend Bob Prince; Bierbauer's, positioned behind home plate, where families can enjoy carvery sandwiches and salads; and Keystone Corner, a billiards bar that stretches alongside the third-base line.

DREYFUSS MEMORIAL

The main concourse level just behind home plate houses the Dreyfuss Memorial, a tribute that honors the first owner in Pirates history, Barney Dreyfuss. He owned the club from 1900 to 1932 and is also credited with playing a large part in the creation of the World Series as it is played today. While Dreyfuss was at the helm, the Pirates collected six National League pennants and two World Series championships (1909 versus Detroit and 1925 versus Washington). Dreyfuss also played a major role in the building of Forbes Field, and on the day it opened, he personally shook hands with the fans as they filed in. He passed away on February 5, 1932, at the age of 66.

DUGOUTS

The visitor's dugout, positioned down the right-field line, features a roof decorated with the logo of the visiting team at each end and "WELCOME TO PNC PARK" sandwiched in the middle. The Pittsburgh side, which is located down the left-field line, features "PIRATES" in official lettering between two Pirates logos.

FORBES FIELD REMINDERS

A couple of elements integrated in PNC Park are a tribute to Forbes Field, the Pirates' previous home from 1909 to 1971. For starters, the dark-blue seats are replicas, and the tall light poles that rise high above the seating bowl mimic the ones at the Oakland, Pennsylvania–based ballpark during its time. The use of natural grass rather than artificial turf is also a first.

HALL OF FAME CLUB

Table seating, a full-service bar with the works, and a lounge chair seating area with 25 embroidered Pirates stools is just the beginning in this comfortable setting. Retractable glass doors give fans the sense that they are viewing the game outdoors. If you elect to be outside, a patio area—boasting a full bar, canopy area, and seating for more than 100—overlooks left-center field and is available to all ticket holders. The Hall of Fame Club officially replaced Outback Steakhouse in 2008, which at 10,000 square feet had the unique distinction of being the largest of its kind in the world.

KENNAMETAL *K* SIGN

Taking a cue from its predecessor at Three Rivers Stadium (The K-Mart "K" Club), the Kennametal *K* sign hangs proudly down the left-field line at the base of the upper deck and tracks strikeouts collected by Pirate pitchers.

Each time a punch-out is recorded, a *K* is revealed from beneath a placard. Once the sign reaches its limit (9), all the *K*s are removed, the number 1 is unveiled at the beginning—to signify double digits—and the *K*s start over.

LARGER-THAN-LIFE BASEBALL CARDS

Encircling the spiral ramp in left field, where fans can congregate and watch the game, there are enlargements of baseball cards that highlight the best of the best in Pittsburgh Pirates history. If you are a serious collector, take the time to examine them closely. Chances are you likely own some of the cards on display.

LEGACY SQUARE

During the first season at PNC Park in 2001, a permanent display honoring members of the Negro National League was dedicated. This exhibit features eight 18-foot-long fiberglass bats with the names of 16 former Negro League players, including Josh Gibson, Cool Papa Bell, Satchel Paige, Buck Leonard, and Smokey Joe Williams, to name a few. The location of this display is over the left-field entrance to the ballpark.

MAIN SCOREBOARD

It's hard to miss the 47-foot by 187-foot main scoreboard, which is just above the Hall of Fame Club in left field. The video board, topped by the words "PNC Park" in blue and sandwiched between advertisements, is often used to display replays and various pregame activities. Just below the video board is where all the in-game information is displayed, providing fans with the score and pitch count, along with the current time and temperature at PNC Park.

NARROW CONCOURSES

If there were one negative factor at PNC Park, it would have to be the tight concourses. The congestion occurs only when the fans come out in droves, so if you are planning on using the facilities or grabbing a hot dog or beverage between innings, be sure to leave plenty of time to do so.

OUT-OF-TOWN SCOREBOARD

Located at the base of the 21-foot-high Clemente Wall in right field and divided into two sections—the National League on left, American League on the right—the out-of-town scoreboard is one of the most complete in the Majors. A small baseball diamond next to each score informs fans of who's on base and which base they are on, while lights make the scoreboard easy to read from anywhere inside the ballpark.

OVERSIZED BOTTLES

Useful features of PNC Park, especially during the hot summer months, are the jumbo cola bottles that overlook the action just above the right-field bleachers. To cool down spectators sitting nearby, the replica bottles are preprogrammed to spray a mist of water at random times throughout the course of a game.

PITTSBURGH BASEBALL CLUB

The Pittsburgh Baseball Club is an exclusive area that offers first-class seating and services. In addition to wide, plush seats, ticket holders have access to three exclusive club lounges and state-of-the-art amenities. Private patios offer all-encompassing views of the skyline, and flat-screened video monitors provide replays and game action. If the sudden urge to shoot billiards arises, don't worry. Pool tables allow fans to play a game of stripes and solids.

PITTSBURGH SKYLINE

The views of the downtown area from any seat in the house are stunning. Resembling a painting, the signature yellow bridges and downtown buildings that have become famous upon PNC Park's opening in 2001, combined with the Allegheny River, make PNC Park's backdrop unique. This one feature not only sets this structure apart from any other, but it defines what an open-air ballpark is all about.

PNC NAMING RIGHTS

On August 6, 1998, Pittsburgh-based PNC Park Corporation announced that it had purchased the rights to officially name the new Pirates ballpark PNC Park when it opened in April 2001. Under the deal, PNC Bank, a financial services company, pays approximately $1.5 million a year through the conclusion of the 2020 baseball season.

RAISE THE JOLLY ROGER!

First started by Pirates broadcaster Greg Brown—who after every win has proclaimed, "Raise the Jolly Roger!"—a ceremonial Jolly Roger flag located in center field rises with each Pirates home or road victory. Brown, who credits former Pirates pitcher and broadcast partner Bob Walk with giving him the idea, came up with the catchphrase after realizing he did not have a signature call to end a game. The flag, which features a skull wearing a bandana with crossbones, is next to the American flag.

RETIRED NUMBERS

The Pittsburgh Pirates organization boasts nine retired numbers, which are on the façade of the second deck, down the right- and left-field lines behind home plate. The men honored include Billy Meyer (1), Ralph Kiner (4), Willie Stargell (8), Bill Mazeroski (9), Paul Waner (11), Pie Traynor (20), Roberto Clemente (21), Honus Wagner (33), and Danny Murtaugh (40).

RIVER WALK

The outfield promenade, commonly referred to as the River Walk, allows fans the opportunity to absorb a panoramic view while admiring where the Ohio, Monongahela, and Allegheny Rivers meet. There are concession stands, picnic tables, benches, and restrooms. On game days, anyone with a paid ticket can enjoy this area. On non-game days, it remains open to the public, allowing people a chance to socialize, eat lunch, or just take a break from the daily grind.

SPIRAL RAMP

A spiral ramp just beyond the left-field wall leads to different seating levels, while also providing a bird's-eye view of the action. Large banners, complete with baseball-card pictures of Pirates from the past and present, wrap around the structure. Blue bulbs encircle the structure and illuminate it at night.

STATUES AT PNC PARK

The Pirates are one of the most traditional teams in baseball, and they do an outstanding job paying homage to their history. Five statues around the ballpark commemorate the greatest players in the team's history.

ROBERTO CLEMENTE: The Roberto Clemente statue greets fans at the North Shore end of the Roberto Clemente Bridge and is hard to miss. The base of the statue, constructed of black granite and stainless steel, features glass blocks representing first, second, and third base. Underneath the glass is soil from Puerto Rico, marked as "hallowed ground," and pays tribute to where he played his first game. Encircling the diamond, and set in stainless steel, is a timeline of Clemente's life. Fifteen inscriptions run counterclockwise around the base of the statue, beginning at home plate and ending between third and home. Interestingly, there is space for a sixteenth inscription, but it will remain empty to symbolize the incomplete circle of Roberto's life. Once a Gate C mainstay at Three Rivers Stadium, his statue faces directly into right field, the position he once patrolled during his playing days.

RALPH KINER: Opening Day 2003 saw the dedication of the team's fourth statue, a bronze sculpture of Pirates slugger Ralph Kiner, which is behind the bleacher seats in left field, along the main concourse level. The statue of Kiner, as well as those of Roberto Clemente and Willie Stargell, was designed by Susan Wagner.

BILL MAZEROSKI: The Bill Mazeroski statue is near the right-field entrance and commemorates one of the single greatest moments in Major League history. Dedicated on September 5, 2010, the 14.5-foot bronze likeness of Mazerozski depicts him frozen in time as he circles the bases following his dramatic home run in Game 7 of the 1960 World Series. The blast ended the series and took down the Yankees, 10–9, clinching the third title in franchise history.

WILLIE STARGELL: On April 7, 2001, the Pirates dedicated their third statue to Willie Stargell, who tragically died on opening day. Located at the left-field entrance on Federal Street, the base of the 12-foot statue displays a quote from him when the team hosted Willie Stargell Day at Three Rivers Stadium on September 6, 1982: "Last night, coming in from the airport, we came through the tunnel and the city opened up its arms and I felt at home." Imprinted in the base of the statue and scattered about are "Stargell's Stars," which recall those he handed out to teammates, particularly during the 1979 championship season.

HONUS WAGNER: Dedicated on April 30, 1955, the Honus Wagner statue became the first monument to grace the grounds of a Pirates ballpark. It holds the distinction of having been on display at three different parks (Schenley Park, Forbes Field, and Three Rivers Stadium) prior to its current resting spot, right outside the home plate entrance to PNC Park.

THE NOTCH

Posing trouble for any fielder who has the inevitable task of chasing a ball in this location, The Notch is an area where the bleachers meet the bullpen in left-center field and, more specifically, where the wall is marked 410. Whenever a ball finds its way into the area, it creates a pinball-like scene with the ball bouncing unpredictably off the wall and around the warning track. More often than not, when a batted ball is struck in this location, the hitter ends up at third base with a triple.

WORLD SERIES SUITES

Located down the left-field line on the Club Level, seven World Series suites provide an unsurpassed view of Pittsburgh's skyline. Each area is equipped with a private, temperature-controlled indoor lounge, complete with high-top tables and bar stools, outdoor balcony seating, and indoor televisions. The best part of all: The suites are catered, and the selection of food is sure to appeal to any appetite.

MEMORABLE GAMES AT PNC PARK

APRIL 9, 2001: FIRST GAME AT PNC PARK

The Pirates christened PNC Park with an opening day loss to the Reds, 8–2. Sean Casey, a Pittsburgh native and former high school standout, collected the first hit—a two-run home run—off Pirates starter Todd Ritchie. The Pirates pulled to within 3–2 after scoring twice in the seventh, but the Reds put it away after tallying four runs in the ninth off reliever Marc Wilkins, powered by a two-run double off the bat of Casey—giving him five runs batted in for the game—and an RBI single by Alex Ochoa. The mood was dampened a bit when it was announced that Pirates great Willie Stargell had passed away that morning, and fans honored him by leaving flowers at the base of his statue, which was dedicated on Opening Day.

JULY 13, 2001: CLOSE, BUT NO CIGAR FOR TODD RITCHIE

In what almost went down as the first Interleague no-hitter, Pirates pitcher Todd Ritchie was a royal pain in the behind, limiting visiting Kansas City to one hit in leading Pittsburgh to a 1–0 win. With the crowd standing in anticipation and hoping for PNC Park's first no-hitter, Kansas City second baseman Luis Alicea ended the bid for history with a solid single on a 1–1 pitch. The first hit for the Royals didn't faze Ritchie, who ended up getting Rey Sanchez to ground into a double play to end the inning. In the bottom half of the ninth, Aramis Ramirez came through for Pittsburgh, lacing an RBI single that scored Brian Giles and gave the Pirates the victory. On the mound, Ritchie faced just two batters over the minimum and threw 65 of 87 pitches for strikes. With the performance, he became the first Pirates pitcher to toss a one-hitter since Paul Wagner did so against Colorado at Three Rivers Stadium on August 29, 1995.

JULY 28, 2001: A COMEBACK FOR THE AGES

A month removed from a dramatic sweep of the Indians, the Pirates pulled off another stunner, winning a game that seemed unlikely. Trailing 8–2 with two outs and nobody on base in the bottom of the ninth against Houston, the improbable comeback began. Kevin Young doubled ahead of a Pat Meares two-run home run, cutting the deficit to 8–4. Pinch hitter Adam Hyzdu singled, Tike Redman walked, and Jack Wilson stroked an RBI single, making it 8–5. Flamethrower Billy Wagner then entered the game and walked Jason Kendall, setting up a classic duel with Brian Giles. On 1–0, Giles connected on a Wagner 100 mph fastball, sending it deep into the right-field seats to complete Pittsburgh's biggest comeback in their 115-year existence. Giles immediately raised his arm, evoking memories of Bill Mazeroski's home run trot following his bottom of the ninth home run to clinch the 1960 World Series against the Yankees.

The comeback, which took place in a span of 16 pitches, was the first of its kind in more than 180,000 National League games. The Pirates became only the second team in National League history to rally and score seven runs in the bottom of the ninth inning to win.

JUNE 20–21, 2003: BACK-TO-BACK 15 INNING WINS OVER CLEVELAND

For the first time since 1996, when the Marlins and Giants played back-to-back fifteen inning contests, the Indians and Pirates duplicated the feat. In the first game, Randall Simon's solo home run to center field off Danys Baez lifted the Pirates to a 5–4 win. By the time the ball disappeared over the fence, the capacity crowd had dwindled down to a little less than 600. In the second game the next day, Abraham Nunez got things going with a leadoff triple, and then scored on a wild pitch to win the contest, 7–6. Credit should be given to Brian Giles, though, who in the top of the eighth, leaped high on the outfield wall to rob Brandon Phillips of a potential two-run home run. In the bottom half of the inning, Reggie Sanders went yard on the first pitch to tie the game at four and helped give the Pirates the boost they were ultimately seeking.

JULY 12, 2008: PIRATES PULL OFF REMARKABLE COMEBACK

The St. Louis Cardinals squandered a 9–3 lead in the seventh, and Jason Michaels hit a game-winning tenth-inning home run to lead the Pirates to a stirring 12–11 win. In a game that appeared to be over early, and at one point had the Cardinals ahead in the hits department, 17–2, Ryan Ludwick was the catalyst in the early offensive charge. He finished 3-for-5, and hit an RBI triple in the third, a two-run homer in the fourth, and an RBI single in the seventh to extend the lead to 9–3. With the score 10–4 in the eighth, Jason Bay hit a two-run blast to center—his second of the game—to pull Pittsburgh closer at 10–6.

In the ninth with two aboard, Nate McLouth brought them all home when he tagged Cardinals relief pitcher Jason Isringhausen for a three-run blast, and later in the inning, Jason Bay tied it at 10 with a fielder's choice, sending it to extra innings. In the top of the tenth, Troy Glaus unloaded for a monstrous home run, helping to temporarily regain the lead for St. Louis at 11–10. But as they had the entire game, the Pirates battled back and Michaels delivered the final shot, much to the delight of Pirates fans remaining at PNC Park.

AUGUST 31, 2008: AFTER FURTHER REVIEW, IT'S STILL A ONE-HITTER

C. C. Sabathia tossed a controversial one-hitter as the Brewers blanked Pittsburgh, 7–0, in a game that could have very well been a no-hitter for the hard-tossing left-hander. The play in question occurred in the bottom of the fifth, when Andy LaRoche led off for the Pirates and tapped a short grounder that rolled between home plate and the mound. Sabathia went to field it bare-handed, dropped it, recovered, and threw it on to first, where LaRoche had already been ruled safe. The official scorer deemed it a hit, stating that LaRoche had already been out of the batter's box and two-thirds of the way down the line as Sabathia made the attempt at picking up the ball. While strong disagreement ensued from the Brewers immediately following the play, Sabathia didn't let it bother him as he finished off the one-hitter. A DVD of the game was sent to Major League Baseball, but the official call first made at the game was not overturned.

APRIL 22, 2010: BREWERS SCORE 20 UNANSWERED

In recent seasons leading up to this game, the Pirates had plenty of difficulty trying to defeat the Brewers, but in this one, they sank to a brand-new low. The Brew Crew banged out 25 hits en route to a complete thrashing of the punchless Bucs, winning 20–0 and establishing the record for worst shutout loss in the Pittsburgh Pirates' 124-year history. Prince Fielder got the ball rolling with a solo home run in the second, and the rest was history. A three-run shot by Ryan Braun in the third kicked off three innings of three runs each, and Jim Edmonds tallied four hits, including a booming three-run home run that made it 16–0. Pitcher Manny Parra provided the exclamation point, connecting for an RBI single through the right side in the top of the ninth inning, extending the lead to 20–0.

"That was just one of those days that just seemed like everything we did worked, even the stupid stuff we did worked."
—*Casey McGhee*

"At first, I was trying to get a hit the first couple of innings because I was not invited to the hit parade. . . . You are not trying to show anybody up, but at the same time, you do not want to give any of your at-bats away."
—*George Kottaras*

SEPTEMBER 28, 2012: FIRST NO-HITTER AT PNC PARK

Cincinnati starter Homer Bailey struck out 10 and became the first Reds pitcher since Tom Browning in 1988—and sixteenth in team history—to throw a no-hitter, collecting the first in the history of PNC Park during a 1–0 victory. Even worse for Pittsburgh, the loss assured the team of a twentieth consecutive non-winning season, extending a North American sports record. The 115-pitch effort culminated with Bailey retiring the Pirates in order in the ninth, the last of which came via a pop-up by Alex Presley to shortstop Brandon Phillips. Cincinnati got all the runs it would require in the first inning, courtesy of a bases-loaded sacrifice fly by Todd Frazier, which scored Phillips.

SEPTEMBER 16, 2013: NEAR BRUSH WITH HISTORY FOR PADRE

Seeking to become the first San Diego pitcher to ever toss a no-hitter—let alone a perfect game—Andrew Cashner faced the minimum 27 batters, but allowed a clean single to right field by Jose Tabata, leading off the seventh inning during a Padres 2–0 win. Tabata, who registered the first hit after the first 18 Pirates were retired in a row, was erased after Andrew McCutchen was seduced into an inning-ending double play. Cashner, who struck out seven during the 97-pitch effort, became the first Padres pitcher to face just 27 batters in a nine-inning complete game victory. In the top of the seventh, Will Venable hit a sacrifice fly that scored Ronny Cedeno, and Jedd Gyorko singled home Cashner, accounting for all the runs San Diego would require in the victory.

OCTOBER 1, 2013: FIRST PLAYOFF GAME AT PNC PARK

Hosting their first playoff game since 1992, the Pirates continued their magical season with a 6–2 victory over Cincinnati, becoming the first home team to stand victorious since the one-game playoff debuted in 2010. Marlon Byrd, playing in his first postseason contest after 1,250 regular season games, homered in the second, and Russell Martin followed a batter later with a blast of his own—and later added another in the seventh—as the Pirates were fueled by a sold-out, standing room–only crowd of 40,487. Pittsburgh starter Francisco Liriano went seven innings and had Reds batters baffled from the get-go, finishing with five strikeouts while allowing only four hits. Cincinnati starter Johnny Cueto appeared rattled in the second, when fans began shouting "Cue-to" in unison. That prompted the right-hander to drop the ball from his glove while on the mound, and Martin proceeded to deposit the next pitch over the wall. Shin-Soo Choo homered to right in the eighth, cutting the Cincinnati deficit to 6–2, but on this night, the Pirates would not be denied in front of the hometown faithful.

OCTOBER 7, 2013: WACHA SCINTILLATING IN DOMINANT WIN

Coming off a one-hitter in his final outing of the regular season, Cardinals rookie Michael Wacha was just as good in this one, retiring the first 15 Pirates consecutively during a 2–1 St. Louis victory in Game 4 of the Division Series. Handed the ball in a must-win situation for the Cardinals, Wacha breezed through the lineup with ease before Pedro Alvarez put an end to the no-hit bid, blasting a majestic home run to center field in the eighth inning, which pulled Pittsburgh to within 2–1. Before then, the only sign of offense came in the sixth, when Matt Holliday launched a two-run blast off Pirates starter Charlie Morton, supplying St. Louis with their only runs of the ballgame. Things got interesting in the ninth after Neil Walker took a free pass with two outs to bring up arguably Pittsburgh's most valuable player, Andrew McCutchen. Looking to put an end to the series with one swing of the bat and emulate Bill Mazeroski in Game 7 of the 1960 World Series, McCutchen hit a fly ball to center field, ending the game.

WHAT THEY'RE SAYING ABOUT PNC PARK

GREG BROWN, BROADCASTER: "I like its fairness. I think it is the fairest ballpark [in the Majors] . . . on any given day. It can change, depending on the wind pattern for the most part, and if a pitcher pitches smart, he can win a ballgame here. I think that is unique in this day and age."

R. A. DICKEY: "[PNC Park] has got a beautiful skyline, the park is really pretty, the clubhouse is nice, and they do a good job there. The playing surface is good and you can walk to the field from the hotel. . . . All of those things come into play with how I evaluate things, and it is top shelf."

LANNY FRATTARE, BROADCAST-ER: "I believe that the powers that be made the correct decision about where this ballpark should be. What we have created here is this channel of the ballpark and then across the Clemente Bridge to the theatre district. We have a lot going on here."

BRYCE HARPER: "I feel like the ball flies [at PNC Park] a little bit better than [at] most ballparks. . . . [It is] one of the more impressive ballparks in the league, and a great ballpark to play at also."

GARRETT JONES: "It can be a little tricky on the hitters because you have got a deep left-center-field part of the field and the high fence in right, but overall, it is more of a pitcher's ballpark, I feel."

JASON KENDALL: "It is a great ballpark for fans to see a game and they did a great job with it. . . . I think one person who does not get enough credit is [former Pirates owner] Kevin McClatchy for basically saving Pittsburgh baseball."

GENE LAMONT: "I think the best ballpark itself is Pittsburgh. . . . They did a really good job there. It plays pretty big, but that is okay."

JIM LEYLAND: "The best ballpark in America is PNC Park in Pittsburgh. . . . They got the bridge there and the boats go up and down the river. They have got the Clemente Bridge lit up at night. It is a cozy ballpark and I think it is the best in the country."

ANDREW MCCUTCHEN: "Overall, it is a nice ballpark to be at, but definitely a pitcher's ballpark. . . . I wish the fences were moved in a little bit, but it is all right."

REGGIE SANDERS: "I would have to say [PNC Park] is the most beautiful ballpark in baseball . . . because you have got the city view and, of course, they keep the field immaculate and the clubhouse is tremendous. . . . I would have to say PNC Park is my favorite."

PNC PARK FACTS AND FIGURES

PNC PARK ADDRESS
115 Federal Street, Pittsburgh, PA 15212

PITTSBURGH PIRATES WEB SITE
www.pirates.com

FIELD DIMENSIONS (in feet)
Left Field: 325', Left-Center: 389', Center: 399',
Right-Center: 375', Right Field: 320'

SEATING CAPACITY (as of 2015)
38,362

ALL-STAR GAMES AT PNC PARK
July 11, 2006: American League 3, National League 2
MVP: Michael Young, Texas Rangers (AL)

PNC PARK FIRSTS
Game: April 9, 2001—Cincinnati 9, Pittsburgh 2
Single: Jason Kendall, Pittsburgh (April 9, 2001)
Double: Michael Tucker, Cincinnati (April 9, 2001)
Triple: Aaron Boone, Cincinnati (April 12, 2001)
Home Run: Sean Casey, Cincinnati (April 12, 2001)*

*Denotes first hit in the stadium.

YANKEE STADIUM

HOME OF THE NEW YORK YANKEES

Yankee Stadium, New York Yankees (*Photographed by Russel Tiffin/Flickr*)

W hen the final pitch was thrown at Old Yankee Stadium on September 21, 2008, it signaled the end of an era at a ballpark that was arguably unmatched by any other team in sports history. From no-hitters to World Series championships won and incredible games, the book was closed on a ballpark that had taken on a life of its own over the decades. "The House That Ruth Built" fittingly ended its tenure with a 7–3 New York victory over the Baltimore Orioles, and many were left to wonder how the new Yankee Stadium could ever follow such a historic structure.

It didn't take long to win over the Yankee faithful.

The new Yankee Stadium, incorporating many structural features of the old ballpark, pumped new life into the Bronx and energized the fans upon its arrival into the big leagues. There were some who thought the original Yankee Stadium would stand the test of time and remain a mainstay for many years, much like Fenway Park in Boston and Wrigley Field in Chicago. While it didn't quite work out that way, the closing of Yankee Stadium paved the way for a new castle to be constructed for baseball's most celebrated franchise.

With a construction cost of $1.5 billion, Yankee Stadium was built on 24 acres of what was once public parkland. The price tag was the third most expensive in the world, next to the famous Wembley Stadium in England and the New Meadowlands Stadium in East Rutherford, New Jersey, home of the NFL's New York Giants and Jets. Construction began in August 2006, but the planning for a replacement was in the works for many years before the first load of soil was moved.

Then-owner George Steinbrenner began his quest to replace the former structure in the 1980s, citing unsafe conditions around Old Yankee Stadium and even suggesting that it would deter fans from coming out to support the team. The organization even toyed with the idea of moving to the West Side of Manhattan, where a new ballpark would be built and the team would be set with a state-of-the-art facility.

Shortly before Mayor Rudy Giuliani left office in December 2001, he announced tentative agreements for both the Mets and Yankees in which state taxpayers would pick up the tab for half of the construction costs for two new ballparks. Both teams would be allowed to retain parking revenues collected throughout the year, keeping 96 percent of ticket revenues and 100 percent of all other revenues, forgo paying sales or property tax, and obtain a low-cost electricity option from New York. This, of course, was met with profound indifference from business officials who disagreed with the plan and thought that too much cash was being given to teams who were already loaded.

When Michael Bloomberg stepped into the mayoral offices in 2002, he dubbed the stadium plans as "corporate welfare" and promptly set into motion an escape clause, enabling the city to back out of both deals with the Mets and Yankees. Bloomberg made it clear that the city could not afford such a gigantic price tag, and that ultimately, publicly funded stadiums were a bad idea. He suggested that if both the Yankees and Mets wanted new ballparks, then the teams themselves should be responsible for banking the money and paying for the construction of their own stadiums.

The first proposal for the ballpark was made public by the New York Yankees in 2004 and featured a retractable roof design, which was later omitted from the final plan, saving approximately $200 million. On August 16, 2006, the fifty-eighth anniversary of Babe Ruth's death, the groundbreaking for the new ballpark took place with many notables in attendance, including Steinbrenner. After many years of planning and proposals for a new ballpark, the wheels were finally set into motion that ultimately signaled the beginning of a new era in New York Yankees Baseball.

SPECIAL FEATURES OF YANKEE STADIUM

ARMITRON CLOCK

As Armitron had been associated with the Yankees organization for over 35 years, it made sense that they would design an old-school clock that would become a prominent part of the Yankee Stadium landscape. The clock, positioned on top of the left-field façade and just to the left of the stadium's name, measures 32 feet wide by 13 feet high, is white with no numbers, and sits on top of a black base featuring "ARMITRON" in yellow.

BABE RUTH PLAZA

Situated alongside East 161st Street between gates 4 and 6 is a tribute to Babe Ruth, arguably the greatest baseball player of all time. The one-of-a-kind "Bambino" is showcased and honored with a series of porcelain images and storyboards scattered throughout the area, recalling his playing days. Babe Ruth became a legend for smacking 714 home runs early in his career and for being an outstanding pitcher. Legend has it that had he not pitched, he likely would have amassed over 1,000 career home runs.

BANQUET AND CONFERENCE CENTER

With 2,400 feet of space and the potential to accommodate up to 200 people, a top-of-the-line conference room awaits those looking to impress their fellow business associates. State-of-the-art technology is a given, while other amenities such as video conferencing are available. You can even schedule your meeting to give your clients the opportunity to see a game after all the work is done.

BLEACHER CREATURES

Lurking in section 203 of the right-field bleachers is a group of Yankees fans who are quite possibly the most dedicated and loyal in all of baseball. With a diehard loyalty to New York and a relentless dislike of opposing teams, these fans often begin the game with a roll call, in which they chant each player's name in the New York starting lineup. Fan Ali Ramirez is credited with beginning the Bleacher Creature phenomenon and being the original member, as he rang a cowbell to inspire the fans during the 1980s and 1990s. It caught on, and now fans in that section are considered among the most passionate in all of baseball.

CENTER-FIELD RESTAURANT

The restaurant, located in center field and overlooking Monument Park, is a sports bar that enables fans to view the game through windows or on high-definition televisions. Oversized, backlit baseball cards highlight players who have had their numbers retired at the elite Monument Park. In 2009, while playing for the Seattle Mariners, Russell Branyan became the first player to ever hit a ball that ricocheted off the restaurant.

CENTER-FIELD SCOREBOARD

Measuring 59 feet by 101 feet and featuring 5,925 square feet of viewing pleasure, this high-definition video board can showcase up to four crystal-clear, 1080p HD images at the same time. The size is second only to the one at Kauffman Stadium in Kansas City.

CHAMPIONS SUITE

Appropriately named for the most successful franchise in baseball history, the Champions Suite has access to the field only a few feet away. The suite, filled with memorabilia, has two lounges and comes complete with complimentary parking, cushioned seats, and a personal concierge service. There are many food options, including standard ballpark grub and other assorted eats.

FAN MARQUEE

Are you interested in making a statement or possibly popping the question to that special someone in a memorable way? The Yankees give you that unique chance for a cool $100. Offered on a first-come basis to fans, the video board in center field allows those with extra cash to display a message of a maximum of 12 words. As an added bonus, the text is announced over the public address system. All the proceeds are donated to the non-profit Yankees Foundation.

FRIEZE

There is a steel-coated frieze along the top of the roof like the one that was once a trademark at the previous ballpark. At the old Yankee Stadium, a copper version once lined the top of the ballpark but was torn down as part of the renovations during 1974–75. According to the *New York Times,* the new Yankee Stadium replicates the frieze in its original location along the upper-deck stands, which also serves as a support system for the cantilevers that hold the top deck and lighting on the roof. The frieze is approximately 1,400 feet long and consists of 300 tons of structural steel.

GOING GREEN

The Yankees organization has made every effort to protect the environment. For starters, the lighting uses 300 fewer watts than a typical stadium. Secondly, control systems and building automation preserve 207,000 pounds of carbon dioxide emission during one night game, which is the equivalent of one tree planted during every pitch of every home game. Another highlight is in the Great Hall, where a natural, more Earth-friendly cooling system replaces air conditioning. All these factors make the new Yankee Stadium one of the most eco-friendly ballparks in all of baseball.

GOLD PLAQUE

The Yankees honored the memory of Ali Ramirez, the man who was credited with being the first and original Bleacher Creature, by placing a gold plaque at section 203, row 7, seat 25. A Bleacher Creature voluntarily cleans the plaque before the start of every home game, ensuring that the memory of Ramirez will last forever.

GREAT HALL

Potentially worth the price of admission alone, the Great Hall is a concourse between gates 4 and 6 that's hard to miss. The 31,000 square feet of retail space is a shopper's paradise, complemented by seven-story ceilings that showcase 20 banners of past and present Yankees ballplayers who have made their mark on the historic franchise. Make sure you get to the ballpark early to fully appreciate all that the Great Hall has to offer!

HALL OF FAME LOUNGE

Fans can kick back and enjoy a cold one at the Hall of Fame Lounge, next to the Audi Yankees Club on the H&R Block level. It is also available on an individual-game basis for private parties. Yankee memorabilia adds plenty of appeal to this particular lounge.

HARD ROCK CAFÉ

Open year-round, the iconic Hard Rock Café restaurant measures 7,000 square feet and is near Gate 6. Decorated with Yankees attire and music-related memorabilia, the eatery offers comfortable seating, an extensive menu, and all the favorites that you would expect to find in any Hard Rock Café. A gift shop offers hats, T-shirts, and other souvenirs. In a tribute to Mariano Rivera, arguably the greatest closer in Major League Baseball history, the Hard Rock franchise retired Metallica's hit song "Enter Sandman"—and Rivera's entrance music from the bullpen—from all other Hard Rock Cafés except for the one at Yankee Stadium.

HOME PLATE CLUB

Behind home plate is another hidden treasure full of top-notch amenities. A climate-controlled lounge highlights this suite, which has some of the best views in the Major Leagues, and a multitude of menu options are sure to impress. An outdoor patio offering one-of-a-kind views of Yankee Stadium is available should you get the urge to venture outside.

LEGENDS SUITE

Boasting a ticket price that could be the equivalent of a down payment on a vehicle, seats in the first eight rows in the lower bowl—known as the Legends Suite—average (as of this writing) anywhere from $510 in advance all the way up to $2,600 on game days. This section is separate from the other lower bowl seating areas, and security keeps a watchful eye. Anyone who doesn't have a ticket in that area is prohibited from entering the Legends Suite. In an effort to fill the seats, ticket prices were slightly lowered in 2009.

MANUAL SCOREBOARDS

Embedded into both the right- and left-field walls is an in-game box score, which gives an inning-by-inning breakdown, tallies the runs scored, as well as tallies the total number of runs, hits, and errors. It also keeps track of which player is at-bat and his position, along with a real-time update on balls, strikes, and outs.

MONUMENT PARK

Retired numbers, monuments, and plaques of former New York greats adorn Monument Park, paying homage to New York Hall of Famers who have left their impression on the franchise. There has been criticism of its current location beyond the center-field fences because it is not as visible as it once was at the previous Yankee Stadium. The current position is meant to emulate that of the pre-renovated Yankee Stadium, when it was actually once a part of the playing field.

The first monuments went up on February 23, 2009, with the others following suit shortly thereafter. There is also a section for non-Yankees, including Jackie Robinson, the three popes who have visited Yankee Stadium, the victims of the tragic September 11 attacks, and Nelson Mandela, whose plaque was added on Jackie Robinson Day in 2014. At the request of Yankees relief ace Mariano Rivera, the team repositioned the home bullpens and added a door so that relief pitchers could pass by the monuments on their way to the field. On game days, fans may access the structures 45 minutes prior to the first pitch.

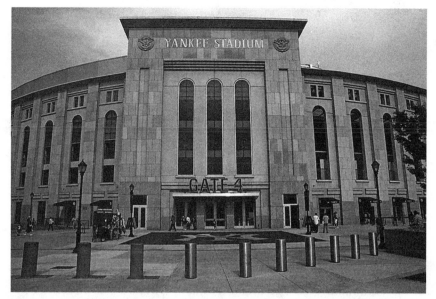

The majestic entranceway welcomes fans to the cathedral known as Yankee Stadium.
(Photographed by Russel Tiffin/Flickr)

NEW YORK YANKEES MUSEUM

The history of the team is chronicled throughout the ballpark, but if you're itching for more, make sure you stop at the New York Yankees Museum. Adjacent to Gate 6 on the main concourse level, the "museum within a museum," as the Yankees call it, displays artifacts and other memorabilia that tell the story of days past when Babe Ruth, Lou Gehrig, and other great Bronx Bombers ruled the New York City spotlight.

PHOTO COLLECTION

Presented by *The Daily News,* the 1,300 photos that line the interior of the stadium showcase the rich history of the team. The *New York Daily News* formally teamed up with the Yankees organization on the project and selected images from a collection of over 2,000. The photographs capture players at the plate and in the field, bringing to life the men and memories that ultimately helped to create the legacy of the New York Yankees and made the team what it is today.

RETIRED NUMBERS

The Yankees, the most storied franchise in baseball history, boast 17 retired numbers, which are inside Monument Park. They are: Billy Martin (1), Babe Ruth (3), Lou Gehrig (4), Joe DiMaggio (5), Joe Torre (6), Mickey Mantle (7),

Yogi Berra (8), Bill Dickey (8), Roger Maris (9), Phil Rizzuto (10), Thurman Munson (15), Whitey Ford (16), Don Mattingly (23), Elston Howard (32), Casey Stengel (37), Mariano Rivera (42), Reggie Jackson (44), and Ron Guidry (49).

SUBWAY TRAINS

The hustle and bustle of everyday life can be viewed right from your seats, thanks to a cutout in the Yankee Stadium center field. This opening allows fans to view subway trains as they pass by on their way in and out of the Bronx. This was a feature carried over from the Yankees' previous place of residence and is a nice visual reminder of life in New York.

TERRACE DECK

A full bar, combined with an assortment of grilled food, complements a picturesque view of the Manhattan skyline at the Malibu Terrace Deck, which is adjacent to section 310. Open to the public until the conclusion of the seventh inning, it's a great place to have a drink while discussing the chances of the Yankees winning another World Series crown.

YANKEES CLUB

The Yankees Club is anchored in left field and provides unparalleled views of the field, along with a full cocktail bar, dining lounge, and cooking and dessert stations. Images of Yankees players spruce up the area and illustrate the tradition of baseball.

MEMORABLE GAMES AT YANKEE STADIUM

APRIL 16, 2009: FIRST GAME AT YANKEE STADIUM

The Cleveland Indians marched into town and stole the spotlight from the opening day festivities, winning the first contest, 10–2. The seventh inning proved to make the difference as the Indians struck for nine runs, capped off by a grand slam off the bat of Grady Sizemore. The game was played in front of a sellout crowd of 48,271, and Yogi Berra was on hand to throw out the ceremonial first pitch. Johnny Damon registered the first Yankees hit (a single) and Jorge Posada went deep for the Bronx Bombers in the fifth inning off Cliff Lee, who picked up the win.

APRIL 18, 2009: INDIANS EMBARRASS YANKEES

The Cleveland Indians continued their mastery of the Yankees in the first home stand at New Yankee Stadium, exploding for 14 runs during the second inning of a 22–4 whitewashing of the Bronx Bombers. New York took an early 2–0 advantage when Mark Teixeira connected for a two-run homer off Indians starter Fausto Carmona. Things changed drastically a half-inning later when the Indians' outburst was highlighted by a three-run bomb off the bat of Shin Soo Choo, a grand slam by Asdrubal Cabrera, and a solo shot by Grady Sizemore. If that wasn't enough, Mark DeRosa—who went 4-for-7 in the game—added a three-run shot of his own in the fifth, and Victor Martinez and Travis Hafner each added solo shots in the contest.

The 14 runs established a Major League record for the most scored in the second inning of a game, and the 13 hits allowed by the Yankees in the frame were the most surrendered in the long chronicle of the storied franchise. The 22 runs surrendered by New York at home tied the franchise record set by—who else?—the Indians on August 31, 2004, when they beat the Yankees, 22–0, at Old Yankee Stadium.

NOVEMBER 4, 2009: YANKEES CAPTURE TITLE NUMBER 27

Behind a record-tying six RBI performance by Yankees designated hitter Hideki Matsui, New York captured its first World Series title since 2000 and twenty-seventh overall, defeating Philadelphia 7–3 in Game 6 of the 2009 Fall Classic. Matsui, who became the first Japanese-born player to take home the World Series Most Valuable Player Award, slugged a two-run home run in the bottom of the second; a bases-loaded, two-run single in the third; and capped his phenomenal evening with a two-run double in the fifth as the Yankees closed the first season of the new Yankee Stadium out with a bang. The six RBI matched the single-game record set by another Yankee, Bobby Richardson, during Game 3 of the 1960 World Series versus the Pittsburgh Pirates, and was later tied by Albert Pujols of the Cardinals during the 2011 Fall Classic versus Texas.

> "I thought it was great because it was the first one in the next ballpark. . . . That was a very, very exciting year wrapped up in a groundball to Robbie Cano at second base. It was very fitting that the Yankees had a championship there right away."
> —*John Sterling, Yankees broadcaster*

JULY 9, 2011: JETER REACHES 3,000 HITS IN STYLE

With one swing of the bat, Derek Jeter rewrote the record books in dramatic fashion by becoming the first Yankee to collect 3,000 hits in a career with a third inning home run off Tampa Bay's David Price during a 5–4 New York victory. With the long ball, he became only the second player ever to reach the milestone that way, ironically joining former Yankee Wade Boggs, who did so against Cleveland's Chris Haney as a member of Tampa Bay on August 7, 1999, at Tropicana Field. But he didn't stop there.

After he singled in the first for career hit number 2,999, he homered in the third for number 3,000, laced a double in the fifth, a single in the sixth, and in the eighth he notched an RBI single that turned out to be the game-winner. In all, it capped a 5-for-5 day that matched Houston's Craig Biggio (who went 5-for-6 on June 28, 2007, at Minute Maid Park in Houston against Colorado) for the most hits on the same day the 3,000-mark was attained.

AUGUST 25, 2011: YANKEES SLAM THEIR WAY TO NEW RECORD

The Yankees became the first team in Major League history to hit three grand slams in one game, and Russell Martin finished 5-for-5 with six RBI as the Yankees stormed back from an early 7–1 deficit to hammer Oakland, 22–9. Robinson Cano got the party started in the fifth when he took Athletics starter Rich Harden deep to pull the Yankees to within 7–6. In the sixth, Martin, who had hit a solo homer in the fourth, matched Cano by swatting a grand slam of his own into the right-field seats off A's reliever Fautino de Los Santos.

Finally in the eighth, Curtis Granderson sent a bases-loaded blast off reliever Bruce Billings that landed in the right-field bullpen, giving New York the grand-slam hat trick and a date with baseball history. For good measure, Andruw Jones followed Granderson's blast with a home run of his own, putting the final touches on the most runs allowed by the A's since April 23, 1955, when the franchise was in Kansas City. They lost that game to the White Sox, 29–6.

SEPTEMBER 19, 2011: RIVERA ALL ALONE IN THE SAVES DEPARTMENT

With a strikeout of Minnesota's Chris Parmelee, Mariano Rivera bypassed Trevor Hoffman for the all-time saves lead and registered number 602 in preserving a 6–4 victory. As he made the trek from the bullpen to the mound, a small Yankee Stadium crowd—the attendance was low as it was a makeup game—stood and cheered his every move during the ninth inning. If Rivera was nervous, he certainly didn't show it. For the Twins in the inning, Trevor Plouffe grounded out, Michael Cuddyer lined out, and Parmelee admired strike three as it zipped on by. The milestone was merely another notch in Rivera's belt and one that solidified his spot in the Hall of Fame.

OCTOBER 10, 2012: YANKEES STUN ORIOLES IN LATE INNINGS OF ALDS

With Baltimore leading 2–1 heading into the bottom of the ninth behind home runs from Ryan Flaherty and Manny Machado, the Orioles turned to saves leader Jim Johnson to close things out. It didn't quite work out. Pinch hitting for Alex Rodriguez in the ninth inning, Raul Ibanez connected for a game-tying home run, then hit a first-pitch, leadoff home run in the twelfth as the Yankees shocked Baltimore, 3–2, in Game 3 of the Division Series. Rodriguez, who had amassed 647 career home runs as of this game, was 1-for-12 with seven strikeouts in the series—numbers that ultimately led New York manager Joe Girardi to make the bold move. Ibanez also became the first player in Major League history to hit two home runs in a playoff game in which he wasn't a starter. With the loss, Baltimore watched their string of 16 straight extra-inning wins and a 76–0 record when leading after seven innings come to a crashing end.

AUGUST 21, 2013: ICHIRO NOTCHES 4,000TH PROFESSIONAL HIT

With a single to left field off Toronto Blue Jays starter R. A. Dickey, Ichiro Suzuki—who had been a model of consistency since he entered Major League Baseball in 2001—became the third player in professional baseball history with 4,000 career hits, joining Pete Rose (4,256) and Ty Cobb (4,189). Suzuki played nine seasons for the Orix Blue Wave of Japan's Pacific League, accumulating 1,278 hits before signing with the Seattle Mariners prior to the 2001 season. All he did in the Pacific Northwest was collect 200 hits in 10 consecutive seasons, set the Major League rookie mark for most hits in a season with 242 in 2001, and break the single season mark previously held by George Sisler (257) with 262 in 2004. For the record, the Yankees picked up the win, 4–2.

SEPTEMBER 20, 2013: RODRIGUEZ SETS SLAMS RECORD

With a high drive deep to right field in the seventh inning off Giants reliever George Kontos, Alex Rodriguez established a new Major League Baseball for career grand slams with 24, breaking a tie with former Yankees great and Hall of Famer Lou Gehrig during a 5–1 New York victory. The grand slam, which came on a 2–1 pitch and traveled 380 feet, accounted for his fourteenth as a member of the Yankees, putting him past Joe DiMaggio for second in that category and behind Lou Gehrig for the franchise lead.

SEPTEMBER 25, 2014: JETER ENDS CAREER AT YANKEE STADIUM WITH A BANG

As if a script had been written prior to the game, New York Hall of Famer Derek Jeter played his final home game by delivering a game-winning single in the bottom of the ninth, helping give the Yankees a stirring 6–5 victory over the Baltimore Orioles. A flair for the dramatics at Yankee Stadium is nothing new to Jeter who, on July 9, 2011, became the second player in Major League history to notch a home run for hit number 3,000 in his career when he connected off of David Price and the Tampa Bay Rays. In this one, New York was ahead 5–2 heading to the top of the ninth before Baltimore struck for three in the frame on two home runs: a two-run shot by Adam Jones and a solo shot by Steve Pearce. In the bottom of the ninth, Jose Pirela hit a leadoff single to left and was lifted for pinch-runner Antoan Richardson, who promptly moved to second on a sacrifice by Brett Gardner. That's when Jeter, already 1-for-4 in the game, struck for the game-winning RBI single, much to the delight of the 48,613 who were in attendance to pay their respects to a player better known as "The Captain."

WHAT THEY'RE SAYING ABOUT YANKEE STADIUM

CURTIS GRANDERSON: All in all, aesthetically, [it is] very nice [and] you are going to have a full crowd unless it is raining. . . . Hitting-wise, it is good and bad at the same time. Obviously, everyone knows about it to right [field], but you very rarely see balls go to center like you do at other ballparks."

TORII HUNTER: "Beautiful . . . very well-built and players love that clubhouse in there for the visiting side [and] I can only imagine what the home side clubhouse looks like. . . . The visiting clubhouse looks like funland because we have got flat screens everywhere and a video arcade room."

RAUL IBANEZ: "Yankee Stadium is great. . . . Obviously, it is a great ballpark to hit in, but it is a great atmosphere [and] great environment [with] a lot of energy—a lot like Philadelphia—that type of intensity."

PAUL KONERKO: "From a player's perspective, the inside, as far as the clubhouse and all the amenities that come along with it, is just second to none at this point. . . . The actual field, it kind of just looks like the old Yankee Stadium, but just brand new with a couple [of] little twists to it."

JIM LEYLAND: "[I] cannot say that I like it. . . . It is gorgeous on the inside, but the only reason I do not like it—I love Yankee Stadium—[but] they took the monuments out of sight [and] I loved to look at the monuments when I went in there. Now they have them underneath and you cannot see them, and it took a lot of charm away for me."

BRANDON PHILLIPS: "That [Yankee Stadium] is priceless. It is just nice to have the opportunity to play in the stadium that Derek Jeter built. . . . It is a great field. The infield is very nice, [and] the atmosphere in Yankee Stadium is great, but I still love the old stadium better than the new one."

JOHN STERLING, BROADCASTER: "They created a perfect ballpark. It is majestic in scope like the old Yankee Stadium . . . [with] the huge boards in the outfield and the HD board, it kind of closes in the ballpark [and] the ball flies out, but I like that because I like offense."

JUSTIN VERLANDER: "The new Yankee Stadium might be a little too business-like, but it is also nice [and] they really spared no expense. . . . The clubhouse is phenomenal and it reminds you of the old ballpark, [but] it just does not have the aura as the old one, but it is something special."

DAVID WRIGHT: "It is a newer old Yankee Stadium, and it has that same feel where you are walking in the footsteps of those Yankee greats. . . . It is just a newer, more classic version of that."

MICHAEL YOUNG: "I like it before and after the game, but during the game, it does not compare to the old place. . . . The new ballpark is great [and] they did a great job with it, spent a ton of money, and it is state-of-the-art, but Babe Ruth did not hit in the new place."

YANKEE STADIUM FACTS AND FIGURES

YANKEE STADIUM ADDRESS
One East 161st Street, Bronx, NY 10451

NEW YORK YANKEES TEAM WEB SITE
www.yankees.com

FIELD DIMENSIONS (in feet)
Left Field: 318', Left-Center: 399', Center: 408', Right-Center: 385', Right Field: 314'

SEATING CAPACITY (as of 2015)
50,291

ALL-STAR GAMES AT YANKEE STADIUM
None

YANKEE STADIUM FIRSTS
Game: April 16, 2009—Cleveland 10, New York 2
Single: Johnny Damon, New York (April 16, 2009)*
Double: Ben Francisco, Cleveland (April 16, 2009)
Triple: Cody Ransom, New York (April 18, 2009)
Home Run: Jorge Posada, New York (April 18, 2009)

*Denotes first hit in the stadium.

GREAT LAKES
REGION

COMERICA PARK
HOME OF THE DETROIT TIGERS

Comerica Park, Detroit Tigers (*Photographed by Mark Whitt/Flickr*)

For 101 seasons, Tiger Stadium had been home to some of the greatest players and moments in Major League Baseball history. But when the legend of "The Corner" officially closed its doors following the 1999 campaign, not many people knew what to expect with the debut of Comerica Park the following season. What the franchise had left behind at Tiger Stadium was not only unrivaled history and tradition, but also one of the few remaining ballparks from the early days of baseball.

Discussion for what would be known as Comerica Park began many years prior to the 2000 season and took the dedication of the organization, local government, and civic officials—along with Detroit residents—to make the project a reality. Groundbreaking ceremonies occurred on October 29, 1997, and jump-started a new sensation in the downtown area. Not long after plans for the ballpark were finalized, a strategy was under way to replace the Silverdome, home of the NFL's Lions, with the current Ford Field.

Comerica Park cost $290 million to build and is in the heart of downtown, east of Woodward Avenue. As opposed to having the taxpayers of the city foot most of the bill, this project was funded through a combination of private (37 percent or $145 million from the Tigers) and public (63 percent, including a 2 percent car rental tax and a 1 percent hotel tax) dollars. In addition, Comerica Bank agreed to fork over $66 million over 30 years in order to have the exclusive naming rights to Detroit's newest structure.

When Comerica Park entered the Major League picture in 2000, it combined the best of both worlds—old and new—while ensuring the city would have a structure that included the latest amenities. At the same time, it immediately embraced the historical nature of the downtown architecture and features a brick-and-steel exterior that recalls the classic look of days gone by. One thing is for certain: The experience begins long before you get to your seat as the main entrance welcomes visitors with a slew of decorative Tigers, ensuring that guests are well aware that it is, indeed, the home of the Detroit Tigers.

SPECIAL FEATURES OF COMERICA PARK

ADAMS STREET LOOK-IN

Similar to the porthole outside AT&T Park in San Francisco, a porthole on Adams Street allows fans to sneak a peek at the action. Free of charge, this is a subtle touch that incorporates essentials from the ballparks of yesterday.

BEER HALL

This sit-down restaurant within the Brushfire Grill can accommodate up to 350 guests at a time. The open-floor plan is flexible, and is a great venue for either business or casual, offering guests a tavern-style menu. The beer hall, a nonsmoking facility, is available for rental by the general public for special events.

BIG BAT COURT

Like a food court in a shopping mall, the circular design offers plenty of choices to make everyone happy, from Little Caesars Pizza (founded on May 8, 1959, in Garden City, Michigan, by Michael and Marian Ilitch) to fair food (elephant ears, french fries) to Mexican selections.

BLEACHERS

The bleacher section is a reasonably priced, potential home run–catching area that spans from the right-center field all the way to the right-field foul pole. Prior to the 2005 season, the bullpens were relocated from right field to an empty area in left—created when the fences were moved in—allowing for the installation of 950 more bleacher seats. Geared to be family-friendly, drinking is strictly prohibited and has helped to keep rowdiness and crude language to a bare minimum.

BRUSHFIRE GRILL

If you're like me, you enjoy heading out to your neighborhood park when the weather is picture-perfect. At Comerica Park, you can enjoy the great outdoors and all the excitement of a baseball game. The Brushfire Grill, conveniently situated near the carousel and Ferris wheel, is an open-air picnic area that provides fans with the chance to entertain friends and family while experiencing all a Major League ballpark has to offer.

CHAMPIONS CLUB

The Champions Club is home to two of the most prized possessions in the Tigers' rich history: the 1968 and 1984 World Series championship trophies. Breathtaking views are just the beginning. Relaxation is the number-one priority, thanks in part to an upscale lounge that encourages fans to kick back and forget about the stresses of everyday life.

CIGAR BAR

For those who love to smoke a stogie with a cocktail in hand, Comerica Park features one of the best cigar bars in all of baseball and combines the best of the 1940s with the technology of today. It is the only indoor smoking area at Comerica Park and has a baby grand piano, a fully stocked bar, and a humidor. There is a similar setup at Tropicana Field in St. Petersburg, home to the Tampa Bay Rays.

ERNIE HARWELL MEDIA CENTER

Named for one of baseball's most legendary announcers—and the best known in the Detroit Tigers' history—the Ernie Harwell Media Center is the official name for the press box, which is on the first level of suites behind home plate. For Tigers fans, nobody painted a better picture of the action than Harwell, whose catchphrases such as "It is long gone!" made him one of a kind. Sadly, Harwell died on May 4, 2010, after a courageous battle with cancer.

ERNIE HARWELL STATUE

A statue of legendary broadcaster Ernie Harwell serves as the unofficial greeter to Comerica Park near the main entrance at Gate A. Designed by Omri Amrany, who is also responsible for creating the Michael Jordan and Harry Caray statues in Chicago, the sculpture was formally dedicated on

September 15, 2002, and is cast in white bronze. It depicts a smiling Harwell standing, with his right hand in his pocket and a microphone in his left hand, ready to call the action.

FERRIS WHEEL

A Ferris wheel in Big Bat Court continues the amusement-park theme and is appropriately situated near the Tiger-themed carousel. The 50-foot structure has 12 baseball-shaped cars and offers a fun alternative to the baseball game. There is a small fee to ride the Ferris wheel, which is free of charge for all kids each time the Tigers play a home game at Comerica Park on Sunday.

FOLLOW THE RED BRICK ROAD

As you make your way toward the Comerica Park main entrance, commemorative bricks pave the way and guide you in the right direction. In 1999, fans were given the opportunity to purchase bricks in two different sizes and have special messages or memories engraved on them. I hate to be the bearer of bad tidings, but if you're hoping to find the Tin Man, you'll have to follow the *yellow* brick road for that one.

FORD FIELD

Next door to Comerica Park, and in plain view for spectators inside the ballpark, is Ford Field, the home of the NFL's Detroit Lions, which opened on August 24, 2002. Owned by the Detroit/Wayne County Stadium Authority, this venue replaced the Pontiac Silverdome, which was utilized from 1975 to 2001. For the record, there is virtually no shot at hitting a foul ball to Ford Field as the distance would be well over 600 feet (distance courtesy of Google Earth).

FOUNTAINS

Much like the waterfalls at Kauffman Stadium in Kansas City but on a smaller scale, Comerica Park boasts one of its own in center field that springs to life following certain accomplishments. The display, preprogrammed and synchronized to music, celebrates home runs and exciting plays. It can spray water up to 150 feet from more than 900 nozzles. Distinctive lighting was installed throughout the park, including beneath the seating decks, to interact with the sound and water.

GRAND ENTRANCE

Eighty-foot-high baseball bats stand on guard at the main gates, and colossal Tiger statues are ready to attack in case someone attempts to sneak in without a ticket. This area is a popular destination for picture-taking or just to admire the structures. Drain spouts—camouflaged to look like a Tiger's head—take a bite into oversized baseballs, which light up during night games.

LIGHTING

The right-field light towers are five stories tall and hold 75 1,500-watt bulbs that measure 20 inches in diameter. During night games, when all 16 towers are lit, they emit a total of 1.4 million watts of energy, illuminating the field.

MAIN SCOREBOARD

Just 12 seasons after Comerica Park opened, the Tigers went back to the drawing board to see how they could enhance the experience for fans. They decided to make the main scoreboard bigger and better than ever. Designed and manufactured by Daktronics, it features multicolored LED lights covering 6,096 square feet, more than 5,088 square feet larger than the previous display. This replacement, elevated 16 feet to allow for a better view, measures approximately 48 feet high and 127 feet wide, most of which is utilized for replays and player statistics.

Other scoreboard-related changes included replacing the 22-foot-tall block-letter "Tigers" logo on top with a 36-foot-tall LED cursive version that can change colors and design. The impressive fiberglass tigers prowling on top of the board were refurbished and polished after weather-related damage. Lastly, the pitch-count board size increased from five feet by 48 feet to five feet by 96 feet, and is now complete with an LED display.

ON-DECK CIRCLE SEATS

The On-Deck Circle comprises the first 13 rows on the lower level between the dugouts and offers cushy seats that measure 22 inches in diameter. These seats, which put the ticket holder front and center for all the action, also allow for easy access to both the Tiger Den Lounge and the Tiger Club.

OUT-OF-TOWN SCOREBOARD

Embedded into the right-center-field wall, the out-of-town scoreboard is an extensive information base that is continuously updated with scores from around the world of Major League Baseball. Fans can also track balls, strikes, and pitch speeds on two boards between the upper and lower decks.

RENAISSANCE CENTER

A recognizable part of the city landscape and visible from certain seats at Comerica Park, the tall, shiny, circular building rising high in the distance is known as the Detroit Marriott. This hotel is an astonishing 727 feet high and holds the distinction of being the tallest building in Michigan while also featuring the largest rooftop restaurant. Located along the International Riverfront, the hotel is part of the General Motors Renaissance Center, and four 39-story office buildings compose the rest of the complex downtown.

RETIRED NUMBERS

The six numbers retired by the Detroit Tigers are on the brick outfield walls in center field. They are: Charlie Gehringer (2), Hank Greenberg (5), Al Kaline (6), Sparky Anderson (11), Hal Newhouser (16), and Willie Horton (23).

STATUES

If you are a die-hard Tigers fan, the center-field area is one spot you won't want to miss. Stainless-steel, 13-foot-tall statues of former Tiger greats capture each player in action. Fine details accentuate some of the most lifelike statues ever produced. The legends represented are, from left to right: Willie Horton, Ty Cobb, Hank Greenberg, Charlie Gehringer, Hal Newhouser, and Al Kaline.

Al Kaline's statue depicts him leaping to take away a home run, but look closely: His glove features tiny pins that if a ball were to hit that area, it would stick right in his glove as if he made the catch. The sculpting of these beautiful larger-than-life statues spruce up the center-field section and give it a sense of nostalgia.

The scoreboard, renovated in 2011, is behind statues honoring great Tigers players. *(Photographed by Alicia Barnhart/Flickr)*

TECHNOLOGICAL ADVANCEMENTS

The program that produces the "liquid fireworks" in center field is programmed through a laptop computer. The fountain, which boasts more than four miles of wire, cable, and pumps, is powered by 500 horsepower and can move up to 15,000 gallons of water a minute.

The matrix board is also run from a laptop-size command center from a control room that resembles a scaled-down TV studio with high-end equipment. By comparison, the scoreboard at Tiger Stadium required three computers, about the size of a refrigerator, to do the same job.

TIGER CLUB

The Tiger Club, arguably the most luxurious restaurant at Comerica Park, features an all-you-can-eat buffet, a glassed-in view of the field, and a private entrance. It is on the lower suite level in right field, and you must pay a premium to enter if your ticket does not have a face value of $60 or more. If food and drink are in your immediate plans, be prepared to spend a few bucks on those, too.

TIGER DEN LOUNGE

Featuring bar and grill food, this area has two big-screen televisions, a private entrance, personal restrooms, and lockers to store all of your personal belongings. The seating also entitles fans—should they choose—to dine at the Tiger Club, which is similar to the center-field restaurant at Tropicana Field. Even though you might have a ticket, you must still pay for any food or drink.

TIGER STADIUM REMINDER

Much like it was at Tiger Stadium, the flagpole was positioned in center field, in play and part of all the action for the first four years at Comerica Park. After the fences were shifted to allow for an equal balance of pitching and hitting following the 2003 season, the flagpole was repositioned to its current location, just behind the outfield wall and out of play. The repositioning also put an end to the possibility of a player running headfirst into the pole while attempting to catch a fly ball.

TIGER-THEMED CAROUSEL

The Tiger-themed carousel, one of the two amusement-park attractions, is in the Big Bat Court, located behind first base. Graced with 30 hand-painted Tigers and two chariots, the carousel is open during all home games and costs a small amount of currency to ride. On the plus side, kids can ride for free during every Sunday home game.

UPPER DECK LOUNGE

Historically, the upper deck has produced sight lines that make fans feel rather distant from the action. At Comerica Park, the Upper Deck Lounge is only one of two bars located on the upper level in any Major League stadium (the other being Angel Stadium of Anaheim). A full-service bar, light food options, and a restroom are just a few of its features.

WALK OF FAME

The main concourse showcases some of the finest moments in baseball history, and takes fans on a self-guided tour throughout the different eras of the game. Starting with the twentieth century and moving onward, highly detailed and brilliantly displayed exhibits educate fans on the history of America's pastime. Decade monuments, spanning from the 1900s to the 2000s, are positioned throughout the concourse, tower from floor to ceiling, and contain artifacts from their respective years.

WRIGLEY FIELD–LIKE IVY

Like Wrigley Field in Chicago, the ivy at Comerica Park engulfs the center-field partition just beyond the outfield wall. The overgrown greenery also serves as the hitter's backdrop, and is sure to make things easy when it comes to picking up the white ball out of the pitcher's hand.

MEMORABLE GAMES AT COMERICA PARK

APRIL 11, 2000: FIRST GAME AT COMERICA PARK

Although the thermometer read a chilly 36°F, it didn't dampen the spirits of the 39,168 who were in attendance to help usher in a new era in Detroit Tigers baseball, a game won by the home team over Seattle, 5–2. In what could become a trivia question on *Jeopardy* some day, Tigers starter Brian Moehler—who picked up the win in the final game at Tiger Stadium—notched the first win in Comerica Park history by allowing two runs on 10 hits while striking out three. Providing the offense for Detroit was Luis Polonia, who drilled the first pitch from Freddy Garcia in the bottom of the first inning to center field for a triple and was promptly driven in on an RBI single by Gregg Jefferies. Tigers closer Todd Jones, who recorded the save and final out at Tiger Stadium, duplicated the feat by registering the first save in Comerica Park history.

SEPTEMBER 9, 2004: RANDA, ROYALS HAVE DAY TO REMEMBER

In Game 1 of a doubleheader, Kansas City third baseman Joe Randa etched his name in the record books by going 6-for-7 and added a Major League–tying six runs during a 26–5 thrashing of the Detroit Tigers. After jumping out to a 6–2 lead after two, things really got out of hand when the Royals matched an American League record by having 13 straight runners reach base during a backbreaking 11-run third inning. Randa led the 26-hit attack by connecting for five singles and a double, while shortstop Angel Berroa also had quite a game by finishing 4-for-5 with five runs batted in. In the process, the Tigers set a dubious franchise record by allowing the most runs in a nine-inning game, while on the flip side, Kansas City set a record of their own for scoring, eclipsing the previous mark of 23, accomplished on April 6, 1974, against the Twins at Kauffman Stadium. For the record, Detroit was victorious in Game 2, 8–0. The six hits recorded by Randa in a nine-inning game tied a Major League mark.

APRIL 4, 2005: INDIVIDUAL POWER DISPLAY HIGHLIGHTS OPENING DAY

Dmitri Young went 4-for-4 with three home runs and five RBI, becoming the third player in baseball history to connect for three long balls on opening day, helping lead the Tigers to an 11–2 win over Kansas City. For the first time since Karl Rhodes of the Cubs did so against the Mets exactly 11 years earlier, Young was locked in, hitting a solo shot in the second and two-run blasts in both the third and eighth innings. In his two other at-bats, he was hit by a pitch in the fifth and singled in the seventh. The only other player, as of this writing, to hit three home runs on opening day was George Bell, who accomplished the feat on April 4, 1988, as a member of the Blue Jays, also against the Royals.

OCTOBER 14, 2006: INCREDIBLE WIN SENDS MOTOWN TO FALL CLASSIC

In one of the most dramatic postseason games in franchise history, Magglio Ordonez provided the fireworks by hitting a three-run shot in the bottom of the ninth, helping lead the Tigers to the American League pennant, a 6–3 win over Oakland, a four-game sweep, and their first trip to the Fall Classic since they won it all in 1984. The A's took a 3–0 lead into the fifth frame when the Tigers offense awoke to the tune of back-to-back RBI doubles by Curtis Granderson and Craig Monroe, which cut the deficit to 3–2. In the sixth, Ordonez connected for a solo blast to tie the contest at three, simultaneously helping breathe new life into a Detroit offense that had sputtered early in the contest. It remained deadlocked until the bottom of the ninth, when Ordonez's blast off A's reliever Huston Street was the first pennant-winning home run since 2003. That's when New York's Aaron Boone victimized the Red Sox with a home run in the eleventh inning of Game 7.

OCTOBER 21, 2006: WORLD SERIES BACK IN DETROIT

The Tigers marched into the World Series on the heels of a dramatic American League Championship Series win, but the magic fizzled out when the Cardinals flexed their muscles and took Game 1 of the Fall Classic, 7–2. For the first time in 102 years, two rookie pitchers took to the mound in the first game, when Anthony Reyes got the call for St. Louis and Justin Verlander for Detroit. Reyes soon took center stage after retiring 17 in a row beginning in the first inning, and Albert Pujols added to his legacy by slamming a two-run jack off Verlander as part of a three-run third. The Cardinals later added three more in the sixth after two errors by Brandon Inge allowed two runs to cross the plate, giving St. Louis a 7–1 lead. Craig Monroe hit a solo home run off Reyes in the bottom of the ninth, but that's all the Tigers could muster as the National League champions won their first World Series game since Game 5 of the 1987 edition.

JUNE 12, 2007: VERLANDER TOSSES INTERLEAGUE NO-NO

For just the second time in the 10-year history of Interleague play, a no-hitter was pitched, this time by Tigers starter Justin Verlander—and 2006 American League Rookie of the Year—who struck out 12 and went the distance, holding the Milwaukee Brewers hitless during a 4–0 victory. In the first no-hitter for the Motor City Kitties since Jack Morris turned in the accomplishment during the 1984 season, Verlander baffled Brewers hitters all night and took it to a team that had an impressive start to the season. In the ninth, he struck out Craig Counsell and Tony Graffanino before getting J. J. Hardy to fly out to Magglio Ordonez, who was waiting for the final out on the warning track in right field. Brandon Inge finished 2-for-2, homered and drove in two RBI for Detroit in a game that was completed in a brisk two hours, 11 minutes.

> "Pure jubilation . . . I was just so excited and when I got the chance to think about being part of history like that, it was a pretty unique moment. Knowing [that] no matter what else I did in my career, I am still ingrained in baseball history was pretty special."
> —*Justin Verlander*

JUNE 2, 2010: GALARAGGA CLOSE TO PERFECTION

In what has arguably become the most controversial finish in baseball history, Detroit Tigers starting pitcher Armando Galarraga retired 26 consecutive batters in a game against the Cleveland Indians before having his date with perfection abruptly ended. With the twenty-seventh batter representing Indians third baseman Jason Donald, he grounded sharply to first, where Miguel Cabrera gloved the ball and threw it to Galaragga, who was covering first base, only to have umpire Jim Joyce rule that Donald was safe.

Television replays later showed that the batter was indeed out—by a step—but in the heat of the moment, Joyce later admitted he had missed the call. Although the Tigers won 3–0, and Galaragga finished with a one-hitter, he showed true sportsmanship by embracing Joyce the next day at home plate before the game. Two batters earlier, center fielder Austin Jackson made an incredible over-the-shoulder catch on a fly ball hit by Mark Grudzielanek that at the time was the hardest-hit ball and toughest out recorded all day.

AUGUST 15, 2011: THOME CEMENTS LEGACY

Sitting on 598 home runs, Twins slugger Jim Thome took aim against the Detroit Tigers and became the eighth player in Major League history to hit 600 home runs, hitting two opposite-field shots to join an elite group of players during Minnesota's 9–6 victory. Only Babe Ruth needed fewer at-bats to accomplish the feat (6,921 to Thome's 8,167). In the sixth inning, Thome came up and struck for a two-run shot off Rick Porcello, giving the Twins a 5–3 advantage. In the seventh with two men on, Thome returned to the plate and drilled a three-run blast on a 2–1 pitch off Daniel Schlereth, allowing him to reach the magical 600-home run plateau. As he rounded the bases, the Detroit crowd gave him a nice ovation; at that point Minnesota took a 9–5 lead and eventually won the game, 9–6.

> "I thought of my mother first, and the journey [it took] to get there . . . the long road, the ups and downs. [It was a] very special night."
> —Jim Thome

OCTOBER 28, 2012: GIANTS SWEEP TIGERS FOR TITLE

The San Francisco Giants, pushed to the limit in the division series and National League championship series, made quick work of the Detroit Tigers, finishing off the sweep with a 4–3 10-inning victory to claim their second title in three seasons. Playing on a chilly 44°F night, Brandon Belt put the Giants ahead 1–0 in the second with a triple to deep right off Tigers starter Max Scherzer, scoring Hunter Pence. Triple Crown–winner Miguel Cabrera struck for Detroit in the bottom of the third, connecting for a two-run homer, but it was matched by Buster Posey in the sixth, helping to regain the lead for San Francisco at 3–2. Detroit evened things up at three when Delmon Young belted a solo shot in the bottom half of the sixth, but Marco Scutaro sent the Giants to another celebration coming up with another clutch hit—

something he had made a habit of doing in these playoffs—connecting for a single to plate Ryan Theriot in the bottom of the tenth for an eventual 4–3 win. The win was San Francisco's seventh straight and their seventh World Series title overall.

JULY 9, 2013: RIOS COLLECTS SIX HITS, WHITE SOX TRIUMPHANT

Chicago's Alex Rios tied an American League record by going 6-for-6 in a nine-inning game, and the White Sox pounded Detroit ace Justin Verlander during an 11–4 victory. In the win, Rios became the thirty-second player overall to accomplish the feat, and the first for the ball club since Lance Johnson turned in a six-hit performance against the Minnesota Twins on September 23, 1995, at the Hubert H. Humphrey Metrodome. Rios, who led a 23-hit attack, collected singles in the first, fifth, twice in the eighth, and ninth while adding a triple in the third. He accumulated two RBI and two stolen bases and became the first player to ever have four hits off Verlander.

WHAT THEY'RE SAYING ABOUT COMERICA PARK

VINCE COTRONEO, BROADCASTER: "I like that it is downtown, but I do not like personally the grade of the way the stadium kind of contours back for the fans. . . . It is not steep enough, it is too gradual, and [as a result], the fans get further and further away from the action."

CHRIS DAVIS: "I love Comerica Park. . . . When you are walking up to it, it has a cool feel and the fact that it is right in the middle of downtown, it kind of adds to the ballpark. One reason it [is one of my favorites] is because the dugouts are huge, and that is something that goes unnoticed a lot of times."

ADAM DUNN: "I like it. . . . It is kind of tough to see during the day, [but] since they moved the fences in, it is a fair ballpark. It is not a good home run–hitting ballpark, but it is a good hitting ballpark."

RAY FOSSE, BROADCASTER: "I think Comerica [Park] is a good ballpark. I had the chance to play at Tiger Stadium and it was a good one. I wish they could have renovated it for [history's] sake. . . . The unfortunate thing [about Comerica Park] is the surroundings and they can only do so much, but it is very nicely done."

RON GARDENHIRE: "It started out bigger, and they have made it a little smaller [and] I really enjoy going there [because] the clubhouses are really nice. The dugout is huge, [and it has] good sight lines in the dugout. . . . Those things are important from my side and being able to see the game and not have to duck over poles."

JONNY GOMES: "It is almost like a circus because you have got the scoreboard with the Tigers on top, the center field with the vegetation, the Pepsi deck in right field. It is almost like a carnival and then a baseball game pops out in the middle of it."

CURTIS GRANDERSON: "It is very big [and] difficult to see in the outfield, but it is a good hitter's ballpark even though people say it is not. . . . It is a good triples ballpark and visually, it is a very nice-looking stadium as well."

JIM LEYLAND: "It is a great ballpark and I love the Tigers up on top and the eyes light up at night. [They have] got a little merry-go-round there for the kids, the field structure is gorgeous, and we pack it pretty good, so it is one of the nicest in America."

JOHN STERLING, BROADCASTER: "Comerica [Park] is different because they built the stands so far away from the field. . . . It is built down into the ground; it is below street level—way below—so when you sit there, you look out into the city because you are kind of beneath it and the lights of the city make it very, very attractive."

JUSTIN VERLANDER: "I love it. I think it is a great ballpark and it is one of the prettiest around because you have got the ivy out there in center field and the fountains. . . . I am kind of partial to it because it is my home ballpark."

COMERICA PARK FACTS AND FIGURES

COMERICA PARK ADDRESS
2100 Woodward Avenue, Detroit, MI 48201

DETROIT TIGERS TEAM WEB SITE
www.tigers.com

FIELD DIMENSIONS (IN FEET)
Left Field: 345', Left-Center: 370', Center: 420', Right-Center: 365', Right Field: 330'

SEATING CAPACITY (AS OF 2015)
41,255

ALL-STAR GAMES AT COMERICA PARK

July 12, 2005: American League 7, National League 5
MVP: Miguel Tejada, Baltimore Orioles (AL)

COMERICA PARK FIRSTS

Game: April 11, 2000—Detroit 5, Seattle 2
Single: Gregg Jefferies, Detroit (April 11, 2000)
Double: John Olerud, Seattle (April 11, 2000)*
Triple: Luis Polonia, Detroit (April 11, 2000)
Home Run: Juan Gonzalez, Detroit (April 14, 2000)

Denotes first hit in the stadium.

MILLER PARK
HOME OF THE MILWAUKEE BREWERS

Miller Park, Milwaukee Brewers (*Photographed by Russel Tiffin/Flickr*)

The doors to Miller Park opened on April 6, 2001, with a celebration of pomp and circumstance for fans, the city of Milwaukee, and everyone involved within the Brewers organization. For a franchise that had worked desperately to bring a brand-new Major League ballpark to the area, the dream finally came through and, in essence, saved Brewers baseball from becoming extinct.

Although Milwaukee County Stadium had character and history, it lacked the brash, new attitude that a Progressive Field in Cleveland or Oriole Park at Camden Yards in Baltimore possessed. The transition from the old ballpark to the new digs was no more evident than on the final day of County Stadium on September 28, 2000 (an 8–1 loss to Cincinnati), as any fan—from any seat—could clearly see the bright, shiny new Miller Park rising in the background.

Construction for Miller Park began in October 1996, and the official groundbreaking took place November 9, 1996. The ballpark, funded by a 0.1 percent sales tax in Milwaukee, Racine, Waukesha, Ozaukee, and Washington

Counties, will eventually total $310 million. The remaining $90 million was covered by the Brewers franchise, ultimately alleviating the rest of the costs.

On July 14, 1999, three ironworkers were killed when a crane dubbed "Big Blue" malfunctioned, ultimately pushing back the opening by a year. Adding even more salt to the wound, an extra $100 million in repairs due to the unfortunate mishap was tacked on to the final cost of building Miller Park. Around this time, many residents were opposed to a temporary sales tax increase necessary to cover the additional costs.

The location, at One Brewers Way, does not have any picturesque sight lines or landscape as at PNC Park in Pittsburgh, but the drive up to the ball-park is like approaching a castle atop a hillside. The large and prominent structure can be viewed from miles away, and as impressive as it is from a distance, it's that much more imposing when you arrive.

It is easily accessed once you are downtown, as a new expressway built in conjunction with Miller Park directs you into clearly marked parking lots around the perimeter. If you enjoy cookouts and barbecues, be sure to get there early to enjoy what is widely regarded around the Major Leagues to be a tailgater's paradise.

The first game was just as memorable as any in team history. The people of Wisconsin embraced Miller Park with open arms and seemed to have no reservations about bidding adieu to Milwaukee County Stadium. Dignitaries were on hand for its opening, among them Commissioner Bud Selig. The event was so high profile that President George W. Bush threw out the inaugural first pitch, marking the first time that a sitting president attended a professional sporting event in the state of Wisconsin.

The Brewers completed the picture-perfect day by defeating the Reds on what turned out to be a dramatic, game-winning home run in the eighth inning by Richie Sexson. The magic continued all weekend as Milwaukee chalked up a sweep of Cincinnati in the first-ever home stand at Miller Park.

SPECIAL FEATURES OF MILLER PARK

BERNIE'S DUGOUT

Miller Park signaled the beginning of a new tradition for Bernie the Brewer, Milwaukee's official mascot. His new setup can be spotted in left field—just look for the yellow slide—and it comes into play whenever the Brewers slam a home run. Whenever that happens, Bernie descends from the top of a curvy, yellow slide as balloons are simultaneously released to simulate bubbles. At Milwaukee County Stadium, he occupied a makeshift cabin and would descend into an oversized beer keg each time after a Milwaukee player went deep.

BOB BETTS PRESS BOX

On April 7, 2001, the Brewers had a formal ceremony to dedicate the press box to the late Bob Betts, the public address announcer for 23 seasons at Milwaukee County Stadium. Betts worked more than 1,700 games and sadly passed away on November 23, 1998, following a battle with a prolonged illness. The Brewers also placed a commemorative plaque in his honor in the hallway entrance. The smoke-free establishment features rolling windows that can open or close, and seven radio and television booths are reserved for home and visiting announcers.

BREWERS MEETING ROOMS

Named for four Milwaukee Brewers greats—Bob Uecker, Hank Aaron, Paul Molitor, Robin Yount, and Warren Abramson, a longtime employee within the organization—these state-of-the-art meeting rooms are on the Club and Terrace levels. On non-game days, they can be rented by the general public for business meetings or other events.

BRONZE STATUES

Immortalized forever in bronze are two Brewers greats and a broadcaster: Robin Yount, Hank Aaron, and Bob Uecker. Yount's likeness is near the home plate plaza and depicts him taking a big cut, perhaps ready to connect for his 3,000th career hit. Nearby, a statue of one of baseball's greatest sluggers is proudly displayed and has become a popular subject for pictures. And in 2012, the Brewers unveiled a seven-foot statue of Uecker near Aaron's, hands in pockets and smiling.

A statue at the main entrance pays tribute to the laborers who built Miller Park and is a fitting dedication to the three men who died tragically in the crane accident.

BUD SELIG STATUE

On August 24, 2010, the Brewers dedicated a statue to a man who was not only instrumental in bringing a Major League team to Milwaukee, but getting Miller Park built to ensure that baseball would be played there for years to come. The seven-foot-tall bronze likeness of Bud Selig stands proudly at the entrance to Miller Park, and depicts the longtime baseball fan with his right arm extended, holding a baseball. Prior to the 1970 season, he purchased the bankrupt Seattle Pilots and relocated them to Milwaukee, where he renamed them the Brewers.

CLUBHOUSE SEATING

A bar and restaurant with a bird's-eye view is on the club level (third deck) and allows fans to take in the game in a sociable and welcoming environment. Access to this particular section of Miller Park is limited to those who, as of this writing, have purchased one of two ticket packages: club-level seats or an annual pass that costs more than $500.

DIMENSIONS AND PLAYING SURFACE

Designed with the special contribution of Hall of Famer and Milwaukee Brewers legend Robin Yount, the field dimensions at Miller Park are asymmetrical. To date, the left-field line measures 344 feet, center field checks in at 400 feet from the plate, and the right-field line comes in at 345 feet. The Brewers also utilize the same infield mix that once was at Milwaukee County Stadium, which at the time was known around the Major League for having one of the best playing fields in all of baseball.

FAMOUS SAUSAGE RACES

Synonymous with the Milwaukee Brewers and dating all the way back to their previous ballpark at Milwaukee County Stadium are the sausage races that take place prior to the seventh inning. What began in the 1990s as cartoons running a virtual race on the scoreboard took on a whole new meaning in 2000, when actual sausages squared off against each other. The original sausages—Bratwurst, Polish, and Italian—were later joined by Hot Dog in the mid-1990s. A new addition, Chorizo, was added in 2007 and joins a cast of characters that leaves fans longing for more with each game.

GREAT TEAMS SUITES

All of the perks of a club suite, along with a larger lounge area to sit back, relax, and enjoy, are available at three party suites named for Milwaukee's playoff teams. The 1957 Braves Suite, 1982 Brewers Suite, and 2011 Brewers Suite are in the right-field corner and subtly honor the best teams in franchise history. This package comes complete with a dinner buffet, which features grilled bratwurst, hot dogs, soft drinks, water, beer, and plenty more.

HANK AARON TRIBUTE

On June 7, 2007, the Brewers dedicated a special plaque in honor of Hank Aaron, located at Brewers Lot 1. The marker commemorates Aaron's 755th and final big league home run, which took place on July 20, 1976, during the seventh inning, when he connected for a 363-foot bomb off California's

Dick Drago at Milwaukee County Stadium. The exact location of where the ball landed was determined by a multitude of studies, which later confirmed the precise spot.

HELFAER FIELD
Constructed in the shadows of Miller Park and on the site of Milwaukee's former ballpark, County Stadium, Helfaer Field is the ultimate venue for youth baseball and softball leagues. The $3.1 million facility—built thanks to a generous $2.1 million grant from the Helfaer Foundation and $1.1 million from the Miller Park infrastructure budget—features 502 bleacher seats and additional seating for 220. Foul poles from Milwaukee County Stadium are utilized, and the fences measure 200 feet from home, while the walls are six feet high with the exception of left field, where it is nine feet tall.

HOME TO HEROES
Displayed proudly throughout Miller Park is a series of colorful murals depicting five great industries of Wisconsin related to the five eras of baseball in the state. Beginning with the American League Brewers of 1901, the murals continue through current and future Brewers teams. This is a great way to educate young fans and get them up to speed on how the franchise came about, along with all of the successes experienced along the way.

OPEN CONCOURSES
The concourse, which encircles the entire field, allows for easy navigation around Miller Park without missing any of the action on the field. Nearby concession stands offer numerous selections ranging from traditional ballpark food like peanuts and Cracker Jacks to bakery items, pizza, and sandwiches.

PLAYGROUND AREA
For the little ones with a lot of energy to expend, a playground area on the field level near the right-field corner offers plenty of options to burn off some steam, including a batting cage, pitching cage, a replica Bernie the Brewer slide, and clubhouse, as well as an interactive game with sausage races and much more. The playground area is open when the gates are at Miller Park, all the way through the end of the game.

The high-definition scoreboard, updated in 2011, is a prominent feature in center field.
(*Photographed by Brian Skversky/Flickr*)

RETIRED NUMBERS

The Milwaukee Brewers have retired five numbers in their franchise's history, and they are positioned on the façade, just below the roof. They include: Bud Selig (1), Paul Molitor (4), Robin Yount (19), Rollie Fingers (34), Hank Aaron (44), and the number 50, which honors Bob Uecker's 50 seasons in professional baseball.

SCOREBOARD

The color replay and full scoreboard located in center field keeps fans informed, and also doubles as an attractive target for batters. In 2011, the Brewers made the structure even better by updating and replacing their video board. The new model measures 105 feet high by 168 feet wide and is more than capable of handling high-definition imaging and, at 5,940 square feet, it is among the largest in baseball. It offers exceptional, crystal-clear views of exciting replays, highlights, player photos, and significant information regarding the action on the field.

SPORTS GRILL

Overlooking the field of play, and positioned in the left-field corner is one of the most popular destinations at Miller Park, the Friday's Front Row Sports Grill. Open 365 days a year (and 366 on leap years), the grill features cuisine favorites. Once reservations are made, the package includes a game ticket, food, and nonalcoholic beverages. In addition, there is a beer garden that has a relaxing atmosphere to kick back and enjoy a cold one.

THE ROOF

The roof, weighing 12,000 tons and covering close to 10.5 acres, is a manufacturing phenomenon that is the first convertible fan-shaped roof of its kind in North America. Seven panels protect spectators from inclement weather, and each is the equivalent in size to the Bradley Center roof (which is the home of the NBA's Bucks). The outside height can rise to an astronomical 330 feet, and the structure can be opened or closed in 10 minutes.

UECKER SEATS

Tickets for the upper stretches of Miller Park, one of the best bargains in the game today, will set you back only one George Washington. Sure, roof pivots obstruct seat views, and players look like they're a mile away, but the Uecker Seats—a mainstay since Milwaukee County Stadium was utilized— offer an affordable alternative. Bob Uecker, a recipient of the Ford C. Frick broadcasting award in 2003, has been a recognizable voice as announcer, and his comedic voice and one-of-a-kind delivery have made him someone fans can truly connect with.

UECKER'S FAMOUS CALL

The famous home run call of legendary announcer Bob Uecker is right above Bernie the Brewer's Dugout. Whenever a Brewers player connects for a home run, in synchronization with Bernie coming down the slide, the words "GET UP, GET UP, GET OUTTA HERE, GONE" in four separate sections come to life and light up.

WALK OF FAME

A plaza near the statues of Robin Yount and Hank Aaron commemorates some of the greatest names in Brewers history. Each inductee is honored with his own granite home plate set into the ground. Since it debuted in 2001, the names in the Walk of Fame include Hank Aaron, Rollie Fingers, Paul Molitor, Robin Yount, and radio announcer Bob Uecker. The recipients are selected by a committee made up of local media members, former winners, and Brewers officials who decide from a ballot of 25 former players, coaches, managers, and front-office brass.

WALL OF FAME

Dedicated in 2014, the Wall of Fame is on the north side of Miller Park and honors Brewers players and managers who have met certain criteria while members of the organization. They include, for players, those who have had: 2,000 or more plate appearances, 1,000 or more innings pitched, 250 appearances as a pitcher, a major award such as MVP or the Cy Young Award. Also included are managers of a pennant-winning ballclub and members who have played for the Brewers and are in the Baseball Hall of Fame. The first inductees were commemorated on June 13, 2014, and included Hank Aaron, Jeromy Burnitz, Geoff Jenkins, Bud Selig, and Bob Uecker, among others.

WINDOWED PANELS

The windowed panels accentuate the overall look of Miller Park and allow sunlight in on nice days. Each windowed panel can be opened for fresh air. The glass is also a good counterpoint for the acres of bricks on the ballpark's exterior.

MEMORABLE GAMES AT MILLER PARK

APRIL 6, 2001: FIRST GAME AT MILLER PARK

Miller Park made a dramatic debut in the Major Leagues as the Brewers fought back and defeated Cincinnati, 5–4. A crowd of 42,024 came out to see the new stadium, and the Brewers did their part, sending them home happy. The Reds staked claim to the first runs ever scored, when Michael Tucker blasted a two-run homer in the second, giving the visitors a 2–0 advantage.

Not to be outdone, Milwaukee struck for three in the bottom half, all of which came on a bases-loaded double off the bat of Jose Hernandez. In the sixth, Jeromy Burnitz added a solo home run to regain the lead for Milwaukee at 4–2. In the seventh, the Reds answered when Dmitri Young homered, and Aaron Boone added an RBI single, knotting the contest at four. With one out in the bottom of the eighth, Richie Sexson sent a long drive that proved to be the game-winner, and David Weathers came on in the bottom half and promptly retired the Reds for the save.

MAY 23, 2002: SHAWN GREEN HAS PRETTY GOOD WEEK IN ONE DAY

Green dazzled the 26,728 in attendance by going 6-for-6, establishing the Major League record for total bases in a game with 19, while hitting four home runs and driving in seven runs during the Dodgers' 16–3 blasting of Milwaukee. What is arguably considered the greatest single-game effort in the long history of baseball, Green started his day by connecting for a two-run shot off Glendon Rusch in the second inning. He proceeded to blast a solo home run off Brian Mallette in both the fourth and fifth innings and for good measure, added another solo blast off Jose Cabrera in the ninth. Green's power rubbed off on Hiram Bocachica, Adrian Beltre, and Brian Jordan, who also connected for long balls throughout the course of the game.

MAY 16, 2004: BEN SHEETS STRIKES OUT 18 BRAVES

It appeared to be just another Sunday matinee until Ben Sheets changed the course of history by fanning 18 Atlanta Braves during a 4–1 complete game victory. In dominating the game, Sheets also established the Brewers all-time mark for most strikeouts in a contest, breaking the record previously held by Moose Haas in 1978. The Brewers struck for three runs in the bottom of the first inning, highlighted by a two-run double by Lyle Overbay, which was more than enough run support for Sheets. In the ninth, Sheets closed the game with a bang, striking out Adam LaRoche, J. D. Drew, and Johnny Estrada in succession to finish off the three-hitter.

SEPTEMBER 25, 2007: AN INDIVIDUAL FRANCHISE FIRST: 50 HOME RUNS

With a two-run homer to deep left off Cardinals reliever Kip Wells in the seventh inning, Prince Fielder became the first Milwaukee Brewer—and youngest player in baseball history—to hit 50 home runs in a single season during a 9–1 victory. Sitting on 48 coming into the game, he quickly moved closer to the big 5–0 when he smoked a two-run shot in the first, giving the Brewers an early 3–0 advantage. His second blast of the game, which came on a 2–2 pitch, sent the fans into celebration mode and made history for a franchise that has seen power hitters such as Gorman Thomas, Robin Yount, and Paul Molitor call Milwaukee home. It also marked the first time in Major League history that a father and son had each surpassed 50 home runs in a single season, with his father Cecil doing so in 1991, when he slammed 51 as a member of the Detroit Tigers.

"It did not sink in until the next day, but I was really happy."
—*Prince Fielder*

SEPTEMBER 14, 2008: FIRST NEUTRAL-SITE NO-HITTER

Thanks to Hurricane Ike wreaking havoc in Texas, the Cubs-Astros game was relocated to Miller Park and turned out to be anything but ordinary. Chicago pitcher Carlos Zambrano hurled the game of his life, taking Houston by storm and throwing a no-hitter during a 5–0 victory. A crowd of 23,441—mostly Chicago fans who made the short trek on I-94—watched Zambrano toss the first no-hitter since Milt Pappas did so against the Padres on September 2,

1972, at Wrigley Field. Striking out 10 and walking one, the closest Houston came to obtaining a hit was in the fifth, but Derrek Lee ended all doubt when he snagged a hot shot off the bat of David Newhan, ending the inning. With the crowd ready to erupt, Zambrano struck out Darin Erstad on a 3–2 pitch to finish off the incredible gem. Making it possible for "Big Z" to notch the win, Alfonso Soriano hit a solo home run in the first, and Lee ignited a four-run third with a two-run double.

SEPTEMBER 7, 2010: HOFFMAN FIRST TO 600 SAVES

Later matched by Mariano Rivera in 2011, Trevor Hoffman added another milestone to his fabulous pitching record when he closed out a 4–2 win over the Cardinals for career-save number 600. With closers such as Lee Smith, John Franco, and Dennis Eckersley known for their ability to close out games with ease, Hoffman took that term to new heights. In a career that began innocently on April 29, 1993, at Fulton County Stadium in Atlanta, the site of his first Major League save, Hoffman became the first to make the climb toward the hallowed 600 mark. Staked to a 4–2 lead in front of 30,000 fans anxiously anticipating the record, the former shortstop-turned-pitcher solidified his legacy when he induced Aaron Miles into a groundout on a 3–2 pitch to end the game.

SEPTEMBER 23, 2011: FIRST DIVISION TITLE IN 19 YEARS

Ryan Braun blasted a three-run home run in the bottom of the eighth inning, and it proved to be the difference in propelling the Brewers to a 4–1 win over Florida and their first division title since 1982. Milwaukee struck early, when Prince Fielder launched a solo home run off Marlins starter Chris Volstad in the second, energizing the crowd in anticipation of capturing the crown. Florida squared things up in the fourth when Bryan Petersen quieted the crowd—albeit for a just a little bit—when he laced a single to shallow center field, tying the game at one apiece.

Things began brewing for Milwaukee in the eighth after Corey Hart doubled with one out, followed by a walk issued to Nyjer Morgan courtesy of Clay Hensley, who had just entered the game as a relief pitcher. That brought up Braun, who snapped a 1-for-16 skid with a knew-it's-gone-immediately home run that clanged off the scoreboard supports, creating a buzz not heard in these parts for quite some time. John Axford pitched a perfect ninth to wrap up the division title and clinch a postseason berth faster than any other Milwaukee team in franchise history.

JUNE 29, 2012: DIAMONDBACKS HILL HITS FOR SECOND CYCLE IN TWO WEEKS

Arizona Diamondbacks second baseman Aaron Hill hit for the cycle twice in 12 days, becoming the first player to hit for two cycles in one season since 1900, matching the mark set by Babe Herman (Brooklyn) in 1931 during a 9–3 Diamondbacks victory. After accomplishing the feat on June 18 against Seattle during an Interleague contest, Hill was back at it again, doubling for career hit number 1,000 in the first, notching a single in the third, and connecting for a two-run home run in the fourth, all off Brewers starter Randy Wolf. In the sixth off reliever Livan Hernandez, Hill hit a shot to deep right in which he easily beat the throw to third, putting the final touches on another cycle. Before 1900, two cycles in the same year were accomplished twice—by John Reilly of the Cincinnati Red Stockings in 1883 and Tip O'Neill of the St. Louis Browns in 1887—both of whom completed theirs in seven days.

WHAT THEY'RE SAYING ABOUT MILLER PARK

RICK ANKIEL: "I am not a big fan of that one only because I do not always hit great there . . . , but it is nice, and you really feel [that] with the dome there, it helps out with the cold weather."

PRINCE FIELDER: "It is a nice park. . . . When I was there, I thought the fans were really good and it is a good ballpark to hit in."

J. J. HARDY: "Great place to play, the fans are awesome there, and the ball carries as a hitter to the gaps really well. . . . Sometimes day games are really tough to see and probably the hardest place to hit during the game with all the shadows."

GARRETT JONES: "I like Milwaukee, but sometimes it can be tough to see there hitting-wise. . . . The crowd gets on you pretty good there [and] it can be loud; other than that, the ballpark is pretty good."

GEORGE KOTTARAS: "Great atmosphere and a great place to hit [in]. It was pretty good going there every day, knowing you are going to get a game in. . . . [The windows behind home plate] make it tough on day games— you have got those weird shadows coming in and sometimes there is a glare in center off the wall."

DUANE KUIPER, BROADCASTER: "I am not a fan. I just do not think that was very well thought out when it comes to playing day baseball and all the shadows.... We had a case [once] where our third baseman almost got beheaded on a line drive because he never saw the ball, so I think that is a flaw and they ought to think about doing something about it."

ADAM LAROCHE: "Excellent ... great hitter's ballpark, good batter's eye, climate-controlled, and the ball flies."

ANDREW MCCUTCHEN: "I am not a big fan of it ... I mean it is a hitter's ballpark, but as far as the field goes, it is a dome so I am not real big into domes; I am more of an outside guy."

JIM THOME: "[It is] unique, a lot of tailgating [and] a lot of excitement.... They love their team [and] you can sense it even as an opponent [when] you go in there and [know] they love their Brewers. The thing that sticks out with me is how it is designed and the shadows that can make it difficult to hit."

BARRY ZITO: "It is a terrible ballpark to pitch in, but it is a gorgeous ballpark.... They have got the windows in center and the windows back behind the third- and first-base side, [and] it does not make much sense, but I think it looks good, but it is the worst park, hands down, in the league for shadows and I do not think they considered that."

MILLER PARK FACTS AND FIGURES

MILLER PARK ADDRESS
One Brewers Way, Milwaukee, WI 53214

MILWAUKEE BREWERS TEAM WEB SITE
www.brewers.com

FIELD DIMENSIONS (IN FEET)
Left Field: 344', Left-Center: 370', Center: 400', Right-Center: 374', Right Field: 345'

SEATING CAPACITY (AS OF 2015)
41,900

ALL-STAR GAMES AT MILLER PARK
July 9, 2002: National League 7, American League 7 (11 innings)
MVP: None selected

MILLER PARK FIRSTS

Game: April 6, 2001—Milwaukee 5, Cincinnati 4

Single: Sean Casey, Cincinnati (April 6, 2001)*

Double: Jose Hernandez, Milwaukee (April 6, 2001)

Triple: Jeff D'Amico, Milwaukee (April 12, 2001)

Home Run: Michael Tucker, Cincinnati (April 12, 2001)

Denotes first hit in the stadium.

PROGRESSIVE FIELD
HOME OF THE CLEVELAND INDIANS

Progressive Field, Cleveland Indians (*Photographed by Russel Tiffin/Flickr*)

[*Progressive Field was previously known as Jacobs Field (1994–2007).*]

For an extended period, the city of Cleveland was popular material for comedians all across the country who relentlessly riffed on how bad a town it was. It wasn't much better closer to home, with local citizens feeling the exact same way. Not only did the metropolis go through atrocious times in the 1960s and 1970s, but the high point of embarrassment came when the polluted Cuyahoga River caught fire at the same time the local government went bankrupt.

But the laughing stopped when Progressive Field opened its doors in 1994. The ballpark had such an impact that it went on to sell out 455 straight games (from 1995 to 2001), while the Indians parlayed it into seven of the greatest seasons the franchise and their fans have ever seen. It seemed as though the comeback magic from the first-ever game against the Mariners would have a carryover effect into the next century as the ball club capitalized on the momentum created to rip off amazing come-from-behind wins straight out of a Hollywood script.

Progressive Field instantly became the blueprint for other teams around the country who were at the drawing board, designing plans for a new stadium of their own, hoping to replicate Cleveland's success. Since it was built, Cleveland has undergone some renovations of its own and, as a result, has attracted new businesses to the area and gained more revenue for the city.

New skyscrapers dominate the skyline, while tourists arrive in droves to visit the Rock and Roll Hall of Fame, among other hot spots. And while it seems as though many franchises have tried, few—if any—have been able to duplicate the success and magic of Progressive Field in transforming the Indians and the region. With a price tag of $175 million and financed through the sale of Gateway Bonds, a 15-year luxury tax in Cuyahoga County on alcohol and cigarette sales, private investments, and prepaid leasing on luxury seating, it's unlikely that any ballpark within that price range will ever come close to what Progressive Field has to offer.

Progressive Field employs asymmetrical dimensions once utilized at older parks, giving it an air of nostalgia. Although it has a capacity of more than 40,000, these proportions give it a cozier feeling than an unwelcoming place such as the cavernous Veterans Stadium in Philadelphia once did, or even Cleveland Municipal Stadium, for that matter. Put simply, Progressive Field is beautiful and full of grandeur. It's an urban ballpark in the truest sense, and the exterior is a microcosm of what the city itself represents. The steel recalls the same look of many of the bridges in the area, and the light towers are similar to others in the downtown area.

The ballpark received a major boost in May 2014, after 56 percent of the voters in Cuyahoga County approved a 20-year extension to the sin tax, which would provide the necessary funding for Progressive Field's capital repairs. According to the Indians, they have spent $63 million for capital repairs and improvements since the ballpark first opened in 1994 and estimated that an additional $60–$70 million will be essential to maintain Progressive Field between 2014 and 2023.

SPECIAL FEATURES OF PROGRESSIVE FIELD

455 THE FANS

From June 2, 1995, to April 4, 2001, the Cleveland Indians and their fans set a Major League record for consecutive sellouts with 455. To commemorate this, the franchise retired the number 455 and placed it alongside the other Indians greats, which are just below the right-field upper deck. The Indians surpassed the previous mark of 203, originally held by the Colorado Rockies. Although many felt the number 455 would stand the test of time, the Boston Red Sox eventually passed it on September 9, 2008.

BLEACHER SECTION

Constructed beneath the left-field scoreboard and reminiscent of the bleacher section in Chicago's Wrigley Field, a 2,731-seat bleacher section offers an affordable seating option for fans. By comparison, it is approximately 100 feet closer to the action than those at the old Cleveland Municipal Stadium. This area is popular because the chances are very high that a home run will find its way into the section throughout the course of a game.

BOB FELLER MEMORIAL SEAT

The Indians have dedicated a seat in the press box to the late Feller, who occupied it during home games. A Plexiglas display case features items that serve as a tribute to the Indians legend. It includes a porcelain figure of him in the windup, jersey patches, a photo of Feller in that very seat, and a sculpture of his hand holding a baseball.

BOB FELLER STATUE

A statue of Bob Feller, the first man in baseball history to toss a no-hitter on opening day, welcomes fans to the Gate C entrance outside the ballpark. The bronze likeness, which depicts Feller in the pitching stance that earned him 266 wins over the course of his 18-year career, is a good likeness of the man who was arguably the greatest right-handed pitcher in Indians franchise history. As of this writing, plans are also in the works to honor Feller with a museum at Progressive Field.

BUDWEISER PATIO

Heading to a baseball game and downing a Budweiser beverage are a match made in heaven. The Indians incorporated the famous brewery into the Progressive Field landscape just in time for the 2011 season, and it has made a splash ever since. The Budweiser Patio, located in the right-field corner of the lower bowl, offers fans the opportunity to purchase tickets that score them an unlimited buffet and Pepsi products for one hour after the first pitch and access to a private cash bar. Aluminum tables and chairs offer plenty of seating for those who want a unique view of the playing field.

DISTINCTIVE CHIME

A distinctive chime is played over the loudspeakers to respectfully prompt fans to stand and remove their caps for the playing of the national anthem. As an Indians front office member explained, it has been something the club has incorporated into the pregame scene since 1996.

ENVIRONMENTALLY FRIENDLY

In 2007, the Cleveland Indians became the first American League team to install solar panels at the ballpark, providing 8.4 kilowatts of renewable energy. According to the Indians, the 42 panels produce enough electricity to power 400 televisions sets throughout Progressive Field. In taking things a step further, the Indians became the first Major League team to feature a wind turbine, which was installed on the right-field roof at the beginning of the 2012 season. However, the 3,000-pound turbine was removed prior to the 2013 season because it had sustained wind damage to its frame.

ERNIE HARWELL RADIO BOOTH

Situated in the Progressive Field press box, the visiting radio booth was re-named in honor of former legendary Detroit Tigers broadcaster, Ernie Harwell. The honor was made official in 2002 after he made his final visit to Cleveland as a broadcaster, and now a bronze plaque just outside the door commemorates him. Harwell was a broadcaster for 55 years—42 of which were with the Tigers—and sadly passed away on May 4, 2010.

EXECUTIVE OFFICES

The Indians office buildings, just behind the left-field stands, house all the executives and other high-ranking officials within the organization. This area cannot be accessed from inside the ballpark, and an attendant greets those who enter the building from the outside.

GATE C RENOVATIONS

Part of a major overhaul to Progressive Field just before the 2015 season, the Gate C entrance underwent a transformation that now offers a more fan-friendly view inside of the ballpark. To enable this, the Market Pavilion and Batter's Eye Bar were both removed, and the entranceway was redone, complete with the statues of Bob Feller, Jim Thome, and Larry Doby there to greet fans as they make their way through the turnstiles.

HAL LEBOVITZ PRESS DINING ROOM

For writers, broadcasters, and credentialed members of the media, the press dining room is behind the press box. It is named after longtime sports-writer and award-winning columnist Hal Lebovitz, whose work spanned six decades. In 2000 he was inducted into the writer's wing of the National Baseball Hall of Fame. Sadly, Lebovitz passed away on October 18, 2005.

HERITAGE PARK

Following the 2006 season, the Indians decided to do away with the Davey Tree Picnic Plaza in the center and erect what's now called Heritage Park. This new home of the Indians Hall of Fame, which bears a striking resemblance to Monument Park at Yankee Stadium, is chock-full of tributes and is open before, during, and after games. On the lower level, a curved brick wall is covered with 100 small plaques, one for each player selected in 2001 as the 100 greatest players in Indians history.

A plaque from League Park, the team's old home, pays tribute to second baseman Ray Chapman, who was the only player ever to die from injuries incurred in a Major League game. On the upper level, personalized bricks purchased by fans pave the way to the Ring of Fame, a section that commemorates members of the Indians Hall of Fame who also had the privilege of being enshrined into Cooperstown. Fences constructed of dark slats surround Heritage Park, allowing for light to filter in without affecting batters' ability to see incoming pitches.

HOME PLATE

Cleveland Municipal Stadium might be long gone, but an item of its history was preserved and is still in play at Progressive Field. Following the conclusion of the 1993 season, the Indians transplanted home plate from the "Mistake by the Lake" to Progressive Field, where it currently sits at the focal point of every batter. Apparently there was no curse in using the old dish, as the Indians left their losing ways at the door of Municipal Stadium when they began playing here in 1994.

HOME RUN PORCH

The home run porch is in left field above the mini-Green Monster, where fans can take in the game while heckling the players from the other team in the outfield. Access to the area, which also has concession stands, is free of charge with paid admission and can get quite crowded during sellouts and playoff games. Fans with standing room–only tickets can also claim their spot in this particular section.

INDIANS KIDS CLUBHOUSE

The Indians Kids Clubhouse, which is on the mezzanine level and winds all the way from right field toward the first-base line, is 10,000 square feet and will keep the little ones entertained. Split into two sections, those six and under will get a kick out of the 4,000-square-foot attraction better known as The Rookie Suite, where there is a climbing wall and playground. For those seven and older, The Slugger's Sandlot is sure to impress with 6,000 square feet of fun featuring a batting cage, pitch game, and more. There is also a concession stand that offers all of the kids' favorites, including juice boxes and peanut-butter-and-jelly sandwiches. It was expanded for the 2015 season, as part of a renovation project.

JIM THOME STATUE

A statue of Jim Thome, placed at Gate C, depicts the slugger in his well-known pose, pointing the bat toward the mound as the pitcher prepares for the windup. It was originally located at the spot of the longest home run in Indians history, where on July 3, 1999, he blasted a 511-foot home run to center off Kansas City Royals pitcher Don Wengert that took a tremendous bounce and landed outside the ballpark on Eagle Avenue. The statue was officially dedicated on August 2, 2014, and is the second one at Progressive Field (the first is of Bob Feller).

JOHN ADAMS, DRUM GUY

As was the case at Cleveland Stadium, Indians diehard John Adams can be found perched faithfully at every home game in the center-field bleachers, in section 183. Whenever the Indians have a man in scoring position or a rally brewing, Adams goes to work beating the drum with passion. The tradition began on August 24, 1973, and has remained a part of Progressive Field history since its inception in 1994. In 2013, the Indians and Adams commemorated his fortieth season as a mainstay in center field, further cementing his legacy in Cleveland Indians history.

LARRY DOBY STATUE

The first African American player in the American League and the second African American manager in Major League history, Larry Doby was a 7-time All-Star who paved the way for future generations. Starring for the Indians from 1947 through 1955, he led the Indians to the 1948 World Championship by batting .318 in the series and accomplished his best season in 1954 after hitting 32 home runs and driving home 126 runs. His number retired by the Indians in 1994, he was elected to the National Baseball Hall of Fame in 1998. As of this writing, the Larry Doby statue was set to be dedicated sometime during the 2015 season.

MINI-GREEN MONSTER

Measuring 19 feet high and resembling a miniature version of the Green Monster at Fenway Park in Boston, the wall in left field has fast become a legend in its own right. Bad caroms offer smaller versions of Green Monster havoc as players have a split-second to judge where the ball will bounce. Embedded into the wall is a new out-of-town scoreboard that was introduced before the 2004 campaign, which gives fans a continual update of other games going on across the Major Leagues.

NAME CHANGE

Formerly known as Jacobs Field and The Jake for short when it opened, the ballpark underwent a name change following the conclusion of the 2007 season. On January 11, 2008, it was made official that Progressive Corporation—an insurance company headquartered in nearby Mayfield Heights, Ohio—had purchased the naming rights to the ballpark through the year 2023 for $57.6 million.

PLAYING SURFACE

The field, which duplicates the specifications for an official United States Association golf green, is composed of 105,000 square feet of sod and four varieties of bluegrass. It contains perforated drain lines that run horizontally in sections of 20 feet, and there are two levels of pea gravel. Even deeper, there is a 12-inch layer of root zone sand, a mixture of peat moss and sand.

During heavy rain, the field can drain water at a rate of 12 inches per hour. The infield clay, a mixture of 75 percent sand and 25 percent clay, is inundated with five tons of soil conditioner to give it a unique look. The warning track in foul territory is a rubberized surface made of angular road rock, two layers of asphalt capped with a rubber-like material. By comparison, the track in the fair ground is simply crushed brick.

PRESS BOX

The press box, positioned directly behind home plate, offers writers and broadcasters a place to get some work done. The structure stretches across the back of the field. The press box came into play during a game I was attending, when the ball ricocheted off the rail in front of one of the windows and settled directly into my hand. My father was at the game with me but had left to take a bathroom break just before I made the grab.

RETIRED NUMBERS

The Cleveland Indians have retired six numbers, which are directly under the right-field upper deck. They include: Earl Averill (3), Lou Boudreau (5), Larry Doby (14), Mel Harder (18), Bob Feller (19), and Bob Lemon (21).

SCOREBOARD SYSTEM

After the 2003 season, the arrival of a new entertainment system with LED capabilities was installed throughout the entire ballpark. The main scoreboard in left field underwent an overhaul, and a new video screen that produces sharper images was installed.

Before the changes took place, the previous out-of-town scoreboard on the left-field wall was difficult to see during the day because the sun reflected off the plastic shield that protected it from the elements. That all

The huge scoreboard overlooks the bleacher section, a popular choice for fans.
(*Photographed by Russel Tiffin/Flickr*)

changed when a full-color, state-of-the-art display was installed, making it easier to read the scores and progress updates from around the Major League. The cost of $7 million made Progressive Field the first ballpark in Major League Baseball to incorporate a full-color display board.

STRIKEOUT METER

A meter on the façade of the right-field upper deck and just to the right of the right-field foul pole records every strikeout Indians pitchers obtain collectively throughout the game. The placards are flipped down by hand to reveal *K*s, but numbers are also available should the total exceed 14. Once a strikeout is completed, the individual in charge of the board usually dances around like he just won the lottery to celebrate the accomplishment.

TERRACE CLUB

A mainstay since the beginning of the Progressive Field era in 1994, the multilevel, glass-enclosed restaurant dubbed the Terrace Club is positioned down the left-field foul line. A valid game ticket and a pass are necessary to enter the restaurant. Inside, Caribbean Calamari, Stuffed Banana Peppers, and a Lobster Club sandwich are just some selections from an extensive menu. On non-game days, it can be rented out and used for special events or business.

UPPER DECK BAR

In an effort to reach out to a younger generation of fans and make Progressive Field a little more cozier, the Indians removed seats in the right field upper deck and created a two-story bar, a privately funded operation that debuted just in time for the 2015 season. While empty hunter green seats became the norm over the years, this newly constructed climate-controlled area offers fans not only a place to hobnob before and during games, but it lends itself to unprecedented views of the downtown Cleveland skyline and field.

MEMORABLE GAMES AT PROGRESSIVE FIELD

APRIL 4, 1994: FIRST GAME AT PROGRESSIVE FIELD

In their first game at Progressive Field, it initially seemed as though the bad karma surrounding the ball club at Cleveland Municipal Stadium had followed the Indians to their new digs, as Mariners left-hander Randy Johnson was busy crafting a no-hitter deep into the contest. With President Bill Clinton in attendance, Seattle's Eric Anthony was responsible for the first runs of the game, hitting a sacrifice fly in the first and solo home run in the third, but the Indians would pull through and stand victorious at the end. With Johnson cruising, Sandy Alomar Jr. broke up the no-hit bid in the eighth inning with a single, and a two-run double later in the inning by Manny Ramirez tied the game at two. In the eleventh, Wayne Kirby put the finishing touches on the comeback, lining a game-winning single that won the game for Cleveland, 4–3. The magic would merely pave the way for bigger and better moments as time went on.

MAY 5, 1995: MARATHON GAME ENDS FAVORABLY FOR INDIANS

In a game that tested the intestinal fortitude of all involved, the Indians outlasted Minnesota in 17 innings after Kenny Lofton singled home Manny Ramirez during a wild 10–9 victory. Totaling six hours and 36 minutes, it appeared as though Cleveland had the game under control after taking an 8–3 lead heading into the top of the seventh. The Twins came back with a vengeance, connecting for five runs and five hits, highlighted by a two-run blast off the bat of Kirby Puckett. From there, the two teams traded runs in the eighth before hitting a drought by going eight straight innings without a run. That set the stage for the seventeenth, when Ramirez singled, stole second, moved to third on a single by Jesse Levis, and scored on Lofton's game-winning RBI.

JUNE 4, 1995: INDIANS STAGE INCREDIBLE COMEBACK

It might have been a month until the Fourth of July, but on this day, regular fireworks just wouldn't suffice. After falling behind 7–0 after one inning and 8–0 after three to Toronto, the Indians regrouped and turned it into one of the more remarkable comebacks in their history, winning the contest, 9–8. Eddie Murray connected for a two-run homer in the fifth that pulled the Indians to within 8–5, and thoughts of coming back became a distinct possibility. During the ninth inning—with two outs and one on—Paul Sorrento came to the plate and sent the first pitch he laid his eyes on from reliever Darren Hall deep into the seats, setting off the pyrotechnics and a premature Independence celebration. Unbeknownest to most, comebacks would become a normal occurrence for the Indians during the 1990s at Progressive Field.

OCTOBER 3, 1995: EXTRA-INNING PLAYOFF THRILLER

When Tony Pena hit a dramatic two-out solo home run in the thirteenth inning off Red Sox pitcher Zane Smith, not only was it well past midnight, but the 5–4 win went down in the history books as the first postseason win for the franchise since October 2, 1954. With Boston leading, 4–3, in the eleventh and seemingly on their way to a Game 1 victory, Albert Belle belted a solo home run that tied the game, which led to Boston manager Kevin Kennedy claiming that Belle's bat was corked. The bat was confiscated, and Belle could later be seen in the dugout pointing to his flexed muscles, an image that fans haven't soon forgotten. Pena's home run propelled the Indians to a sweep of Boston and paved the way for the rest of the postseason.

OCTOBER 24, 1995: INDIANS WIN FIRST WORLD SERIES GAME SINCE 1948

With the Fall Classic returning to Cleveland for the first time since a four-game sweep at the hands of the Giants in 1954, the Indians made it one to remember. Eddie Murray capped an Indians comeback after slicing a single to right field, driving in a hustling Alvaro Espinoza from second base for a 7–6 victory. Atlanta took a 6–5 lead after tallying three runs in the eighth, but Sandy Alomar Jr. connected for an RBI double, tying the game and setting the stage for Murray's heroics. The victory was made possible thanks in great part to Jose Mesa, who worked two effective innings down the stretch in shutting down the Atlanta Braves offense.

APRIL 31, 1997: THE FAMOUS BUDWEISER SHOT

When Mark McGwire stood in during the third inning against Indians pitcher Orel Hershiser, it seemed like just another at-bat with the anticipation of a monster blast. What proceeded was a home run that not only left the fans in awe, but is still being talked about to this day. McGwire, who became the first player to strike the scoreboard with a home run during a game, unloaded a 485-foot two-run blast that cleared the 23 rows of bleachers in left field with ease and hit off one of North America's largest freestanding information bases. The ball slammed into the Budweiser sign, then into the lower midsection of the scoreboard with so much force that it put a dent between the *e* and *i* in "Budweiser." The game itself was a back-and-forth affair, with Oakland standing victorious in 11 innings, 11–9 after McGwire and Geronimo Berroa hit back-to-back bombs leading off the eleventh.

> "I remember Jim Thorne sending over a 12-pack of Budweiser and I still have it at my house right now and he signed it. . . . I believe it was a hanging slider."
> —*Mark McGwire*

OCTOBER 11, 1997: INCREDIBLE WIN OVER ORIOLES IN ALCS

It wasn't a base hit or home run that won this one but a missed squeeze bunt by Omar Vizquel that scored Marquis Grissom, who was officially awarded a steal of home, helping Cleveland stun the Orioles in the twelfth inning, 2–1. The Indians couldn't get a hit early in the contest, mainly because Baltimore starter Mike Mussina was busy crafting a masterpiece that saw him strike out a total of 15 Cleveland batters. When they did scratch one out, it came in the bottom of the seventh after Matt Williams singled home Jim Thome, helping stake Cleveland to a 1–0 lead. Baltimore tied the game in the ninth, after Brady Anderson doubled home Chris Hoiles, ultimately sending the game into extra innings. In the game, the two teams combined for a total of 33 strikeouts, establishing an American League Championship record.

OCTOBER 21, 1997: WILD NINTH IN WORLD SERIES VERSUS FLORIDA

With the series shifting from the tropical weather of Florida to the subfreezing climate of Cleveland, the change on the thermometer wasn't the only crazy thing happening in the World Series. With the game tied 7–7 heading into the ninth inning, the Marlins went on a scoring binge, tallying seven runs off the bullpen for a commanding 14–7 lead. In the bottom of the ninth, the Marlins bullpen proceeded to allow four runs, but Florida ultimately held on to win by a final margin of 14–11. Gary Sheffield led the Marlins' offensive charge, hitting 3-for-5 with a single, double, home run, and five runs batted in.

MAY 7, 1999: RAYS GET LAMBASTED

What seemed like a comfortable lead for Tampa Bay turned into one incredible rally by the Indians. Trailing 9–1 heading into the sixth inning, Cleveland tallied four runs in the sixth, seven in the seventh, and seven more in the eighth to defeat the Rays in unbelievable fashion, 20–11. Roberto Alomar and David Justice each collected five RBIs for Cleveland, who had five players attain three hits or more. Tampa Bay's Fred McGriff made some noise for the Rays and got in on the action by blasting a home run that turned out to be one for the record books. For McGriff, Progressive Field became the thirty-fourth ballpark in which he homered, setting a then–Major League record for most ballparks homered in.

AUGUST 5, 2001: A COMEBACK FOR THE AGES

The Indians equaled a Major League record and became the first team in 76 years to overcome a 12-run deficit, defeating the Seattle Mariners, 15–14. With NFL Hall of Fame coach Don Shula in attendance to throw out the ceremonial first pitch, the Indians quickly fell behind 14–2 through six innings, but Cleveland came back with a vengeance to score three in the seventh, four in the eighth, and five in the ninth. Unbelievably, with two outs in the bottom of the ninth and the bases loaded, Omar Vizquel tripled down the right-field line on a 3–2 pitch just out of the reach of first baseman Ed Sprague, driving in three and tying the game at 14, seemingly the only way possible that the runs could have scored other than a grand slam. In the eleventh, with no more than 1,000 fans remaining in the ballpark, Jolbert Cabrera stroked a broken bat single to left field, driving in Kenny Lofton for the incredible victory.

> "Whenever you come to a ballpark, you may see something that night that you have never seen before and that game was a perfect example. . . . You are down 14–2, that game is over, especially when you were talking about being down 12 runs in the seventh inning and that was a ball club that won 116 games. It was an incredible night."
> —*Tom Hamilton, Indians broadcaster*

JULY 8, 2003: INDIANS ROOKIE DOMINANT IN WIN OVER YANKEES

Cleveland rookie starter Billy Traber flirted with perfection and flat-out dominated the Yankees, allowing one hit during a 4–0 complete game win. Needing just two hours and 11 minutes, Traber allowed a single to leadoff batter John Flaherty, who was facing a 1–2 count, in the third inning before settling down to retire the final 21 in a row and 27 of 28 overall. The Indians offense assisted Traber in the effort, scoring two runs in the first courtesy of an RBI double by Jody Gerut and RBI single by Casey Blake, and added two insurance runs in the eighth, thanks to Matt Lawton's solo home run and an RBI single by Victor Martinez. Traber also became the first Indians pitcher to toss a complete game, one-hitter at home since Tom Candiotti on

August 3, 1987, against the Yankees at Cleveland Municipal Stadium. Candiotti missed his chance at throwing the no-hitter after allowing an eighth-inning single to Mike Easler.

JULY 27, 2011: SANTANA NO-HITS TRIBE

Despite allowing a run to score in the first inning on a wild pitch, Los Angeles starter Ervin Santana settled down and went on to throw the first solo Angels no-hitter since Mike Witt pitched a perfect game on September 30, 1984, during a 3–1 Angels victory. Santana struck out 10, and the only true danger of losing it came in the sixth. That's when second baseman Howie Kendrick made a backhand grab of a sharp grounder hit by Jason Kipinis, throwing from his knees to Mark Trumbo for the out.

The offense did their part: in the fifth, Trumbo lofted a sacrifice fly that scored Peter Bourjos tying the game at one. In the sixth, Torii Hunter scored on a passed ball, giving L.A. a 2–1 lead and in the ninth, Bourjos singled to center field, which scored Kendrick for an insurance run. In the bottom of the ninth, Santana showed no signs of nervousness, masterfully getting Travis Buck to watch strike three fly by for the first out. Ezequiel Carrera then grounded out, and with two outs, Michael Brantley connected for a soft fly ball to center that settled in the glove of Bourjos, notching the ninth no-hitter in team history, and the first to be pitched at Progressive Field.

APRIL 5, 2012: LONGEST OPENING DAY GAME IN HISTORY

J. P. Arencibia connected for a three-run home run in the bottom of the sixteenth inning, and Toronto outlasted Cleveland in the longest Opening Day game in Major League Baseball history, 7–4. The Indians jumped out to a quick 4–0 lead in the second inning, highlighted by a three-run home run off the bat of Jack Hannahan that traveled an estimated 350 feet. With Justin Masterson on the mound for the Indians and cruising—he allowed one run, two hits, and struck out 10—closer Chris Perez was summoned from the bullpen to close out the game in the bottom of the ninth. That's when the trouble started. A sacrifice fly by Jose Bautista scored Yunel Escobar, and three batters later, Edwin Encarnacion knotted the game at four with a two-run double, before Arencibia struck seven innings later.

MAY 20, 2013: INDIANS WIN WILD ONE

In what proved to be a game of "Can you top this?" the Indians scratched out a 10–8 victory over Seattle after Yan Gomes slammed a three-run blast in the bottom of the tenth. With the Indians holding a 6–5 lead in the top of the eighth, Kyle Seager blasted a solo home run, tying the game at six. All hell then broke loose in the top of the ninth, when Mariners pinch hitter

Endy Chavez connected for a go-ahead home run off Indians closer Chris Perez, staking Seattle to a 7–6 lead. Not to be outdone, Cleveland tied the game courtesy of an error in the bottom of the ninth, but as had been done in the previous two frames, Seattle went ahead with another solo home run, this time off the bat of Justin Smoak. The craziness ended in the bottom of the tenth, when the first two batters got aboard for Cleveland, setting the stage for Gomes's home run into the left-field bleachers.

WHAT THEY'RE SAYING ABOUT PROGRESSIVE FIELD

SANDY ALOMAR JR.: "When it was built, it brought a different aura to the city of Cleveland. [It is a] beautiful ballpark to begin with and similar to Camden Yards. . . . I always loved to play here [at Progressive Field]."

MARTY BRENNAMAN, BROADCAST-ER: "It is a sensational ballpark and to me, there is no negative to it. . . . I can remember the first time I went in there and I walked from the clubhouse and into the dugout and looked at the ballpark and thought, 'Oh My God, it does not get any better than this.'"

JACK CORRIGAN, BROADCASTER: "Having grown up in Cleveland, it was like being a 10-year-old kid on Christmas morning when they opened the place in 1994. . . . I just loved how it had that small-ballpark feel and yet had more than enough seats to handle the crowd."

TOM HAMILTON, BROADCASTER: "I think the reason why it is one of the best ballparks [in baseball] is how it has stood the test of time, and with all the new ballparks in baseball, I still have not seen one that I like better. . . .

It has got its own characteristics and its own feel and really has not been duplicated, nor did it duplicate anything else. It is truly an original."

JIM LEYLAND: "We were the first team to play here against the Indians [in 1994] when I was managing the Pirates, and we came up for an exhibition game before the season started so we broke this ballpark in . . . and of course, we [the Marlins] ended up winning a couple of big games here in the 1997 World Series, so I have always liked it."

RICK MANNING: "I like everything about [Progressive Field]. I have been here since it opened. I like the broadcast booth and sitting behind home plate because it is a great view. . . . It is still just as nice now as [it was] when it first opened."

MARK MCGWIRE: "It was the bomb back in the day when they had all those sellouts in a row. It was just unbelievable. . . . Again, it was the new trend of stadiums [and] it was a great ballpark to hit in [and] had great fans."

JOHN ROONEY, BROADCASTER: "It is a really attractive ballpark. I like the high wall in left, left-center field and the gigantic scoreboard above the bleachers in left [field]. . . . I think it has a lot of character and that is another good ballpark to work in. I always enjoy going to Progressive Field."

JIM THOME: "[Progressive Field] is very special, I played a long time there. . . . I remember a lot of the years it [was called] The Jake, so I had a lot of great memories always and definitely for me, it was one of the better ballparks I have played in for my career."

MATT WILLIAMS: "That is a special situation because every seat was filled every night, [and it was] a lot of fun to play in front of a packed house and we won, went to the World Series, and all of that stuff. . . . [It had a] great surface and [was] a great place to play [at]."

PROGRESSIVE FIELD FACTS AND FIGURES

PROGRESSIVE FIELD ADDRESS
2401 Ontario Street, Cleveland, OH 44115

CLEVELAND INDIANS TEAM WEB SITE
www.indians.com

FIELD DIMENSIONS (IN FEET)
Left Field: 325', Left-Center: 370', Center: 405', Right-Center: 375', Right Field: 325'

SEATING CAPACITY (AS OF 2015)
35,400

ALL-STAR GAMES AT PROGRESSIVE FIELD
July 8, 1997: American League 3, National League 1
MVP: Sandy Alomar Jr., Cleveland Indians (AL)

PROGRESSIVE FIELD FIRSTS
Game: April 4, 1994—Cleveland 4, Seattle 3 (11 innings)
Single: Mike Blowers, Seattle (April 4, 1994)
Double: Manny Ramirez, Cleveland (April 4, 1994)
Triple: Ken Griffey Jr., Seattle (April 7, 1994)
Home Run: Eric Anthony, Seattle (April 4, 1994)*

Denotes first hit in the stadium.

ROGERS CENTRE
HOME OF THE TORONTO BLUE JAYS

Rogers Centre, Toronto Blue Jays (*Photographed by Brian Skversky/Flickr*)

[*The Rogers Centre was previously known as the SkyDome (1989–2005).*]

When it made its much-awaited debut in 1989, sports personalities and fans all across Canada viewed the structure as the greatest thing since sliced bread. Touted as "The World's Greatest Entertainment Center" with its retractable roof, there's no denying that the Rogers Centre is one of the most impressive structures Major League Baseball has ever seen, and the awards back it up: from 1990 to 1993, it was named stadium of the year. A lot has changed since the Blue Jays first took the field.

For starters, it appears as though the Rogers Centre was an "aftershock" from a 1970s era that produced greatest hits such as Three Rivers Stadium in Pittsburgh and Busch Memorial Stadium in St. Louis, among others. Secondly, the expansive concrete, combined with spacious seating, gives the ballpark a desolate feel, and it's even worse when games aren't sold out, especially in Level 500, located in the upper tank. However, despite all of those factors, Blue Jays management has gone out of their way to ensure everyone has an enjoyable baseball experience, and that alone shows their dedication to the fans.

The Rogers Centre, which is next to the CN Tower near the shores of Lake Ontario, was designed by Rod Robbie and Michael Allen. Constructed by Ellis-Don Construction of Toronto, the actual time frame for completion took just over three years and cost $500 million, which was paid for by the Canadian federal government, the Ontario provincial government, and many corporations.

When the construction began in 1987, the site was discovered to be a landfill from the 1850s, and many ancient artifacts were unearthed in the process. Among the treasures found was a mustard bottle over 100 years old, vintage tools, and a French cannon that was said to have been used during the War of 1812. When Robbie was asked to describe his design of the Rogers Centre, he described it as "A social place similar to a cathedral, a place where people meet, a place with activity. We can build something that will be here for 100 years. We will build a secular cathedral. This building will be a signature for the city, the province, the country." While it might be a landmark in that respect, it certainly went through its share of difficulties throughout the 1990s.

It soon became public knowledge that the companies who had helped fund the ballpark had amassed a huge debt, and in an effort to alleviate it, they were given a substantial and controversial amount of government financial aid. Still left with a huge debt to repay, Rogers Communications, a parent company of the Blue Jays, swooped in and came to the rescue in 2004, agreeing to acquire the stadium for approximately $21.3 million, roughly 1/24th of the cost of construction.

The ballpark was named the Rogers Centre and on February 2, 2005, Ted Rogers, president and CEO of Rogers Communications, announced that his company would significantly increase the team payroll and that a three-year corporate contract to change the name of the ballpark would officially be set into motion.

The Rogers Centre appears massive when viewed on TV, but in reality, it's not as large as one might think. There are different seating sections, with decent views down the first- and third-base line and also along the outfield, which give a view of the whole field.

SPECIAL FEATURES OF ROGERS CENTRE

ARTWORK

Canadian artwork in Rogers Centre include *The Audience* by Michael Snow and *The Art of the Possible* by Mimi Gellman. *The Audience* is staged at the northeast and northwest corners of the ballpark and pays tribute to the fans of Toronto baseball. *The Art of the Possible,* on Level 100 at the north end, is a sculpture made of glass and steel that honors the men and women who built the world's first retractable-roof ballpark.

CHAMPIONSHIP BANNERS

Banners paying tribute to American League East championships, the 1991 American League All-Star Game, and World Series titles hang proudly above the video board. Color-coded banners are a nod to the glory days in which the Blue Jays ruled the roost. White banners signify division titles captured and pay tribute to the All-Star Game held in 1991; blue denotes the back-to-back World Series titles won in 1992 and 1993.

CN TOWER

If you're sitting in a seat left of home plate with the roof open, you'll be able to spot the CN Tower, the world's tallest freestanding structure. Rising over 1,815 feet and looming high above the Rogers Centre like a watchdog, the CN Tower offers visitors the chance to take a 58-second ride to the top for an incredible view of the city. The 360 restaurant sits 1,150 feet above the ground and provides an unprecedented view of Toronto and Rogers Centre.

HARD ROCK CAFÉ—UNTIL 2009

When it existed, the Hard Rock Café was at the very top of the right-field seats. Fans were able to grab a bite to eat in the world-renowned restaurant during the game or simply admire the music memorabilia displayed inside. In 1998, Carlos Delgado gave the fans an up-close-and-personal look at a Major League baseball when he smacked a home run that bounced off a Hard Rock Café window, an estimated 468 feet from home plate. Sadly, the Hard Rock Café closed following the conclusion of the 2009 season after the lease had expired.

HYDRAULIC MOUND

The pitcher's mound boasts an innovative 18-foot fiberglass hydraulic mound set in place by a holding chamber in which water fills to the top, raising the mound and locking it in place. At the end of the game, the water is drained and the mound is lowered below the field of play.

IMPRESSIVE STRUCTURE

Although it has been over 20 years since the Rogers Centre made its debut into the Major League Baseball world, the ballpark continues to amaze. Providing more proof are these statistics, courtesy of the Blue Jays Media Guide:

- Rogers Centre was built from enough concrete that you could dismantle it and build a sidewalk that would stretch all the way from Toronto to St. Louis.
- When the roof is completely closed, a 31-story building could fit inside, while 743 Indian elephants could fit side by side on the field.
- Nearly 9,000 light bulbs and 776 field lights surround the Rogers Centre.

No matter which way you look at it, Rogers Centre is an impressive technological advancement.

LEVEL OF EXCELLENCE

Positioned on Level 500 of Rogers Centre is the Level of Excellence, a section that honors Blue Jays players throughout the years who have made the biggest impacts. As of this writing, nine members have been inducted and are acknowledged with large banners at the top of the seating areas, flanking the championship banners. The men honored are: Roberto Alomar (inducted in 2008), Paul Beeston (2008), George Bell (1996), Joe Carter (1999), Tom Cheek (2004), Carlos Delgado (2013), Tony Fernandez (2001), Cito Gaston (1999), Pat Gillick (2002), and Dave Stieb (1996).

MASSIVE SCOREBOARD

The $17 million scoreboard, one of the largest video display boards in North America, offers picture-perfect replays and vital in-game statistics. Built by Daktronics, the structure is right above the Rogers Centre hotel and measures a gigantic 33 feet high by 110 feet wide. The viewing area is created by an astonishing number of trinilights—67,200 to be exact. In 2005, an integrated display and scoring system, also produced by Daktronics, was incorporated into the scoreboard.

OVERSIZED PLAYER POSTERS

Larger-than-life player posters featuring action shots of the current 25-man roster line the exterior of the Rogers Centre and brighten an otherwise bland gray façade.

PLAYING FIELD UPGRADE

In 2005, the playing surface was upgraded from Astroturf to Field Turf, and management took it a step further in 2010 with the unveiling of Astro Turf Game Day 3D, a synthetic turf. According to Blue Jays officials, the synthetic grass has a roll-up system, with each panel consisting of crumb rubber and sand to recreate the consistencies of a natural grass field. Overall, 97 panels create the baseball layout, and the largest roll measures 170 feet long.

RAILWAY TRACK SYSTEM

Rogers Centre is a multipurpose facility that can be easily altered to accommodate either baseball or football. The seats on Level 100, sitting on a track system, can be rotated within hours to accommodate the higher capacity for football games, or be reverted back to regular configurations for Blue Jays baseball games.

RETIRED NUMBERS

The Blue Jays have retired one number to honor a man who was truly a legend in his time with Toronto. Roberto Alomar's number 11 is alongside the championship banners above the video board in center field.

ROGERS CENTRE HOTEL

The 348-room hotel, known as the Renaissance Toronto, is built into the back portion of the stadium and features 70 rooms overlooking the field. Legend has it that an unsuspecting couple checked into the hotel and had forgotten to close the curtains. What ensued was a big enough show that it diverted the fans' attention from the field to their hotel room. Now the rooms facing the field have one-way windows, preventing such an occurrence from ever happening again. During his days with the Blue Jays, Roberto Alomar called the Rogers Centre hotel his home for a few seasons, as do many of the players who don a Toronto uniform.

ROGERS CENTRE RESTAURANT

A restaurant, complete with a 300-foot open-air bar and all seats facing the playing field, is positioned 60 feet up from center field and comes complete with a buffet. A strange, but true fact: On May 31, 1998, Jim Thome of the Cleveland Indians plastered a home run that flew into an open window of the restaurant, over three rows of tables, and plopped down at the feet of a man who was filling his plate with dessert.

The hotel (on the same level as the scoreboard) and restaurant (below the scoreboard) highlight the center-field area. (*Photographed by Brian Skversky/Flickr*)

ROGERS CENTRE TRIBUTE

There is a plaque at the north end of the Level 100 concourse to honor the hard work of all the workers who constructed Rogers Centre. These men and women—who logged a combined 10,000 person-years in constructing the ballpark—built a structure that has housed Blue Jays baseball since 1989 and assisted in paving the way for other retractable-roof stadiums in the future.

SEAT WASHING

Although Dodger Stadium in Los Angeles is widely regarding as being so clean you could eat off the floor, the Rogers Centre is the only Major League ballpark in which every seat is washed thoroughly following each and every home game. The 37,000 seats, along with all other surrounding areas, are soaked down and disinfected before the next game. This job takes approximately 14 workers eight hours to complete.

LEVEL 500

The highest seating level at Rogers Centre might seem like it's a mile away from the action, but home runs have traveled into that particular area before. One of the more memorable shots came when Oakland slugger Jose

Canseco connected for a shot off Toronto pitcher Mike Flanagan during Game 4 of the 1989 American League Championship Series, sending it 480 feet into the left-field sky deck. Not to be outdone, former Athletics teammate and fellow bash brother Mark McGwire duplicated the feat in 1996, sending it 488 feet off Blue Jays pitcher Huck Flener.

TOM CHEEK TRIBUTE

To honor former Blue Jays broadcaster Tom Cheek, a blue banner with the inscription "4306 TOM CHEEK" in white was raised in the Rogers Centre Level of Excellence deck. This number pays tribute to the amount of games called consecutively by Cheek from April 7, 1977, to June 3, 2004, when he ended his 27-year run following the death of his father. Cheek, who was the radio voice since the franchise was born in 1977, passed away on October 14, 2005.

THE ROOF

The Rogers Centre roof was the world's first fully retractable roof when it debuted in 1989, ultimately setting the stage for others to follow. Weighing a hefty 11,000 tons, held together by 250,000 bolts, and covering 340,000 square feet, it can open and close in approximately 20 minutes. Three movable panels and one stationary panel are powered by a series of motors that can generate over 750 horsepower, moving along a steel-track system. The roof has a patent that was officially registered on December 1, 1992.

MEMORABLE GAMES AT ROGERS CENTRE

JUNE 5, 1989: FIRST GAME AT ROGERS CENTRE

After spending their first 12 seasons at Exhibition Stadium, the Blue Jays welcomed the world to the highly anticipated Rogers Centre in front of 48,378 fans, but the Milwaukee Brewers picked up the win, 5–3. Paul Molitor got things rolling for the Brew Crew by becoming the first player to register a hit—a double to center field—in Rogers Centre history and was later driven in on a groundout by Gary Sheffield. In the bottom of the second, Blue Jays first baseman Fred McGriff cracked a solo home run—the stadium's first—to tie the game at one, but Milwaukee was too much to handle this day despite Blue Jays pitcher Jimmy Key going the distance.

OCTOBER 6, 1989: FIRST PLAYOFF GAME AT ROGERS CENTRE

The new ballpark propelled the Blue Jays to their first postseason since 1985, and the playoff game against the mighty Athletics was a success too. Toronto took the contest 7–3 behind the strength of a four-run fourth inning and a three-run seventh. Tony Fernandez, who connected for two doubles, provided the offensive spark for the Blue Jays, and Jimmy Key turned in yet another solid pitching performance in limiting the powerful Oakland offense to only three runs.

JUNE 29, 1990: OAKLAND ACE TOSSES FIRST NO-HITTER AT ROGERS CENTRE

With a sellout crowd on hand and cheering for him by game's end, Athletics starter Dave Stewart pitched the game of his life, striking out 12 in holding the Blue Jays hitless during a 5–0 Oakland victory. After walking the first two Toronto batters—Junior Felix and Tony Fernandez—Stewart proceeded to retire 26 in a row before walking Felix again with two outs in the bottom of the ninth before retiring Fernandez on a fly ball. Rickey Henderson, who went 1-for-2 with a home run and three RBI, powered the A's offense while another Henderson—Dave—homered and accounted for the other two runs. Later that night, Los Angeles Dodgers starter Fernando Valenzuela matched Stewart, pitching a no-hitter of his own against the Cardinals at Dodger Stadium.

AUGUST 28, 1992: BREWERS RECORD 31 HITS IN WIN

Not only did Milwaukee come into Toronto and embarrass the Blue Jays, 22–2, but they also set an American League record in the process by collecting 31 hits, the most knocks in a game since 1901. Of the 31 hits, 26 were singles and were good enough to set the record in that particular category as well. For Milwaukee, Kevin Seitzer and Scott Fletcher each collected five hits while combining for eight RBI and seven runs scored, as the Brewers scored in every inning except the fifth. The fourth inning proved to be the difference when six runs were scored by the Brew Crew, highlighted by five straight singles from Seitzer, Fletcher, Pat Listach, Darryl Hamilton, and Paul Molitor, which extended the lead to 12–1 at that point.

OCTOBER 14, 1992: BLUE JAYS WRAP UP FIRST AMERICAN LEAGUE PENNANT

After facing Oakland in the first-ever postseason contest at Rogers Centre, the Blue Jays added another first to the record books: an American League pennant. Joe Carter hammered a two-run home run in the first, and Candy Maldonado stroked a three-run shot of his own, helping Toronto jump to a 6–0 lead. From that point on, they never looked back, simultaneously ending the Athletics' season and heading to their first-ever Fall Classic with a 9–2 triumph. Juan Guzman was solid on the mound for Toronto, striking out eight and allowing five hits in picking up the pennant-clinching win.

OCTOBER 20, 1992: FIRST WORLD SERIES CONTEST OUTSIDE THE UNITED STATES

As if the contest and series weren't exciting enough, the Fall Classic made history when it was the first one to be held outside the United States. In a classic pitcher's duel, Steve Avery (Braves) and Juan Guzman (Blue Jays) each went eight solid innings, but it was Blue Jays left fielder Candy Maldonado who came through in the clutch. He connected for a two-strike, game-ending single in the bottom of the ninth inning with the bases loaded to drive in Roberto Alomar, securing a 3–2 Toronto victory in front of 51,813 charged-up fans at Rogers Centre.

OCTOBER 23, 1993: CARTER HOME RUN WINS TITLE

For only the second time in Major League and World Series history, the Fall Classic ended on a dramatic home run after Joe Carter went deep in the bottom of the ninth, propelling Toronto to an 8–6 victory. Carter joined Pittsburgh's Bill Mazeroski (Game 7 of the 1960 World Series versus New York) as the only other player to accomplish that feat. After Rickey Henderson and Paul Molitor reached base against Phillies closer Mitch Williams, Carter took a 2–2 slider and deposited it into the left-field bullpen, setting off a wild celebration inside the Rogers Centre as Toronto captured its second consecutive championship in dramatic fashion.

JULY 5, 1998: ROCKET MAN REACHES 3,000 STRIKEOUTS

It might have been the summer of the home run ball, but Roger Clemens was too busy adding pitching accomplishments to his résumé to notice during a 2–1 Toronto win. With a strikeout of the Tampa Bay's Randy Wynn in the third, Clemens became the eleventh pitcher to attain the 3,000-strikeout mark. Pumping his fist as he walked off the mound, his teammates congratulated him, and catcher Darrin Fletcher gave him the ball as he pointed to his wife when he entered the dugout. Needing five strikeouts to accomplish the feat, Clemens didn't waste any time. In the first, he struck out Quinton McCracken and Wade Boggs and then came back with a vengeance to strike out the side in order consisting of Mike DeFelice, Miguel Cairo, and Wynn consecutively. With the score tied at one, Tony Fernandez connected for an RBI single in the bottom of the eighth that scored Shannon Stewart, giving Toronto the win.

SEPTEMBER 27, 1998: A NEAR NO-HITTER ON THE LAST DAY OF THE SEASON

We all know Roy Halladay as a consistent pitcher today, but his second start in the Major Leagues was more than impressive—it was downright incredible. Halladay was dominant, going the distance and allowing only one hit during a season-ending 2–1 Blue Jays victory. Having faced just one Detroit Tigers batter over the minimum going into the ninth inning, Gabe Kapler lined out to left, and pinch hitter Paul Bako grounded out to second for two quick outs. With the fans standing in anticipation, pinch hitter Bobby Higginson stepped in and connected for an opposite-field, first-pitch home run that landed just over the left-field fence, ending the no-hit bid and shutout. Despite the long ball, Halladay went on to finish the game in picking the first win of his Major League career. Alex Gonzalez and Shawn Green, who blasted solo homers in the third and sixth innings off Detroit starter Justin Thompson, respectively, led the Blue Jays offense.

SEPTEMBER 25, 2003: DELGADO ENTERS THE RECORD BOOKS
Carlos Delgado became the first Toronto Blue Jays player—and fifteenth overall in Major League history—to hit four home runs in one game, doing so against Tampa Bay during Toronto's 10–8 victory. Delgado, who connected for career-blast number 300 off Tampa Bay starter Jorge Sosa with his first home run of the game, victimized him again with a solo shot leading off the bottom of the fourth. With reliever Joe Kennedy on in the sixth, Delgado sent a 386-foot home run to right field, while tying the game at six. Lastly, in the bottom of the eighth facing Lance Carter, it was more of the same when Delgado smashed one to straightaway center, an estimated 445 feet, once again tying the game—this time at 8—and a date with the record books. Toronto won the game, thanks to a sacrifice fly by Bobby Kielty that scored Eric Hinske and a solo home run by Mike Bordick, all coming in the bottom of the eighth.

SEPTEMBER 23, 2010: BAUTISTA CRANKS FIFTIETH OF THE SEASON
Wasting no time to make history, Jose Bautista continued his stellar 2010 campaign by blasting a home run in the first inning—the only runs of the game—to become the first Toronto hitter to amass 50 home runs in one season during a 1–0 win over Seattle. With two outs, Bautista turned on a 2–1 pitch against Mariners flamethrower Felix Hernandez, depositing the ball into the left-field bullpen to reach the historic plateau. He became the twenty-sixth player in Major League history to hit 50 in one season and extended his own Blue Jays record, a mark formerly held by George Bell, who connected for 47 in 1987. It was also his thirty-first home run at Rogers Centre, breaking the team record formerly held by Carlos Delgado in 2000.

"Quite honestly, I did not realize it until it was about halfway out of the ballpark and all of a sudden I just thought, 'That's 50!' . . . Bautista's fiftieth home run will always be remembered not only because it was a milestone home run, but because it was against Felix Hernandez in a 1–0 game."

—*Buck Martinez, Blue Jays broadcaster*

MAY 7, 2011: VERLANDER TOSSES ANOTHER NO-NO

Detroit Tigers starter Justin Verlander registered his second career no-hitter, this time coming close to perfection after shutting down Toronto, 9–0, on a sunny afternoon. With the only base runner for the Blue Jays coming via a 12-pitch walk issued to J. P. Arencibia in the eighth—and who was erased by a double play—Verlander was unstoppable on the mound during an 108-pitch, 12-strikeout masterpiece. Alex Avila and Jhonny Peralta, who both cashed in on home runs, led the Tiger offense, and Austin Jackson also chipped in by going 3-for-5. With a Rogers Centre crowd of 23,453 standing and cheering in anticipation during the bottom of the ninth, Verlander ended the game on a high note after getting Rajai Davis to strike out swinging on a 2–2 pitch.

SEPTEMBER 13, 2013: DAVIS JOINS ELITE COMPANY

Baltimore slugger Chris Davis connected for his fiftieth home run of the season, tying the franchise record set by Brady Anderson, and joined Babe Ruth (59 home runs, 44 doubles in 1921) and Albert Belle (50 home runs, 52 doubles in 1995) as the only players to accumulate 40 doubles and 50 home runs in a single season during a 5–3 victory over Toronto. Davis, who became the first player to hit 50 since Toronto's Jose Bautista did so in 2010, became the twenty-seventh player to accomplish the feat after leading off the eighth with a 430-foot blast to center field off Blue Jays pitcher Steve Delabar. The long ball put Baltimore ahead 4–3, and later in the inning an insurance run was added when Danny Valencia singled home Adam Jones for the final margin of victory.

WHAT THEY'RE SAYING ABOUT ROGERS CENTRE

GEORGE BRETT: "It was better than the football field we played on [Exhibition Stadium]. . . . It was state-of-the-art when it first came out and you did not think you could ever find a better stadium. Unfortunately, they built a lot of good stadiums now."

JASON GIAMBI: "I like Toronto—it is a great town . . . great hitter's ballpark, [and] I definitely think the ball travels a lot better with the dome opened than closed, but [overall], I like playing there."

CURTIS GRANDERSON: "The ball carries pretty well there to all fields—center, left, and right—the dome is probably the easiest to see out of all of them. . . . The only thing I have noticed is when it is open, it can be really bright [because] the sun seems to reflect off that turf pretty good."

PAUL KONERKO: "Not a fan. . . . About the only thing you can say about it is that it is a dome and you do not have to worry about rain delays, although one year we had a rain delay because it rained quick enough to where they could not shut the roof, [but] I never really played well there."

DON MATTINGLY: "Not a big fan of Rogers Centre. . . . I do not know why, [but] it just never really did much for me there, probably because I did not swing the bat good there either."

MARK MCGWIRE: "Great hitter's ballpark. [The] ball jumps out of there [and] it was just [a] great, great background and everything. . . . [I] had a lot of great playoff games there back in the day—in the early 1990s—and I think I can still hear the roar of the fans there when they beat us in 1992."

ERIC NADEL, BROADCASTER: "I remember when it opened, and it really was the eighth wonder of the world and we would sit there and watch the retractable roof take 20 minutes to open and close and we thought it was the greatest miracle of all time. . . . Now you realize it is not a great place to watch a game unless there are 50,000 people in it."

RICK RIZZS, BROADCASTER: "Toronto was the eighth wonder of the world and they wanted a situation where [they could have] the best of both worlds [an indoor and outdoor-type ballpark] and they built a retractable, domed stadium. It was amazing and I could not wait for it to open. . . . Now it has changed over the years, but it is still a remarkable stadium."

ROBIN VENTURA: "That was a pretty exciting time because their team was pretty good at the time and then getting an indoor stadium like that . . . they were selling out every night and with the hotel in center field, it was a futuristic ballpark at that time."

JUSTIN VERLANDER: "I like it when the roof is open, [and] you have got the CN Tower sitting over top of you and it almost looks like it is leaning into the stadium. That is a unique view that you will not see anywhere else."

ROGERS CENTRE FACTS AND FIGURES

ROGERS CENTRE ADDRESS
1 Blue Jays Way, Toronto, ON, Canada M5V 1J1

TORONTO BLUE JAYS TEAM WEB SITE
www.bluejays.com

FIELD DIMENSIONS (IN FEET)
Left Field: 328', Left-Center: 375', Center: 400',
Right-Center: 375', Right Field: 328'

SEATING CAPACITY (AS OF 2015)
49,282

ALL-STAR GAMES AT ROGERS CENTRE
July 9, 1991: American League 4, National League 1
MVP: Cal Ripken Jr., Baltimore Orioles (AL)

ROGERS CENTRE FIRSTS
Game: June 5, 1989—Milwaukee 5, Toronto 3
Single: Kelly Gruber, Toronto (June 5, 1989)
Double: Paul Molitor, Toronto (June 5, 1989)*
Triple: Jay Buhner, Seattle (June 18, 1989)
Home Run: Fred McGriff, Toronto (June 18, 1989)

Denotes first hit in the stadium.

TARGET FIELD
HOME OF THE MINNESOTA TWINS

TARGET FIELD, MINNESOTA TWINS (*Photographed by Mark Whitt/Flickr*)

W hen the Minnesota Twins departed the Hubert H. Humphrey Metrodome in 2009 after 28 seasons, what they had left behind was anything but an ordinary Major League ballpark. From the crazy, unconventional bounces only a carpeted surface can produce, to a white Teflon roof that wreaked havoc on any outfielder trying to track down a fly ball, it was less than suitable for the game of baseball. So when plans were drawn up to replace the indoor ballpark, management decided to go back in time and create the first open-air stadium in the Twin Cities since Metropolitan Stadium, the home of Twins Baseball from 1961 to 1981.

Twins management got the ball rolling and began to plant the seeds for new digs in 1995, when a potential site was located with large acreage just north of the Metrodome, along the Mississippi River. The idea ultimately fell through, and the area was later cleared for the current Gold Medal Park, a facility open to the public. The mid-1990s were trying times for the ball club, and losing seasons were the norm. In 1997, a potential sale to a North Carolina businessman, who would have relocated to the team to the Greensboro area, left fans on edge, but the idea ultimately went by the wayside.

In 2001, Major League Baseball announced that the contraction of the Twins was a distinct possibility (along with the Montreal Expos), and it certainly didn't help that fellow American League Central teams either had a new stadium already or were in the process of building one. For a while, things were appearing bleak for the franchise and its fan base, but to Minnesota's credit, they never gave up. In 2005, their patience and persistence proved to be the key when the push for a new ballpark started to pick up steam, and a light at the end of the tunnel began to appear.

On April 26, 2005, the Minnesota Twins and Hennepin County had tentatively reached an agreement that consisted of the Twins footing one-third of the overall cost of the stadium while the rest would be covered by a 0.15 percent sales tax within the borders of Hennepin County. With the full endorsement of the mayor of Minneapolis, the board voted in favor (by a 4–3 margin) for the stadium deal on May 3, 2005, and it passed a second vote on May 9, when the House committee of Minnesota's legislature gave the okay (by a 17–5 vote) that the referendum be sent to the floor. Although the vote of the full legislature was delayed several times because other issues took precedence, the bill was approved during a 2006 session that saw it pass by a 71–61 count in the House and a narrow margin of 34–32 in the Senate.

Under the legislation, $392 million in public subsidy would be generated through the Hennepin County sales tax increase for the $522 million needed to build Target Field. The final hurdle was cleared on May 21 and signed into law by Gov. Tim Pawlenty in a ceremony that was full of pomp and circumstance before a May 26 home contest at the Hubert H. Humphrey Metrodome. For Twins players, management, and all of the die-hard fans, the dream of having a new baseball-only facility to call their own had finally become a reality.

On June 20, 2006, the county board showed its approval, voting 5–2, and in mid-February 2007, despite a holdup regarding the purchase price of the land, which was later resolved, the Twins made the official design of the ballpark public on April 12. For a franchise that had hit rock-bottom in the middle of the 1990s and weathered the storm of a possible sale and contraction, it was a victory that signaled a new era for Minnesota Twins Baseball.

SPECIAL FEATURES OF TARGET FIELD

ADVANCED HEAT
When baseball in April and October hits the Twin Cities, Target Field is prepared with plenty of spots for fans to warm up. The number of radiant heaters, which made their debut in 2010, was increased in the home run

porch and terrace levels in 2011. The big heaters engulf fans with warm air and allow them to stay connected to the game with the field in plain view. The Metrodome may have offered a safe haven from the elements, but the heaters are the next best solution at Target Field.

BONFIRE

The Twins took a backyard, summertime tradition and incorporated it into the ballpark by instituting the first-ever bonfire for fans at a Major League ballpark. The 4-foot by 10-foot elevated rectangular structure is useful during those cold nights in Minnesota, but don't forget the graham crackers, marshmallows, and chocolate! (A special thanks to the Twins for double-checking the exact dimensions of the bonfire pit for me.)

CAPTAIN'S DECK

The Captain's Deck, a hot spot and fan favorite that overlooks left field, is a full-service bar that offers plenty of choices when it comes to selecting just the right drink for the occasion. The view, similar to that of being on the captain's deck in a ship, is from a great vantage point, and the bird's-eye perspective of the action on the field is unsurpassed.

CHAMPIONS CLUB

Seeking comfortable leather chairs and a wine collection that would put five-star restaurants to shame? Look no further than the Champions Club, a top-notch location that may make you forget why you're even at the ballpark in the first place. The highlight of the Champions Club—the two World Series trophies won in 1987 and 1991—are displayed separately in glass-enclosed wooden cabinets. A door leads to first-class outdoor seating positioned directly behind home plate.

CHAMPIONSHIP REMINDERS

Small flagpoles behind the home run porch located just beyond left field pay homage to each division, league, and World Series title won by the franchise since its arrival in the Twin Cities in 1961. Blue flags with white numbers outlined in red denote division and league championships won, while red flags with blue numbers outlined in white symbolize Fall Classics captured by Minnesota.

DIVISION STANDINGS

The Minnesota Twins have incorporated flags as part of their own system of displaying up-to-date standings within the division. Small flagpoles, located on the upper rim in right-center field, display each team's position

A bronze statue of a massive gold glove sits a mere 520 feet from home plate.
(*Photographed by Brian Skversky/Flickr*)

and are arranged by the order in which they currently sit within the division once each game has been played.

FLAGPOLE

The primary flagpole in right field, which proudly flies the United States flag, has a bit of history. It was originally at Metropolitan Stadium, the outdoor home of Twins baseball from 1961 to 1981, before being relocated to the Bloomington VFW following the demolition of "The Met." Hall of Famer Harmon Killebrew had the honor of raising the flag for the first time at Target Field, and on September 6, 2010, slugger Jim Thome took aim and blasted a tape-measure home run off of it.

GOLDEN GLOVE

A bronze statue of a massive gold glove, a tribute to all the Twins players who have excelled in the field and collected the Gold Glove Award, sits precisely 520 feet from home plate in the Target Plaza. A popular destination for photos, the old-style, vintage glove is slightly tilted back and features "TWINS" written in cursive on the right-hand side. As for its distance from home plate, that's no coincidence: it's the exact length of a home run once smashed by slugger Harmon Killebrew at Metropolitan Stadium during his playing days with the Twins.

HRBEK'S BAR AND GRILL

Hrbek's Bar and Grill, located in section 114, is decorated in Minnesota Twins memorabilia, including every Twins logo ever used on the ceiling, and is dedicated to Kent Hrbek, the Bloomington native and Twins Hall of Fame first baseman. The favorite dishes of Hrbek, a frequent visitor to the establishment, are on the menu. The restaurant offers a full-service bar and outdoor patio for fans when the weather is nice and warm.

LEED CERTIFIED

After Nationals Park in Washington, Target Field became the second professional sports stadium to be recognized as LEED certified. LEED, an acronym for Leadership in Energy and Environmental Design, provides third-party verification that a structure was designed and constructed using plans that improved energy savings, water efficiency, and other environmentally friendly practices. Target Field collected 36 certification points—the most awarded to a Major League ballpark at the time—and, as a result, was awarded a silver certificate.

LEGENDS CLUB

Upscale lounges are part of the membership services offered by the Delta SKY360 Legends Club. Most notably, the Kirby Puckett Lounge, positioned by section C, and the Rod Carew Lounge by section P and 573 near section J are two of the most popular destinations for fans. Each one does an outstanding job of displaying memorabilia and photos of two of the most successful players in franchise history.

LIMESTONE GALORE

Looking to differentiate itself from the other newer ballparks and to avoid the repetition of a brick exterior, Target Field utilizes 100,000 square feet of Mankato limestone, which was delivered by the truckload from nearby Mankato, Minnesota. The distinctive limestone continues on top of both the home and visitor's dugouts and is also integrated down the first- and third-base lines.

METRODOME TRIBUTES

They may not play there anymore, but the Twins made sure they incorporated a few attributes from the Metrodome before they departed for greener pastures. Following Game 3 of the American League Division Series on October 11, 2009 (a 4–1 loss to New York), which turned out to be their final game ever in the climate-controlled dome, home plate was uprooted and later set into place at Target Field. The Twins also took a few buckets of dirt from the sliding pit and pitcher's mound and added it to the dirt in those areas at Target Field.

METROPOLITAN CLUB

The Metropolitan Club, a nod to Metropolitan Stadium, the former home of Twins baseball, is located on the club level along right field and is one of the exclusive restaurants at Target Field. Floor-to-ceiling windows complement the spacious setting. A display case, complete with a chair from "The Met," a panoramic view of the stadium, and an old sign that once designated section 32 enhance the setting. A full-service bar and a buffet are one of the many choices available to season-ticket holders, who may enter by showing their season-ticket ID card.

MINNIE AND PAUL LOGO

One of the most recognizable parts of Target Field, the 46-foot-tall, animated Minnie and Paul logo is displayed in center field against a backdrop of the outline of the state. Two players donning uniforms of the Minneapolis Millers and St. Paul Saints—the two Minor League franchises that ruled the roost before the Twins came along—are depicted shaking hands across the Mississippi River with a small bridge in the background.

Whenever a Twins player goes yard, the logo comes to life. As strobe lights flash, Minnie and Paul shake hands and the Mississippi River appears as though it is flowing. When a Twins player crosses home plate, strobe lights trace the border of the sign as if a player rounded the bases; for a strikeout, the outside corners flash symbolizing the strike zone; and following a win, the *T* and *s* in "Twins" illuminate, and the players shake hands, and the river flows as if a homer were hit.

NAMING RIGHTS

Target Corporation, one of the most recognizable and popular shopping destinations for many people, decided to team up with the Minnesota Twins and agreed to a 25-year deal on September 15, 2008, for sole rights to the ballpark title. The Minneapolis-based Fortune 500 company also owns the naming rights to the NBA's Minnesota Timberwolves arena (Target Center) and is the second largest discount retailer in the country. Financial terms of the deal were not disclosed.

RETIRED NUMBERS

Seven numbers have been retired to honor the greatest Minnesota Twins players, and they can be found on the front of the executive offices, positioned down the left-field line and displayed in white circles and red numbers. They include: Harmon Killebrew (3), Tony Oliva (6), Tom Kelly (10), Kent Hrbek (14), Bert Blyleven (28), Rod Carew (29), and Kirby Puckett (34).

RETRACTABLE ROOF PLANS SCRAPPED

Considering that the temperatures in Minnesota during April and October hover around the freezing mark, it makes sense that a retractable roof was one of the ideas being considered when plans were released. It was said that the roof would have added $100 million to the total budget, and Hennepin County, the Twins, or the Minnesota legislature were not even slightly interested in paying that added expense. There was even talk of adding a Major League–first—heated seats—but that idea was scrapped as well.

ROOF DECK

The left-field corner of Target Field is home to the roof deck, a spot that not only offers incredible views of the picturesque Minneapolis skyline, but was also designed to give fans the ultimate outdoor experience. There is a 120-seat capacity, a bar, and a party-like atmosphere. One hundred more could be accommodated with standing room–only tickets.

SPRUCE TREES

In Target Field's first season, 14 six-foot-high black spruce trees were planted in front of the batter's eye in center field. Throughout the season, players complained that they were too much of a diversion while they were in the batter's box, and as a result, the trees were uprooted, with two saved and planted elsewhere on the Target Field grounds. As for the other 12, 10 were given as gifts to state parks, one was auctioned off to the general public, and the final one was a contest prize for season-ticket holders. The backdrop was later covered in a black material to help reduce glare—and complaints.

STATUES AT TARGET FIELD

As of this writing, eight statues designed by local artist Bill Mack add character to Target Field and honor individuals who have left a lasting impression on Minnesota Twins baseball throughout the years.

FORMER OWNERS: Instrumental in the success of the Twins organization, former owners Calvin Griffith (statue located outside Gate 29), Carl Pohlad, and his wife Eloise Pohlad (statues positioned at Target Plaza, outside Gate 34) are also honored for their contributions to the franchise. Griffith's statue was dedicated on September 3, 2010, while the Pohlads' took place on October 3, 2010.

HARMON KILLEBREW: Positioned on the Target Plaza, this Hall of Famer's statue is a perfect representation of what he stood for: power. It portrays him taking a massive swing—and most likely connecting—for what would be a majestic home run. Killebrew's statue was dedicated on April 3, 2010.

KENT HRBEK: Located appropriately outside Gate 14 (the number he wore his entire Twins career), this fan favorite was the latest player to be immortalized. The statue captures him with his arms raised in celebration. Fast fact: Hrbek connected for the first home run in Hubert H. Humphrey Metrodome history with a blast on April 3, 1982, against the Phillies in an exhibition game. Hrbek's statue was dedicated on April 14, 2012.

KIRBY PUCKETT: Positioned on Target Plaza right outside Gate 34, this Minnesota legend's bronze likeness captures one of the most recognizable images in Twins history. His legendary fist-pump as he headed around first base following his dramatic eleventh-inning home run in Game 6 of the 1991 World Series versus the Braves is preserved forever. Puckett's statue was dedicated on April 12, 2010.

ROD CAREW: Located outside Gate 29, near 7th street, the statue of Rod Carew displays the one-of-a-kind batting stance that enabled him to collect 3,053 hits throughout his big-league career. His consistency also earned him a prestigious spot in Cooperstown. Carew's statue was dedicated on April 2, 2010.

TONY OLIVA: Placed outside Gate 6, the statue of Tony Oliva shows him following through on a smooth swing, most likely connecting for an extra-base hit. The former Twins right fielder was a menace at the plate, smacking 220 career home runs to go along with 329 doubles and a lifetime .304 batting average. Oliva's statue was dedicated on April 8, 2011.

TARGET PLAZA

Target Plaza, the most popular gathering area for fans, is behind the right-field gate and features an assortment of displays. A monument commemorates all the previous ballparks used by Minnesota baseball, and a pedestrian walkway nearby is home to the Twins Tradition Wall, a partition littered with pennants featuring rosters of all the Twins teams throughout the years and pennants of players, coaches, and staff.

TOWN BALL TAVERN

Best known among Minneapolis natives for serving the ever-popular Jucy Lucy burger, the Town Ball Tavern is a full-service bar in the left-field corner of the upper concourse that celebrates amateur baseball in Minnesota. Don't want to miss a score? A real-time scrolling scoreboard keeps fans up-to-date on all the action around the league. For a touch of nostalgia, the floor is from the basketball court once used by the Minneapolis Lakers before they bolted for the glitz and glamour of Los Angeles.

TWINS FAMILY LOUNGE

What many fans won't see is the tunnel that leads to the Twins clubhouse, and that's the spot designated as the Twins Family Lounge. A large floor-to-ceiling mural depicts great moments in Minnesota Twins baseball over the years. The pictures are the focal point of the brown-carpeted walkway, which is a gathering spot for the families of Twins baseball players.

TWINS TRADITION WALL

During the construction of Target Field, fans were given a one-of-a-kind opportunity to send in, for a fee, personalized 35-character messages to family members, friends, or even the Twins on the inscription wall. Located at the Target Plaza, the 60-inch by 101-inch glass panels were so popular that the first 2,400 slots sold out in September 2009, prompting a second section of glass to be built. Once panels are added to the wall, fans can check the Twins Web site to find the precise location of their message.

WI-FI ZONES

The Twins have wired Target Field for Wi-Fi connection throughout the entire ballpark. The service is free, and the coverage area is widespread. The Twins have also ensured that all cell phones in the building will receive a signal.

WOOD-BACK SEATS

Part of the Legends Club, this private seating option has wood-backed seats, a subtle tribute to baseball played in days past when the entire seat was constructed of wood. The dark-green padded seats stand out in the crowd and for a quick view of them, look directly beneath the press box, where the seats surround the concourse.

MEMORABLE GAMES AT TARGET FIELD

APRIL 12, 2010: FIRST GAME AT TARGET FIELD

A sold-out crowd of 39,715 clad in Twins gear witnessed the first outdoor baseball game in Minneapolis since the days of the Metropolitan Stadium 28 years ago, and they went home happy after Minnesota defeated the Red Sox, 5–2. Marco Scuturo, leading off and playing center for the Red Sox, lined a sharp single to center for the ballpark's first official hit but was promptly picked off moments later attempting to steal second. In the bottom of the first, the Twins tallied two runs on the strength of back-to-back RBI singles by Michael Cuddyer and Jason Kubel, and a double by Joe Mauer in the bottom of the second increased the lead to 3–0.

David Ortiz, a former Minnesota Twin, connected for an RBI double in the fourth for Boston that made it 3–1, but in the bottom half, Mauer would return to the scene of the crime and cash in on an RBI single, increasing the lead to 4–1. Kubel finished off the Twins, scoring with a home run in the bottom of the seventh to right field. Boston added a run in the top of the eighth on a Dustin Pedroia sacrifice fly, but it wasn't enough as the Twins made history by winning their first-ever game at Target Field.

SEPTEMBER 2, 2010: TWINS DROP HIGH-SCORING AFFAIR

In a game that lasted four hours and 47 minutes, Minnesota blew a late lead and in due time lost to Detroit, 10–9, in a game that featured five long balls by the visiting Tigers. With the Twins ahead 7–3 heading into the top of the eighth, the boys from Motown tapped into their power source when Johnny Peralta and Ryan Raburn went back to back with solo shots, and Will Rhymes added an RBI single that scored two, tying the game at seven. In the bottom half, the Twins added a run on an RBI single by Alexi Casilla to regain the lead, but Detroit came right back in the top of the ninth, when Casper Wells slammed a solo shot to deadlock the score at eight.

It stayed that way until the top of the eleventh, when Raburn singled in Brandon Inge to give the Tigers a 9–8 advantage momentarily. The Twins, taking an "anything you can do I can do better" approach, retaliated in the bottom half on a Delwyn Young groundout with the bases loaded, which scored Denard Span, knotting the game at nine apiece. The Tigers ended the charade in the thirteenth, when Gerald Laird hit the Tigers' fifth home run of the game—a solo shot off Nick Blackburn—and Jose Valverde pitched a perfect frame to secure a 10–9 Detroit victory.

SEPTEMBER 21, 2010: TWINS WRAP UP ANOTHER DIVISION TITLE

The Twins captured their sixth American League Central Division title in nine years with a come-from-behind win over the Indians, 6–4, in front of their seventy-third straight sellout of the year. With Minnesota trailing 4–1 in the bottom of the sixth, Danny Valencia singled to score former Indian Jim Thome, who had homered earlier in the game, making it 4–2. The Twins rose to the occasion in the bottom of the eighth, when Delwyn Young laced an RBI double, and pinch hitter Jose Morales came on to hit a game-tying sacrifice fly. Denard Span sent Target Field into delirium after his eventual game-winning RBI single plated Valencia, and Orlando Hudson added an RBI double for good measure that scored Span, propelling the Twins to the 6–4 win. The division championship became official long after the game ended, when the Chicago White Sox lost on the West Coast to the Oakland Athletics, 7–2.

OCTOBER 6, 2010: FIRST PLAYOFF GAME AT TARGET FIELD

The New York Yankees waltzed in and spoiled the first-ever postseason game at Target Field, defeating the Twins 6–4 on the strength of a two-run home run by Mark Teixeira in the top of the seventh, which proved to be the difference. Minnesota struck first in the bottom of the second when Michael Cuddyer blasted a two-run home run and in the third inning, Orlando Hudson scored on a passed ball, giving the Twins a 3–0 lead. Undaunted, the Yankees took their first lead of the contest when they tallied four runs in the top of the sixth, highlighted by Curtis Granderson's two-run triple off Twins ace Francisco Liriano, who was pulled following that hit. Danny Valencia walked with the bases loaded in the bottom of the sixth, tying the game at four, setting the stage for Teixeira's go-ahead homer. The Yankees would go on to sweep the Twins and advance to the ALCS against Texas.

WHAT THEY'RE SAYING ABOUT TARGET FIELD

VINCE COTRONEO, BROADCASTER: "I just love what they did with the ballpark and they seem to make everything work . . . large concourses, fans close to the action, every bell and whistle that you could possibly want as a fan, and for us [the broadcasters], we are literally directly behind home plate."

RON GARDENHIRE: "A lot of thought went into it. It was a long process and I think they just about covered everything they could cover. They made it as nice a ballpark as you could ever want to be in . . . and the one thing they wanted to make sure [about was that] Target Field was all about Minnesota."

JONNY GOMES: "It is just mind-boggling how they put that where they put it and they are even shocked about it. It almost looks like they dropped it from a helicopter. . . . [It has a] real good batter's eye and it seems like all the seats are pretty good for the fans."

J. J. HARDY: "Target Field is a great place with the fans. [It is a] bigger ballpark and not a hitter's ballpark at all. . . . [It is] beautiful [and] more of a pitcher's ballpark, but a great place to play [at]."

TORII HUNTER: "It is awesome. It is something that I saw as a plan and to see it built and to see a structure there, it is like a dream come true. . . . Just to see it built and the fans coming to the games and selling [it] out . . . was pretty awesome."

ADAM JONES: "Minus the bugs that come from the lakes, it is actually a pretty nice ballpark. . . . [It has a] big outfield, the fans are pretty close to you, and they have got a good view. The clubhouse is nice and they did a pretty good job on the construction of it."

JOE MAUER: "It plays a little bigger than most, but it is a beautiful place [and] it is definitely an upgrade from the Metrodome. . . . From a player's perspective, the clubhouse and the facility itself [are] definitely an upgrade."

A. J. PIERZYNSKI: "They did a good job with not a lot of room to work with. They had to squeeze it into a good spot. . . . I know those guys coming from the Metrodome to there was a huge achievement, and it was a huge accomplishment for the Twins organization."

BUCK SHOWALTER: "I love it. [It is] the best new ballpark going. . . . I look at it as baseball functional—the dugouts are great, their clubhouses are where they are supposed to be, the hitting background is right. That is probably the best new ballpark out there."

JIM THOME: "[I] love the way they constructed it, the way they built it. I think it is very unique the way it sits in the city, and I think it has been great to have outdoor baseball in Minnesota. . . . It has brought a lot of excitement and I think people there really, really love going there and visiting teams love coming there as well."

TARGET FIELD FACTS AND FIGURES

TARGET FIELD ADDRESS
1 Twins Way, Minneapolis, MN 55403

MINNESOTA TWINS TEAM WEB SITE
www.twinsbaseball.com

FIELD DIMENSIONS (IN FEET)
Left Field: 339', Left-Center: 377', Center: 411',
Right-Center: 365', Right Field: 328'

SEATING CAPACITY (AS OF 2015)
39,021

ALL-STAR GAMES AT TARGET FIELD
July 15, 2014
American League 5, National League 3
MVP: Mike Trout, Los Angeles Angels

TARGET FIELD FIRSTS
Game: April 12, 2010—Minnesota 5, Boston 2
Single: Marco Scutaro, Boston (April 12, 2010)*
Double: Dustin Pedroia, Boston (April 12, 2010)
Triple: David DeJesus, Kansas City (April 16, 2010)
Home Run: Jason Kubel, Minnesota (April 12, 2010)

Denotes first hit in the stadium.

U.S. CELLULAR FIELD
HOME OF THE CHICAGO WHITE SOX

U.S. Cellular Field, Chicago White Sox (Photographed by Mark Whitt/Flickr)

[*U.S. Cellular Field was previously known as New Comiskey Park (1991–2003).*]

I f a Major League ballpark had feelings, U.S. Cellular Field would no doubt express its discontent with getting the short end of the stick. After the completion of Chicago's new digs on the South Side in 1991, there was an explosion of retro-style facilities, beginning with Baltimore's Camden Yards in 1992, which ultimately altered the landscape of ballparks around the Major League.

Conspicuous by their absence at U.S. Cellular Field were the recognizable quirks and other amenities that have gone a long way toward making ballparks such as Coors Field and Nationals Park one of a kind in their own way. However, credit should be given to the White Sox organization for upping the ante and making the necessary changes to not only make the ballpark more fan friendly, but also turning it into a more enjoyable experience for those who walk through the turnstiles.

Construction began on May 17, 1989, and when it was completed, the $167 million U.S. Cellular Field became the first new stadium of any kind in Chicago since 1929. That's the year the NBA's Chicago Stadium opened its doors and later was home to the great Michael Jordan–led Chicago Bulls teams of the early 1990s. When Old Comiskey Park was replaced, the tradition started by Bill Veeck in 1960, known as the "exploding scoreboard," was carried over and incorporated into U.S. Cellular Field. A nostalgic-looking façade in the upper deck is a subtle shout-out to the White Sox's previous home.

One of the major concerns early on was the vertigo-inducing slope of the upper deck's steps. One of the highest—if not the highest in all of baseball—the pitch and the angle of the steps created one heck of a conundrum for fans whose seats happened to be in that location. One of the main reasons this was an issue in the first place was because the upper tank was set back over the lower deck, and as a result, the first row of chairs were equal in height to the highest row of seats at the original Comiskey Park. As a general note, the White Sox are strict about their seating policies and venturing into the lower deck to take vacant seats is a no-no. To gain access, one must have a ticket clearly marked "lower level."

Despite all the skeptical feedback from fans, the Chicago White Sox organization stepped up to the plate and, in 2001, decided to kick off a series of improvements and upgrades that have made the stadium more of a retro-style Major League ballpark.

Dubbed Phase 1, three rows totaling close to 2,000 seats were added along the field between the dugouts and foul poles to give fans a closer perspective of the game, increasing the capacity from 44,321 to 45,936. The outfield structure was altered slightly to extend the seating to the fence. The bullpens were also relocated, enabling fans to view the pitchers making their warm-up tosses. Their former location was replaced by seating.

In 2002, there were several interior changes, including a brick façade, stainless-steel countertops, and new lighting installed in the main concourse. Other additions included new carpet, and a new heating and air conditioning system in the Club Level concourse, which is now enclosed. In 2003, $20 million was spent, and many items, including the outfield steel framework, the underside of the canopy roof, and the concrete in all the seating levels, were painted a dark gray.

In 2004, the upper deck was assessed. As a result, eight rows equaling 6,600 seats were removed from the very top. A roof, elevated 21 feet and covering 13 of the 21 rows above the chairs, replaced the preexisting overhang, which had provided little coverage from inclement weather. As a result, the stadium's capacity was reduced to a more baseball-like number at 40,615.

As the years have gone on, other improvements have changed the face of U.S. Cellular Field. It's true that it missed the boat in taking on the look of a retro-type, baseball-only ballpark, but with the enhancements made since its opening in 1991, fans should be proud and happy to attend a baseball game on the South Side of Chicago. The response from management to initiate and make all the changes over the years simply shows they are listening to the fans and are committed to making the U.S. Cellular Field experience enjoyable for all.

SPECIAL FEATURES OF U.S. CELLULAR FIELD

2005 WORLD CHAMPIONS REMINDER
At the main entrance of U.S. Cellular Field, a baseball diamond–shaped plaza honors the 2005 World Series championship, and legacy bricks emblazoned with individual messages from fans highlight the walkway. The red-bricked, white-lettered messages proclaim excitement for the championship team, which finished the postseason with an 11–1 record. In addition, a white bronze-and-granite sculpture weighing 25 tons has been placed at the forefront and honors the first title on the South Side since 1917.

BLUE SEATS
Blue seats used to be the standard at U.S. Cellular Field before they were phased out over the years in favor of a dark green shade. However, two originals still remain to mark two of the greatest moments in White Sox history. In Game 2 of the 2005 World Series, Paul Konerko connected for a grand-slam home run, and the spot is marked in section 159, row 7, seat 4. Later in that same contest, Scott Podsednik took aim and launched a game-winning home run that is commemorated in right-center at section 101, row 1, seat 13. (I want to personally thank the White Sox staff for scouting out the exact locations of those seats for me.)

CHAMPIONSHIP REMINDERS
Banners commemorating the championships won by the White Sox are on the outfield light towers and honor the extraordinary teams from 1906, 1917, and 2005. All the American League pennants and one with strictly division championships are displayed as well. The championships were once listed on flags, but the existing banners replaced them, and all the logos in franchise history are now displayed on the flags.

COMISKEY PARK GRILL
Comiskey Park Grill, a nod to the previous ballpark's name, was added before the 2011 season and is near Gate 5. This high-tech, modern restaurant features 64 flat-screen televisions, and is open before, during, and after

games. Among the tasty options are standard ballpark favorites such as hamburgers, hot dogs, and ribs, as well as other choices.

DISPLAY CASE

To honor Hall of Fame baseball writer Jerome Holtzman, the White Sox have placed a display case in front of the entranceway to the Stadium Club, on Level 300, located down the right-field line. Artifacts on display commemorate a man whose nickname was "The Dean," and some of the items include photographs, books, and pictures. Holtzman, who wrote for over 50 years, served as baseball's official historian for nine seasons from 1999 to 2008, the year he passed away.

ENCLOSURE

A steel-beamed wall, spanning from the Fundamentals deck in left field to the right-field foul pole, serves as a barrier to the outside. It is also a space for advertisements and video boards that display pertinent information about the game being played on the field. The main scoreboard, positioned in center field, is the primary showpiece and features a video board flanked by two advertisements on each side.

FAN PAVILION

The fan pavilion is a first-come, first-serve party deck located directly above the batter's eye in center field. The two-tiered structure, which offers a bird's-eye view of the action and incredible sight lines of the entire ballpark—not to mention a great view of those signature pinwheels on the scoreboard when they are set in motion—is also available on non-game days for private events.

GOLD COAST CLUB

Tickets purchased in the Gold Coast Club, the premium-seating area, include extended use of the private lounge following a game, four rows of extra-padded seats directly outside, and an in-seat wait service so you won't have to miss any of the action. Perhaps the best part is an all-inclusive buffet that has plenty of incredible food choices.

HISTORY LESSON

The upper deck concourse provides a view of White Sox history with a very comprehensive and thorough mural. The display takes a look back at some of the greatest players, teams, managers, and owners who have made their mark and left a lasting impression on the South Side. The pictures do an exceptional job of proving just how important baseball is in the Windy City.

INFORMATION BOARD

An information board, located in left field, delivers vital facts about the on-going game to those in attendance at U.S. Cellular Field. Player statistics, the official linescore, and other important information are displayed here, including any special announcements or bulletins for fans and any unique accomplishments attained by a player.

INSTRUCTIONAL BASEBALL

Geared toward the little ones and open through the sixth inning is an extensive 15,000 square-foot Fundamentals section, which includes a youth-sized Wiffle ball diamond, batting and pitching cages, and spots for running the bases. The section, which was added in 2005, is interactive in every sense of the word. Perched above the left-field concourse, it offers kids the chance to gain valuable baseball advice from Chicago White Sox Training Academy coaches.

LEARNING CENTER

In the Chicago area and looking to host your next meeting in a place everyone will remember? The Conference and Learning Center at the ballpark comes equipped with state-of-the-art technology, lots of space, and a business center fully outfitted with copiers, fax machines, and other useful tools for presentations. If the scheduling is done strategically, perhaps a baseball game could follow a day of meetings!

OLD COMISKEY PARK TRIBUTES

U.S. Cellular Field was built directly across the street from Old Comiskey Park, which was later demolished to make room for a parking lot for the current ballpark. As a tribute to its former digs, a marble plaque on the sidewalk marks where home plate used to be, and the old foul lines are painted on the pavement to indicate where they once were. In addition, an observation ramp situated across 35th Street closely replicates the outline of Old Comiskey Park's first-base grandstand.

OUT-OF-TOWN SCOREBOARD

Positioned right above the right-field concourse is the out-of-town scoreboard, which keeps fans in attendance up to date on other games ongoing in Major League Baseball. Installed in 2009, the scoreboard measures approximately 23 feet high by 68 feet wide, according to the White Sox Media Guide. Color and clarity is not an issue as 913,000 LED bulbs illuminate and keep track of light balls, strikes, outs, runners on base, who is currently at-bat, and the scores.

PINWHEELS

The colorful pinwheels that once were a signature of the scoreboard at Old Comiskey Park were transported to U.S. Cellular Field in 1991 and remain one of the most identifiable features of the ballpark. Seven in all light up and shoot fireworks immediately following a home run or White Sox victory. According to the White Sox Media Guide, the scoreboard is loaded manually but is then activated by computers. The concept was first introduced by one-time owner Bill Veeck at Old Comiskey Park, and since its inception has instantly become a fan favorite and recognizable feature. The outermost pinwheels are blue, the second from the outside are red, the third from the outside are green, and the center is yellow.

PRESS BOX

As part of renovations during the 2007 off-season, a brand-new, technologically advanced press box was constructed and is now on the first-base side, on Level 400. Flat-screen televisions, wireless Internet access, and other necessities to get the job done are available in this media working area, which can seat up to 100. A "Welcome to U.S. Cellular Field, Home of the Chicago White Sox" sign dominates the front of the press box.

RETIRED NUMBERS

The White Sox organization boasts nine retired numbers, which can be easily spotted on the left-center-field wall. They are: Nellie Fox (2), Harold Baines (3), Luke Appling (4), Minnie Minoso (9), Luis Aparicio (11), Paul Konerko (14), Ted Lyons (16), Billy Pierce (19), Frank Thomas (35), and Carlton Fisk (72).

SCOUT SEATS

The very ultimate in comfort, 314 leather seats positioned directly behind home plate offer the chance to take in a Major League Baseball game like no other. Behind-the-scenes access for ticket holders to U.S. Cellular Field is just an added bonus to an already impressive package that includes top-notch services and only the best money can buy, not to mention—and best of all—a great view of all the action!

SHOWERHEAD

A shower area on the main level near section 161, a carryover feature from Old Comiskey Park, offers fans a one-of-a-kind opportunity to cool down during the dog days of summer. Simply pull a lever and presto! Water cascades on your body as if you were at home in the privacy of your very own bathroom. Don't forget the shampoo and conditioner!

The press box, on Level 400, was renovated in 2007. (*Photographed by Russel Tiffin/Flickr*)

STADIUM CLUB

Positioned in right field, the Stadium Club has a capacity of 750 and is a members-only restaurant that offers superior dining before or during the course of a game. From steak to fresh fish or—my favorite—an antipasto station, there's something for everyone. The seating quarter is arranged in such a way that diners get great views no matter where they are seated.

STATUES

The White Sox have eight statues to honor their greatest players in franchise history. The Legends Sculpture Plaza features larger-than-life monuments to Minnie Minoso (located at section 164, added in 2004), Carlton Fisk (section 164, added in 2005), Billy Pierce (section 164, added in 2007), Charles Comiskey (section 100, added in 2004), Luis Aparicio (section 100, added in 2006), Nellie Fox (section 100, added in 2006), Harold Baines (section 105, added in 2008), Frank Thomas (section 157, added in 2011), and Paul Konerko (added in 2014).

THE PATIO

A patio, visible just beyond the right-field fence, is a picnic-like setting at field level that can accommodate between 50 to 100 people. Primarily a seating and dining section for group outings, the view of the action is unprecedented and is a perfect place to see every little detail in right field. Often when the ball is hit in this section, and opposing right fielders are on the move for the ball, it gives fans an excellent time to add a little heckling into the mix.

WHITE SOX HALL OF FAME

The White Sox Hall of Fame, which pays tribute to players who have left a lasting impression and also doubles as a gift shop, is on Level 100 behind home plate and is open Monday through Saturday, even when the White Sox are on the road.

MEMORABLE GAMES AT U.S. CELLULAR FIELD

APRIL 18, 1991: FIRST GAME AT U.S. CELLULAR FIELD

The anticipation of the inaugural game at U.S. Cellular Field was high, but the Detroit Tigers came into town and put an old-fashioned butt-whooping on the hometown Sox, 16–0. It was scoreless until the third and fourth innings came along, which is exactly when the bottom dropped out for Chicago. Six runs were recorded by the Tigers, highlighted by a grand slam from Cecil Fielder and a two-run jack by Rob Deer. It got worse in the fourth, when 10 runs crossed the dish, thanks to another two-run shot from Rob Deer, and a three-run bomb by Tony Phillips off relief pitcher Ken Patterson. The Tigers, who accumulated 19 hits, received a complete game performance from Frank Tanana, who allowed seven hits and three walks in the contest.

JUNE 22, 1993: FISK SETS MAJOR LEAGUE MARK

Carlton Fisk, a man best known for his Game 6 dramatics during the 1975 World Series in which his desperate wave seemingly kept a ball fair, cemented his legacy even further as one of the greatest catchers of all time by catching in his 2,226th game, breaking the record formerly held by Bob Boone. Fisk finished 0-for-2 in the game, lining out in the second inning to center field in his first at-bat, and flying out to deep center in the bottom of the eighth with a sacrifice bunt sandwiched between those at-bats in the fifth. In the top of the ninth, Mike LaValliere replaced Fisk and assumed the catching duties. The White Sox won the game in dramatic fashion, after Lance Johnson singled to score Frank Thomas in the bottom of the ninth for a 3–2 win over Texas.

MAY 2, 2002: CAMERON ALMOST GOES YARD FIVE TIMES

Seattle's Mike Cameron homered in his first four at-bats—and nearly connected for a fifth in the ninth inning—as the Mariners cruised over the White Sox with ease, 15–4. After making history earlier in the game by going back to back twice in the *same* inning with Bret Boone as part of a 10-run first, Cameron set his sights on being the first to ever hit five in a game. He crushed four in the first five innings—all solo shots—to become the first Major Leaguer to hit four home runs in a contest since Mark Whiten did so for St. Louis at Cincinnati on September 7, 1993. In the ninth inning and with U.S. Cellular Field buzzing, he sent a drive to deep right field that ended up falling just short of a new Major League record.

OCTOBER 22, 2005: FIRST WORLD SERIES AT U.S. CELLULAR FIELD

In their first World Series home game since 1959, the White Sox jumped on Houston starter Roger Clemens right away, striking for one in the first on a solo shot by Jermaine Dye and two in the second highlighted by an RBI by Joe Crede during a 5–3 victory. While the Astros wouldn't go away tying the game at three in the third, the White Sox answered right back when Crede hit a home run and Scott Podsednik put the finishing touches on a Game 1 win with an RBI triple in the eighth, scoring catcher A. J. Pierzynski. Clemens, who left after the second inning due to a sore hamstring, threw only 53 pitches in setting his own personal record for shortest World Series start. The White Sox would ride the momentum of the first game all the way to a four-game sweep of the Astros, collecting their first World Championship since 1917.

OCTOBER 23, 2005: DRAMATIC WIN PUTS CHICAGO IN DRIVER'S SEAT

A day after capturing their first World Series win since 1959, the White Sox topped that performance by a dramatic win over Houston, 7–6. With the Astros ahead 4–2 in the bottom of the seventh, Houston reliever Chad Qualls was abruptly greeted by Paul Konerko, who connected for the eighteenth grand slam in World Series history, regaining the lead for the White Sox, 6–4. With their backs against the wall in the ninth and two outs, Astros pinch hitter Jose Vizcaino smacked an opposite-field, two-run single off Bobby Jenks, tying the contest at six and setting the stage for one of the more dramatic finishes in Fall Classic history. That's when Scott Podsednik, who had hit no home runs during the regular season, sent a game-ending bomb flying over the wall in right-center field to account for the fourteenth walk-off home run in World Series history, but, more importantly, the 7–6 win and two games to none lead in the series.

APRIL 18, 2007: BUEHRLE MAKES HISTORY ON THE SOUTH SIDE

Powered by a grand-slam home run from Jermaine Dye and two solo shots by Jim Thome, Mark Buehrle shut down the Texas Rangers with a dominant pitching performance, throwing a no-hitter and facing one batter over the minimum (a fifth inning walk to Sammy Sosa) during a 6–0 White Sox victory. Buehrle, who dominated throughout, retired the final 12 batters and induced Rangers catcher Gerald Laird into a groundout to finish the masterpiece. It was the first no-hitter in the history of U.S. Cellular Field and a sign of things down the road to come for Buehrle, who finished the game with eight strikeouts.

SEPTEMBER 16, 2007: THOME JOINS THE 500-HOME RUN CLUB

Jim Thome became the twenty-third player to join the 500-home run club—and the first to do so in walk-off style—as the White Sox defeated the Angels in dramatic fashion, 9–7. Sitting on 499 home runs, the slugger strode to the plate with the 29,010 White Sox faithful on their feet. Seizing the moment, Thome drove a 3–2 pitch from reliever Dustin Moseley deep to left-center field and when the ball finally landed, he became a part of baseball lore. What's more, Thome completed the feat needing only 6,809 at-bats, fourth behind Harmon Killebrew (6,671), Babe Ruth (5,801), and Mark McGwire (5,487).

SEPTEMBER 30, 2008: ONE-GAME PLAYOFF DECIDES DIVISION

Needing 163 games to decide the American League Central division crown, Jim Thome provided all the offense necessary for the White Sox with a seventh inning solo home run to center field, propelling the White Sox to a 1–0 triumph over the Minnesota Twins, clinching the division title and a berth in the postseason. On the mound, Sox starter John Danks was as good as gold, tossing eight innings of shutout baseball while allowing only two hits. The game ended in dramatic fashion with Brian Anderson making a diving catch in right-center field, setting off a wild celebration for the newly crowned American League Central Division champions.

JULY 23, 2009: BUEHRLE AT IT AGAIN

Two years removed from his no-hitter against the Texas Rangers, Mark Buehrle bested his own performance by throwing the first perfect game since Randy Johnson did so as a member of the Diamondbacks against the Braves in 2004, shutting down the Rays in a 5–0 win in front of 28,036 fans. In the top of the ninth, Dewayne Wise replaced Carlos Quentin in the outfield and came up with arguably the greatest catch of all time to save a no-hitter. Leading off the ninth, Tampa Bay outfielder Gabe Kapler sent a drive to left-center field that looked like it was headed out, but Wise leaped high and robbed Kapler, helping keep the perfect game intact. Jason Bartlett hit a ground ball to shortstop Alexei Ramirez to finish off the crisp two-hour, three-minute contest in which Buehrle struck out six and recorded 11 outs via the ground ball.

"I knew he [Gabe Kapler] hit it pretty good and I just said, 'If it is go-ing to be catchable, it is going to be in the first couple rows. Just give him [Dewayne Wise] a chance to catch it,' and he did."
—*Mark Buehrle*

"When Kapler hit the ball, Dewayne was playing very shallow and he hit another gear . . . and when he went up and got the glove on it, then I saw the ball pop out and he held onto it. For that kind of circumstance, it is the greatest catch I have ever seen."
—*Ken "Hawk" Harrelson, White Sox broadcaster*

MAY 3, 2011: WHITE SOX HELD HITLESS

Minnesota Twins starter Francisco Liriano came into their game with the White Sox, sporting a 9.00 ERA with no career complete games to his credit. That all changed over the course of one game when he tossed the first no-hitter by an opposing pitcher at U.S. Cellular Field, shutting down Chicago, 1–0. Twins designated hitter Jason Kubel hit a solo home run in the fourth inning off White Sox starter Edwin Jackson, accounting for the only run in the game. Although Liriano was wild in walking six batters, he struck out two during the 123-pitch performance and lowered his ERA to 6.61 by game's end. He became the first Twins pitcher since Eric Milton on September 11, 1999, at the Hubert H. Humphrey Metrodome to throw a no-no, and the first to do so on the road since August 25, 1967, when Dean Chance no-hit Cleveland in the second game of a doubleheader that was called after five innings due to rain.

WHAT THEY ARE SAYING ABOUT U.S. CELLULAR FIELD

SANDY ALOMAR JR.: "Actually, U.S. Cellular Field is one of my favorite ballparks because they redid it after U.S. Cellular invested to renovate the stadium. . . . Before, it was a little bland, but now they have steel and it is all dark, and the infield there is very nice and they take care of it very well."

MARK BUEHRLE: "Loved it—more of a hitter's ballpark than a pitcher's ballpark. . . . Whether the wind is blow-ing in or out that day, you just try to keep the ball on the ground."

ERIC COLLINS, BROADCASTER: "I love U.S. Cellular. It was awful when it first opened up and they just did not know what they were doing and figured they could build anything that was new and people would come to it. . . . It is amazing how little things like changing the color of the seats [makes a difference]."

ADAM DUNN: "I think there is a big misconception about how everyone says the ball flies there—it is a very fair ballpark—but when you have home run–hitting teams like the White Sox have had, I think that is why people say that."

KEN "HAWK" HARRELSON, BROAD-CASTER: "I love it. I think it is one of the better ballparks in the league. . . . They had some structural deficiencies when they built it that they corrected, and since they corrected it, it is awesome, especially underneath with the guts of the ballpark."

PAUL KONERKO: "I think it is a beautiful ballpark. . . . I have been with the team long enough to see some of the changes they have made over the last 10 years and it is really improved. . . . Now I think it is one of the most beautiful ballparks on the inside of it [as well]."

A. J. PIERZYNSKI: "It is a good ballpark. Since it was built 20 years ago, they have done a lot to improve it [and] make it more fan-friendly and player-friendly. . . . It is a fair pitcher's/hitter's ballpark, and there is a lot of excitement when we play there."

ALEX RODRIGUEZ: "I will tell you, U.S. Cellular [Field] really made a nice comeback. . . . They have made some really, really nice improvements, and I say they are the most improved [ballpark]."

JOHN ROONEY, BROADCASTER: "U.S. Cellular Field, in its original form, was brand new and according to a study the team did, that is what the fans wanted. The problem was, Camden Yards was coming up next and it was a new ballpark that looked like an old ballpark. . . . Years later when they knocked down about eight rows of seats from the upper deck and changed the color of the seats, they made it a lot more attractive."

ROBIN VENTURA: "It was exciting for us, having gone from older Comiskey to the new one. . . . It [U.S. Cellular Field] was a regular one that looked like the others, just newer stuff."

U.S. CELLULAR FIELD FACTS AND FIGURES

U.S. CELLULAR FIELD ADDRESS
333 West 35th Street, Chicago, IL 60616

CHICAGO WHITE SOX TEAM WEB SITE
www.whitesox.com

FIELD DIMENSIONS (IN FEET)
Left Field: 330', Left-Center: 377', Center: 400',
Right-Center: 372', Right Field: 335'

SEATING CAPACITY (AS OF 2015)
40,615

ALL-STAR GAMES AT U.S. CELLULAR FIELD
July 15, 2003: American League 7, National League 6
MVP: Garret Anderson, Los Angeles Angels (AL)

U.S. CELLULAR FIELD FIRSTS
Game: April 18, 1991—Detroit 16, Chicago 0
Single: Alan Trammell, Detroit (April 18, 1991)*
Double: John Shelby, Detroit (April 18, 1991)
Triple: Tony Phillips, Detroit (April 18, 1991)
Home Run: Cecil Fielder, Detroit (April 18, 1991)

*Denotes first hit in the stadium.

WRIGLEY FIELD
HOME OF THE CHICAGO CUBS

Wrigley Field, Chicago Cubs (*Photographed by Russel Tiffin/Flickr*)

[*Wrigley Field was previously known as Weeghman Park (1914–20) and Cubs Park (1920–26).*]

If you checked a dictionary for a definition of the term "baseball palace," it's a good bet that if there was a picture, it would be of Wrigley Field. Since Oriole Park at Camden Yards in Baltimore debuted in 1992, new ballparks have been constructed all across Major League Baseball replacing older, outdated models. On the north side of Chicago, Wrigley Field has withstood the test of time and continued to be a place where fans have passed through the turnstiles for over a century and counting.

In 1914, Charles Weeghman, the owner of the Federal League's Chicago Whales, orchestrated the building of Wrigley Field, a task accomplished in six weeks at a total expenditure of $250,000. The man behind the design of the Friendly Confines was Zachary Taylor Davis, an architect who, four years prior, was responsible for the building of Old Comiskey Park in Chicago, the previous home of the White Sox.

At the time, Weeghman had signed a lease that stated the club would enter into a 55-year relationship with the newly built Wrigley Field at a cost of $18,000 per season. It lasted a little over one year when, in 1915, the Federal League folded and Weeghman formed an association with William Wrigley Jr. to purchase the Cubs organization from Charles Taft for $500,000.

In 1918, Wrigley gained complete control of the club, and it remains the only Federal League ballpark today.

In 2013, the Chicago Cubs struck a deal with the city of Chicago to make $500 million worth of renovations to the ballpark, a transformation that will change the iconic structure forever. Among the changes was a proposal to construct a 5,700-square-foot Jumbotron in left field, just above the famous ivy-covered walls. By comparison, the manually operated scoreboard in center field measures just less than 2,000 square feet. An advertising sign will be placed in left field, alleviating some of the costs of the upgrades. According to Cubs officials, an upgrade was necessary, and basic repairs each season have cost around $15 million per year.

Also in the works are a 175-room hotel, a plaza, and an office building, complete with retail space, all of which would be located across from Wrigley Field. Under the terms of the renovation deal, the Cubs would be allowed to increase the number of night games it plays each season from 30 to 40.

Before the agreement was made, the reality of the Cubs leaving Chicago for a nearby city was a real possibility. To that end, the mayor of nearby Rosemont stated that a 25-acre area near O'Hare International Airport would be given to the team free of charge to build a replica of Wrigley Field. When that idea went by the wayside, purists rejoiced that Wrigley Field would remain in place, and that the upcoming renovations would help make the landmark better than ever.

SPECIAL FEATURES OF WRIGLEY FIELD

BATTING PRACTICE GLIMPSE

As time goes on, it seems as though ballparks all across Major League Baseball are incorporating a one-of-a-kind view that allows fans to sneak a peak at the indoor batting cages. It's no different here, where a viewing plaza was constructed just beneath the center-field bleachers. This unique vantage point allows fans the opportunity to check in on their favorite players as they hack away during a pregame batting practice session.

BLEACHERS

First formed in 1966 by 10 fans, the outfield bleachers are now home to some of the most passionate fans in all of baseball. Accessible via the corner of Waveland and Sheffield avenues, this seating area is always buzzing with fans commonly known as the Bleacher Bums, and they had an exceptional time in 1998 after Sammy Sosa deposited many home run balls into the left-field section during his summer-long battle for home run supremacy with Mark McGwire. If you're planning on sitting in this area, tickets are distributed on a first-come, first-served basis and are categorized as general admission. Due to their popularity, it's a good idea to make sure you arrive early to ensure getting a seat.

CENTER-FIELD RESTAURANT

The Batter's Eye restaurant, which can accommodate between 75 and 100 individuals, is in center field, is a completely enclosed structure, and offers a full-service bar and televisions so none of the action will be missed. Reservations must be made ahead of time, and included in the package are 10 VIP parking passes and a voucher for food and nonalcoholic beverages.

ENTRANCE SIGN

The solid red marquee, one of the most recognizable images at Wrigley Field, was originally installed in 1934 and serves as a formal welcome to fans entering the ballpark. "Wrigley Field, Home of Chicago Cubs" is painted in white lettering and at night, lights illuminate the "Wrigley Field" portion of the display. Blue until the 1960s, the two-line announcement board was once changed by hand, but was later replaced with an electronic version. The backlit panel was once used for advertising, but was later painted a solid red. In 2010, the entire marquee was painted purple for Northwestern University, when they took on Illinois in a college football game won by the Fighting Illini, 48–27.

FAN BRICKS

As you stroll around Wrigley Field and enjoy all of the sights and sounds the historic ballpark has to offer, take a look at the brickwork. There are commemorative bricks with engraved messages in various locations around the stadium. At one time fans were offered the opportunity to submit their own personalized messages, which allowed them, in a sense, to become an official part of the stadium.

FOUL POLES

While the Cubs have paid homage to one broadcaster in the form of a statue for Harry Caray, another one has been immortalized in a different kind of way. Jack Brickhouse, who handled the play-by-play duties for the Cubs on WGN from 1948 to 1981, was well known for regularly saying "Hey hey!" on the air. As a tribute to him, his signature line is now affixed to both foul poles to remind fans of his legendary battle cry.

FRIENDLY CONFINES CAFÉ

The Friendly Confines Café, open to the public and situated along the first-base side of the main concourse, is another outdoor bistro that features a wide array of sandwiches and beverages. Another fan favorite nearby is the Friendly Confines Beer Garden, which is outside Wrigley Field and across from Gate D.

ICONIC SCOREBOARD

The 27-foot-high, 75-foot-wide center-field scoreboard serves as the primary information base for fans and has been a mainstay at Wrigley Field since it was first introduced in 1937. Aside from Fenway Park in Boston, it is the only hand-operated main scoreboard left in the big leagues. Constructed of sheet metal, a trap door at the bottom serves as the entrance to the non-heated, non-air-conditioned unit, and three individuals have the honor of working each home game. The 10-foot-diameter clock arrived in 1941, and just beneath it the numbers of the umpiring crew are displayed.

Below the umpires, the current batter, balls, strikes, and outs are tracked by electronic numbers, and the number of hits accumulated by both the Cubs and the visiting team are in yellow at the very bottom. On the left side, the score outlined in red indicates the current Cubs game on the field.

Throughout its history, only one individual has hit the scoreboard: professional golfer Sam Snead, who teed it up at home plate and sent a golf ball dinging off the historic landmark. Two baseball players have come close with a batted ball during a game. In 1948, Chicago's own Bill Nicholson hit a shot that landed on Sheffield Avenue, and 11 years later in 1959, Pittsburgh's Roberto Clemente drilled one onto Waveland Avenue. According to unofficial measurements, a ball would have to travel 457 feet to leave a mark on the scoreboard.

In 2004, an electronic video board was added at the very bottom, and prior to the 2010 campaign, the back of the scoreboard was fully renovated for the first time since its inception in 1937.

IVY WALLS

Bill Veeck, the mastermind around the baseball world, decided that the Wrigley Field outfield wall needed a little something extra. In 1937, he planted a combination of 350 Japanese bittersweet and 200 Boston ivy plants in the hopes they would one day grow into a more imposing presence. He also planted eight Chinese elm trees on the bleacher steps to complement the ivy, but later removed them because an erratic wind off Lake Michigan wreaked havoc with the leaves. By rule, in the event a baseball is hit into the shrubbery and can't be found, the batter is awarded a ground-rule double.

LAKEVIEW BASEBALL CLUB

Founded in 1988, the three-level Lakeview Baseball Club, located on Sheffield Avenue, is the only private section of rooftop seats around and is home to the Eamus Catuli counter, which diligently keeps track of the Cubs' success on the field. Incredible sight lines are just the beginning. A bevy of food options, drink selections, and an indoor bar, just in case the wind is a little more than one can handle, highlight this setting exclusive to the famous Wrigley Field landscape.

OUTDOOR CAFÉ

Touted as the largest outdoor café within Wrigley Field, this indoor and outdoor hotspot, located at the corner of Addison and Sheffield streets, provides plenty of options. Food choices ranging from salads to burgers to sandwiches satisfy hunger, and a full bar highlighted by a premium, top-shelf selection goes above and beyond in wetting your whistle. To keep things interesting and patrons guessing, there is a rotation of specialty cocktails.

OUT-OF-TOWN SCOREBOARD

On both the left (National League) and right (American League) side of the main center-field scoreboard is the hand-operated out-of-town portion, which keeps the individuals in charge of maintaining that section busy throughout the course of a game. The updates arrive by computer, and are then displayed in forest green-and-white numbers. Markings at the very bottom of the board denote the starting pitcher (SP) and relief pitcher (RP), while the innings are represented with the numbers 1–10. The number system used for starting pitchers runs from 1 to 16, and in order to crack the code and find out who's taking the hill, a scorecard must be purchased.

RETIRED NUMBERS

The Chicago Cubs have honored six men who have come through the organization by flying their numbers on top of the flagpoles. These men are:

The rooftop seats high above right field provide a bird's-eye view of Wrigley Field. (*Photographed by Russel Tiffin/Flickr*)

Ron Santo (10), Ernie Banks (14), Ryne Sandberg (23), Billy Williams (26), Ferguson Jenkins (31), and Greg Maddux (31).

RIGHT-FIELD PATIO
Installed for 2012, the right-field bleacher section now offers Cub fans more bang for their buck. The right-field patio area—with room for 150—is an elevated seating section that features an all-inclusive food-and-beverage package for those with standing room–only or seated tickets. At the base, a 75-foot LED board showcases baseball information, in-game statistics, and other relevant material pertaining to the action on the field. The changes were made to improve views over obstructions, which were once an issue with the original configuration.

ROOFTOP SEATS
The apartment buildings across from Waveland Avenue and Sheffield Street have been a place for fans to congregate and enjoy the action from an unparalleled vantage point. In the 1990s, despite Cubs management not outwardly approving the arrangement, owners of the complexes began constructing seating areas on top and charged fans a small fee to take a seat, sit back, and enjoy the game. When ownership learned of what was transpiring, they weren't too happy and attempted to shut down the arrangement. Years

later, a settlement was ultimately reached, and the building owners agreed to share a percentage of their profits with the Chicago Cubs organization.

SEATS ADDED FOR 2013

Needing to first acquire formal permission from the Commission on Chicago Landmarks, the Cubs moved the brick wall closer to home plate, adding 56 more seats to the fold and ultimately reducing the amount of foul territory by three feet. In 2005, the Cubs had requested a similar arrangement, which resulted in the addition of three rows of seats and a foul territory reduced by 10 feet.

SEVENTH INNING STRETCH

Following the passing of legendary broadcaster Harry Caray just before the start of the 1998 season, the Cubs decided to carry on his legacy of singing the seventh inning stretch by inviting guests in the booth to sing the famous "Take Me Out to the Ballgame." Since then, unforgettable renditions of the age-old song have been sung by the likes of Mike Ditka, Bill Murray, and Ozzie Osbourne. However, in 2013, the Cubs decided to limit the participants to only those hailing from Chicago, but the song and Caray's legend live on.

STANDINGS FLAGS

To display the current standings in the National League, team flags in their official colors fly high atop the scoreboard and indicate the current standings in the East, Central, and West. Following the end of a game—and depending on how the hometown Cubbies fared—a W flag (Win) or L flag (Loss) is raised. Once completed, the National League team flags come down for the day and are again hoisted the following day after all the action around baseball has concluded. The American flag tops the display.

STATUES AT WRIGLEY FIELD

Four statues honor Chicago Cubs legends and serve as unofficial greeters in their respective locations.

ERNIE BANKS: The Cubs honored Hall of Famer Ernie Banks with a statue on the corner of Clark and Addison streets. All Banks did was play 19 seasons with the club (hence the name Mr. Cub), and accumulate 512 home runs, 407 doubles, 1,636 RBI, and a lifetime batting average of .274. Following the 2011 season, his statue was sent back and re-polished because the metal was turning green and oxidizing too quickly. Banks's statue was dedicated on March 31, 1998.

HARRY CARAY: Outside the entrance to the bleacher section—in an area where we would occasionally call a game—one of baseball's most legendary announcers is captured in bronze forever. The statue depicts him with a microphone in hand, presumably leading the fans during a rendition of "Take Me Out to the Ballgame" during the seventh inning stretch. It stood previously at Sheffield Avenue and Addison Street but was later transported to make room for the Williams statue. Caray's statue was dedicated on August 12, 1999.

RON SANTO: A beloved Cub in every way, Santo's statue was positioned at Sheffield Avenue and Addison Street right outside Wrigley Field and captures the third baseman preparing to throw the ball, perhaps to first base for an out. Santo was a nine-time All-Star for 14 seasons on the north side, captured five Gold Gloves, and finished with 342 home runs. Santo's statue was dedicated on August 10, 2011.

BILLY WILLIAMS: Positioned at the corner of Sheffield Avenue and Addison Street, this Hall of Famer played for the Cubs from 1959 to 1974 and was also a part of their coaching staff on three separate occasions: 1980–82, 1986–89, and 1992–2001. His best season occurred in 1970, when he captivated Cubs fans by hitting .322 to go along with 42 home runs, 129 RBI, and 205 hits, a career high. William's statue was dedicated on September 7, 2010.

THE BASKETS

The baskets, an extension of the outfield wall, first became a part of the Wrigley Field scene on May 7, 1970, in a game versus the Philadelphia Phillies. The inspiration for such an idea came when overzealous fans and a security guard, who was trying to save them from taking the plunge, took a dive out of the right-field bleachers and onto the playing field after an opening day win on April 14, 1970. The baskets extend five feet from the wall and although it's a lot safer than tumbling down to the grass, fans still manage to find a way to stumble into the basket area.

UPPER DECK FLAGS

Flags on the roof serve as a tribute to the special moments that have taken place over the years. Playoff appearances and games are commemorated on the left-field shingles, while on the right side, specific individuals, followed by numbers, commemorate unique situations over the years. For example, SAMMY-66 refers to the 66 home runs blasted by Sammy Sosa in 1998, and KW-20 is a direct reference to Kerry Wood's 20 strikeouts during his dominating performance against Houston on May 6, 1998.

WALL OF FAME

The main concourse across from Field Box aisles 126–127 is home to the Cubs Wall of Fame, a display that honors past Cubs players who have left their mark on the organization. There are framed photos, each with a player's photo above his name and the years he played. Some of the men include Ernie Banks, Andre Dawson, Ryne Sandberg, and Hack Wilson.

WIND FACTOR

Chicago is best known as "the windy city," and this is true at Wrigley Field more so than at any other ballpark in the Major Leagues today. Nearby Lake Michigan and unpredictable wind patterns can either turn into a pitcher's duel, thanks to a stiff wind blowing in, or a slugfest with it blowing out as it does so often during the warm summer months. When Candlestick Park in San Francisco was around, it had a wind pattern similar to that of Wrigley Field.

WIN FLAG

The Cubs raise a flag on the scoreboard to indicate whether they won or lost the game. This practice, which originated in the 1940s, has become a tradition at Wrigley Field. To date, the current Win flag has a white background with a large blue *W*, while the Loss flag has a blue background and huge white *L*. While I'm sure Chicago fans would love to see a *W* raised after every game, the Cubs remain the only franchise that does this to inform passers-by of how the game went.

YEAR OF THE CUB

A placard posted just beyond the right-field wall of the rooftop seating section near Sheffield Avenue tallies the number of years it's been since a Chicago Cubs team won anything significant. The banner, which features "EAMUS CATULI," is Latin for "Let's go Little Bears." The sign is blue with white numbers and letters, and features "AC" first which, spelled out, is "Anno Catuli" in Latin, translating into "Year of the Cub." From there, the numbers refer to the years since they last won a division championship, National League pennant, and World Series crown respectively. The sign was first installed in 1995 and has been a mainstay at Wrigley Field ever since.

MEMORABLE GAMES AT WRIGLEY FIELD

APRIL 20, 1916: FIRST CUBS GAME AT WRIGLEY FIELD

Although technically the first game to be played at the Friendly Confines involved the Federal League's Chicago Whales in 1914, Major League Baseball's Cubs took to the field and defeated the Cincinnati Reds in 11 innings, 7–6. While there aren't any detailed play-by-play reports of this contest, Chicago was managed by Joe Tinker (of Tinker-to-Evers-to-Chance double-play fame) and featured players such as first baseman Vic Saier, who banged out 25 doubles that season; outfielder Cy Williams, who stroked a team-high 12 home runs; and pitcher Jim "Hippo" Vaughn, who compiled a record of 17–15 to go along with a stellar 2.20 ERA.

MAY 2, 1917: DUAL NO-HITTERS STEAL THE SHOW

Cubs pitcher Jim Vaughn and Reds starter Fred Toney each made Major League history by tossing a no-hitter through nine innings, but Olympian Jim Thorpe drove in the game's only run during the tenth inning of Cincinnati's 1–0 win in front of a sparse crowd of 3,500. In the tenth frame, Vaughn retired the first two hitters, but proceeded to allow a single to Larry Koph, and Hal Chase followed with a fly ball to right field that was muffed, setting the stage for Thorpe, the 1912 decathlon champion in Stockholm, Sweden. In the bottom of the tenth, Toney preserved his no-hitter by retiring the Chicago Cubs in order, ending the contest and baseball's only instance of a feat of this magnitude.

AUGUST 25, 1922: CUBS-PHILLIES SLUGFEST, PART I

As of this writing, it is still the highest-scoring game in Major League history. The Cubs and Phillies combined for 49 runs in a game that saw Chicago hold on after leading by 19, eventually winning 26–23. The Phillies took an innocent 4–1 lead heading into the bottom of the second, which is exactly when all hell broke loose. The Cubs struck for 10 in the frame, teeing off on Philadelphia starter Jimmy Ring in taking the 11–3 advantage. The Phillies answered with two in the third and one in the fourth but were promptly answered by Chicago in the bottom of the fourth, when they plated 14 runs and took a 25–6 lead.

As if that wasn't enough for a storyline, the Phillies would go on to outscore the Cubs 17–1 over the final five innings, even stranding the lead run at the plate, but Chicago held on for the wild win. Offensive stars for the Cubs included Cliff Heathcote, who went 5-for-5 with two doubles and four RBI, and Charlie Hollocher, who enjoyed a 3-for-6 day while driving in a team-high six RBI. For Philadelphia, Russ Wrightstone and Curt Walker combined for eight hits (four each) and each added a triple.

OCTOBER 1, 1932: RUTH CALLS HIS SHOT

Although nobody really knows for sure what Babe Ruth was pointing at, the legend of the Bambino grew when he called his shot during a fifth inning at-bat versus Cubs pitcher Charlie Root during Game 3 of the World Series. Ruth stood at the plate and pointed toward the center-field bleachers, presumably suggesting he would be depositing the next pitch in that area. As fate would have it, he clobbered the very next pitch from Root deep to center field—the ball is said to have gone 440 feet—beginning a debate that continues today about whether or not he actually called the hit. The Yankees went on to win the game, 7–5, and finished off the four-game sweep for the crown in the following game with a 13–6 victory.

AUGUST 19, 1969: HOLTZMAN NO-HITS BRAVES

Despite an Atlanta lineup that boasted slugger Hank Aaron, Cubs starter Ken Holtzman dominated from start to finish and no-hit the potent Braves, 3–0. A brisk northerly wind would prove to be a big assist to Holtzman, who became the first Cubs pitcher to toss a no-hitter since Don Cardwell did on May 15, 1960, in the second game of a doubleheader victory versus the St. Louis Cardinals. After breezing through the first six innings with relative ease, Aaron strode to the plate, desperately looking to make something happen for the Braves.

He nearly did, sending a deep drive that had Waveland Avenue written all over it before the wind knocked it down, allowing the ball to settle into the glove of a leaping Billy Williams for the out. The jolt didn't faze Holtzman, who finished off the Braves by retiring none other than Aaron on a harmless groundball to end the game. A three-run home run by Ron Santo in the bottom of the first proved to be the only runs Chicago would need in the victory.

SEPTEMBER 2, 1972: NEAR PERFECTION FOR PAPPAS

Chicago starter Milt Pappas came within a strike of tossing a perfect game, overcoming a controversial ball four call to dominate the San Diego Padres and claim the no-hitter, 8–0. After retiring the first 26 San Diego batters with relative ease, Larry Stahl was inserted to pinch hit for pitcher Al Severinsen, and little would he know that he'd be right smack-dab in the middle of controversy. After working the count full, Pappas unloaded a pitch that everyone inside Wrigley Field thought was a strike, but was called a ball by umpire Bruce Froemming. Despite that, Pappas would go on to retire the next batter—pinch hitter Garry Jestadt—via the fly ball to finish off the no-hitter. The offense gave him plenty of run support and added insurance runs in the bottom of the eighth after already leading 4–0. That's when Bill North stroked an RBI single and Don Kessinger cleared the bases with a three-run double to left field.

APRIL 17, 1976: CUBS-PHILLIES SLUGFEST, PART II

With the strong wind blowing in from the south, the Phillies overcame an 11-run deficit to knock off the Cubs, 18–16, in 10 innings. Philadelphia slugger Mike Schmidt put on a show, finishing 5-for-6 at the plate, blasting four home runs and driving in eight RBI to help lead a 24-hit attack. When Rick Monday stroked a solo home run in the bottom of the fourth inning to give the Cubs a 13–2 lead, it appeared as though the rout was on. However, the Phillies equaled the National League record for the largest comeback after chipping away slowly and surely to eventually give Philadelphia a remarkable 15–13 lead heading into the bottom of the ninth.

In that frame, Steve Swisher proved "it's never over 'til it's over" by lacing a two-run single to send the wild game into extras. Mike Schmidt connected for a two-run shot—his fourth long ball of the game—and Dave Cash added a sacrifice fly to help put the Phillies back on top, 18–14. A double by pinch hitter Mike Adams and an RBI double by Bill Madlock sandwiched between two outs pulled the North Siders to within two, but the comeback stalled out there. With the win, Philadelphia exacted a little revenge for having lost the 26–23 classic played between the two teams 54 years prior.

MAY 17, 1979: CUBS-PHILLIES SLUGFEST, PART III

Much like the previous two games between the clubs, which resembled more of a local softball game than a baseball contest, the Phillies came into town and simply outscored the Cubs, 23–22. Like the 1922 and 1976 contests, scoring was the name of the game and was evident following the first inning in which the Cubs led, 7–6. The Phillies then broke out for eight runs in the third, punctuated by a three-run home run off the bat of Garry Maddox, which put them back on top, 15–6. The lead eventually grew to 21–9 after four runs crossed the plate in the fifth, which is exactly the time Chicago's bats got hot.

Facing reliever Tug McGraw, Bill Buckner unloaded for a grand slam, and Jerry Martin connected for a two-run blast, helping to pull the Cubs to within five at 21–16. In the bottom of the sixth, Dave Kingman hit his third home run of the game—a solo shot—after two runs were already in, closing the gap even more. Incredibly, the Cubs tied the game at 22 in the bottom of the eighth, but it was Philadelphia basher Mike Schmidt who was responsible for the final blow after connecting for a solo home run in the tenth off relief ace Bruce Sutter, helping to end the high-scoring affair.

SEPTEMBER 8, 1985: ROSE TIES COBB WITH 4,191ST HIT

Sitting three hits from surpassing one of baseball's most hallowed records, Pete Rose notched two singles to tie Hall of Famer Ty Cobb's record of 4,191 but missed a date with history by striking out in the ninth during a 5–5 tie in a game halted by darkness. In fact, Rose wasn't expected to be in the lineup because the Cubs had left-handed pitcher Steve Trout on the mound; Rose played only when right-handers took to the hill. As luck would have it, Trout was involved in a bicycling accident with his family the previous night and, as a result, was scratched from the lineup card and replaced by right-handed tosser Reggie Patterson.

Despite a home stand consisting of 10 games looming for Rose and the Reds at Riverfront Stadium, he inserted himself as a part of the starting nine in an effort to make history on the North Side. The two knocks came in the first and fifth innings, but not before a little second-guessing. Although accounts have Cobb's hit total at 4,191, independent research conducted over the years has speculated that 4,189 is the actual number of hits Cobb collected, which would mean Rose would have broken the hit record following his first hit. Three days later in front of the hometown faithful, Rose notched the record-breaker with a base hit off San Diego's Eric Show.

AUGUST 9, 1988: LET THERE BE LIGHT, TAKE 2!

After 5,687 consecutive day games had been played at Wrigley Field, the Chicago Cubs finally experienced a home night game, defeating the New York Mets in the process, 6–4. It was scheduled for the night before (August 8, 1988), but Mother Nature had other plans, and play was suspended in the fourth inning with the Cubs leading the Philadelphia Phillies, 3–1. The next day, rain was not a factor as the two teams played to a 2–2 tie into the bottom of the seventh, when Chicago stepped it up with a four-run outburst. A pinch hit RBI double by Jody Davis, and back-to-back-to-back RBI singles from Ryne Sandberg, Mark Grace, and Andre Dawson gave the Cubs a 6–2 lead they would not relinquish.

MAY 6, 1998: WOOD PITCHES A MASTERPIECE

When rookie Kerry Wood took to the mound against the Houston Astros, he turned in a performance that went down as one of the greatest ever. Facing just two batters over the minimum, Wood cut down the Astros like a lumberjack, striking out 20 and finishing with a one-hitter during Chicago's

2–0 win. In just his fifth Major League start, he looked like a veteran striking out the first five Houston batters on strikeouts, setting the tone early for what was to come.

Only two base runners were fortunate to reach for Houston: An infield single by Ricky Gutierrez, which could have easily been ruled an error as the ball ticked off the glove of Cubs third baseman Kevin Orie, and Craig Biggio, who gained access to first base after he was hit by a pitch with two outs in the sixth. Fittingly, Wood ended the game with his patented wicked curve, making Derek Bell look silly in finishing off visiting Houston. When all was said and done, he had matched Roger Clemens's record for strikeouts in a nine-inning game and shattered the mark by a rookie pitcher set by Bill Gullickson in 1980.

JULY 26, 2005: MADDUX NOTCHES 3,000TH STRIKEOUT

Greg Maddux became the thirteenth player in Major League history to strike out 3,000 batters when he fanned San Francisco's Omar Vizquel to end the third frame during the Giants 3–2 victory. Although rain had delayed the start for two hours and 43 minutes, it didn't prevent the ageless Maddux from adding another record to his Hall of Fame résumé. Having clinched his 300th win a week earlier in San Francisco, he also became the ninth player to post both 300 wins and 3,000 strikeouts. As for the game, Chicago's Michael Barrett led off the bottom of the eighth inning with a game-tying home run off Giants reliever LaTroy Hawkins, but San Francisco got the last laugh when Jason Ellison notched an RBI single in the eleventh, which would be the determining factor in San Francisco's 3–2 win.

WHAT THEY'RE SAYING ABOUT WRIGLEY FIELD

JACK CORRIGAN, BROADCASTER: "It sounds sacrilegious and it really has nothing to do with the ballpark itself, but the worst place to broadcast now is Wrigley Field. . . . The booth is like climbing into a World War II submarine, and going down a little stairway that seems dangerous."

DICK ENBERG, BROADCASTER: "I love the fact that you can still smell beer from 25 years ago. . . . It has a sound and a smell and a feel that no other ballpark has today, and that comes with age; time and age brings all those things and it continues to grow the way the ivy climbs the walls of the outfield."

LANNY FRATTARE, BROADCASTER: "I never felt that the Wrigley Field mystique was all that they made it out to be. I thought it was more hype and more spin than it was in reality. . . . One thing about Wrigley [Field] is that everyone makes a big deal about the scoreboard in center field. Well, many times there are no other games going on because the Cubs are playing in the daytime."

ANDREW MCCUTCHEN: "It feels like you are playing in the backyard at your house. . . . It does not have a lot of things going, but I [also] really love playing there too."

MARK MCGWIRE: "I did not mind it. The playing field was actually a small playing field, [a] small cutout infield, and the batter's box was a little uncomfortable there. . . . They did not really have a good clay surface, and it was sort of difficult at times to get your footing in there and it felt like the pitcher was right on top of you."

TIM NEVERETT, BROADCASTER: "When I go to Wrigley [Field], every time I take my walk from the visitor's clubhouse, down the stairs and through the labyrinth that gets you to the first base dugout, you think of all the guys that have taken that walk. . . . [It] brings you back to [the] reality that this place is pretty special."

MIKE PIAZZA: "For me, I came up and that was my first big league game [at Wrigley Field]. . . . I just like the feel of the stadium, and I feel it is more of a stadium and there is just something special about the energy in the air. It is a cool place to play and I think it is a fun place to watch a game, too."

PAT SAJAK, *WHEEL OF FORTUNE* HOST: "Wrigley Field was kind of a day trip for me. There were buses for me to take and I felt like I was going to the ritzy part of town. . . . I do not necessarily believe that old is good, [but] I understand the history and tradition and it will never leave there and get torn down."

TROY TULOWITZKI: "I know there is a lot of history, but the infield does not play well, [and] it is always cold when we go there . . . and the locker rooms are small."

MATT WILLIAMS: "I have always been partial to Wrigley Field because it is still a little of the old-time baseball and they play the organ in between innings. . . . Those of us who love the history of the game love the old ones because you get the chance to sit on the same bench that a lot of Hall of Fame players have sat on, so it is a lot of fun."

WRIGLEY FIELD FACTS AND FIGURES

WRIGLEY FIELD ADDRESS
1060 West Addison Street, Chicago, IL 60613

CHICAGO CUBS TEAM WEB SITE
www.cubs.com

FIELD DIMENSIONS (IN FEET)
Left Field: 355', Left-Center: 368', Center: 400',
Right-Center: 368', Right Field: 353'

SEATING CAPACITY (AS OF 2015)
41,019

ALL-STAR GAMES AT WRIGLEY FIELD
July 8, 1947: American League 2, National League 1
MVP: Not awarded until 1962
July 30, 1962: American League 9, National League 4
MVP: Leon Wagner, Los Angeles Angels (AL)
July 10, 1990: American League 2, National League 0
MVP: Julio Franco, Texas Rangers (AL)

WRIGLEY FIELD FIRSTS
Game: April 23, 1914—Chicago Whales 9, Kansas City Packers 1
Single: John Potts, Kansas City (April 23, 1914)*
Double: Rollie Zeider, Chicago (April 23, 1914)
Triple: Rollie Zeider, Chicago (April 25, 1914)
Home Run: Art Wilson, Chicago (April 10, 2006)

*Denotes first hit in the stadium.

Note: These firsts represented are from the Federal League; the Chicago Cubs first began play at Wrigley Field in 1916.

SOUTH-CENTRAL
REGION

BUSCH STADIUM
HOME OF THE ST. LOUIS CARDINALS

Busch Stadium, St. Louis Cardinals (*Photographed by Brian Skversky/Flickr*)

If anything, few franchises rival the rich history and tradition linked with the St. Louis Cardinals organization. From the great championship teams of 1982 and 2011 to players like Lou Brock, Albert Pujols, and Ozzie Smith, many have contributed to the Cardinals' legacy. And now the new Busch Stadium, completed in 2006, is part of one of the most well-known franchises in Major League Baseball.

After spending 39 seasons at the rounded, cookie-cutter ballpark lovingly known among Cardinals fans as Busch Memorial Stadium, the folks in St. Louis felt it was time for change, and rightfully so. Those taking a quick peek at the NL Central in 2001 would have been quick to point out that, other than the wonder that is Wrigley Field in Chicago, the Cardinals were the only team who didn't have a new stadium, while innovative structures had been built in Houston (2000), Milwaukee (2001), and Pittsburgh (2001), and Great American Ball Park was under way in Cincinnati for 2003. And while the older Busch Stadium proved to be a decent stage for America's pastime during its existence, everyone within the organization knew that the key to keeping up with the rest of the pack revenue-wise was to erect a brand-new, state-of-the-art ballpark of their own in the downtown district.

From the beginning, management put together an arrangement that successfully integrated improved sight lines and upgraded services, while at the same time incorporating the best that Minute Maid Park, PNC Park, and other recently built facilities had to offer. The end result turned out to be a Major League ballpark fit only for the die-hards who make up Cardinals Nation.

When construction began in January 2004, the Cardinals became the first Major League Baseball team to fund their own ballpark since the San Francisco Giants completed the same agreement with AT&T Park. When the building began, it actually overlapped some of the old ballpark, much like Great American Ballpark did when Riverfront Stadium was still being utilized in Cincinnati. When Busch Memorial Stadium was demolished following the 2005 season, construction resumed and was finished just in time for Opening Day 2006.

Attention was given to every detail, including the fact that Busch Stadium is located on the northern edge of the old stadium and gradually slopes down 40 feet to reveal breathtaking views of the city's skyline. This meant that home plate could lie in the southwest corner of the site with lowered seating in many areas, and there are plenty of sections in which fans can sit back and take in the city's historic Gateway Arch.

SPECIAL FEATURES OF BUSCH STADIUM

ANHEUSER-BUSCH

A long-standing relationship began when August A. Busch Jr. purchased the ball club from previous owner Fred Saigh on February 20, 1953. Anheuser-Busch has maintained a prominent role in both the Cardinals franchise and their ballparks. Busch Jr., who was president of the famous brewery whose main headquarters are in St. Louis, put together a World Series winner in 1964. From there, he was instrumental in the building of the $26 million Busch Memorial Stadium, which opened on May 12, 1966. Over the years, Anheuser-Busch has become synomous with Cardinals baseball, and that partnership was extended in 2004 when they signed a new 20-year marketing agreement.

BALLPARK VILLAGE

Although the opening of Ballpark Village did not coincide with the debut of Busch Stadium in 2006, phase one of the 10-acre development next to the ballpark was completed in time for the 2014 season and has instantly become an integral part of the fan experience. Designed with their rivals to the north in mind, 330 rooftop seats sit 500 feet from home plate and offer a unique vantage point. There is also a 30,000-square-foot three-level restaurant and other entertainment options.

The preliminary brainstorm began in 1999 after the Cardinals began exploring the idea of a new ballpark. Various snags over the years ultimately delayed its expected completion in 2006. Further development of the area is scheduled to include even more retail and entertainment features, along with potential residential and office developments.

BIG MAC LAND

Instituted in 1998 at Busch Memorial Stadium to honor Mark "Big Mac" McGwire and his march toward the single-season home run record of 61, this seating section was duplicated at the new digs in 2006 and is currently positioned in left field at section 272. The 181-seat location sits 405 feet away from home plate, and each time a Cardinals player peppers that spot, fans in the section can redeem their game tickets for a free Big Mac sandwich at a McDonald's restaurant. On May 21, 2009, Albert Pujols sent a drive that clocked the *I* in "BIG," shattering lights in the process.

BULLPEN MEMORIALS

Two black round circles, with the initials "DK 57" and "JH 32" in white, are tributes to two players who passed away while they were in the Cardinals organization. Darryl Kile, who pitched 11 seasons in the big leagues for Houston, Colorado, and St. Louis, died during the 2002 season while the team was on a road trip in Chicago. Josh Hancock, a pitcher who played six seasons with Boston, Philadelphia, Cincinnati, and St. Louis, tragically perished after a car accident on April 29, 2007.

BUSCH STADIUM REMINDERS

Without question, the current Busch Stadium has a lot more character than the previous model, and showcases the city while providing both the team and fans with up-to-date amenities. However, there are a few subtle reminders of its predecessor around the new version. Cardinal red seats encircle the field and help remind out-of-town fans that they are, indeed, in Cardinals country. The grassy knoll, which doubles as the batter's eye in center field, is a carbon copy of the old setup. The old scoreboard, previously a mainstay in the upper deck, is showcased in the main concourse and was a creative way to reuse rather than destroy it during the demolition.

CARDINALS CLUB

This exclusive, high-class seating area is the most expensive option at Busch Stadium and tickets in this section (as of this writing) for an entire season will set the buyer back $14,000—but there's a catch. Two seats must be purchased at the same time, and for a 10-year lease, which works out to $280,000 over the length of the term agreement. A bronze statue of August "Gussie" Busch welcomes ticket holders at the entrance, and there is a full-size restaurant, along with an extensive collection of spirits. As an added bonus, members never have to pay for any food they order, whether it is inside or from their green seats situated directly behind home plate.

CHAMPIONS CLUB

The start of the 2008 season brought the arrival of the freshly remodeled 382-seat Champions Club, a premium seating option anchored down the left-field line. In addition to Cardinals memorabilia—which include displays featuring the best moments from their World Series titles and the actual 2006 World Series trophy—there is an all-you-can-eat buffet, a lounge with big-screen televisions, and two full-service bars offering only the best spirits. Seats feature the Cardinals logo carved into wooden chair backs, and there is a broadcast booth that ticket holders can enter.

CHAMPIONSHIP FLAGS

The Cardinals could be considered the National League's version of the New York Yankees and boast of more World Series championships won over the course of their rich tradition than any other National League franchise. On top of the out-of-town scoreboard, located in right field, are displayed the words "WORLD SERIES CHAMPIONS," and behind the scoreboard are vertical oversized baseball bats on which are marked the championship years in white numbers in a red oval. Red Cardinals flags fly high on mini-flagpoles.

CONFERENCE CENTER

This impressive business center can be utilized as a single area or divided into three smaller boardrooms. The main meeting room can host up to 120 guests. Each room comes equipped with drop-down screens, televisions, Wi-Fi Internet access, and projectors for presentations.

A view of the city and Busch Stadium from inside the Gateway Arch—630 feet above the ground. (*Photographed by Alicia Barnhart/Flickr*)

FAMILY FUN

Gate 5 is the home to one place that kids will surely love—the Family Pavilion. There are plenty of attractions that will leave the little ones wanting more—full-size batting cages, pitching games, and ever-popular video games. It is open on game days and can also be rented for birthdays or other parties.

GATEWAY ARCH

One striking difference that distinguishes Busch Stadium from that of its predecessor is the open outfield, which gives spectators a view of the St. Louis skyline. In the distance, the Gateway Arch rises high above center field and can be seen from most seats, giving a one-of-a-kind view. The Arch, which is the centerpiece of the Jefferson National Expansion Memorial, is the tallest human-made monument in the United States and stands 630 feet high.

HOMER'S LANDING

One of the more popular destinations for long home run balls, the appropriately named Homer's Landing boasts a relaxed atmosphere and is just above the bullpen in right-center field. Square aluminum tables dominate the front part, while a long wooden table, complete with silver chairs, stretches across the back and provides seating in the second row. Snack buffets include standard ballpark favorites, and a wide selection of beer is available.

JACK BUCK TRIBUTE

A striking tribute outside of Busch Stadium honors one of baseball's most legendary announcers, Jack Buck. A statue shows him behind a podium, speaking into a microphone. It is the main focal point, while behind it seven photographs show a younger Buck. His oversized signature—along with his famous line "That's a winner!"—complete the memorial that honors the man who handled Cardinals broadcasts for KMOX for 40 seasons.

MAIN SCOREBOARD

The main video board, located in right-center field, displays high-quality replays and graphics, while five smaller boards list statistics of the ongoing game. Below the video board is a spot for real-time line score that keeps an inning-by-inning register of runs scored by each team along with total runs, hits, and errors. Balls, strikes, and outs are tallied on the right side. On top is a clock between two official Cardinals logos facing each other, with the famous Budweiser logo displayed below.

MUSIAL BRIDGE

If you're taking a stroll around the ballpark prior to the first pitch, make sure to stop by the Gate 3 entrance, where the Cardinals have incorporated one of the city's most historic structures. A replica of the Eads Bridge—known as the Musial Bridge and named for Stan Musial, one of the greatest baseball players ever—is a tribute to the real thing and arches over the entrance. The actual Eads Bridge connects St. Louis to East St. Louis, Illinois, and is a combined road and railroad that spans the Mississippi River.

MUSIAL PLAZA

Musial Plaza, named for one of the greatest Cardinals ever, the Gate 3 entrance-way was dedicated to Stan Musial on May 18, 2008, and is a popular gathering spot for fans. The plaza features 3,630 personalized bricks—the number of hits he attained in his career—and includes an oversized granite baseball with his signature in the middle, his achievements detailed on the upper portion, and his family tree on the lower half. A larger-than-life statue depicts Musial in his batting stance, presumably waiting patiently for the baseball to arrive.

OUT-OF-TOWN SCOREBOARD

To the right of the main scoreboard is the out-of-town scoreboard, which offers a comprehensive look at other games going on around Major League Baseball. Topped with flags representing championships won by the organization, the brightly colored structure showcases the logo of each team on the left side, the score of the game, the current batter and inning, and a baseball diamond on the right side that shows how many are currently on base.

PLAQUES AROUND THE BALLPARK

Plaques embedded in the brickwork around the exterior of Busch Stadium recall the history of the franchise. Ones bearing previous logos used by the Cardinals and a placard recognizing the World Series titles won by the team are just a few that can be spotted. One in particular, entitled "Traces of the Past," shows the old cookie-cutter Busch Stadium overlapping the new Busch, serving as a tribute to the Cardinals' old home.

PRESS BOX

Positioned directly behind home plate is the double-deck press box, which was renamed the Bob Broeg-Rick Hummel press box in 2007 to honor two local writers who were inducted into the National Baseball Hall of Fame. A plaque honoring Mike Shannon hangs on the wall and honors the former baseball player who, as of this writing, currently serves as the lead voice for the radio broadcasting team.

REDBIRD CLUB

A casual dining experience, combined with an extensive menu and limited bar options, await those who have a ticket in this section. The wallpaper is composed of Cardinals baseball cards collected by one of the owners, Bill DeWitt. The Redbird Club's seating areas are divided into three parts: sections 247 to 253 are near home plate, 241 to 246 are down the first-base line along the infield, and 254 to 257 are down the third-base line, also near the infield.

RETIRED NUMBERS

The St. Louis Cardinals have 14 National League–leading retired numbers, which are beneath the right-center field scoreboard and are painted in red on the brick wall above the scoreboard patio. These men are: Rogers Hornsby (the letters "SL"), Jack Buck (image of a microphone), Ozzie Smith (1), Red Schoendienst (2), Stan Musial (6), Enos Slaughter (9), Tony LaRussa (10), Ken Boyer (14), Dizzy Dean (17), Lou Brock (20), Whitey Herzog (24), Bruce Sutter (42), Bob Gibson (45), and August Busch Jr. (85).

SCOREBOARD PATIO

The Scoreboard Patio, positioned directly underneath the main scoreboard and accessible via the main concourse level, has a backyard barbecue feel while providing magnificent views of the baseball diamond. Ten tables—five on the right, five on the left—complete with four red chairs, provide fans with the opportunity to grab a bite to eat, sit down, relax, and take in the game at hand from a unique perspective.

SHELTER AREAS

On July 16, 2006, the Cardinals were in the middle of hosting the Atlanta Braves when a vicious storm ripped through St. Louis and made a stop at Busch Stadium. High winds knocked over concession stands, and plastic coverings put in place to protect the press box were torn apart, with one landing in the stands. As a result, management has incorporated shelter areas in ramps and stairways for fans to retreat to in the event another storm of that magnitude rolls through. Also installed was a weather radar on the outfield video board, which gives fans plenty of warning in case any potential storms should approach the ballpark.

SOLAR PANELS

One hundred-six solar panels producing close to 32,000 kilowatt hours of solar energy per year were installed in 2012. Two solar arrays, positioned on the roof of the Clark Street ticket building and atop a canopy in the left center-field bleachers, give off enough juice to power food, beverage, and retail shops in Busch Stadium. The solar energy offsets grid power utilized by the stadium, thus reducing both power use and electricity costs.

STATUES

There are nine statues on the northwest corner of Busch Stadium (Gate 4). Likenesses of Cardinal greats "Cool Papa" Bell (depicting him watching a baseball in flight), Lou Brock (following through on a swing), Dizzy Dean (in the windup), Bob Gibson (hurling a 100 mph fastball), Rogers Hornsby (admiring one of his long home runs fly out of the ballpark), Stan Musial (following through on a swing), Red Schoendienst (turning a double play), George Sisler (making a great, one-handed catch), Enos Slaughter (sliding into a base), and last but not least, Ozzie Smith (making a signature over-the-shoulder catch) surround the area. This impressive collection represents the legendary players who starred in a Cardinals uniform over the years.

MEMORABLE GAMES AT BUSCH STADIUM

APRIL 10, 2006: FIRST GAME AT BUSCH STADIUM

The St. Louis Cardinals began a new era in their glorious history by notching a win over the Milwaukee Brewers, 6–4, in their first game at the new

Busch Stadium. Mark Mulder started for the Cardinals and had a day to remember, going eight innings on the mound while allowing two runs on seven hits. At the plate he was just as dangerous, finishing 2-for-3 with a double in the fifth and a two-run home run in the seventh.

Milwaukee got on the board first when Carlos Lee singled, and Bill Hall promptly followed with a two-run blast, giving the Brew Crew an early 2–0 lead. It lasted until the third when Albert Pujols lined a solo shot and Yadier Molina added a sacrifice fly, tying the game at two. An RBI double by Scott Rolen in the fourth and the homer by Mulder in the seventh increased the advantage to 6–2. Two runs in the ninth on RBI singles by Rickie Weeks and Prince Fielder were too little, too late as the Cardinals held on for the first victory in their new digs.

OCTOBER 14, 2006: THE NLCS ROLLS INTO TOWN

After splitting the first two games in New York, the National League Championship Series made its first appearance at Busch Stadium, and fans in attendance weren't disappointed. The Cardinals scored all the runs necessary to win the game in the first two innings, taking the contest by a 5–0 margin. In the bottom of the first, Scott Spiezio got things going by smacking a two-run triple off Mets starter Steve Trachsel, staking St. Louis to a 2–0 lead. In the bottom of the second, Cardinals starter Jeff Suppan connected for a solo home run, helping extend the advantage to 3–0. After the bases were loaded, Mets reliever Darren Oliver uncorked a wild pitch that enabled David Eckstein to come home, and later a Jim Edmonds groundout allowed Preston Wilson to score, putting the Redbirds up 5–0. That's all the support Suppan would require, pitching eight shutout innings and allowing only three hits. Five days later, the Cardinals would clinch the series in New York, with a 3–1 Game 7 victory.

OCTOBER 27, 2006: REDBIRDS BRING TITLE BACK TO ST. LOUIS

The Cardinals quest to capture their tenth World Series championship ended successfully, defeating the Detroit Tigers in Game 5 of the Fall Classic, 4–2. Facing Tigers ace Justin Verlander, the Cardinals struck first when David Eckstein hit an infield single that Tigers third baseman Brandon Inge couldn't handle, allowing Yadier Molina to register the first run of the game. Detroit answered in the fourth, fueled by a two-run blast off the bat of Sean Casey to give the Tigers a brief 2–1 lead. It didn't last long as the Cardinals answered in the bottom half with two of their own when pitcher Jeff Weaver reached by way of error, allowing Molina to score, and a batter Eckstein later grounded out to plate, So Taguchi, giving St. Louis a 3–2 lead. An insurance run in the form of a Scott Rolen RBI single in the seventh made it 4–2, and Adam Wainwright's strikeout of Brandon Inge in the ninth sealed the deal. With the win, the Cardinals became the fourth team in Major League history to win a championship in a stadium's first season, joining the 1909 Pirates (Forbes Field), 1912 Red Sox (Fenway Park), and 1923 Yankees (Yankee Stadium).

JUNE 13, 2008: PHILLIES TIP THE SCOREBOARD

Three home runs in the top of the first with two outs from Chase Utley, Ryan Howard, and Pat Burrell got the offense rolling for Philadelphia, and they would never look back during their 20–2 rout of the Cardinals, which also saw them pile on 21 hits. An RBI double by Carlos Ruiz in the second made it 4–0, and the Phillies scored nine runs in the fourth, highlighted by RBI singles from Utley and Howard, and an RBI double by Shane Victorino, pushing the lead to 13–1. After extending the lead to 14–1 in the fifth, Howard inflicted even more damage in the sixth by slamming a three-run blast to give Philadelphia an insurmountable 17–1 lead. Three more runs in the eighth, capped off by a RBI single by Ruiz, pushed the visitors to the 20-run plateau for the second time in the season (having done so May 26 versus Colorado). Howard finished the game 3-for-5 with five RBI and four runs scored.

APRIL 17, 2010: MARATHON GAME LASTS 20 FRAMES

It took 20 innings and lasted six hours and 53 minutes to determine a winner, but when the smoke cleared, the visiting New York Mets came away with a 2–1 win. The game was scoreless until the top of the nineteenth when the Mets broke through first, with Jeff Francoeur hitting a sacrifice fly to enable Jose Reyes to trot home for the game's first run. Amazingly, the Cardinals offense also came to life in the inning, and the score was once again tied after Yadier Molina singled home Albert Pujols, and just like that it was on to the twentieth.

Angel Pagan got it going for the Mets with an infield single, advanced to third on base hit by Mike Jacobs, and came home on a sacrifice fly by Reyes, helping regain the lead for New York at 2–1. That's where it would stay as Mike Pelfrey, the nineteenth pitcher used between both teams, came on and pitched a scoreless inning in notching his first career save. The Cardinals had their chances, loading the bases in the tenth, twelfth, and fourteenth innings only to come away empty-handed each time.

OCTOBER 27, 2011: CARDINALS COME BACK TWICE IN DRAMATIC FASHION

Down to their last strike twice at two separate points in the game, St. Louis would not be denied and staged an incredible rally to take Game 6 and force a Game 7, winning 10–9 in 11 innings. With Texas in front 7–5 and the champagne on ice, Albert Pujols laced a one-out double off Rangers closer Neftali Perez ahead of a walk to Lance Berkman. After Allen Craig was caught looking at strike three, Perez quickly got two strikes on hometown hero David Freese. Facing a 1–2 pitch with two outs, Freese then lined a two-run triple, tying the game at seven and sending it into extra innings.

Not to be denied, Rangers slugger Josh Hamilton regained the lead for Texas with a two-run home run to right to help Texas take a 9–7 lead, but St. Louis responded in dramatic fashion. Following an RBI groundout by Ryan Theriot, Berkman—facing a 2–2 count and the possibility of the series being over with one more strike—lined a single to center that brought home Jon Jay, who had singled earlier, and once again the game was tied and headed to the eleventh inning. After a scoreless frame from Texas, Freese, who before made it possible for the game to continue, ended it with the fourth game-ending home run in Game 6, and the Cardinals stood improbably victorious, 10–9.

> "I was just trying to stay focused at that part of the Series, that part of the game, part of the year. It is tough to stray away from the task at hand . . . you remind yourself to do the whole one-pitch-at-a-time thing and stay focused. It is a whole pressurized situation, but if you keep it simple, you have got a chance."
> —*David Freese*

OCTOBER 28, 2011: MISSION COMPLETE, CARDINALS CLAIM ELEVENTH TITLE

The only possible way to follow up their unbelievable win in Game 6 the night before would be to win Game 7. That's exactly what the Cardinals did, finishing up their incredible journey through the postseason with a 6–2 World Championship–clinching victory. Texas, trying their best to forget about Game 6, jumped out to an early 2–0 lead on the strength of back-to-back RBI doubles by Josh Hamilton and Michael Young off St. Louis starter Chris Carpenter, who became the first player since Curt Schilling in 2001 to make three starts in a World Series.

The Cardinals answered with two of their own in the bottom of the first on a two-run double by Series MVP David Freese and slowly distanced themselves from Texas with one in the third on a solo home run by Allen Craig, two in the fifth, and the icing on the cake, an RBI single by Yadier Molina to score Lance Berkman. In the ninth, a fly ball by David Murphy into the glove of the left fielder Craig finished off one of the greatest World Series ever and increased the Cardinals' National League–leading championship total to 11.

> "That was amazing. There is nothing that could beat it—maybe another ring. That would top the first one as far as how that went down, coming back from 10-and-a-half back [from the playoffs], and just taking it all the way to getting the ring. It was absolutely special."
> —*David Freese*

JULY 21, 2012: CARDINALS GIVE CUBS A CASE OF DOUBLE VISION

Through six innings, it appeared to be just a normal scoreless affair between rivals Chicago and St. Louis. Everything changed in the bottom of the seventh, when the Cardinals erupted for seven doubles—tying a 76-year-old Major League record set by the Boston Bees in 1936 *against* St. Louis—en route to tallying 12 runs in the inning during a 12–0 victory. The fun began after Allen Craig hit an innocent double to left and four batters later, Carlos Beltran connected for a ground-rule double, giving the Cardinals a 3–0 lead. What followed were two-baggers by David Freese, Jon Jay, Craig (his second of the inning), Skip Schumaker, and Matt Holliday as the Cardinals would go on to rack up 10 hits in the seventh inning alone.

MAY 10, 2013: CARDINALS PITCHER MILLER PERFECT— AFTER FIRST BATTER

When rookie pitcher Shelby Miller took to the mound against the Rockies, Eric Young Jr. smacked an innocent leadoff single to start the game. What followed was truly impressive as Miller buckled down, retiring the next 27 in a row during a 3–0 St. Louis victory. Blowing through the Colorado lineup, Miller tied a Cardinals rookie record by striking out 13 while throwing 113 pitches in the dominant performance. The final out—fittingly—was a strikeout of Young Jr. The Cardinals offense was led by Carlos Beltran, who connected for a solo home run off Colorado starter Jon Garland, who also went the distance in the loss. The next day, Cardinals starter Adam Wainwright pitched no-hit baseball into the eighth before giving up a clean single to Nolan Arednado—the Rockies first hit in 49 at-bats—ending quite a streak. St. Louis pitching also tied a Major League mark, held by Texas against Detroit in 1996, by retiring 40 straight batters in a row.

SEPTEMBER 24, 2013: WACHA NEARLY ETCHES NAME IN RECORD BOOK

In yet another scintillating pitching performance by a Cardinals rookie (see May 10, 2013), Michael Wacha lost a no-hitter with two outs in the ninth inning as the Cardinals took care of the Nationals, 2–0. With the crowd on their feet and two outs in the ninth, Nationals third baseman Ryan Zimmerman chopped a ball just over the outstretched glove of the six-foot six-inch Wacha. Shortstop Pete Kozma charged and barehanded it, firing a bullet to first, but Zimmerman just beat it out for the infield single, accounting for Washington's only hit of the contest. Trevor Rosenthal replaced Wacha and picked up the final out when Jayson Werth grounded out to first. Wacha, who was making his ninth career start, threw 112 pitches and struck out nine while allowing only two walks. St. Louis scored their runs after an RBI single by Shane Robinson in the third and a run-scoring double by Yadier Molina in the fourth.

OCTOBER 18, 2013: CARDINALS TAKE NL PENNANT

After squandering a 3–1 NLCS lead a year ago against eventual World Series champion San Francisco, the Cardinals righted the ship with a dominating 9–0 win over the Los Angeles Dodgers in Game 6 of the NLCS. Facing Dodgers ace Clayton Kershaw, the Cardinals wasted no time obtaining their nineteenth National League pennant by striking for four in the third, and five in the fifth in taking a commanding 9–0 lead. The offensive attack was led by postseason superhero Carlos Beltran, who finished 3-for-4 with a double and two RBI. Once again, it was Cardinals rookie Michael Wacha who was spectacular on the mound, putting in seven strong innings of two-hit, five-strikeout ball. He exited after the seventh and gave way to relievers Carlos Martinez (eighth inning) and closer Trevor Rosenthal, who sealed the deal in the ninth by retiring the side in order.

OCTOBER 26, 2013: OBSTRUCTION CALL GIVES CARDS BIZARRE WIN

In a World Series game to remember, St. Louis was assisted by a one-of-a-kind call in the bottom of the ninth and ended up taking Game 3, 5–4. With runners on second and third in the bottom of the ninth with one out, Jon Jay (Cardinals) hit a fielder's choice to Dustin Pedroia, who threw home to get Yadier Molina for the second out of the inning. What followed was insanity. Red Sox catcher Jarrod Saltalamacchia proceeded to throw wide of third baseman Will Middlebrooks in an attempt to get Allen Craig, but Middlebrooks was called for obstruction after he raised both legs while on the ground, helping give the Redbirds the one-run win. Craig, who scampered home before realizing what the call was, would have been out on the tag at home (left fielder Daniel Nava picked up the ball and threw a dart to home plate). The situation was made possible after Yadier Molina singled to right with one out, and Craig jumped on the first offering by Boston closer Koji Uehara for a double, enabling the winning run to reside 90 feet from home plate.

WHAT THEY'RE SAYING ABOUT BUSCH STADIUM

RICK ANKIEL: "At the old Busch Stadium, the ball might have flown a little more, . . . but [the new Busch Stadium] is nice and I think being able to see the Arch is pretty cool through the outfield there."

CARLOS BELTRAN: "Busch Stadium is a very nice atmosphere, the fans really support the team, [and the] facilities are great too. . . . As ballplayers, [the] fans really make the atmosphere of [the stadium] being a good ballpark or being a bad ballpark."

STEVE BERTHIAUME, BROADCAST-ER: "Really like it, great food choices. . . . St. Louis really nailed it; they did a great job with the skyline and you can see the Arch, [and] I think that it is probably underrated [as far as ballparks around the league go]."

BOB CARPENTER, BROADCAST-ER: "[It is] near and dear to my heart because I am from St. Louis. . . . You have to hit it good to get it out and one thing people do not think about a whole lot is the field sits way down below street level, so the air can be dead down there sometimes."

ERIC COLLINS, BROADCASTER: "I like being at Busch Stadium because you get the sense that there is some tradition in St. Louis. The ballpark does not do a ton for me, the red bricks are unique, and you get a view of the Arch, but it looks a lot like the previous one that had turf."

EVAN LONGORIA: "St. Louis was the best. . . . I loved playing [Interleague games] in St. Louis. The fans there are not cheering for anybody else, but they know good baseball when they see it, and they do not boo or yell negative things. It was just fun."

RYAN LUDWICK: "I really enjoyed playing in St. Louis [as a member of the Cardinals from 2007 to 2010]. . . . It was a great place, always packed and a sea of red and white, just a great baseball town. That is probably my favorite place that I have played [at]."

STEVE LYONS, BROADCASTER: "I was a pretty big fan of the old Busch Stadium. I know it was getting older and it was part of the cookie-cutter stadiums in the 1970s. . . . I think there [are] a lot of complaints in St. Louis that they threw the new one up there a little too quickly and did not pay attention to detail."

TIM NEVERETT, BROADCASTER: "It is beautiful, and Cardinal fans are great [and] they show up en masse.... I do not think there is a bad sight line in that ballpark [and] from our standpoint in the broadcast booth, we have got a great seat right behind home plate."

JOHN ROONEY, BROADCASTER: "Busch Stadium is a very busy ballpark—there is so much going on—and you have the different all-inclusive areas in the ballpark where the fans can take in a game and have all the food and drink included in the ticket price ... [and] we have a broadcast booth that is probably the biggest booth in the history of radio."

BUSCH STADIUM FACTS AND FIGURES

BUSCH STADIUM ADDRESS
700 Clark Street, St. Louis, MO 63102

ST. LOUIS CARDINALS TEAM WEB SITE
www.cardinals.com

FIELD DIMENSIONS (IN FEET)
Left Field: 336', Left-Center: 375', Center: 400', Right-Center: 375', Right Field: 335'

SEATING CAPACITY (AS OF 2015)
43,975

ALL-STAR GAMES AT BUSCH STADIUM
July 14, 2009: American League 4, National League 3
MVP: Carl Crawford, Tampa Bay Rays (AL)

BUSCH STADIUM FIRSTS
Game: April 10, 2006—St. Louis 6, Milwaukee 4
Single: Carlos Lee, Milwaukee (April 10, 2006)*
Double: Bill Hall, Milwaukee (April 10, 2006)
Triple: David Eckstein, St. Louis (April 13, 2006)
Home Run: Bill Hall, Milwaukee (April 10, 2006)

Denotes first hit in the stadium.

GLOBE LIFE PARK
HOME OF THE TEXAS RANGERS

Rangers Ballpark in Arlington, Texas Rangers (*Photographed by Matthew D. Britt/Flickr*)

[*Globe Life Park was previously known as The Ballpark in Arlington (1994–2004), Ameriquest Field in Arlington (2004–07), and Rangers Ballpark in Arlington (2007–13).*]

When the quest began to replace the deteriorating Arlington Stadium in the early 1990s, Rangers management wanted to continue the trend of retro-style ballparks, which were being constructed throughout the Major League. Beginning with Oriole Park at Camden Yards in Baltimore, which ultimately set the tone for all the ballparks that followed in later years, the Rangers wanted to use the same concept for a state-of-the-art baseball-only facility. Not only did they accomplish that goal, but they ended up creating a new palace in the Dallas-Fort Worth area that quickly became one of the crown jewels in all of baseball.

On October 24, 1990, a mutual agreement was made official between the Rangers and the City of Arlington that a new ballpark would be built, and in 1991, the City of Arlington approved funding for the $191 million Globe Life Park. The financing for the stadium consisted of $135 million in bonds issued by the Arlington Sports Facilities Development Authority, and the remaining was raised through the sale or lease of luxury boxes and other seating options, loans as promised by the Rangers, and the concessions contract with city street funds.

Additionally, the annual debt for the municipal bonds is paid by a $3.5 million rental payment from the Rangers, combined with a one-half cent sales tax by the City of Arlington. On January 19, 1991, the Arlington municipal election approved the sales tax by a 65 percent majority, and it later expired when the debt was fully paid in November 2001.

The ground was broken on April 2, 1992, and construction officially began on April 24, 1992, on the 270-acre site, which includes a 12-acre lake and is a short distance from their previous ballpark, Arlington Stadium. Overall, the project took less than two years to complete, and the first official game occurred on April 1, 1994, when the Rangers welcomed the New York Mets for an exhibition contest.

SPECIAL FEATURES OF GLOBE LIFE PARK

ARLINGTON STADIUM TRIBUTES

The Rangers brought over home plate, the foul poles, and the bleacher seats—used until 2011—from Arlington Stadium, their previous home, and incorporated them into their new digs. In a ceremony, home plate was put into place by Richard Greene (the mayor of Arlington at the time), Elzie Odom (later the mayor of Arlington), and former Rangers owner and later the president of United States, George Bush. The current location of Globe Life Park sits on what once was a former parking lot of the now-defunct Arlington Stadium.

BATTER'S EYE CLUB

The Batter's Eye Club, new for the 2012 season and part of a $12 million renovation project, is in center field atop Greene's Hill and affords fans an exceptional view of the action. With seating for up to 100, this air-conditioned restaurant boasts a buffet and bar, as well as other dining options. A shaded deck area and open-air seating, complete with tables and chairs, afford fans the option of staying cool during the sweltering summer months.

BLEACHER SECTION—UNTIL 2011

The bleacher section, which once was a carry-over item from Arlington Stadium, was eliminated following the 2011 season as part of the renovation. The aluminum was replaced with individual stadium seats in an area now referred to as the Outfield Plaza. As a result of the modifications, seating in the section decreased from a capacity of 1,075 to 424.

BRONZE STATUES

Two statues in Vandergriff Plaza were dedicated in 1997 to honor the men who have made the most significant impact in the history of Texas Rangers baseball. Tom Vandergriff, the former mayor of Arlington from 1951 to 1977 and for whom the plaza is named, is credited with being the driving force in bringing Major League Baseball to Texas, as well as playing a major role in the construction of Globe Life Park. The other individual honored is one of baseball's greatest pitchers, Nolan Ryan. His bronze likeness depicts him tipping his cap to the fans and is on top of a marble mound encircled by a marble ring highlighting the many accomplishments he attained through-out the course of his magnificent 27-year career.

CHAMPIONSHIP FLAGS

Pennants commemorating division and league championships fly high on flagpoles on the roof of the stadium. Red flags signifying the division titles, and blue flags symbolizing the American League pennants won are alongside the official Texas flag. Atop the scoreboard are flags of the United States, the National and American League, and the State of Texas.

EXTRA SAFETY PRECAUTIONS

Just before the 2012 season began, the Rangers raised the railings in the front row at all levels to 42 inches, ensuring that no fans will accidently fall over. The decision was prompted as a result of a tragic accident in 2011, when Texas fan Shannon Stone died from injuries suffered after he fell over a railing while attempting to retrieve a baseball.

FOUR-STORY OFFICE BUILDING

One of the most recognizable structures in baseball, the white four-story office building is at the perimeter of the stadium and stretches from left-center to right-center field. Each level has 35,000 square feet of space and is occupied throughout the course of the year. On the first floor, fans can access the new restaurant, while the third and fourth floors house the Rangers executive offices. Atop the building are eight ad panels and a windscreen, measuring 42 feet by 430 feet, which was installed to slow down incoming winds.

Greene's Hill, named for former mayor Richard Greene, sits in the foreground of a new restaurant erected before the 2013 season and the four-story office building in center field. (*Photographed by Matthew D. Britt/Flickr*)

GREENE'S HILL

Greene's Hill, officially named for Richard Greene, the former mayor of Arlington, and dedicated in November 1997, is directly behind the center-field wall and is an angled section of grass that primarily serves as the batter's eye. Original plans called for a picnic area to be installed for fans, but that idea never came to fruition. When home runs are launched into that area, fans closest to the hill dive over the partition in hopes of retrieving the baseball.

HOME RUN PORCH SCOREBOARD

With high-definition scoreboards replacing older technology all around baseball, the Rangers made the transition just in time for the 2011 season. The new scoreboard, placed on the green roof of the home run porch in right field, measures 42 feet by 120 feet (5,040 square feet), dwarfing the previous model, which was 24 feet by 36 feet (864 square feet). Sectioned into three parts, the left side displays the visiting team's roster, the middle part streams live in-game video and instant replays, and the right side lists the Rangers lineup. An in-game box score and pitch count is beneath the center section.

INTERACTIVE SPORTS PARK

Kids will love the interactive sports park, part of the Vandergriff Plaza in center. T-ball cages, speed pitch, and a Wiffle ball park are just a few of the many options that kids can enjoy for $1 tokens. The sports park opens two hours before the first pitch and has varying closing times, depending on the particular month. Picnic tables make it easy for parents to sit back and relax while their kids have fun.

LEATHER CHAIRS

Is it possible to combine all the comforts of home at the old ball game? Without a doubt! Texas management has incorporated 72 soft leather recliners in the front section of the Cuervo Club on the Mezzanine Level. The package also features a complimentary buffet and in-seat beverage service. Just remember: There's a baseball game taking place on the field, so forget any thoughts of taking a nap.

LUXURY BOXES

A white-paneled, tile-floored luxury box encircles the length of the seating bowl and occupies sections 217–35. Amenities include 22-inch-wide padded seats and specialty food items not offered anywhere else in the ballpark. Valet parking, available at a cost, is one of the services offered as part of this particular package.

OUT-OF-TOWN SCOREBOARD

Prior to the 2011 season, a manual scoreboard embedded in the left-field wall just below the seating area displayed scores from around baseball. That has since been replaced with the latest and greatest from Daktronics, one of the worldwide leaders in video board technology. The new out-of-town high-definition scoreboard measures 12 feet high by 84 feet wide and features the number of each team's current pitcher along with a three-letter abbreviation of the teams playing, the current score, and inning.

RANGERS FAN STATUE

Outside the home plate gate are bronze life-size statues that pay tribute to Rangers fans Shannon and Cooper Stone and depict the father and son walking hand in hand. This honors Shannon, who, while at a Rangers game, tragically fell from the stands attempting to obtain a foul ball tossed to him.

RANGERS HALL OF FAME

Rangers management reconfigured the former Legends of the Game Baseball Museum behind right field and renamed the two-leveled structure the Texas Rangers Hall of Fame. Plaques honoring Rangers Hall of Famers, pictures worth a thousand words, and glass cases displaying game-used jerseys, baseballs, and other important artifacts in the franchise's history are in the 13,000-square-foot museum. A 235-seat theatre featuring a 30-foot screening wall occupies the second floor, and can be rented for meetings or presentations.

RESTAURANT

The first floor of the four-story office building in left-center was completely remodeled during the 2011 off-season and now has a new two-level restaurant and sports bar. Open to the public and not requiring a ticket to gain entrance, this 9,152-square-foot eatery features an extensive menu and drink selections. The general public can rent it out on days when the Rangers are away from the ballpark.

RETIRED NUMBERS

The Texas Rangers have retired the numbers of two men in the franchise's history, and their numbers are on the left-field façade, just above the windows of the Diamond Club. These men are Johnny Oates (26) and Nolan Ryan (34).

TEXAS FLAVOR

The exterior granite fascia is a product of Marble Falls, Texas, and the upper arches feature "Ranger Red" bricks, also from the area. Upper arches around the perimeter of the ballpark feature a grand total of 21 Lone Stars and 35 steer heads constructed of cast stone. Murals between the lower and upper arches on the outer façade showcase scenes from Texas.

THE NAME GAME

Once known as The Ballpark in Arlington upon its debut in 1994, the stadium has undergone a few name changes since its inception. On May 7, 2004, Ameriquest, one of the leading wholesale lenders in the United States, purchased the naming rights and it became Ameriquest Field in Arlington. On March 19, 2007, the Texas Rangers announced that they had broken their relationship with Ameriquest and decided that the the stadium would be called Rangers Ballpark in Arlington until 2013, when the name was changed to Globe Life Park.

TIGER STADIUM TRIBUTE

One of the most nostalgic features at Globe Life Park is a two-level seating area in right field with a roof that serves as an appealing target for left-handed batters and evokes memories of the seating arrangement that was once at Tiger

Stadium in Detroit. Although as of this writing no player has blasted a baseball that hit the roof or went over it, many shots have landed in the upper portion of the seating deck, making it a great area for seekers of home run baseballs.

VANDERGRIFF PLAZA

Renovated after the 2011 season and named for former Arlington mayor Tom Vandergriff who served in office from 1951 to 1977, the center-field area is a hot spot for mingling before and after games. Vandergriff is credited with bringing the Washington Senators to Texas and played a pivotal role in the planning and construction of Globe Life Park. A statue unveiled in his honor during the 1997 season greets fans as they walk around the plaza.

VISITORS' BULLPEN CHANGED

In Game 5 of the 2011 World Series, Cardinals manager Tony LaRussa phoned the bullpen for a pitching change, was misheard, and the wrong player was inserted into the contest. The Rangers took note, and their renovation project following the 2011 campaign included altering the location of the visitors' bullpen. Before the change, pitchers warmed up with their backs to the field, but the bullpen now runs parallel to the field and should help prevent any mix-ups in the future.

MEMORABLE GAMES AT GLOBE LIFE PARK

APRIL 11, 1994: FIRST GAME AT GLOBE LIFE PARK

The Texas Rangers began a new era in their franchise history in front of more than 46,000, but the Milwaukee Brewers played the role of spoiler by standing victorious, 4–3. Scoreless until the fifth, the Brewers got on the board when Dave Nilsson staked his claim to history by hitting the first home run—a solo shot—off Kenny Rogers for a 1–0 Milwaukee advantage. Both teams traded runs over the course of the next few innings, but the go-ahead run was registered in the eighth when Kevin Seitzer greeted reliever Cris Carpenter with an RBI single that extended the Brew Crew's advantage to 4–2. It's a good thing; in the bottom half of the eighth Jose Canseco drew a bases-loaded walk, pulling Texas to within one, but the rally was snuffed out after Juan Gonzalez grounded into a double play to end the inning.

JULY 28, 1994: ROGERS THROWS PERFECT GAME

In a game that left Los Angeles Angels batters clueless at the plate, Rangers pitcher Kenny Rogers became the fourteenth player in Major League Baseball history to retire 27 consecutive, defeating visiting California 4–0 during a masterful 98-pitch effort. Rogers, who struck out eight, received the majority of his run support by way of three solo home runs, including back-to-back jobbies by Ivan Rodriguez and Jose Canseco in the bottom of the third.

After cruising through six innings with no difficulty, the seventh proved to be a test. Chad Curtis, Spike Owen, and Jim Edmonds all worked the count full at 3–2 before registering outs: Curtis on a groundout, Owen on a fly ball to left, and Edmonds by way of a swinging strikeout. In the bottom of the ninth with the crowd cheering in anticipation, Rogers coaxed Gary DiSarcina into a fly ball to center that settled into the glove of Rusty Greer, wrapping the first perfecto since Dennis Martinez pulled the stunt as a member of the Expos at Los Angeles on July 28, 1991.

JUNE 13, 1997: FIRST INTERLEAGUE GAME IN MAJOR LEAGUE HISTORY
For the first time since 1871, two teams from separate leagues met in the regular season, and San Francisco defeated Texas in the historic first, 4–3. San Francisco leadoff hitter Darryl Hamilton registered the first hit in the top of the first—a sharp single to right—but was ultimately left stranded. The Rangers got on the board in the bottom of the second when Billy Ripken singled home Damon Buford for an early 1–0 advantage. San Francisco answered in the third on a solo home run by Stan Javier off Texas starter Darren Oliver, but Texas answered emphatically with two in the sixth powered by an RBI triple by Mark McLemore that drove in Will Clark, and two batters later, Ripken notched another RBI single, helping push the favor back to Texas, 3–1. The lead was short-lived; the next half-inning saw the Giants tally three highlighted by Javier inflicting more damage, this time with an RBI double that put the Giants ahead for good.

JULY 5, 1998: GONZALEZ HITS 100 RBI BEFORE THE BREAK
With two-run home runs in the first and seventh innings, Rangers slugger Juan Gonzalez eclipsed the 100-RBI mark before the All-Star Game during an 8–4 Texas win. In accomplishing the feat, he became the second player in Major League history to do it, joining legendary Detroit Tigers slugger Hank Greenberg (who had 103 at the break in 1935 en route to finishing with 170). The first shot, a two-run blast off Randy Johnson in the bottom of the first, staked Texas to an early 2–0 lead. In the seventh, with the Rangers leading Seattle 6–5, he once again took Johnson deep, providing the final margin of victory and a spot in the record books. Although Gonzalez was on pace to break the Major League record of 190, set by Hack Wilson in 1930 while he was a member of the Chicago Cubs, he finished with 157 and ultimately was awarded the Most Valuable Player Award after leading Texas to the AL West title.

JULY 29, 2008: ICHIRO NOTCHES 3,000TH CAREER PROFESSIONAL HIT

In his first at-bat, Ichiro Suzuki knocked a single to left-center field on the first pitch for his 1,722nd Major League hit; the fact that it was career-hit number 3,000 as a professional baseball player is what proved noteworthy. As a member of the Pacific League's Orix Blue Wave for nine seasons, he had accumulated 1,278 hits before signing with the Seattle Mariners beginning with the 2001 season.

While Major League Baseball won't officially recognize the milestone and invite him with open arms to the exclusive 3,000th-hit club, there's no denying his model of consistency at the plate will undoubtedly earn him a spot in baseball's most coveted museum one day: The Hall of Fame. Seattle, who led 10–9 entering the bottom of the ninth, ended up losing the contest after closer J. J Putz allowed back-to-back singles by Marlon Byrd and Chris Davis before surrendering a game-winning, two-run double by Ramon Vazquez, giving Texas an 11–10 win.

APRIL 15, 2009: KINSLER HAS CAREER DAY

On Jackie Robinson Day, Rangers second baseman Ian Kinsler turned in a performance that Robinson himself would be proud of, becoming the first American League player in 119 seasons to hit for the cycle and finish with six hits (6-for-6) during a nine-inning game as Texas beat up Baltimore, 19–6. He doubled in the first, connected for a solo home run in the third, collected two singles—one of which drove in a run—in the fourth during an eight-run inning, tripled in the sixth to complete the cycle, and connected for an RBI double in the eighth. For the triple, he worked the count to 3–2 before hitting a shot that landed just in front of the 407-foot sign and caromed just enough for Kinsler to make it to third. As an added note, he became the first right-handed batter in Texas history to hit for the cycle. Other players to collect six hits and hit for the cycle in a single game include Rondell White (1995 with the Montreal Expos), and Bobby Veach (1920 with the Detroit Tigers).

OCTOBER 22, 2010: RANGERS CLINCH FIRST PENNANT

Before this season's playoffs, the Rangers had never won a series, let alone defeated the Yankees in the postseason. They made up for that and more by capturing Game 6 and advancing to their first World Series with a 6–1 victory over the Bronx Bombers. Vladimir Guerrero provided the offense early, driving in an RBI via a groundout in the first, and a two-run double with two outs in the fifth pushed the lead to 3–1. The biggest blow came when Nelson Cruz launched a two-run blast off New York reliever David Robertson, also in the bottom of the fifth, unofficially kicking off the celebration.

Arguably the real hero was starter Colby Lewis, who went eight innings in limiting the vaunted Yankees' offense to one run on three hits. New York's only run came courtesy of a wild pitch in the third, which allowed Alex Rodriguez to trot home.

"[My] favorite moment was the Rangers winning the pennant for the first time in 2010. . . . Neftali Perez striking out A-Rod—that is above all others anywhere in my baseball career."
—*Eric Nadel, Rangers broadcaster*

OCTOBER 15, 2011: RANGERS WIN SECOND PENNANT IN A ROW

Nelson Cruz led an offensive onslaught with his Major League record sixth League Championship Series home run, and the Texas Rangers wrapped up their second straight American League pennant with a 15–5 trouncing of the Detroit Tigers. Miguel Cabrera and Jhonny Peralta each hit solo home runs in the first and second innings respectively, but the Rangers answered with a nine-run third punctuated by two two-run doubles by Michael Young to open—and close—the scoring. Ahead 12–4 in the seventh, the Rangers put the icing on the cake when Young connected for a solo home run, and Cruz, the ALCS MVP, hit a two-run blast for the record breaker and thirteenth RBI of the series, eclipsing the previous mark of 12 held by New York's Bobby Richardson during the 1960 World Series and Boston's John Valentin in the 1999 American League Division Series.

OCTOBER 22, 2011: PUJOLS HAS EPIC WORLD SERIES PERFORMANCE

Considered by many to be the greatest single-game hitting performance in World Series history, St. Louis slugger Albert Pujols put on a show in Game 3 of the Fall Classic, finishing 5-for-6 with three home runs and six runs batted in during the Cardinals 16–7 thrashing of Texas. Joining Babe Ruth, Reggie Jackson—and in 2012, Pablo Sandoval of the Giants—as the only four to slam three taters in a World Series contest, Pujols struck in the sixth with a three-run blast off Alexi Ogando, a two-run shot off Mike Gonzalez in the seventh, and just for the heck of it, a solo rocket off Darren Oliver. If that wasn't enough, he added two singles and established World Series records for total bases with 14 and hits registered in four consecutive innings in the fourth (single), fifth (single), sixth (home run), and seventh (home run).

SEPTEMBER 9, 2013: PIRATES END 20 YEARS OF MISERY

Behind a stellar pitching performance from rookie Gerrit Cole, who allowed three hits and no runs over seven innings, the Pirates clinched their first winning season since 1992 with a 1–0 victory over Texas. After playing scoreless baseball through six, Marlon Byrd slapped a two-out double off Rangers starter Yu Darvish and was driven in by Pedro Alvarez, who followed with a double of his own to account for the only runs of the game. The victory ended a dubious North American record of 20 straight losing seasons, and put the franchise in the win column for the first time since Barry Bonds roamed the outfield at Three Rivers Stadium as a member of the Pirates.

JUNE 9, 2014: CHISENHALL HAS A GAME FOR THE AGES

Cleveland third baseman Lonnie Chisenhall had a historic night, finishing 5-for-5 with three home runs, nine runs batted in, helping propel the Indians to a 17–7 thrashing of the Rangers. The night started off innocently as Chisenhall singled in the first inning, but then from there it became evident that it was about to be a special game. He proceeded to hit a two-run blast in the second, added another two-run shot in the fourth, connected for an RBI double in the sixth, and in his final plate appearance, notched a three-run blast to right field.

His performance tied two club records: the nine RBI in a game matched that of Chris James, who accomplished the feat on May 4, 1991, at O.co Coliseum in Oakland, and the three home run performance was the first such accomplishment since Shin-Soo Choo did it on September 17, 2010, at Progressive Field. Chisenhall is also the fourth Major Leaguer to accumulate at least five hits, three home runs, and nine RBIs since Fred Lynn of the Red Sox did so in 1975.

WHAT THEY'RE SAYING ABOUT GLOBE LIFE PARK

SANDY ALOMAR JR.: "Pretty big ballpark. The ball travels very well similar to all the new stadiums . . . brick, very large, and now it kind of reminds me a little bit of Comerica Park if you walk around the stadium; it takes you a while."

JASON GIAMBI: "A great hitter's ballpark. You cannot wait to get to that place to go hit. . . . It can be hot, [and it is] kind of sunken a little bit, so you do not really get that breeze down in there, but I enjoy playing there."

CURTIS GRANDERSON: "Dark stadium—I remember a couple of guys saying a few years back that it was one of the stadiums where you could just stare at the lights and not really have to worry about blinking or anything. . . . The ball carries pretty well there. It is going to be hot, so you are hoping that you get a night game there."

JOSH HAMILTON: "Good place to hit [and] the ball carries well . . . just the overall atmosphere. There is something about the older configuration—the last couple of years they have done some renovations—[and they] improved it with the restaurant in center field and the bullpens; it just adds a lot more character to the ballpark."

RAUL IBANEZ: "Great ballpark to hit in, [and] it is always nice and hot there. . . . Good atmosphere now that they have been winning. It is a really good, fun ballpark to play in."

DAVID MURPHY: "It is a great place to play, great place to hit. Obviously, much has been made about the jet stream to right-center, so for me it is perfect as a left-handed hitter. . . . It is just a comfortable place to play 81 games [a year] in."

ERIC NADEL, BROADCASTER: "I love the ballpark. I think of the newer waves of ballparks and it is one of the more unique with the home run porch out in right field and the office building in center field is different. The fact it is fully enclosed in center field gives it a different look than some of the other ones."

ALEX RODRIGUEZ: "Great hitter's place, great fans. . . . [What stands out] is how hot it is, and how much we used to always love to hit there."

JOHN STERLING, BROADCASTER: "When they built it, they built a very deep outfield and they wanted it to be a triples ballpark. Well, little did they realize the ball was going to fly in the Texas heat. . . . They have a Fenway left field, and an old Tiger Stadium right field, and they did not know what to do in center, so they built an office building."

MICHAEL YOUNG: "Texas is a good ballpark and in the postseason they can pack 50,000 in there and it gets really loud. . . . [Overall] it is a nice ballpark. It just gets smoking hot and if they had a roof on that thing, it would be incredible."

GLOBE LIFE PARK FACTS AND FIGURES

GLOBE LIFE PARK ADDRESS
1000 Ballpark Way, Arlington, TX 76011

TEXAS RANGERS TEAM WEB SITE
www.texasrangers.com

FIELD DIMENSIONS (IN FEET)
Left Field: 332', Left-Center: 390', Center: 400', Right-Center: 377', Right Field: 325'

SEATING CAPACITY (AS OF 2015)
48,114

ALL-STAR GAMES AT GLOBE LIFE PARK
July 11, 1995: National League 3, American League 2
MVP: Jeff Conine, Florida Marlins (NL)

GLOBE LIFE PARK FIRSTS
Game: April 11, 1994—Milwaukee 4, Texas 3
Single: David Hulse, Texas (April 11, 1994)*
Double: Dean Palmer, Texas (April 11, 1994)
Triple: Kevin Seitzer, Milwaukee (April 11, 1994)
Home Run: Dave Nilsson, Milwaukee (April 11, 1994)

*Denotes first hit in the stadium.

GREAT AMERICAN BALL PARK

HOME OF THE CINCINNATI REDS

Great American Ball Park, Cincinnati Reds (*Photographed by Brian Skversky/Flickr*)

Great American Ball Park sits proudly along the banks of the Ohio River. This state-of-the-art facility, which replaced the multipurpose and concrete-laden Riverfront Stadium, was the catalyst for development along the Ohio River, helping to pump much-needed revenue into the downtown district. Plans for building this jewel were in the works for nearly 10 years, but after many struggles and controversies, the vision finally became reality when the first pitch was thrown on March 31, 2003.

Talks for a new ballpark began in August 1993, when then-General Manager Jim Bowden argued that a modern facility was necessary in order to keep up with the other baseball clubs' construction of new, baseball-only structures. In addition, the Reds, along with the NFL's Bengals, complained that Riverfront Stadium lacked the high-end amenities that other teams were enjoying, and in order to increase payroll and contend for championships, new stadiums were essential.

In the summer of 1995, Hamilton County commissioners suggested increasing the sales tax county-wide by one percentage point for the next 20 years, which would provide the funding necessary for building the stadiums for the two franchises. It was also a surefire way to bring in extra cash essential for a jail expansion, and the county-wide tax would provide some relief for taxpayers in the Hamilton County district.

In May 1996, a historic vote took place when the Hamilton County voters took to the ballots and elected to keep the Bengals and Reds in town—a major ruling in its own right—by agreeing to a tax that would be an extra half-penny on the dollar for nearly everything purchased. Another vote was cast in 1998, when citizens decided that the best place for the new ballpark to be constructed would be along the riverfront instead of an area known as Broadway Commons. Although the votes were tallied, and the results were official, there were still arguments concerning the location of the ballpark and its financial state.

Cincinnati City Council members argued and were opposed at how much the city should contribute to the county-owned stadiums (for both the Reds and the NFL's Bengals) and how the sales tax revenue should be allocated. While all this was going on, the Reds had a quarrel of their own when former owner Marge Schott, along with other Reds officials, threatened to relocate the franchise to northern Kentucky because they felt the Reds were getting the short end of the stick, while the Bengals were getting most of the attention in the stadium plans.

A year after the sales-tax vote, a lease still hadn't been negotiated. Reds ownership began to voice their concern once again in February 1997 about the Bengals getting better treatment than the Reds, and said they wanted to construct what would later be known as Great American Ball Park on the banks of the Ohio River, just like the Bengals were planning to do. Later, an option called The Wedge was considered. It called for some of Riverfront Stadium to be demolished in order for the new ballpark to be built.

The project was finally agreed upon, ground was broken, and as planned, some of Riverfront Stadium was altered to allow for the new stadium to be constructed. The project was completed in time for Opening Day 2003, when the Reds took the field in front of a packed house. It may have been a long road to the first pitch, but it became one of the significant moments in the long and storied history of the Reds franchise.

SPECIAL FEATURES OF GREAT AMERICAN BALL PARK

BIG RED MACHINE TRIBUTE

A stunning mosaic that depicts the 1975 World Champion Reds team and pays tribute to a team better known as the Big Red Machine is just one of several pieces of art in Great American Ball Park. With downtown Cincinnati, the late Riverfront Stadium, and the Roebling suspension bridge in the background, players depicted in the mosaic include Ken Griffey Sr., Johnny Bench, Pete Rose, and Joe Morgan, all of whom contributed in a magical season capped off by a stunning World Series win over Boston in seven games.

BLEACHER SEATS

Following the blueprint as set forth by the likes of Wrigley Field and later Progressive Field, this left-field bleacher section is an outfield seating area and doubles as a throwback to the old days. If you're thinking that it might get pretty hot during the summer, you're absolutely right. To help alleviate the problem, water misters—located beneath the smokestacks and also doubling as a decoration on the main scoreboard—cool off the crowd during scorching afternoon contests.

BRIDGE IN THE GAP

The bridge, one of the more creative and innovative standing room–only sections in the game of baseball today, is just off home plate in the upper deck and provides incredible sight lines. A 35-foot-wide break in the stands between home plate and third base, known as The Gap, is bridged by the concourse on each level. Aligned with Sycamore Street, it provides unparalleled views into the stadium from downtown and out to the skyline from within the park.

CENTER-FIELD PAVILION

Similar to that of the center-field restaurant at Tropicana Field in Tampa Bay, the center-field portion of Great American Ball Park is highlighted by an enclosed party area that has become one of the most visible features in all of baseball. The climate-controlled eating establishment features a non-reflective glass shield, which doubles as a batter's eye. State-of-the-art amenities provide comfort and luxury. The price of admission includes a game ticket, catered buffet, and beverages. In 2006, a 7,500-square-foot riverboat-themed roof deck was added atop the Pavilion, creating a one-of-a-kind feature in the game of baseball.

With the Ohio River in the background, the center-field pavilion area is a popular spot for fans before, during, and after a Reds game. (*Photographed by Brian Skversky/Flickr*)

CHAMPIONSHIP BANNERS

Installed just before the 2005 season, banners displaying the five World Series Championships won by the organization are on the façade in left field, just beneath the Machine Room Grille. The banners—in the Reds' colors of black, white, and red—are in descending order from left to right: 1990, 1976, 1975, 1940, and 1919, the year of the infamous "Black Sox Scandal."

CLUB 4192

The Club 4192 lounge, dedicated in honor of Pete Rose's historic hit, is available to all premium-seat customers and offers a wide range of services before, during, and after the contest. Measuring a total of 13,000 square feet, Club 4192 has a menu big enough to satisfy everyone, and there is a large sit-down bar if you want to enjoy a cold one while taking in the action. Traditional dining seats are also available for meals before or after the game.

CLUB RED

An open-air patio on the concourse in center field is a great place to hobnob before, during, and after games while downing a couple of beverages. Drink specials are available from the time the gates open until the first pitch of the ballgame. What really makes this location so exceptional is that it offers great views of the Ohio River and glimpses of riverboats as they float by.

CROSLEY TERRACE

The main entrance to Great American Ball Park has four statues from the Crosley Field era that combine history, art, and baseball. An acre in length, the area is masterfully landscaped with grass and trees, and as a symbolic tribute, the turf inside the terrace is sloped at the same incline as Crosley Field's outfield. Banners pay tribute to six memorable events that took place during that era, including baseball's first night contest (May 24, 1935) and Johnny Vander Meer's consecutive no-hitters (June 11 and 15, 1938).

FAMILY SECTION

The Family Section on the Terrace Level in left field, one of the spots in which alcoholic beverages are prohibited, offers families the opportunity to enjoy the action without having to worry about things getting out of hand. This might be a great place to take little kids who are attending a game at Great American Ball Park for the first time, as the controlled atmosphere may be a little easier to handle.

FAMOUS CLOCK

A replica of the Longines clock, a famous, well-known centerpiece of Crosley Field, adorns the main scoreboard at Great American Ball Park. The replica, which sits atop the structure, comes to life and is larger than its predecessor. This simple timepiece evokes life in earlier, less complicated times.

FAN ZONE

An interactive fan zone, part of the final phase of Great American Ball Park, is on the Terrace Level along the west side of the ballpark. A playground, picnic deck, and two additional entrances were constructed on the site of the Reds' previous home, Riverfront Stadium. The Rose Garden, which pays tribute to hits leader Pete Rose, is also here.

FREEDOM

Fans can wander from section to section without having to show proof of ticket purchase. They can explore all the amenities of Great American Ball Park without missing any action on the field.

HOME PLATE CLUB

It may seem like every ballpark has one of these, but the management at Great American Ball Park goes to great lengths to make people feel as though they are VIPs. A gourmet buffet, which occupies the first eight rows behind home plate, has an in-seat dining option. There are exclusive views into the tunnel leading from the Reds Clubhouse to the dugout.

MACHINE ROOM GRILLE

A brewpub, located in the left-field corner, pays homage to the Big Red Machine and the 1970s. The spacious bar and grille, with its distinctive architecture featuring brick and steel finishes along with an exposed ceiling, has a fan-friendly, blue-collar feel. There is plenty of memorabilia, including mock foul poles, a zamboni once used at Riverfront Stadium, and a mini electronic scoreboard.

MOSAICS

Fans entering the main gates at Great American Ball Park can view historic images from the 1869 team. There are two mosaics, but one in particular seems to steal the show, so make sure you have your camera ready! With historic Cincinnati as the backdrop, this mosaic features the original starting nine of the Cincinnati Red Stockings in their traditional uniforms and is made of Italian marble tiles.

POWER ALLEY PATIO

Power Alley Patio, above the Cincinnati bullpen in center field, offers exceptional views of the field. It can accommodate up to 70, and has a semi-retractable roof in case the weather turns bad. Tickets entitle fans to a catered buffet and beverages. Perhaps the best of all is an up-close-and-personal view of Reds relievers warming up.

PRIVATE SUITES: THE ULTIMATE IN COMFORT

Private suites, which come with 12 exterior seats and four optional bar stools, help fans feel as though they are royalty. The suites are available in different decors that boast of Reds history and other paraphernalia. Clearly, citizens were anxious to reserve their own because the previous record of selling out suites was 61 days, held by PNC Park in Pittsburgh; the record was broken by the Reds, who eclipsed the mark in 27 days. Some of the features include a buffet counter, a bar and icemaker, three television screens, a private phone line and restroom, and gourmet food and beverage options.

REDLEGS LANDING

The ultimate place to be seen before or during a game is the Redlegs Landing, an ideal place for mingling and downing a cold one. Located on the view level concourse near section 537, it has spectacular views and a state-of-the-art digital video scoreboard that offers out-of-town scores. The ticket includes a catered buffet and beverages and probably the best feature of all—plenty of fun!

REDS HALL OF FAME

This extensive exhibit pays tribute to both the great teams and players in Cincinnati Reds history and is an attraction that can't be missed if you love the history of baseball. The Hall of Fame is on the west side of Great American Ball Park, along Main Street, and will fascinate anyone who yearns to know more about the oldest franchise in Major League Baseball. Every detail about the franchise—from the tribute to Pete Rose to the 1919 World Series—is available at this location.

RETIRED NUMBERS

The Cincinnati Reds have retired seven numbers throughout the course of their history. The numbers are in circles beneath the press box windows. They include: Fred Hutchinson (1), Johnny Bench (5), Joe Morgan (8), Barry Larkin (11), Ted Kluszewski (18), Frank Robinson (20), and Tony Perez (24). For a more detailed look at the retired Reds numbers, pick up a copy of the first edition of *The Baseball Stadium Insider: A Comprehensive Dissection of All Thirty Ballparks, the Legendary Players, and the Memorable Moments,* published in 2012.

RIVER BLAST

At PNC Park in Pittsburgh, the distance from home plate to the Allegheny River measures 443 feet, so it's entirely possible for a batter to reach it on the fly, but a batter would have to crank a shot down the right-field line for 616 feet (distance courtesy of Google Maps), which is something possible only in video games or with a golf ball.

However, honorable mention goes to Adam Dunn, who as a member of the Reds in 2005, clobbered a Jose Lima offering and sent it to straightaway center field. According to HOK Sport, the builders of Great American Ball Park, a study concluded that by the time the ball landed, it found its way to a street called Mehring Way, an estimated 535 feet from home plate. It then bounced along for another 200 feet, ultimately coming to rest on a piece of driftwood along the banks of the Ohio River. According to local geographers, what had occurred was the unthinkable: the ball started its flight in Ohio and ended up in the state of Kentucky. Now *that's* a home run!

RIVERBOAT

A riverboat drops off guests who wish to arrive by water at a dock just beyond the center-field barrier. The dock is decorated by a sculpture that features a riverboat paddle wheel with the trademark smokestacks that give off blasts of steam visible from inside of the ballpark. Of course, if your seat is in the upper deck section, you can watch the boats pass by or on clear days, even sneak a peek at the city of Covington, Kentucky.

RIVERFRONT CLUB

The Riverfront Club, in the right-field section of the ballpark and over-looking the Ohio River, offers world-class cuisine and luxury. Access to the upscale restaurant and bar requires a membership, but those who already have one are invited to enjoy a meal before or after the contest or view the game from one of the three terraces.

ROSE GARDEN

Pete Rose is not in the Hall of Fame as of this writing (yet), but a Rose Garden on the western part of Great American Ball Park contains a circle of roses that sits accurately on the spot in which his historic 4,192nd hit landed. His date with destiny came on September 11, 1985, when his first inning single off San Diego starter Eric Show during a 2–0 win at River-front Stadium made history and put him in a class all by himself. Will his hits record ever be surpassed? Don't bet on it!

SCOREBOARD MURAL

The back of the main scoreboard features a massive mural depicting a photograph of a weathered baseball and bat. It's a photo of the actual ball and bat used by Pete Rose when he collected his record-breaking 4,192nd hit on September 11, 1985, which surpassed Ty Cobb's long-standing mark.

SCOREBOARDS

Measuring 217 feet across, the six-part scoreboard includes a 26-foot by 167-foot main matrix board, two ribbon boards along the first- and third-base line measuring 4 feet high by 232 feet long, an out-of-town scoreboard, a pitch board, and two boards shaped like paddle wheels flanking replicas of old-fashioned riverboat smokestacks. The permanent out-of-town score-board spans the entire wall from left to left-center field, has enough room to account for every game, and is a one-stop shop for up-to-the-minute progress of all other ongoing baseball contests.

SCOUT BOX SEATS

Situated behind the plate beginning with row nine, these seats were once occupied by Major League Baseball scouts who hoped to find new talent. In-seat food and beverage services, combined with exceptional up-close-and-personal views, padded seats, and access to the Scouts Alley private lounge make this a one-of-a-kind experience.

SCOUTS ALLEY

With a maximum capacity of 1,000, this private lounge offers a wide array of drinks, and historic photographs and various displays of baseball equipment offer fans a trip down memory lane. There is also a replica scouting map, and authentic contracts tell the story of what Major League scouting is all about.

SECOND STREET BANNERS

A series of banners line the streets outside Great American Ball Park and commemorate famous moments in the history of the Cincinnati Reds franchise. Each banner features the name, date, and description of each significant event and reminds true Reds fans of the highlights and moments that will be forever a part of not only Cincinnati lore, but Major League Baseball as well.

SMOKESTACKS

Just to the right of the Batter's Eye Pavilion in center field, two smokestacks come to life and are set in motion whenever certain accomplishments occur throughout the course of a game. When a Cincinnati Reds pitcher records a strikeout, puffs of smoke fly out of the stacks, signifying the achievement. Conversely, when the Reds blast a home run or register a victory, fireworks shoot from the smokestacks.

STATUES

There are six statues featuring Cincinnati baseball greats on the Crosley Terrace. Fans were asked to vote on four players from the categories of catcher, pitcher, and two hitters. After more than 17,000 votes were cast, the players selected to become bronzed forever were Ted Kluszewski, Ernie Lombardi, Joe Nuxhall, and Frank Robinson. The statues were sculpted by Thomas Tsuchiya and were added to the terrace throughout the 2003 season and into 2004. On September 17, 2011, the Reds unveiled a statue of catcher Johnny Bench, and on September 6, 2013, one of Joe Morgan joined the group.

THE GREAT AMERICAN NAME

On July 7, 2000, the Reds and Great American Insurance Company, one of the oldest establishments in the United States, agreed to a 30-year deal that enables the company to own the naming rights to the ballpark.

THE SPIRIT OF BASEBALL

Located on the west end of the Reds administration building is a limestone display that stands 50 feet tall and measures 20 feet across. The structure pays tribute to the game of baseball, with the Cincinnati riverfront in the background and four characters in the front. Three of the characters, shown in the form of clouds, symbolize a catcher, batter, and fielder, while the fourth is a child dressed in uniform with a bat. The actual image varies, depending on the sunlight, clouds, and other lighting.

TRADEMARK QUOTE

Joe Nuxhall has a storied career in baseball, having logged over 60 years in the business. His famous line of "Rounding third and heading for home . . ." is proudly immortalized on the north side of the ballpark, positioned on the back of the third-base stands. Nuxhall, whose dedication to the organization was evident, was a Cincinnati pitcher in 1944 and again from 1952 to 1960. Upon his retirement from the game, he became a full-time Reds radio broadcaster from 1967 through 2004, and on a part-time basis until he passed away in 2007.

MEMORABLE GAMES AT GREAT AMERICAN BALL PARK

MARCH 31, 2003: FIRST GAME AT GREAT AMERICAN BALL PARK

The Pittsburgh Pirates exacted a little revenge on Cincinnati with a 10–1 thrashing in the opening game at Great American Ball Park, paying the Reds back for spoiling the inaugural game at PNC Park two years prior. After a scoreless first that saw Ken Griffey Jr. register the stadium's first official hit, a double, Pittsburgh went to work on the offensive end during the second inning, scoring six runs on the strength of three home runs: a two-run shot by Reggie Sanders, a three-run blast by Kenny Lofton, and a solo bomb by Jason Kendall.

The Reds scratched a run across in the third on a bases-loaded walk, pulling to within 6–1, but it was the Pirates' bats that remained hot. A bases-loaded walk in the fifth to Pokey Reese increased the lead to 7–1, and a two-run double by Randall Simon in the seventh put the contest out of reach. This wasn't the first time Cincinnati lost big in the opening of a new stadium; the debut of Riverfront Stadium on June 30, 1970, had the same script with Atlanta taking it to the Reds, 8–2.

JUNE 30, 2006: OHIO SHOWDOWN FAILS TO DISAPPOINT

Trailing 7–0 after seven innings, Adam Dunn blasted a grand slam off Cleveland closer Bob Wickman in the bottom of the ninth to cap a five-run rally, helping propel Cincinnati to a stunning 9–8 victory. The Indians jumped out to an early 5–0 lead after one, and it looked as though they would cruise to the victory. Todd Hollandsworth connected for a solo home run in the top of the eighth for Cleveland to push the lead to 7–0, but the Reds responded with four runs in the bottom of the eighth, powered by a three-run home run by pinch hitter Juan Castro. After scoring a run in the bottom of the ninth, the Reds were trailing 8–5 when the bases were loaded for Dunn, who connected on the second pitch of the at-bat, sending it into the right-field stands for the win. The walkoff four-run homer was the first of its kind with a team trailing by exactly three runs with two outs in the bottom of the ninth since Brian Giles victimized Billy Wagner of the Astros on July 28, 2001, at PNC Park.

JUNE 20, 2009: CIVIL RIGHTS GAME COMES TO THE QUEEN CITY

After two years in Memphis, Major League Baseball moved the Civil Rights Game to Cincinnati, and the Chicago White Sox slugged their way to a 10–8 win, as both teams sported their jerseys from the 1965 season. Trailing 5–0 heading into the fourth, the White Sox turned their offense into home run derby mode, beginning with a three-run shot off the bat of Gordon Beckham that closed the gap to 5–3. Two more long balls in the fifth, solo shots by Scott Podsednik and A. J. Pierzynski, knotted the contest at five. Alexei Ramirez ended the home run binge when he took Reds reliever Nick Masset deep for a three-run bomb, giving Chicago their first lead of the afternoon at 8–5.

Back-to-back singles by Wilkin Castillo and Ramon Hernandez in the bottom of the seventh brought the Reds to within one at 8–7, but the White Sox responded with a two-run eighth, thanks to an RBI single by Podsednik and RBI double from Ramirez. Jay Bruce hit a solo home run in the bottom of the ninth, but it wasn't enough as the White Sox walked away from this Interleague contest with a signature win.

SEPTEMBER 28, 2010: DRAMATIC BLAST CLINCHES DIVISION

With one powerful swing of the bat, Reds slugger Jay Bruce slammed the door emphatically on 15 years of frustration, and helped send Cincinnati back to the postseason with a dramatic 3–2 win over Houston. With the opportunity to clinch the National League Central, the Reds got off to a quick start in the bottom of the first, courtesy of Scott Rolen, whose infield single allowed Bruce to scamper home for the first run of the game. Not to be outdone, the Astros put a two-spot on the board when catcher Jason Castro registered an RBI single, and a bunt groundout by pitcher Wandy Rodriguez gave Houston a 2–1 lead.

Interestingly enough for the Reds, it was another infield single, this time by Brandon Phillips, that pushed across the tying run in the sixth in the form of Orlando Cabrera, helping set the scene for the division-clinching victory. After a 1–2–3 ninth by Reds flame-thrower Aroldis Chapman, Bruce crushed the first pitch he saw, leading off the bottom half to become the fifth player—and first since Steve Finley did so for the Dodgers in 2004—to blast a walk-off home run during the regular season to clinch a division title and postseason appearance.

OCTOBER 10, 2010: FIRST POSTSEASON ACTION AT GREAT AMERICAN

The magic that enabled the Reds to clinch their first trip to the playoffs in 15 years ended early, as the Phillies made quick work of Cincinnati with a 2–0 series-clinching win. In Game 1, it was Roy Halladay who stole the show and joined Yankees great Don Larsen by becoming the second player in baseball history to toss a no-hitter in the postseason. This time, Cole Hammels mastered the Reds offense, firing a complete game, a five-hitter complemented by nine strikeouts.

Singles by Placido Polanco and Ryan Howard put Philadelphia runners aboard quickly in the first, and set the stage for Jayson Werth. He promptly reached on a throwing error by Reds second baseman Orlando Cabrera, allowing Polanco to score and giving the Phillies a 1–0 lead. That's all they would need, but just in case, Chase Utley added a little insurance by clocking a solo home run off Reds starter Johnny Cueto in the fifth for a 2–0 advantage and eventual victory. With two outs in the seventh, Reds catcher Ramon Hernandez doubled, but Jay Bruce, representing the tying run, lined out to end the scoring threat.

OCTOBER 11, 2012: GIANTS COMPLETE STUNNING COMEBACK

San Francisco catcher Buster Posey hit a grand slam as part of a six-run fifth, and the Giants became the first National League team in Division Series play to win a series after trailing two games to none after a 6–4 victory over the Reds. For Cincinnati, opportunity knocked in the form of having the tying run at the plate from the sixth inning on but was unable to capitalize in front of the hometown faithful. San Francisco, who lost the first two games of the series at home, was aided by outstanding defensive plays the entire game, including a diving catch in the eighth inning by Giants center fielder

Angel Pagan that snuffed out a potential rally. The Reds made it interesting after an RBI single by Ryan Ludwick in the bottom of the ninth, but Scott Rolen, representing the winning run, struck out with two on to end the season for the National League Central Division champions.

JULY 2, 2013: BAILEY CASHES IN ON SECOND CAREER NO-HITTER

After tossing a no-hitter on September 28, 2012, at PNC Park in Pittsburgh, Cincinnati starter Homer Bailey was at it again, this time shutting down the San Francisco Giants, 3–0. Allowing only one base runner the entire night, Bailey was perfect until Gregor Blanco coaxed a leadoff walk in the seventh inning. The Reds offense did their part, powered by a solo home run off the bat of Shin-Soo Choo in the bottom of the first and a two-run shot by Brandon Phillips in the sixth. The only scare of losing the no-no came in the top of the seventh, after Buster Posey hit a broken-bat blooper toward first baseman Joey Votto. With no one covering first, Votto instinctively whipped the ball over to third for the force-out of Blanco, keeping the no-hitter intact. Bailey joined Nolan Ryan (1974 and 1975) as the last pitcher to throw baseball's two most recent no-hitters.

WHAT THEY'RE SAYING ABOUT GREAT AMERICAN BALL PARK

MARTY BRENNAMAN, BROAD-CASTER: "It is light years better than [Riverfront Stadium], and it does not get any better when you compare those two ballparks, . . . but the ballpark we are in now has big shoes to fill because Riverfront [Stadium] was the home to this team in its greatest period of prosperity."

THOM BRENNAMAN: "I love it. It has changed dramatically ever since they opened it in 2004. . . . The new ownership has poured a ton of money into it; it is a great place to come watch a ballgame at—I love it."

JAY BRUCE: "I think it is a beautiful place . . . the grounds crew does a great job and I think that has a lot to do with how you feel about a ballpark. It is comfortable as far as the dimensions go, and there are not a lot of quirks in the ballpark."

ADAM DUNN: "[Great American Ball Park] is one of the better hitting ballparks. . . . Not only does the ball carry really well, but you [can] really see the ball well there."

DICK ENBERG, BROADCASTER: "I think it has interesting dimensions and the right field with the water beyond. . . . It is such a hitter's ballpark and everyone loves to go there and play. I do not think it stands out with some of the others, but it certainly is a considerable giant step ahead of the old cookie-cutter ballparks."

RYAN LUDWICK: "More of a hitter's ballpark. Once again [it is] a ballpark that is right downtown and on the river. . . . They have done a good job keeping it clean and [it has] a lot of baseball history there."

ANDREW MCCUTCHEN: "It is all right—definitely another hitter's ballpark . . . that is definitely one you love to hit at."

BRANDON PHILLIPS: "It is a great ballpark, it is real nice, and they have got a lot going on there. . . . It is a lot of history with the Reds Museum there, and it is just a beautiful atmosphere."

DREW STUBBS: "Nice place to play, especially as a hitter, because the ball flies pretty well and it is one of the better offensive ballparks in the league. . . . As player[s], we have a good setup in the clubhouse and so forth."

JOEY VOTTO: "When it is a place you play at on a consistent basis, you know all the little ins and outs, but you always fall back on it as the place that is close to your heart. . . . There are some emotional ties to it—my first home run there [at Great American Ball Park], my first at-bat there, so it means a lot to me more than just the ballpark itself."

GREAT AMERICAN BALL PARK FACTS AND FIGURES

GREAT AMERICAN BALL PARK ADDRESS
100 Main Street, Cincinnati, OH 45202

CINCINNATI REDS TEAM WEB SITE
www.reds.com

FIELD DIMENSIONS (IN FEET)
Left Field: 328', Left-Center: 379', Center: 404', Right-Center: 370', Right Field: 325'

SEATING CAPACITY (AS OF 2015)
42,319

ALL-STAR GAMES AT GREAT AMERICAN BALL PARK

None

GREAT AMERICAN BALL PARK FIRSTS

Game: March 31, 2003—Pittsburgh 10, Cincinnati 1
Single: Pokey Reese, Pittsburgh (March 31, 2003)
Double: Ken Griffey Jr., Cincinnati (March 31, 2003)*
Triple: Rob Mackowiak, Pittsburgh (April 3, 2003)
Home Run: Reggie Sanders, Pittsburgh (March 31, 2003)

Denotes first hit in the stadium.

KAUFFMAN STADIUM
HOME OF THE KANSAS CITY ROYALS

Kauffman Stadium, Kansas City Royals (Photographed by Mark Whitt/Flickr)

[*Kauffman Stadium was previously known as Royals Stadium (1973–93).*]

If there ever were a ballpark in Major League Baseball that could be considered the best-kept secret, it would be Kauffman Stadium. Built during the cookie-cutter era in the 1970s, Kauffman Stadium has successfully withstood the test of time, while undergoing facelifts over the years to keep up with the newer and brasher stadiums. An exception rather than the rule, it's simply known as a stunning structure with a peaceful landscape and long tradition.

Even when it opened for the first time to fans on April 10, 1973, it was recognized throughout all of baseball as being one of the most beautiful ballparks. And while it was built in the same era as Three Rivers Stadium, Veterans Stadium, and others with a cereal bowl–like appearance, one characteristic separated it from the rest of the pack: it had an open outfield.

It was considered a shot in the dark at the time to build a baseball-only stadium, but the Royals decided to go out on a limb and test the waters. Cedric Tallis, who was the general manager at the time, was knowledgeable about stadiums and worked closely with builder HOK Sport to design a structure that took the best of Dodger Stadium, Anaheim Stadium (now known as Angel Stadium), and their own ideas to successfully create a ballpark that would be admired for years to come.

The project was completed in 1973 in conjunction with Arrowhead Stadium (home of the NFL's Chiefs) as part of the Harry S. Truman Sports Complex. The two stadiums share the same parking lots and access routes, but there aren't any traffic headaches because the Royals and Chiefs don't play at the same time. If there's one factor that makes Kauffman Stadium that much more attractive to fans, it would have to be the straightforward access to highways I-70 and I-435, which provides a quick getaway in case of a sellout crowd. Parking is plentiful—just make sure you remember where you parked!

After turning 40 years old in 2013, the beauty and mystique remain. Although four decades have passed quickly, through upgrades and renovations, Kauffman Stadium has remained one of the most attractive ballparks in all of Major League Baseball.

SPECIAL FEATURES OF KAUFFMAN STADIUM

.390 BAR AND GRILL

Previously known as the Stadium Club, the .390 Bar and Grill is named after George Brett's remarkable 1980 season in which he batted .390, the highest tally since Ted Williams hit .401 during the 1941 campaign. Located on the loge level, the .390 Bar and Grill's extensive menu features soup, salad, and sandwiches, plus a wide selection of beverages available at the full-service bar. With 65-inch televisions scattered throughout and windows that overlook the game, this is one place that's sure to impress!

BLUE "HUSSEY LEGEND" SEATS

When Kauffman Stadium debuted in 1973, orange seats were a common sight in the seating bowl area, which made the stadium sparkle and stand out. After a while, it was concluded that not only did that particular shade make it tough on the eyes, but it also made it easier to spot all the vacant seats during games in which tickets did not sell as well as the front office would have liked.

The seats were eventually phased out, and in 2000 blue Hussey Legend chairs replaced them. The darker color scheme provided a more sophisticated look and softened the overall interior look of the ballpark.

BUCK O'NEIL LEGACY SEAT

In 2007, Kansas City Royals management placed a single red seat at section 127, row C, seat 9 to honor legendary Kansas City baseball player, Buck O'Neil, who once occupied that chair on a daily basis. The former first baseman and manager for the Kansas City Monarchs of the Negro Leagues from 1938 to 1955 was awarded the prestigious Presidential Medal of Honor by George W. Bush in 2006 and had a lifetime achievement award in his name created by Major League Baseball in 2007. During each game, the Royals select a fan who best exemplifies what O'Neil stood for to occupy the seat for the game.

CAROUSEL

The Kansas City Royals have taken a page out of Comerica Park's book and have their own carousel positioned behind the Royals Hall of Fame, part of the section known as the "Little K." All of the carousel animals were meticulously hand-carved and appropriately dressed in Royals gear. It is one of the more popular destinations at Kauffman Stadium for youngsters.

CHAMPIONSHIP FLAGS

While the Royals Hall of Fame dominates the left-field portion of the ballpark, flags fly proudly atop the structure commemorating league and World Series championships that Kansas City has won. Three flags fly high in the Kansas City wind and commemorate the American League titles won in 1980 and 1985, as well as the only championship to date in franchise victory, a memorable seven-game series win over the crosstown St. Louis Cardinals in 1985.

CROWN CLUB

The Crown Club, added as part of the Vision 2000 renovations, is available exclusively to Crown Seat ticket holders, who can relax in the comfort of the air conditioning, order a drink at the bar, or have a seat at one of the private tables. A complimentary pregame buffet is available, but there is a menu just in case you're seeking a specialty item. Whatever you choose, you'll truly feel like royalty in this place!

CROWNVISION

As part of their continuing improvements to help make Kauffman Stadium a great place for baseball for years to come, the Royals completely restructured the center-field scoreboard as part of a $250 million renovation completed just in time for Opening Day 2008. It is now the largest high-definition scoreboard in the Majors. Measuring 84 feet by 104 feet, CrownVision is visually pleasing from any seat in the house and produces crystal-clear video. An interactive crown sits proudly on top, rising 40 feet above the scoreboard. Lights illuminate the display.

EWING AND MURIEL KAUFFMAN STATUE
In a ceremony held on June 25, 1999, the team unveiled a statue of Ewing and Muriel Kauffman at the northwest corner of the stadium by Gate A. Created by Tom Corbin, a local artist and sculptor, the sculpture depicts the couple holding hands, as if they were taking a relaxing walk around the concourse of Kauffman Stadium.

EWING M. KAUFFMAN
Ewing Kauffman, an ambassador of Royals baseball in Kansas City, helped lay the groundwork for the Kansas City franchise in 1968 after he purchased the team. Kauffman founded Marion Laboratories in his mother's basement and built it into a billion-dollar industry. Over the years, he was the recipient of many awards for his leadership, and was inducted into the Missouri Sports Hall of Fame. Royals Stadium was formally renamed Ewing M. Kauffman Stadium during a ceremony on July 2, 1993. Sadly, he passed away on August 1, 1993, nearly a month after the dedication ceremony.

FOUNTAIN SEATS
Spanning 421 seats in sections 201–3 is a ticketed area known as the fountain seats. While the action is quite far from that particular location, it does provide an incredible close-up view of the gorgeous waterfalls. These tickets are considered a great bargain in a Major League game and allow the ticket holder relatively easy access to the outfield concession areas and bars throughout the concourse.

GEORGE BRETT LOUNGE
Named for arguably the franchise's greatest player of all time, the George Brett Lounge, which can accommodate between 20 and 80 people, can be accessed from Gate C and has many luxurious amenities. The price of a ticket includes both a buffet and draft beer. Whether you sit inside at one of the oval tables or outside to be closer to the action, the George Brett Lounge will make your visit to the ballpark a memorable one.

GEORGE BRETT STATUE
The famous batting stance that earned George Brett over 3,000 career hits is immortalized outside Kauffman Stadium and pays tribute to a man who prided himself on hard work and dedication. The important contributions

Brett made throughout his career toward finding a cure for ALS are engraved on his statue. In 21 seasons with Kansas City, Brett accumulated a lifetime batting average of .305 to go along with 3,154 hits, 665 doubles, 317 home runs, and 1,596 runs batted in.

INTERSTATE 70
Pick any seat behind the plate or upper deck and not only will you have a great view of the action, but also a peek at Interstate 70, which runs just behind the outfield wall. I-70, one of the busier highways in America, is truly the gateway to the Gateway City, and a little over three hours' drive on it would take you to St. Louis, where that *other* Missouri team calls Busch Stadium their home. In case you were wondering, a batted ball would have to travel 1,119 feet in order to land on the highway (distance courtesy of Google Earth).

JOE MCGUFF PRESS BOX
The press box was dedicated to Joe McGuff on April 21, 2006. He played an instrumental part in Kansas City, receiving a Major League franchise after the Athletics bolted for Oakland, and was an active board member with the Royals. McGuff, a longtime civic leader, was named Missouri's most outstanding writer five times by the National Association of Sportswriters. In 1948, he began his employment with the *Kansas City Star* and later became the sports editor in 1966, eventually becoming editor of the *Star* 20 years later in 1986. McGuff was elected to the sportswriter's wing of the National Baseball Hall of Fame in 1985, the same year he had the honor of throwing out the first pitch during Game 7 of the World Series.

RENOVATIONS IN 2009
At a cost of $250 million, Royals management completely overhauled Kauffman Stadium and made it one of the most striking facilities in all of baseball. Capacity was reduced from 40,775 to 38,177, extra suites were added, concourses were expanded (now 37 feet compared to 24 feet previously), and both the crown and stadium clubs were completely revamped. In addition, two new eateries—the Diamond Club and a new sports bar in right field, just beyond the outfield fountains—were also installed. The Royals marked the occasion by dedicating the "new" Kauffman Stadium before their home opener versus New York on April 10, 2009, a game they lost, 4–1.

RETIRED NUMBERS
The Kansas City Royals have retired three numbers. The four-foot-high bronze numbers are displayed just below the message board in center field. They include: George Brett (5), Dick Howser (10), and Frank White (20).

For a more detailed look at the retired Royals numbers, pick up a copy of the first edition of *The Baseball Stadium Insider: A Comprehensive Dissection of All Thirty Ballparks, the Legendary Players, and the Memorable Moments,* published in 2012.

RIGHT-FIELD SPORTS BAR

A sports bar, added in 2009, is just behind the majestic waterfalls in right field and offers an exceptional setting to kick back and unwind. It offers unmatched views of the game through floor-to-ceiling windows and a 360-degree bar and lounge features retractable doors that are open during warm days. The Royals incorporated a 103-inch television into the mix that is hard to miss.

ROYALS ALL-STAR BARBEQUE

The Royals All-Star Barbeque, created in 2009, is located in right-center field and features Kansas City rib-eye sandwiches; a one-of-a-kind hot dog loaded with pulled pork, coleslaw, pickle slices, and barbecue sauce; and burnt ends, a fan favorite consisting of slices of smoked brisket.

ROYALS HALL OF FAME

The 7,000-square-foot Royals Hall of Fame, located at Gate A on the west side of the ballpark, is in left field and debuted in 2009. This museum provides a comprehensive and educational experience for those who want to know more about Kansas City's roots in professional baseball. Artifacts, pictures, and other memorabilia of the team are showcased. Some of the displays include:

- Cooperstown Corner, with items on loan from the National Baseball Hall of Fame;
- Clubhouse Lobby, a two-story setup that shows the greatest moments in Kansas City history;
- Dugout Theater, which gives fans the chance to view movies on a 36-foot-wide by 9-foot-tall screen while sitting in a re-creation of the Royals dugout;
- Royals Way, which highlights the success of founder Ewing Kauffman;
- Taking the Field, a look back at the previous ballparks that Kansas City once called home; and
- Crowning Moments, a recap of the Royals' greatest years, complete with a display of the division and American League pennants and the 1985 World Series trophy.

The Hall of Fame Gallery pays homage to all the elite members elected to the Kansas City Royals team Hall of Fame. There is also a tribute to two

The Royals Hall of Fame, located in left field, debuted in 2009 and provides a link to Kansas City's rich tradition. (*Photographed by Kansas City Royals*)

of the Royals' greatest players ever, George Brett and Frank White, which looks back at their playing days and relives their best moments in a Kansas City uniform. The Royals Hall of Fame is also open on non-game days and can be accessed through gates 2 or 6 of the Truman Sports Complex.

SOLAR PANELS

The Royals incorporated solar panels in 2012 in an effort to do their part by becoming more environmentally friendly. As part of the outfield canopy, 120 solar panels provide roughly 36,000 kilowatt hours of renewable energy each year and have the distinct achievement—as of this writing and according to the Royals Media Guide—for being the largest in-stadium solar array in all of the Major League.

THE LITTLE K

Complete with authentic field turf to give it an official feeling, the Little K gives kids plenty of options to let loose and have a ball. From batting and pitching cages, a five-hole baseball-themed mini-golf course, and a kid-friendly lounge featuring baseball video games, it's a good bet that come game time, kids will not want to vacate the premises. The carousel is also located in this vicinity, and is sure to provide great thrills for the little ones.

VISION 2000: A LOOK BACK

The Royals looked to the future in 1999 with a project dubbed Vision 2000, which was an undertaking that saw the birth of Crown Seats, Dugout Suites, and an exclusive restaurant and lounge known as the Crown Club. State-of-the-art facilities and clubhouses were also built to modernize the structure and maintain its appeal for years to come. There's no question that management's commitment to excellence has paved the way for future generations to enjoy their time at Kauffman Stadium and for further expansions in the future to ensure the ballpark remains beautiful.

WATER FOUNTAINS

The majestic waterfalls in the outfield serve as a serene background while offering a sense of comfort and amusement. The aqua officially measures 322 feet wide and spans almost the entire outfield. A 10-foot-high waterfall flows from an upper pond to two lower sections, providing water for the fountains. Between innings, this renowned display, with pine trees behind it, brings the Kansas City skyline to life. It is the largest privately funded fountain in the world—Ewing Kauffman spent $1.5 million to build the structure.

MEMORABLE GAMES AT KAUFFMAN STADIUM

APRIL 10, 1973: FIRST GAME AT KAUFFMAN STADIUM

Despite temperatures hovering in the upper eighties, the Royals were hot at the plate and debuted Kauffman Stadium with a bang by thrashing the Texas Rangers, 12–1. Led by first baseman John Mayberry, who batted 2-for-3 with four runs scored and four runs batted in, the Royals started off quickly by tallying four runs in the first and never looked back. Kansas City led 8–0 after four behind back-to-back doubles by Freddie Patek and Cookie Rojas, along with RBI singles from Hal McRae and Lou Pinella to highlight the inning. It was 12–0 after eight innings of play when Texas tallied their only run, a solo home run by Jeff Burroughs off Kansas City starter Paul Splittorff, who ended up pitching a complete game five-hitter.

MAY 15, 1973: NOLAN RYAN TOSSES FIRST NO-HITTER OF HIS CAREER

Although only 12,205 were in attendance at Kauffman Stadium (and I'm sure many more will claim they were there), they were about to be treated to what would become a normal occurrence for Nolan Ryan throughout the course of his career. Ryan pitched the first no-hitter in the Angels' history—and the first at one-month-old Kauffman Stadium—defeating overmatched Kansas City, 3–0. In cutting down the Royals, Ryan was so dominant that between the left fielder, third baseman, and shortstop, only two baseballs were hit in their direction. It also helped that the Angels sprinted out to an early 2–0 lead after one inning on back-to-back RBI singles by Bob Oliver and Al Gallagher. Oliver later added a home run in the top of the sixth inning to finish the scoring output for California. The final out was a hard-hit fly ball to the right-field warning track by Royals outfielder Amos Otis, fielded cleanly by Ken Berry to seal the first of seven career no-hitters for Ryan, who struck out 12 and walked three.

OCTOBER 17, 1980: FIRST WORLD SERIES AT KAUFFMAN STADIUM

Seven years after it opened, Kauffman Stadium had the honor of hosting Game 3 of the 1980 Fall Classic between the Royals and National League champion, Philadelphia Phillies. Fans were just settling into their seats when George Brett got things going in the bottom of the first with a home run into right field, giving the capacity crowd something to cheer about. In the seventh, a solo home run by Amos Otis gave the Royals a 3–2 advantage, but not to be outdone, Hall of Famer Mike Schmidt tied the contest at three with a blast of his own in the eighth, ultimately sending it into extra innings. In the tenth, Willie Aikens sent the faithful home happy with a walk-off, RBI double into the left-center field gap that scored Willie Wilson and gave the Royals a triumphant 4–3 victory.

OCTOBER 27, 1985: ROYALS CAPTURE THE CROWN

Things looked bleak for Kansas City in the World Series after they had fallen behind three games to one against crosstown rival St. Louis in what was dubbed the I-70 Showdown Series. However, the Royals stuck together and pulled off one of the more remarkable comebacks in series history, defeating the pesky Cardinals, four games to three and 11–0 in a winner-take-all Game 7. In the deciding game, Bret Saberhagen proved his worth by going the distance and tossing a five-hit shutout, while the offense started early and never let up. Darryl Motley connected for a two-run blast off St. Louis starter John Tudor in the second, giving the Royals a 2–0 lead, a bases-loaded walk to Jim Sundberg, and a two-run single by Steve Balboni in the third increased the advantage to 5–0. With Saberhagen cruising, the Royals added six more runs in the form of extra insurance in the fifth inning off five Cardinals pitchers, and the rout was on as Kansas City collected the trophy and set off a wild celebration at Kauffman Stadium.

APRIL 4, 1988: TORONTO DH BELL HITS THREE HOME RUNS

On opening day, it is the goal of many players to try and jump off to a good start in the hope that it will continue for an entire season. For George Bell, not only did he start the season off on a good note, but he ended up setting a Major League record by becoming the first to collect three home runs in the first game of the year as part of a 5–3 Blue Jays win. Bell victimized Bret Saberhagen three times: in the second inning with a solo shot to left, in the fourth inning with a two-run blast to left center, and in the eighth with another solo shot to left. In his only other at-bat in the sixth, Bell made his only out of the game when he hit a fly ball out to left field. For those wondering, he finished the season with 24 home runs.

AUGUST 26, 1991: SABERHAGEN NO-HITS WHITE SOX

Six years removed from his dramatic Game 7 pitching performance during the 1985 World Series, Bret Saberhagen added another accomplishment to his résumé defeating the Chicago White Sox 7–0 and pitching a no-hitter in front of 25,164 fans at Kauffman Stadium. Saberhagen started off on a high note by retiring the first seven White Sox batters in succession before allowing a one-out walk to Ron Karkovice, who ended up being stranded at second base. Moving forward, he settled down, breezing all the way to the ninth inning, where it was a 1–2–3 frame that saw Tim Raines ground out, Joey Cora fly out to right, and slugger extraordinaire Frank Thomas harmlessly ground out to second. Meanwhile, the Royals offense was humming, led by a 3-for-4 effort from Kirk Gibson and three runs batted in from Todd Benzinger.

JUNE 16, 1996: RIPKEN JR. BREAKS WORLD RECORD

With the Major League record in the books for consecutive games played, Cal Ripken Jr. topped the World Record of 2,216 games in a row set by Japan's Sachio Kinugasa as the Orioles defeated Kansas City, 6–1. Ripken Jr., who was given a standing ovation when the game became official at the start of the sixth inning, went 0-for-4, striking out once and grounding into a double play in the seventh. Baltimore starter Mike Mussina pitched a complete game, seven-hitter—the only hiccup coming in the second, when he allowed a solo home run—and settled down to retire the final 13 Royals in a row to end the contest.

SEPTEMBER 16, 1996: MOLITOR MAKES HISTORY TWICE IN ONE AT-BAT

Minnesota's Paul Molitor became the first player to triple for a 3,000th hit, but the Kansas City Royals spoiled the momentous occasion by winning the game, 6–5. Molitor singled in the first inning for career hit number 2,999, and with one out in the fifth, hit an opposite-field fly ball to the alley off the Royals pitcher Jose Rosado. Center fielder Rod Myers and right fielder Jon Nunally both initially tried to run it down, but slowed as they got closer to each other. As a result, the ball dropped behind them and allowed Molitor to hit the afterburners and head for the hot corner. The Kansas City crowd showed their respect by giving him a standing ovation just as his Minnesota teammates came rushing out of the dugout to greet baseball's newest member of the 3,000th-hit club. The Royals offense was paced by Jose Offerman, who finished the game 2-for-4 with a double and Keith Lockhart, who connected for a two-run home run in the bottom of the sixth.

OCTOBER 3, 2012: CABRERA WRAPS UP TRIPLE CROWN

Tigers slugger Miguel Cabrera became the first American League triple-crown winner since Boston's Carl Yastrzemski in 1967, and Detroit wrapped up the Central Division championship with a 1–0 win over Kansas City. Although Cabrera went 0-for-2 in the game—a fly out in the first and strike out in the fourth—he exited the game in the fourth to a standing ovation from the Kauffman Stadium faithful. One of just 12 in modern major league history to accomplish the feat, Cabrera finished with 44 home runs, 139 RBI, and a .330 batting average. Detroit's lone run came courtesy of Austin Jackson, who doubled home Omar Infante in the fifth inning.

OCTOBER 15, 2014: ROYALS STORM BACK TO WORLD SERIES

Emphatic. That is the only way to describe the Kansas City Royals' return to the World Series after a 29-year absence as they swept the Baltimore Orioles with a 2–1 victory, raising their 2014 postseason record to an incredible 8–0. After many finishes under .500, this year's edition scratched and clawed their way to the playoffs thanks to unmatched defense, a shutdown bullpen, and clutch hitting. This fall classic-clinching game was no different as Kansas City accumulated the only runs they would require in the first, thanks to a missed catch by Baltimore catcher Caleb Joseph that enabled a 2–0 Kansas City lead. A home run by Ryan Flaherty in the third brought Baltimore to within one, but it was lights out after that, and a dream season continued for the upstart Royals.

OCTOBER 29, 2014: GIANTS RECLAIM WORLD CHAMPIONSHIP

Behind the incredible pitching performance of Series MVP Madison Bumgarner, the San Francisco Giants captured their third World Series championship in five years with a 3–2 victory over the Kansas City Royals and became the first team since the 1979 Pittsburgh Pirates to win Game 7 on the road. San Francisco took an early second inning 2–0 lead, but Kansas City struck right back with two in the bottom half, tying the contest. In the bottom of the fifth, the nearly unhittable Bumgarner entered on two days rest for a relief stint, one that would last five innings and go down as the longest in World Series history. What would turn out to be the winning run was produced by Michael Morse, who, in the top of the fourth, singled home Pablo Sandoval for a 3–2 lead and eventual final margin of victory. Bumgarner, who allowed a single to Omar Infante in the fifth, retired the final 14 batters in a row and for the series hurled

21 innings and allowed just one run while accumulating an ERA of 0.43, the lowest since Hall of Famer Sandy Koufax's 0.38 ERA in the 1965 World Series.

WHAT THEY'RE SAYING ABOUT KAUFFMAN STADIUM

GEORGE BRETT: "I loved it then and I love it even more now because we do not have the Astroturf that I played on for 21 years there. . . . It was the biggest ballpark in the American League, it was a fast ballpark, and our team was built for speed and that is why I think we were so successful there."

MARK BUEHRLE: "To me, [it is] probably one of the most underrated stadiums, especially once they redid it. . . . I am a little biased because Missouri is my hometown, so I am a little more favorable of Missouri stuff. I love where the ballpark is at—it is not in the middle of downtown—and there are no big buildings around like a downtown."

JOHNNY DAMON: "It was built way before its time. . . . It is my favorite stadium and it still was even before they did all the new renovations. They did a great job from the start and that is why it is still my favorite."

RON GARDENHIRE: "[It's] probably my favorite of all of them other than Target Field. . . . They make improvements every year and it just keeps getting nicer and nicer. [I love] the fountains—of course they are spectacular—I never tired [of] looking at those."

KEN "HAWK" HARRELSON, BROAD-CASTER: "That was a masterpiece... . The construction company that built it did an unbelievable job, but the new changes they have made as far as the broadcast facilities are overpar."

REX HUDLER: "[Kauffman Stadium] is a beautiful venue . . . and unlike any other ballpark in the world, they have fountains and during batting practice or the game, you hear that soothing sound of water and you almost think you are at Yosemite National Park. It is unique and one of the most beautiful ballparks there is."

TORII HUNTER: "The Royals Stadium is always beautiful. . . . They redid it and it looks nice. They have got the fans out there in the outfield now—they did not have that back in the day. It just keeps looking better and better every year, and that is one stadium that people love to play in."

PAUL KONERKO: "I think Kansas City is one of the most underrated in all of the big leagues—most people do not even think of that one. It was nice before they made the changes to it and it is even nicer now, . . . but I think that is one that has kind of gone under the radar as it is just a beautiful stadium to watch a game at."

A. J. PIERZYNSKI: "It is one of the best for being as old as it is. All the improvements they have made, continually updating, continually trying to make it better, they have done a great job there with the fountains and now they have the sports bars in the outfield. . . . It is one of the best older ballparks out there."

JUSTIN VERLANDER: "That has come a long, long way. . . . I had my first opening day there and was just in awe of everything and then they started doing all the renovations. Every time we go there, I make it a point to tell somebody that they have done a fantastic job with that ballpark."

KAUFFMAN STADIUM FACTS AND FIGURES

KAUFFMAN STADIUM ADDRESS
One Royal Way, Kansas City, MO 64129

KANSAS CITY ROYALS WEB SITE
www.royals.com

FIELD DIMENSIONS (IN FEET)
Left Field: 330', Left-Center: 387', Center: 410',
Right-Center: 387', Right Field: 330'

SEATING CAPACITY (AS OF 2015)
37,903

ALL-STAR GAMES AT KAUFFMAN STADIUM
July 24, 1973: National League 7, American League 1
MVP: Bobby Bonds, San Francisco Giants (NL)
July 10, 2012: National League 8, American League 0
MVP: Melky Cabrera, San Francisco Giants (NL)

KAUFFMAN STADIUM FIRSTS
Game: April 10, 1973—Kansas City 12, Texas 1
Single: Amos Otis, Kansas City (April 10, 1973)*
Double: Amos Otis, Kansas City (April 10, 1973)
Triple: Jeff Burroughs, Texas (April 10, 1973)
Home Run: John Mayberry, Kansas City (April 10, 1973)

Denotes first hit in the stadium.

MARLINS PARK
HOME OF THE MIAMI MARLINS

Marlins Park, Miami Marlins (Photographed by Russel Tiffin/Flickr)

When the Marlins organization embarked on building a new stadium, they had two goals in mind: to move out of cavernous, multipurpose Sun Life Stadium and play on a baseball-only field, and—perhaps the biggest factor—to help solidify the franchise and keep it a Major League Baseball team, ending any and all doubts about whether or not it could survive. Suffice it to say, Marlins Park accomplished both of those goals. The Marlins and their fans now have a state-of-the-art facility that is one of the finest in all of the big leagues. Both contemporary and bold in style, it truly captures what the spirit of Miami is all about.

On the heels of a World Series championship in 1997, and toward the end of the 1990s, then-owner John Henry announced his intention to build a baseball-only venue and subsequently, a couple of plans for prospective venues were created. The success of the 2003 team, combined with their World Series win over the mighty Yankees, led the management to hope that the quick success of the Marlins would help catapult them right into a brand-new ballpark of their own.

In late 2003, Miami-Dade County officials, in conjunction with team management, decided that a new ballpark would be a spectacular idea and announced they would help fund the new stadium. However, shortly after that announcement, the City of Miami reneged, and Marlins officials were left wondering what their next move should be in their quest for a ballpark.

In February 2005, Miami-Dade County officials made public a financial plan for a $420–$435 million ballpark, complete with parking deck, but in May 2005, that idea was nixed and a request for $450 million to help fund the stadium was rejected. The Marlins were getting frustrated, and once again, it was back to the drawing board for a team that desperately wanted to break out of the shadows of the NFL's Dolphins and Sun Life Stadium to pursue a life of their own.

The year 2005 became a breaking point for the team, and negotiations with the City of Miami officially went down the drain. The lack of success in seeking funding options caused key players to pack their bags and ditch their Marlins uniform. Although Marlins management remained committed to staying in Miami, they were still reviewing other avenues if all else failed.

As time went on, in 2006 management rejected an offer from San Antonio, Texas, officials, who hoped to lure the franchise to the Lone Star state. A light at the end of the tunnel began to appear when Florida's governor and mayor made an effort to revisit the project and, as a result, they got the ball rolling.

In December 2007 officials from the Miami-Dade County Commission voted in favor of two proposals that would help fund the ballpark project. After all was said and done, a grand total of $634 million was necessary to build shiny new Marlins Park. Miami-Dade County was responsible for $376.3 million; the City of Miami $132.5 million ($10 million of which was put toward demolition of the old Orange Bowl and $94 million to construct parking facilities); the Miami Marlins were held accountable for $125.2 million, but may spend up to $89.5 million of their contribution for fees for consultants, designers, attorneys, and the like.

Marlins Park, situated in Little Havana and west of downtown Miami, incorporates some of Sun Life Stadium's features, most notably the outfield dimensions in which the farthest part of the ballpark is 422 feet from home plate to straight-away center field. On the flip side, the easiest way to hit a home run is down the right-field line where batters can lick their chops at the distance of 335 feet. The Bermuda Triangle is replicated at Marlins Park, and the shallow left and right field at Sun Life Stadium have been reversed at Marlins Ballpark.

Groundbreaking took place in July 2009 on the 17 acres of the historic 42-acre Orange Bowl site. The 37,000-seat retractable-roof ballpark was set to open in 2012. Thanks to the persistence of city officials and team management, the Marlins accomplished their goal of creating a beautiful facility right in the heart of Miami, while at the same time cementing their place in the ranks of Major League Baseball as they continue their success.

SPECIAL FEATURES OF MARLINS PARK

AQUATIC BACKSTOPS

A first in Major League Baseball history are the aquariums, built on each side of home plate, with 100 fish in each. The tank on the right side measures 34 feet long, 36 inches high, and contains over 600 gallons of seawater; the left one is 24 feet wide and is filled with 450 gallons of seawater. A foul ball or errant pitch won't set the fish free, thanks to a bulletproof and virtually indestructible material installed in both the front and back of the aquariums.

BERMUDA TRIANGLE

Marlins Park recreated a feature from the Marlins' previous multipurpose ballpark. The Bermuda Triangle is an area in left-center field where the rounded section of the outfield wall meets the straight wall in center. This, in turn, creates a small alcove that can cause interesting bounces for an outfielder should a ball venture into this territory. This was a major feature at Sun Life Stadium, and often the unpredictable journey of the baseball turned doubles into triples.

BOBBLEHEAD MUSEUM

A bobblehead lover's dream, this museum, located on the Promenade Level near sections 14 and 15, features over 700 bobblehead dolls of current and former Marlins players, as well as baseball mascots and past and present players representing all 30 Major League teams. The oversized glass case is moved automatically just enough to allow for the head on each doll to shake.

CHAMPIONSHIP SUITES

The Championship Suites, which pay tribute to the World Series winning teams of 1997 and 2003, give fans the chance to enjoy a game with friends, family, or business associates. There is limited seating for 40 in the 2003 Championship Suite, which is positioned down the first-base line, while the 1997 version, located down the third-base line, seats 62.

CLIMATE CONTROL

When the Marlins moved from multipurpose Sun Life Stadium to Marlins Park in 2012, not only did they upgrade to a baseball-only facility, they also installed a retractable roof that allows games to continue regardless of the weather. The roof, combined with air conditioning, guarantees a comfortable temperature for each and every game.

COLORFUL TILES

Mimicking that of its Florida neighbor, Tropicana Field, the West Plaza features four acres of colorful paving patterns in the walkway approaching Marlins Ballpark. Created by Carlos Cruz-Diez, it is one of the largest displays of its kind in any stadium in United States history. Cruz-Diez captured the Floridian surroundings by creating a walkway based on color, line, and viewer perception, giving his artwork a true "wow" factor.

DIAMOND CLUB

Dubbed by the Marlins as the "most exclusive premium entertainment experience," the Diamond Club is on the field level, just 47 feet from home plate. Have a taste for a dessert? It's there, and can be ordered at any time. How about a sit-down meal while you take in the action? Sure, that's available, as well as all-inclusive high-end dining whenever you want it. With 379 seats, there's enough room for all of your friends and your friends' friends. If you stick around until after the game, complimentary beverages are available and include beer, wine, and nonalcoholic drinks.

DUGOUT CLUB

The Dugout Club, situated next to both the first- and third-base dugouts, puts fans close to the action while offering a diverse menu. The first-base Dugout Club seats 144, and the third-base option has room for 152. Fans who purchase seats in that area can reserve it on non-game days for birthday parties, wedding showers, or other events.

EXISTING BALLPARK FLAVOR

Borrowing from the pages of existing ballparks, a swimming pool in left field emulates that of the one in Chase Field, and a double-deck porch design in right field pays homage to the one that used to be a mainstay at Tiger Stadium. Also in left field, a glass wall like the one at Minute Maid Park in Houston slides and gives fans a firsthand glimpse of downtown Miami.

FANS' WALK OF FAME

Before the ballpark opened, fans were given the unique opportunity to be a part of the ballpark's history with the chance to purchase individual engraved pavers. These pavers make up the walkway near the entrance of the East Plaza and feature special messages from fans or other inscriptions.

FOUNDERS AND LEGENDS SUITE

Positioned directly behind home plate and featuring five-star eats and top-notch furnishings, the Founders and Legends Suite is among the finest in all of Major League Baseball. The 720-square-foot suite is complete with oversized and cushioned chairs for added comfort. Assorted artwork adds a special Marlins flavor, and 63-inch and 46-inch flat-screen televisions are available for your viewing pleasure.

GOING GREEN

Marlins Park, one of the most environmentally friendly ballparks in the big leagues, has a recycling program. More than 20 percent of the total material used to build the new stadium was from recycled materials, and the stadium also recycles asphalt, cardboard, concrete, and wood, among other materials.

HIGH-DEFINITION MAIN SCOREBOARD

The main scoreboard measures 51 feet tall by 101 feet wide and features 1,080 lines of resolution and 4.4 trillion shades of color, according to the Marlins Media Guide. This information center is in full high definition, providing comprehensive in-game information, along with crystal-clear video replays for all those close calls on the base paths and at home plate.

HOME RUN DISPLAY

The Marlins have their own display when the home team blasts a home run. Center field has a lively, 72-foot-high art piece, created by Red Grooms, and features moving parts in bright pink, blue, aqua, and orange pastels.

Following a home run, the animated structure rises from a pool of water. There are clouds, pelicans, seagulls, and aquatic life forms. Marlins jump out of the water while laser lights shine for 34 seconds. The piece chimed in at a cost of $2.5 million and was within the overall budget of the stadium.

HUGE WINDOWS

Six giant windows, stretching all the way from left to center field, measure 60 feet high by 40 feet wide and can be opened or closed in three to five

The lively and colorful home run display springs to life whenever a Marlins long ball is hit. (*Photographed by Russel Tiffin/Flickr*)

minutes to create a 240-degree sweeping panoramic view of downtown Miami. The windows can be opened even with the roof closed, allowing for increased comfort and a gentle breeze for fans.

HURRICANE-READY

Management designed the ballpark to withstand hurricane winds of up to 146 miles per hour. Strategically placed roof panels—two of which feature 10-foot gaps and the other 16 feet—avoid an imbalance of pressure inside and outside. In addition, 96 sets of tie-downs—of which 70 percent are automatically set—secure the roof, while workers manually set the others into place via turnbuckles. Minute Maid Park in Houston is also hurricane-ready, but can withstand winds of up to only 110 miles per hour.

ILLUMINATION

Four huge columns that support the retractable roof come to life at night when they are illuminated. Programmed LED lights fade up and down in different patterns to give the illusion that the columns are being concealed and revealed, providing a nice visual for fans as they enter or exit the ballpark.

MVP SUITE

At Marlins Park, they make a concerted effort to make the fans feel as though they are very valuable to the franchise. The MVP suite has 480 square feet of entertainment space and two flat-screen televisions, plus comfortable seats. With an incredible view of the action and access to a patio, the MVP suite truly makes the fan feel like a VIP.

ORANGE BOWL TRIBUTE

Many great college football games were played in the Miami Orange Bowl, and to commemorate that structure, a 10-foot marker that showcases letters from the original sign was placed in the East Plaza. As fans work their way around it, new words appear to create an ever-changing display. Speaking of legendary games, who could ever forget Boston College's Doug Flutie, who launched a Hail Mary pass in the closing seconds of their game against Miami on November 23, 1984, which was caught for a touchdown, giving the Eagles a stunning 47–45 victory?

PARKING GARAGE ARTWORK

The Marlins have used the artwork of Christian Moeller to spruce up the four main parking garages at Marlins Park, covering approximately 8,900 square feet of space. Moeller involved residents in taking photographs of children peering through a ballpark fence and then designed large-scale murals that now cover the sides of the garages facing the ballpark.

RETIRED NUMBERS

The franchise had initially retired the number 5 in 1993 to honor Carl Barger, the man responsible for overseeing the newly formed Marlins organization. On December 9, 1992, Barger collapsed at the winter meetings and later passed away. His favorite player was Joe DiMaggio—who wore the number 5—which is why that particular number was immortalized.

Just before the 2012 season began, the Marlins unretired the number for outfielder Logan Morrison, who wanted to wear this number to honor his father, whose favorite player was Royals Hall of Famer George Brett (who happened to also wear the number 5). Subsequently, Morrison was traded following the 2013 season to Seattle.

The franchise now honors Barger with a plaque inside Marlins Park.

ROOF

Marlins Park's roof is the sixth retractable roof introduced in the Major Leagues. Three panels that stretch over the playing field and span 547 feet from track to track consist of 8,300 tons of steel. The roof takes 13 minutes to fully close and open and the panels can be operated individually to create shading effects over the field of play.

STADIUM TURF

A high-performance Bermuda grass called "Celebration" was installed over the 110,000-square-foot space and is also used on the field at the Marlins Spring Training home in Jupiter, Florida. The shade-resistant turf was installed in February 2012, and the retractable roof remained open to allow it to grow and be ready by Opening Day.

THE CLEVELANDER

The Marlins incorporated a private seating and lounge area called The Clevelander, a nightclub that includes a four-foot-deep swimming pool behind the left-field wall. Enjoy a clear view of the action along with poolside service. A DJ presides over the action as fans grab a drink at the extensive bar, float around in the aqua, or watch relief pitchers warm up in the bullpen.

WEST PLAZA

The West Plaza, which is as long as three-and-a-half football fields and is the largest of any stadium in the United States, has food courts that offer a plethora of dining options and is open every day of the year. There is the possibility of expanding and adding a hotel, retail stores, and other fine eateries.

MEMORABLE GAMES AT MARLINS PARK

APRIL 4, 2012: FIRST GAME AT MARLINS BALLPARK

St. Louis pitcher Kyle Lohse took a no-hitter into the seventh, and 2011 World Series MVP David Freese provided the early offensive punch for the Cardinals, who spoiled the debut of Marlins Park with a 4–1 victory. With a capacity crowd in attendance, Lohse retired the first 10 batters in succession, keeping the Miami bats quiet all night before Jose Reyes singled in the seventh for the Marlins' first hit. Freese lined a two-run single in the first, and Rafael Furcal added an RBI single in the second to stake St. Louis to a 3–0 lead. Miami got on the board in the eighth, when John Buck doubled to deep right field, scoring Omar Infante. The early reviews were that Marlins Park favored pitchers, and Lohse proved that theory to be correct in cruising along through the first six frames.

OCTOBER 2, 2012: GREENBERG GIVEN A SECOND CHANCE

In his first Major League at-bat with the Cubs in 2005, Adam Greenberg was struck in the head with a pitch, resulting in his prompt exit from the game of baseball. As the years went on, Greenberg worked hard to have the opportunity for one more at-bat, and the Marlins gave him the chance he had been waiting for. Signed to a one-day contract, Greenberg strode to the plate in the sixth inning, striking out on three pitches courtesy of Mets pitcher and eventual National League Cy Young winner R. A. Dickey, but not without realizing the dream of having that elusive at-bat that had escaped him seven years before. The Marlins, perhaps inspired by the story of Greenberg, defeated the Mets after Donovan Solano singled in Jose Reyes in the bottom of the eleventh for a 4–3 victory.

MAY 18, 2013: FIRST PITCH HOMER MAKES HISTORY

As fans were settling into their seats at Marlins Park, Diamondbacks right fielder Gerardo Parra promptly deposited the first pitch of the game from Marlins pitcher Tom Koehler 387 feet over the right-field wall, giving Arizona an early 1–0 lead that would eventually hold up. The real story of the game would be the score, as the last time such an instance occurred where a leadoff home run accounted for the only runs of the game was on September 2, 1963, when Cincinnati rookie Pete Rose connected off Mets starter Jay Hook in the second game of a doubleheader at the Polo Grounds. Arizona starter Brandon McCarthy held the Marlins to three hits and received a major assist from—who else?—Parra, who cut down Derek Dietrich trying to score in the bottom of the first inning.

SEPTEMBER 29, 2013: A NO-HITTER TO FINISH THE SEASON

Marlins pitcher Henderson Alvarez sent the Marlins into the off-season on a high note, tossing a no-hitter against the Detroit Tigers during a wild 1–0 victory. Scoreless heading into the bottom of the ninth, Miami promptly loaded the bases with two outs for pinch hitter Greg Dobbs. Detroit reliever Luke Putkonen proceeded to uncork a wild pitch that allowed Giancarlo Stanton to score, securing the win and the no-hitter. Alvarez became the fourth pitcher since 1900 to throw a no-hitter on the final day of the season, joining California's Mike Witt, who threw a perfect game for California at Texas on September 30, 1984; Oakland's Vida Blue, Glenn Abbott, Paul

Lindblad, and Rollie Fingers, who threw a combined no-no at California on September 28, 1975; and Bumpus Jones of Cincinnati, who no-hit Pittsburgh all the way back on October 15, 1892.

WHAT THEY'RE SAYING ABOUT MARLINS PARK

HEATH BELL: "It is definitely Miami—it is very colorful and shiny, and I think it is great for the Marlins. . . . You have got everything from nightlife [The Clevelander] to the bobblehead museum, and all the different types of food, [and] I think center field has the coolest center-field seats because they are right over the field."

STEVE BERTHIAUME, BROADCASTER: "I think architecturally it is fantastic. I think color-scheme wise it is hideous, but it is okay because that is Miami and I think that was the intention because it screams Miami at you and gets in your face."

BOB BRENLY: "That is an interesting place. . . . There is a lot of eye candy there between The Clevelander out there in left-center field and the activities that go on there during a ballgame [and] the artwork out there in center field. Compared to where they used to play—the multi-named stadium—it is a gem."

KIRK GIBSON: "It is way better than the first ballpark. . . . It is big [and] it always rains in Miami, so having a roof is definitely a plus. It is probably a little bigger than most would like, but it is a big improvement."

JOSH LEWIN, BROADCASTER: "I know the traditionalists go wacko when they see the lime green, the sculpture, and the other nonsense, but it is bold. . . . To me, it is a 'W' hotel as opposed to a Hilton, [and] it is almost too 'hip for its own good' kind of vibe, but I think that is emblematic of Miami anyway."

JAMES LONEY: "It is a little different [and] obviously with the roof there, [there] are no rain delays. . . . It is a big ballpark too. [There is] a lot of room out there and [maybe they] will bring those fences in pretty soon."

STEVE LYONS, BROADCASTER: "It is somebody's bad dream [and] that color belongs in someone's kitchen—in fact, it is in my kitchen, which is kind of crazy. That is kind of a stupid color for a kitchen, but that is my color—[and] that is just too much of the lime green. And that monstrosity that is in left-center field that is their home run feature—it looks like a pinball machine."

GIANCARLO STANTON: "It is huge, but it has its perks and basically everybody is always in scoring position because [when] you hit a ball in the gap, they are scoring from first. . . . You have got to get all of it if you are going to hit a home run."

CHARLEY STEINER, BROADCASTER: "The lime-green background reminds me of Grandpa's pants at the early-bird special with the white patent-leather shoes. . . . I still have no idea what that stucture is supposed to be in left-center field and if somebody someday would be kind enough to explain the significance, I am all for it."

DAVID WRIGHT: "I would say that it is stimulating to the senses . . . the colors, the fish tank, but they did a great job with it and it is just a great place to play [at]."

MARLINS PARK FACTS AND FIGURES

MARLINS PARK ADDRESS
501 Marlins Way, Miami, FL 33125

MIAMI MARLINS TEAM WEB SITE
www.marlins.com

FIELD DIMENSIONS (IN FEET)
Left Field: 340', Left-Center: 384', Center: 422', Right-Center: 392', Right Field: 335'

SEATING CAPACITY (AS OF 2015)
36,742

ALL-STAR GAMES AT MARLINS PARK
None

MARLINS PARK FIRSTS
Game: April 4, 2012—St. Louis 4, Miami 1
Single: Carlos Beltran, St. Louis (April 4, 2012)*
Double: Lance Berkman, St. Louis (April 4, 2012)
Triple: Anibal Sanchez, Miami (April 15, 2012)
Home run: J. D. Martinez, Houston (April 13, 2012)

Denotes first hit in the stadium.

MINUTE MAID PARK

HOME OF THE HOUSTON ASTROS

Minute Maid Park, Houston Astros (*Photographed by Mark Whitt/Flickr*)

[*Minute Maid Park was previously known as the Ballpark at Union Station (2000), Enron Field (2000–02), and Astros Field (February–July 2002).*]

W hen Minute Maid Park burst onto the scene just in time for the 2000 season, there was no denying that it had some major shoes to fill. After all, trying to replace a stadium known as "The Eighth Wonder of the World" isn't exactly the easiest thing to do.

Like every situation with teams pleading for the funding necessary for a new ballpark, it appeared as though the Astros were on their way to greener pastures following the 1995 season due to the lack of support for their efforts to replace the Houston Astrodome. As time wore on, the discussions picked up steam and began to produce results, keeping the hope alive of not only keeping the team in Houston, but building a new facility to replace the indoor domed ballpark that had quickly become outdated.

Talks began in 1996, when ideas for a private-public ballpark were broached. In an effort to make the dream a reality, 14 leading Houston companies joined forces to form the Houston Sports Facility Partnership. Through this effort, the Partnership agreed to provide the Astros with a $35 million interest-free loan with no repayment due until 10 years after the ballpark's opening.

The initial partnership seemed to kick-start the entire project as the Harris County-Houston Sports Authority had the support it needed to make a formal ballpark presentation to the public. After successfully demonstrating why a new ballpark would help the city flourish, the public bought the plan and approved the project.

With a final price tag of a little under $250 million, Houston's new digs could be considered a bargain as it's relatively inexpensive for a retractable-roof ballpark as compared to Miller Park in Milwaukee ($352 million), Chase Field in Arizona ($342 million), and Safeco Field in Seattle ($474 million). The debut of the retractable-roof ballpark meant that for the first time in 35 seasons, when Colt Stadium housed the .45's, Houston fans could be exposed to the sun and sky.

Minute Maid Park was built just on the cusp of the downtown area on a 25-acre historic site incorporating the 1911 Union Station, which currently forms the ballpark's main entrance. This preexisting structure, located at the corner of Crawford Street and Texas Avenue, was once the cornerstone of Houston's railroad industry. The brick-and-limestone exterior, with arched windows, gives the ballpark a nostalgic air.

The railroad essentially created Houston and flourished with trading while establishing a base of wealth and culture. By 1910, the railroad was the city's largest industry and in 1911, Union Station was redesigned and reopened for business. The site was dedicated on March 2, 1911, and the station was built at a cost of $500,000—a lot of money during those times. It is estimated that between 7,000 and 10,000 Houston patrons passed through the front doors into the lobby, and by the mid-1940s, Union Station was handling close to 5,000 passengers on a daily basis.

Minute Maid Park earned three awards during its first year. For starters, the Greater Houston Preservation Alliance recognized "The Juice" with the 2000 Good Brick Award, which was presented to owner Drayton McLane, the Astros, and the Harris County-Houston Sports Authority for their renovation of the 1911 Union Station building. The Good Brick Award is given annually to recognize leadership and excellence in historic preservation. The Most Outstanding Civil Engineering Project Award came from the Texas section of the American Society of Civil Engineers and was given for the engineering of the structure and the great development of the building.

Finally, Minute Maid Park won the National Honor Award for Engineering

Excellence when it was named one of the Top 24 engineering projects among all buildings and civil work projects nationally. Like Marlins Park in Miami, Minute Maid Park was built to withstand hurricanes much better than a standard ballpark.

SPECIAL FEATURES OF MINUTE MAID PARK

422-FOOT MARKER

Perhaps in an effort to entice home run hitters to really power one out, a sign with the marking "422 ft" is positioned directly above the Crawford Boxes, just below a window. The significance? The window is part of the administrative office, which tempts players to take a crack at shattering one of the windowpanes.

ASTROS SUITES

Between the Club Level and Terrace Deck are the Astros suites, which offer a bar/buffet. Sliding glass doors open to two rows of outdoor seats. If you wish to entertain guests, private suites are available.

ASTROS WALK OF FAME

The Walk of Fame, unveiled during the 2012 season as part of the team's fiftieth season celebration as a Major League franchise, is a Hollywood-style pathway located on the sidewalk on Texas Avenue, right outside Minute Maid Park. The first player given the honor—and who was most associated with the original Colt .45's team—was Bob Aspromonte. Twelve others followed that year, including Nolan Ryan, Joe Morgan, Jeff Bagwell, and Craig Biggio, to name a few.

CHAMPIONS PAVILION

If you're feeling like a champion (and I know you are), then you can rest easy because there are accommodations for you. Champions Pavilion is a multipurpose banquet room located on the mezzanine level, just above the center-field area. With a seating capacity for 300 people, the room's windows overlook the beautiful ballpark, while also providing a unique view of the downtown area.

CLOSED-CAPTION DISPLAY

Minute Maid Park was the first Major League ballpark to incorporate a message board strictly for closed captioning. The board is just below and to the right of the main scoreboard. The display shows PA announcements, in-game information, and other announcements. Up to three lines of data can be displayed, with up to 28 characters per line. The display board measures 9 feet high by 30 feet six inches wide.

CONFERENCE CENTER
Minute Maid Park's conference center, which is on the second and third floors of the ballpark, is open 365 days a year. It provides plenty of convention rooms and state-of-the-art facilities for business meetings.

CRAWFORD BOXES
The Crawford Boxes are sections 100–105 in left field that run parallel to Crawford Street in downtown Houston. They sit atop the 19-foot wall, and at 315 feet, they are part of one of the shortest home run porches in the Major Leagues. The seats are highly sought after and give fans an exceptional opportunity to snag a home run ball throughout the course of a game.

DIAMOND CLUB
If you are a big shot in the corporate world, you can wine and dine your guests in style by utilizing the Diamond Club at Minute Maid Park. It features a private conference room, a phone/fax room, and all the amenities you need to sway a client one way or another. If you're interested in taking in the Astros game, there are extra-wide seats behind home plate. These particular seats are available only if you purchase season tickets.

FIVESEVEN GRILLE
The name is a tribute to two of the greatest Houston Astros of all time, Jeff Bagwell (5) and Craig Biggio (7). This center-field establishment replaced the former Ruggles Restaurant and combines great food with a laid-back atmosphere. Fans can sample some of Jeff and Craig's favorite dishes. An upstairs loft has a pool table, and televisions ensure that visitors will not miss any of the action on the field.

GIANT BILLBOARDS
Prior to the 2013 season, giant billboards were added in left center that obstructed the view of the famous replica locomotive, leaving many to wonder if the train would be headed straight out of the town. Just before the 2014 season, their positions were altered and they now sit below the train, giving fans a clear view once again. The billboards, which are a part of what is called a "community leaders program," is an $18 million investment by the Houston Astros toward youth baseball and softball.

HIGH-DEFINITION SCOREBOARD

During the 2010 off-season, the Astros replaced the old scoreboard above the right-field seats. Dubbed "El Grande" due to its sheer size, the new high-definition video board measures 54 feet high and 124 feet wide and was the fourth largest in all of baseball when it debuted. One can expect to see unprecedented images and exceptional replays from every angle of Minute Maid Park.

HOLY COW!

Beginning with the 2006 season, Chick-Fil-A cows took over Minute Maid Park and made their way onto the foul poles. The cows wear Astros hats and carry a sign that states "Eat Mor Fowl." Whenever an Astros player slams a home run off the pole, every fan in attendance receives a free chicken sandwich from the popular establishment. In 2007, Hunter Pence became the first to cash in on the promotion, accomplishing the feat twice.

HOME RUN PORCH

Located along the main concourse in left field is the home run porch, which juts out, allowing fans to stand in anticipation of catching a potential home run. Nearby, the Home Run Alley above left field gives those passing by the opportunity to learn more about four of the most prolific sluggers in Astros franchise history: Jeff Bagwell, Craig Biggio, Jose Cruz, and Jimmy Wynn. Opportunities are also present to learn about the history of Houston baseball. As a sidenote, this section was rebranded midseason 2013.

MANUAL SCOREBOARD

An old-fashioned, manually operated scoreboard is embedded into the 19-foot-high left-field wall just below the Crawford Boxes. It displays line scores from other games going on in the world of Major League Baseball, and a staff person behind the board updates each score by hand.

MEDIA WALL OF HONOR

Nestled on the club level at Minute Maid Park, the Houston Baseball Media Wall of Honor "pays tribute to a current or former member of the Houston media who has made substantial and lasting contributions to the landscape of Houston baseball through their work in journalism or broadcasting," according to the Astros Media Guide. Those nominated include Anita Martini, who was a pioneer for women in broadcasting, and Milo Hamilton, the longtime Astros broadcaster who spent 59 years behind the microphone before retiring at the end of 2012.

NAME GAME

When the ballpark opened, it was called Enron Field. However, on February 22, 2002, all that changed when the Astros bought back the naming rights for $2.1 million when the Enron Corporation went bankrupt. The stadium was renamed Astros Field until the rights were resold to Minute Maid on June 5, 2002. The 28-year partnership agreement also stipulated pouring rights for products of The Coca-Cola Company, as well as ongoing advertising and marketing programs. Talks in the beginning focused on the name The Ballpark at Union Station, which was later scrapped after the team decided to find a sponsor for the naming rights.

The old-style gas pump in center field tallies the total number of home runs hit since 2000. (*Photographed by Alicia Barnhart/Flickr*)

OLD-STYLE GAS PUMP

The home run porch in center field has a signature gas pump symbolizing Houston as the oil capital of America. The purpose? It keeps a tally of the total number of home runs hit since the ballpark's inception. Unless you're right next to it, plan on using a pair of binoculars to view the digits as they have low visibility.

PAINTED BRICKWORK

Outlines of flag pennants symbolizing the division championships won in the Houston's history are painted on the brickwork, just below the light poles. A white baseball with the initials "D. K." painted on the masonry pays tribute to Darryl Kyle, who died prematurely, is positioned just to the left of the home run pump.

PLAZA

This 27,000-square-foot plaza, just outside the left-field wall, is open year-round to the general public and is complete with a regulation infield, bronze likenesses of Craig Biggio and Jeff Bagwell, and outfield bleachers. The Astros history wall displays championship pennants commemorating wild card, division, and championship pennants. Halliburton, Houston's third largest employer and for which the outdoor attraction is named, played a significant role in the construction of Minute Maid Park, overseeing the massive project.

REPLICA LOCOMOTIVE

The locomotive in left field has quickly become a fan favorite at Minute Maid Park. Taking a cue from the 1911 Union Station, a replica 1860s-style locomotive provides a nostalgic link to the past and pays homage to the former railroad site.

Weighing 50,000 pounds and operating on a 500-foot track above left field, this 57-foot train combines sight, sound, and motion to create a dynamic celebration whenever an Astros player goes deep or the team picks up a win. It rolls slowly toward the left-field line, and then returns to its original position. The car that usually houses the coal is filled instead with around 25 to 30 pumpkin-sized fake oranges (Minute Maid orange juice).

RETIRED NUMBERS

Nine numbers have been retired by the Houston Astros, all of which are displayed in the upper-level third-base grandstand. They include: Jeff Bagwell (5), Craig Biggio (7), Jimmy Wynn (24), Jose Cruz (25), Jim Umbricht (32), Mike Scott (33), Nolan Ryan (34), Don Wilson (40), and Larry Dierker (49).

ROOF DECK

Groups of 100 or more can enjoy an amazing view of the Houston skyline while watching the action on the sixth level of the stadium at the roof deck and clubhouse. The clubhouse section consists of an upscale sports bar where fans can come together and talk sports or simply drink a beer while watching the game.

SQUEEZE PLAY

Updated for the 2013 season, Squeeze Play is a free interactive exhibit especially for kids under the age of 12. At Squeeze Play, located on the northeast corner of the ballpark at the right-field entrance near section 113, kids can test their pitching speed, take batting practice, and enjoy slushies at the Minute Maid juice bar. The chance for a photo-op is also available with Orbit, the lovable mascot of the Astros.

TAL'S HILL

Named for the former director of baseball operations Tal Smith, the 10-degree hill in center field pays tribute to his creativity and contribution to the ballpark project. A flagpole on top of the hill provides a patriotic touch as well as a possible disaster and career-ending situation for an outfielder. It helped Brewers catcher George Kottaras, who, during the ninth inning of a game on September 3, 2011, needed a double for the cycle and hit a ball that bounced on the hill in such a way that it went over the fence for the ground-rule double.

THE ROOF

The $65 million, three-paneled retractable roof in Houston, which stands 252 feet high, can, of course, be opened on nice days, but it is also transparent. A wall of windows in left field allows the air conditioning to circulate better on hot and humid days. Even with it closed, fans can still catch a glimpse of the Houston skyline. The roof can open in less than 20 minutes, revealing the largest open area of any retractable-roof ballpark. Uni-Systems provided the technical expertise in developing the roof for Minute Maid Park's unique layout.

HOW THE ROOF WORKS

Mechanized roof panels move back and forth an estimated 160 times a year, which is equal to a distance of 14.6 miles. Steel panels roll along the tracks located on the east and west sides. When the roof is open, the north and south panels, which measure 537 feet by 127 feet and weigh 1,905 tons, rest at the north end. In addition, the three panels roll on 140 forged steel wheels, each measuring 35 feet in diameter. Each wheel has its own braking mechanism, and 60 are equipped with electric motors.

UNION STATION ENTRANCE

The 45-foot-high Union Station vestibule was once a busy train station in the nineteenth century before it was converted into office buildings prior to the construction of Minute Maid Park. When the Astros organization took over, a reconfiguration of Union Station was needed to meet the needs of the organization. In the midst of the remodeling, arches and vintage designs were discovered. They were restored and are now part of the finished product.

WORLD'S LARGEST SLIDING GLASS DOOR

Minute Maid Park's hurricane-resistant, 50,000-square-foot sliding door stretches all the way across the entire left field and still allows for views of the skyline, even with the roof closed.

MEMORABLE GAMES AT MINUTE MAID PARK

APRIL 7, 2000: FIRST GAME AT MINUTE MAID PARK

Although the patrons of Houston were treated to a new setting for the first time since the team's inception in 1962, it was the Philadelphia Phillies who ended up celebrating after they cashed in on the first win in the history of Minute Maid Park, 4–1. Behind home runs from Ron Gant and Scott Rolen in the late innings, Randy Wolf pitched seven strong innings to notch the win.

Among those in the sellout crowd of 41,583 were former President George H. W. Bush and then-president-elect George W. Bush, but even with the big guns in attendance, the Astros lost.

JULY 5, 2000: GONZO HITS FOR THE CYCLE

Luis Gonzalez became the first Diamondbacks player—and first to do so at Minute Maid Park—to hit for the cycle as part of a 12–9 Arizona win. He doubled in the first, collected a single in the third, got the hardest hit out of the way by cashing in on a triple in the eighth, and thanks to the offense, which gave him a chance to squeeze in one more at-bat, topped it off by hitting a home run in the ninth, garnering nice applause for the former Astro from those in attendance at Minute Maid Park. Diamondbacks Travis Lee (2-for-5, 3 RBI) and Steve Finley (3-for-5, single, double, and an RBI) also had a nice game in lifting Arizona to the win.

OCTOBER 4, 2001: BONDS GOES YARD FOR NUMBER 70

Barry Bonds matched what was once thought to be an unreachable figure when he collected his seventieth home run of the season in the ninth inning of a 10–2 Giants victory. Bonds connected, leading off the frame with a solo shot off the Houston reliever Wilfredo Rodriguez to right-center field. Having collected three walks in the contest, he took a 1–1 pitch and promptly drilled it 450 feet, much to the delight of the Astros fans, who showed their respect by giving Bonds a standing ovation as he rounded the bases. Upon returning to the dugout, he was summoned for a rare road curtain call.

OCTOBER 8, 2005: MARATHON NLDS GAME 4

With the Astros one win away from moving on to the National League Championship Series to take on the Cardinals for a second consecutive season, both the Astros and Braves fought tooth and nail for five hours and 50 minutes, totaling 18 innings during a 7–6 Houston victory. The contest, which once set the record for the longest postseason game before the 18-inning San Francisco vs. Washington Marathon in 2014 surpassed it, saw two grand slams hit (one by the Atlanta's Adam LaRoche in the top of the third inning and the other by the Houston's Lance Berkman in the bottom of the eighth), marking the first time that had occurred. The Astros trailed 5–0 and 6–1 at one point, but Berkman's slam cut the deficit to 6–5, and Brad Ausmus tied it with a homer to left center in the bottom of the ninth with two outs. The war waged on for nine more innings before Houston's Chris Burke sent the Braves packing once again in the first round with a homer to left field off Joey Devine in the bottom of the eighteenth.

OCTOBER 17, 2005: PUJOLS SPOILS THE CELEBRATION

Trailing 4–2 in the bottom of the ninth with two outs and two on, Albert Pujols sent a message loud and clear to the screaming Astros fans in attendance at Minute Maid Park: Houston, we have a problem. What followed was Pujols crushing a dramatic three-run home run off Astros closer Brad Lidge in the top of the ninth, capping an unlikely comeback and a 5–4 victory that postponed Houston's berth to the World Series. Down to their final strike, the Cardinals refused to quit as David Eckstein connected for a single, and Jim Edmonds walked, setting the stage for Pujols's dramatics. Although the Cardinals would fall in Game 6 at Busch Memorial Stadium, it was a moment that both Lidge and the fans wouldn't soon forget.

OCTOBER 25, 2005: LONGEST WORLD SERIES GAME EVER

After playing a marathon division series game against Atlanta earlier in the playoffs, the Astros found themselves in a dogfight again before falling in 14 innings to Chicago, 7–5. Going 14 innings by length and a record-breaking five hours, 41 minutes, the Chicago White Sox received a clutch home run from Geoff Blum off Houston reliever Ezequiel Astacio in the top half of the fourteenth, breaking a 5–5 tie and putting the White Sox closer than ever to their first World Series Championship since 1917. Houston had their chances to win the game, most notably in the bottom half of the ninth inning, when they failed to capitalize with the bases loaded.

OCTOBER 26, 2005: WHITE SOX FINALIZE SWEEP OF ASTROS

In 2004, the Boston Red Sox ended 86 years of turmoil by winning baseball's ultimate prize, sweeping the St. Louis Cardinals. It's apparent that the Chicago White Sox took notes because not only did they take four straight from the Astros, but ended an 88-year title drought of their own by capturing the World Series with a 1–0 shutout of Houston. Jermaine Dye drove in the only run of the game during the top of the eighth, driving in Willie Harris with an RBI single, and closer Bobby Jenks went on to pitch a scoreless bottom of the ninth as Chicago took home the crown. The White Sox were led by ace Freddy Garcia, who was stellar throughout the entire postseason. As though he saved his best game for last, he shut out the Astros in seven innings of spectacular pitching.

> "I did not go to the World Series, but I watched it. . . . When the last out was made, my wife and I both had tears in our eyes because it was so meaningful."
> —Ken "Hawk" Harrelson, White Sox broadcaster

"That is as good as it gets and there is nothing that can get any better than that unless you do it again. . . . You spend your whole life trying to get to that moment. It was definitely the highlight of my career by far."
—*Paul Konerko*

JUNE 28, 2007: LIFELONG ASTRO HAS DATE WITH HISTORY

For a man who played his entire career in a Houston Astros jersey, it was only right that Craig Biggio collect his 3,000th hit in front of the hometown faithful. It happened when he singled in the seventh inning off Colorado Rockies starter Aaron Cook—after already connecting for singles in the third and fifth innings—setting off a party-like scene at the sold-out Minute Maid Park. Biggio, who was thrown out trying to stretch number 3,000 into a double, became the twenty-seventh player in history to accrue 3,000 for a career and was greeted at second base by his teammates, who rushed out of the dugout to celebrate the accomplishment. He added two more hits to cap an incredible 5-for-5 day, and Carlos Lee blasted a walk-off grand slam in the bottom of the eleventh to give Houston an incredible 8–5 victory.

MARCH 31, 2013: ASTROS MAKE AMERICAN LEAGUE DEBUT

After spending their first 50 seasons in the National League, the Astros started 2013 as a member of the American League West. Fueled by a pinch hit three-run home run by Rick Ankiel and two triples from Justin Maxwell, the Astros successfully infiltrated the new league assignment with an 8–2 victory over Texas. After three scoreless frames, Houston went to work when Maxwell connected for a two-run triple in the fourth, and RBI singles from Ronny Cedeno and Jose Altuve in the fifth extended the lead to 4–0. Starting pitcher Bud Norris held the Texas bats at bay, scattering five hits over 5⅔ innings. Reliever Erik Bedard came in to pitch 3⅓ innings of one hit ball, picking up the extended save.

APRIL 2, 2013: NEAR PERFECTION FOR DARVISH

Bidding to become the twenty-fourth pitcher in contemporary history to toss a perfect game, Texas starter Yu Darvish retired the first 26 batters in succession before allowing a clean single up the middle to Marwin Gonzalez, but the Rangers easily defeated Houston by a touchdown, 7–0. In Texas's second game of the season, Darvish was brilliant, throwing 111 masterful pitches and striking out 14, becoming the first Texas pitcher to strike out that many since Nolan Ryan in 1991 versus the Angels. The hit by Gonzalez went through the legs of Darvish, who wasn't able to get the glove down in time. Elvis Andrus, who connected for two triples, and Ian Kinsler, who connected for a two-run home run in the seventh, led the Rangers' offense.

JULY 20, 2013: MARINERS VICTORIOUS 4–2 DESPITE ONE HIT

In a game that proves anything can happen throughout the course of a Major League season, Seattle collected one hit—a two-out, two-run double by Michael Saunders in the seventh—during a wacky 4–2 victory over the Houston Astros despite striking out 15 times collectively as a group. After being held hitless by Astros starter Erik Bedard through 6⅓ innings, Jose Cisnero came in on relief and walked Seattle's Mike Zunino before allowing the two-bagger to Saunders. The other two runs scored by the Mariners were courtesy of six walks and a passed ball. Even more impressive, the last time a team scored four runs on one hit while not registering an error was all the way back in 1914, when the Chicago White Sox pulled it off during a 5–4 loss against Detroit.

WHAT THEY'RE SAYING ABOUT MINUTE MAID PARK

RICK ANKIEL: "I think it is a nice ballpark, and [it] can get loud because of the dome."

JASON BAY: "It caters to a right-handed hitter a little bit, [and] we appreciate the dome stadium, especially in Houston when it is 150 degrees in the summer. . . . It is very loud when the dome is closed, and it definitely has the baseball atmosphere."

CARLOS BELTRAN: "I think it is a good ballpark. It is good for hitters, it is nice playing inside every day, [and there are] no rain delays. . . . It is just a fun place to play at."

THOM BRENNAMAN: "I really like [Minute Maid Park] a lot. . . . They have the retractable roof and I think it adds an element and ultimately, you are trying to cater to the fans, who spend their hard-earned money to come to a ballpark. I love some of the things they did with Tal's Hill and the railroad tracks above left field."

BOB CARPENTER, BROADCASTER: "I have got a lot of thoughts on [Minute Maid Park]. . . . The main thing is there are cheap home runs and then there are balls you absolutely kill and you do not get rewarded for that. To me, the ballpark is too quirky and does not play fair."

PRINCE FIELDER: "It is a cool ballpark because they have got the train on top. . . . I like ballparks that make you feel like you are not in the traditional baseball atmosphere, and it is something different."

GARRETT JONES: "The ball gets out of there pretty well. . . . It is a pretty cool stadium with the roof closing and a good atmosphere."

RYAN LUDWICK: "To me, it feels kind of like Disneyland. . . . It is just big, closed, [and there] is a lot going on in there. It is just a busy stadium."

NATE MCLOUTH: "I like playing a lot in Houston and I like the city of Houston, but the ballpark is great and it is just a comfortable place to play."

JOEY VOTTO: "That is probably my favorite ballpark to hit in. . . . I like to have some space when I hit the ball and typically if I hit the ball [well], it is going to be a home run—not always, but usually. Houston is good to me both in the balls that fall in either gap and [I can] turn into doubles or triples."

MINUTE MAID PARK FACTS AND FIGURES

MINUTE MAID PARK ADDRESS
501 Crawford Street, Houston, TX 77002

HOUSTON ASTROS TEAM WEB SITE
www.astros.com

FIELD DIMENSIONS (IN FEET)
Left Field: 315', Left-Center: 362', Center: 435',
Right-Center: 373', Right Field: 326'

SEATING CAPACITY (AS OF 2015)
42,060

ALL-STAR GAMES AT MINUTE MAID PARK
July 13, 2004: American League 9, National League 4
MVP: Alfonso Soriano, Texas Rangers (AL)

MINUTE MAID PARK FIRSTS
Game: April 7, 2000—Philadelphia 4, Houston 1
Single: Doug Glanville, Philadelphia (April 7, 2000)*
Double: Rico Brogna, Philadelphia (April 7, 2000)
Triple: Tim Bogar, Houston (April 8, 2000)
Home Run: Scott Rolen, Philadelphia (April 8, 2000)

*Denotes first hit in the stadium.

TROPICANA FIELD
HOME OF THE TAMPA BAY RAYS

Tropicana Field, Tampa Bay Rays (Photographed by Mark Whitt/Flickr)

At the outset, having a domed stadium in Florida makes just as much sense as eating tomato soup with a fork. And while most Floridians opt to participate in other outdoor events and activities where the sun shines bright, the attendance numbers at Tropicana Field normally leave a lot to be desired. On any given day, there is a sea of vacant green seats, which is an unwelcome sight for Tampa Bay Rays ownership.

When the city of Tampa was awarded an NFL franchise in the form of the Buccaneers, St. Petersburg wanted to be home to a professional baseball franchise. Multipurpose stadium designs were created for the area as early as 1983, and one ballpark proposal even had an open-air, tent-like roof with fountains similar to that of Kauffman Stadium in Kansas City. Ultimately, the ideas were shot down, and it was decided that in order to attract a Major League franchise, the ballpark had to have a dome in order to shield the players and fans from the intense heat and thunderstorms during the summer.

Ground was broken on November 22, 1986, and the building later known as Tropicana Field was constructed on a site that was once home to a coal-gasification plant. As a result, millions of dollars were spent to ensure the proper elimination of chemicals to make it safe for everyone.

When it was completed in 1990, St. Petersburg's hopes of convincing existing teams such as the Chicago White Sox, Pittsburgh Pirates, and San Francisco Giants went by the wayside and at the end of the day didn't come to fruition as expected. The city was left with nothing else but to move on to Plan B.

Taxpayers in the area helped fund $138 million of the stadium, which sat vacant for seven years other than hosting occasional fair-related events such as tractor pulls, motor cross-racing, and concerts. Executives knew that in order for the stadium to be Major League Baseball–ready, a serious chunk of change would have to be spent to make over a building that had stood unoccupied and had never hosted a baseball contest. To convince Major League Baseball higher-ups that it would be a good place for America's pastime would be quite a task.

Although St. Petersburg was a finalist for a franchise in 1993, they were passed over. After years of lobbying, Major League Baseball finally decided to expand again, and in 1995, both Arizona and Tampa Bay were the final two contenders for brand-new franchises. In order to create an atmosphere as close to a ballpark as possible, management pumped $70 million into a renovation project in which the construction firm used Ebbets Field, the legendary one-time home of the Dodgers, as its blueprint.

At long last, following years of talks, speculation, and hope, Tropicana Field opened on March 31, 1998, and the city of St. Petersburg and its fans finally got what they wanted all along: a professional baseball team to call their own.

SPECIAL FEATURES OF TROPICANA FIELD

162 LANDING

In 2011, the Rays staged one of the greatest turnarounds in baseball history, rebounding from a nine-game deficit on September 3 to steal away the wild card from Boston with a dramatic 8–7 win on the final day of the regular season over New York. The 162 Landing is appropriately placed in the left-field concourse, where Evan Longoria's dramatic walk-off home run landed, and pays tribute to the come-from-behind win and sequence of events that had to happen in order for Tampa Bay to capture the playoff berth. A series of 11 images against a blue background depict the action, while captions at the bottom recount all the dramatic events and honor one of the greatest games in Tampa Bay franchise history.

ASTROTURF

One of the many downsides to playing on artificial turf is the number of cheap hops and bad bounces the carpet allows. The Rays management team was determined to find a better alternative. Enter Gameday Grass 3D60H, the latest and greatest in carpet technology. Resembling natural grass, the plushy, soft-cushioned surface is said to provide all the true bounces that a natural grass field would.

Installed in three weeks following the 2010 season, the durable new surface has a perky appearance, and the material has a memory feature that allows it to pop back up despite being stepped on repeatedly. As an added bonus, the turf decreases surface temperatures by up to 18 degrees, allowing teams to stay cool, calm, and collected.

BEACH BAR

The left-field Beach Bar is alongside the visitor's bullpen and can accommodate between 75 and 135 guests. Premium catering and food options merely enhance the attractiveness of this selection, but heed this as a fair warning: Heads up! Every so often, a player will venture into the section in the hopes of snagging a fly ball hit down the line for an out.

BREW HOUSE

The Budweiser Brew House is open to the public for two hours before the game and one hour after the final pitch, and is the place to be if you've had a long day. Whether you're drowning yourself in the sorrows of a Rays loss, or simply attempting to take a load off, this is one popular spot that has become one of the most refreshing and easily accessible eateries at Tropicana Field.

BULLPEN CAFÉ

This unique café, located behind the Rays' bullpen, offers picnic-style seating and a full Checker's menu. It is down the right-field line and offers an incredible view of the field, along with an opportunity to heckle the players. Be on the lookout as baseballs tend to gravitate toward this area quite frequently throughout the course of a game.

BULLPENS

The Rays took a page out of days gone past, electing to position both the home and away bullpens down the right- and left-field lines. This not only serves as a challenge to fielders who might happen to chase a ball into the area, but also catchers who are helping to get a pitcher warmed up. In order to prevent an injury, batboys are stationed nearby to prevent a screaming liner from hitting a catcher from behind.

CENTER-FIELD RESTAURANT

Located on the upper level and holding the distinction of being the first Major League restaurant to be located directly in center field when it debuted, this dining hall offers fantastic views and a full buffet. With sitting room for 350 people, the restaurant overlooks the playing field and was built during the 2013 off-season. It has an open-air patio for enhanced views, along with a new bar and concession stand that are partially draped by a dark hitter's background. The new configuration also connects the Rays Touch Tank and another fan deck, allowing for easy navigation during a game.

On a historical note, Ben Grieve was the first player to ever hit a home run *over* the establishment, as it glanced off the "D" catwalk in center and landed on the walkway behind the restaurant, traveling an estimated 463 feet.

CHAMPIONSHIP FLAGS

Suspended just below the left-field roof, white flags with blue inscriptions commemorate the best seasons in Tampa Bay Rays' history—the years in which the team captured the wild card, the American League East division title, and their greatest season to date in 2008, in which they brought home their first American League pennant with a stirring seven-game series win over defending champion Boston.

COMMEMORATIVE SEATS

In Tropicana Field, the Rays have painted three seats—two yellow and one white—to commemorate the greatest moments in the franchise's history. A yellow chair in section 148, row V, seat 6 honors Wade Boggs after he connected on the first home run in Tampa Bay Rays history on March 31, 1998, against the Detroit Tigers. The blast, which occurred during the sixth inning, was a two-run shot off Tigers pitcher Justin Thompson and was also the first run recorded in the Rays' history.

In honor of Wade Boggs's 3,000th career hit on August 7, 1999, a yellow seat in right field marks the spot where his historic home run landed. The chair—in section 144, row V, seat 6—features a small plaque with the inscription: "Site of Wade Boggs 3,000th Hit, August 7, 1999." (A special thanks to the Tampa Bay Rays Media Relations department for double-checking and confirming the exact spot for me.)

Lastly, in right field at section 140, row T, seat 10, a white seat commemorates a historic home run hit on the final day of the regular season in 2011 by Dan Johnson. With Tampa Bay's season down to their final out, down 7–6 to New York and needing a miracle to extend the game—and their wild card hopes—they called on Johnson to pinch hit. With only one home run to his credit and down to his final strike, he connected on a pitch and sent it down the right-field line, tying the game at seven, and eventually the Rays would win the game, wild card, and a playoff berth.

CONCOURSES

Wide concourses and more than 290 concession stands offer an extensive variety of foods to choose from. When Tropicana Field was first designed, the original number of concession areas was set at 90, but in later years was tripled to enable fans to make a quick purchase so they could get back to their seats and not miss any of the action.

CUESTA-REY CIGAR BAR

The first cigar bar in the Major Leagues when it debuted, this area offers baseball fans and cigar enthusiasts the opportunity to watch the game on TV from leather chairs and sofas while savoring the finest cigars. It is also a great meeting place before, during, or after the game and is on the upper level of Center Field Street, which is directly across from the center-field restaurant.

EBBETS FIELD REMINDERS

Taking a page from Ebbets Field, the asymmetrical outfield is nearly a replica of the Dodgers' old home, and this fact was determined only *after* the measurements were completed in the stadium. Another distinct Ebbets Field reminder is the presence of the grand, eight-story-high rotunda entrance that was constructed from the blueprints for the now non-defunct ballpark in Brooklyn.

EXTREME ZONE

Given all the activities available for fans on game day, it seems hard to believe that the main attraction at Tropicana Field is baseball. Perhaps the topper of them all is where fans can play a game of stickball in a quarter of the ballpark that was built and constructed to resemble a New York alley. The attraction is part of a quadrant referred to as Left-Field Street, an area whose features are described later in this section.

FAN-FRIENDLY SEATS

One factor that can be appreciated at Tropicana Field is the seating arrangements and the views they offer. Entire sections were repositioned as part of the renovation project and are now angled toward the infield. While the seating area behind home plate brings you close to the field, most seats have a decent view of the action now that they have been repositioned. The ballpark has seating in every pricing category that far exceeds the standards required in a Major League ballpark.

FAN WALL OF FAME

Everyone is familiar with the Hall of Fames that honor only the best athletes. In Tampa Bay, the Rays have instituted a Wall of Fame for only the biggest and most die-hard fans of the team. Family members or friends can nominate individuals, and inductees for this exceptional honor receive recognition on the Wall of Fame, a dedicatory plaque, and two tickets to a Rays game.

HOME PLATE CLUB

Some of the seats at Tropicana Field that are closest to the action make you feel as if you are on deck and waiting to take your spot in the batter's box. A mere 50 feet separates the fans from the backstop and puts you up close and personal with the hitters, umpires, pitchers, and all the action. Be prepared to shell out big bucks because as of this writing, a seat in that exclusive section starts at $210 per ticket.

HOME RUN DISPLAY

Similar to the oversized apple that rises from a top hat at Citi Field in New York following a home run, when the Rays blast a dinger, a giant glass of orange juice, complete with a straw, illuminates from beyond the right-field fence to celebrate the round-tripper. What would make things a lot more interesting is if actual orange juice was shot out of the straw and sprayed all over the fan base near the display!

LEFT-FIELD STREET

A baseball-themed game show, a Topps baseball card maker, and the chance to broadcast a play-by-play of baseball highlights are all available at this interactive fan attraction. If you're a video-game buff, there's something for you as well with the newest games ready to play, or if you appreciate a throwback from yesteryear, Nintendo and Atari games are also there for your enjoyment.

RAYS TANK

The Rays Tank made its debut on July 21, 2006, and is the first tank of its kind in a professional sports facility that houses cow-nose rays. A 35-foot, 10,000-gallon tank is just behind the right center-field wall and is accessible to fans. Throughout the game, fans have a one-of-a-kind opportunity to touch and feed over 30 rays, thanks to a partnership forged between the

Tampa Bay Rays and the Florida Aquarium. Between each session, workers take 10 minutes to test the water and make sure everything is okay before the next group of people is admitted. Each time a Tampa Bay player splashes a home run into the massive tank, the Rays donate $5,000, $2,500 of which goes to the Florida Aquarium and the other half goes to the charity selected by the player who hit it.

As of this writing, only three players have homered into the tank:

1. Luis Gonzalez (Los Angeles Dodgers) on June 24, 2007
2. Miguel Cabrera (Detroit Tigers) on June 30, 2013
3. Jose Lobaton (Tampa Bay Rays) on October 7, 2013, versus Boston (a walk-off home run off Koji Uehara in Game 3 of the American League Division Series)

For the record, no rays were harmed as a result of any of the splashdowns.

RENOVATIONS 2006–07
An $18 million pledge by Rays management to make Tropicana Field even better following the 2006 season culminated with major overhauls to all the restrooms on the 100 and 200 levels, the installation of new lighting, video boards, a sound system, fixtures, and a premium seating club. Baseball-themed interaction zones were also added and have been a major hit ever since.

RENOVATIONS 2014
Although presently the Rays are tied into a lease to play their home games exclusively at Tropicana Field through the 2027 season, that hasn't prevented management from making changes to ensure the ballpark is as fan friendly as it can be. Before the start of the 2014 campaign, another round of renovations—costing $750,000 and paid for by the Rays—was completed to make the ballpark that much more appealing to fans. Almost 3,000 seats in the lower bowl were removed to create a new 360-degree walkway around the field, enhancing the fans' view of the games. As a result, the capacity within the ballpark dropped from 34,000 to around 31,000. As mentioned earlier in this section, the center-field restaurant was altered and now features an open-air patio. A small portion of the funding came from the $1.3 million that was approved by St. Petersburg City Council, but most of that money was earmarked for standard maintenance and infrastructure improvements.

RETIRED NUMBERS
The Tampa Bay Rays have retired one number in their franchise's history: Wade Boggs (12).

RIGHT-FIELD STREET

Right-Field Street, another interactive area for the little ones, offers attractions such as the "St. Petersburg Times press box" and "Bats, Balls and Brushes." Perhaps the most fascinating—and one that rivals the carnival theme of Comerica Park in Detroit—is the Rays Baseball Carnival. Games such as plinko (à la *The Price Is Right*), skee ball, and spin-the-wheel are available, and fans can also test their batting skills against computer images of real Major League pitchers.

SCOUT SEATS

Some of the most technologically advanced seats in baseball are right behind home plate, where 100 high-backed, upholstered "Scout Seats" combine great views and luxury. Did you happen to miss a play? Want to know a player's statistics for that current game? Hungry? Not a problem. Individual monitors on each of the seats show replays from all angles, statistics, and special concession menus.

TED WILLIAMS MUSEUM

The Ted Williams Museum and Hitters Hall of Fame became a permanent part of Tropicana Field in 2006 and is part of the Center Field Street festivities. There are various artifacts and images of Williams, highlighting his time in the military all the way through his playing days in the game of baseball.

THE ROOF

While Toronto's Rogers Centre lays claim to having the tallest dome in the Major Leagues, Tropicana Field boasts the *world's* second-largest cable-supported dome roof. Measuring 225 feet high over second base to 85 feet at the center-field wall, the translucent, Teflon-coated fiberglass roof is illuminated orange in the evenings when the Rays have an off day, register a victory, or are on the road.

Another unique aspect of the roof—and easily noticeable from the outside—is the fact that it is slanted to provide better protection in case of a hurricane and to decrease the interior volume, which enables the reduction in cooling, ultimately saving money.

Many players seem to dislike the catwalks suspended from the roof. Many have hit either the "A," "B," "C," or "D" catwalks with towering pop-ups, either robbing them of a home run or creating an unnecessary out. It gets a little confusing because many are designated to be home runs when hit, but some can be played off a bounce or ricochet, while others may count as a ground-rule double.

Here is a specific look at the ground rules pertaining to what's in play as far as the roof and catwalks go, courtesy of the Rays Media Guide.

Tropicana Field is home to the only permanent roof structure remaining in the big leagues. (Photographed by Brian Skversky/Flickr)

CATWALKS, LIGHTS, AND SUSPENDED OBJECTS

Batted ball strikes catwalk, light, or suspended object over fair territory:

Batted ball that strikes either of the lower two catwalks, lights, or suspended objects in fair territory: HOME RUN

Batted ball that is not judged a home run and remains on a catwalk, light, or suspended object: TWO BASES

Batted ball that is not judged a home run and strikes a catwalk, light, or suspended object in fair territory shall be judged fair or foul in relation to where it strikes the ground or is touched by a fielder. If caught by a fielder, batter is out, and runners advance at their own risk.

Batted ball strikes catwalk, light, or suspended object over foul territory:

Ball to be judged foul, regardless of where it strikes the ground or is touched by a fielder.

If caught by a fielder: Foul Ball, cannot be caught.

THE TROPICANA NAME

The Tropicana Field naming rights became official on October 3, 1996, when the Rays and Tropicana Dole Beverages North America announced an agreement to rename the Thunderdome Tropicana Field. When the deal was inked, the City of Saint Petersburg collected more than $13 million. When the stadium was first built, it was known as the Florida Suncoast Dome before being renamed the Thunderdome in 1991.

TROPICANA ROOM

No, the Tropicana room is not devoted to displaying the history of Tropicana Orange Juice through pictures and interactive taste sampling, although that would be an exceptional idea! It is the most versatile venue in the stadium, mostly because it features a dazzling array of food to choose from. If a buffet featuring carved meats, pasta salads, and (of course) Tropicana juice tickles your fancy, this is the place to be. The area is available on game days to fans who have Field Box, Lower Club Box, Diamond Club, or suite tickets and is on the mezzanine level behind the home plate area.

WALKWAY

Fans coming in through the rotunda will note that the Rays have done an exceptional job in creating a true Florida atmosphere. The 900-foot walkway has the biggest outdoor terracotta mural in Florida and is one of the five largest in the United States. According to the Rays Media Guide, there are 1,849,091 vibrantly colored 1-inch by 1-inch tiles that depict the sun, sea, and beach.

MEMORABLE GAMES AT TROPICANA FIELD

MARCH 31, 1998: FIRST GAME IN RAYS/TROPICANA FIELD HISTORY

The Detroit Tigers put a damper on the first Major League Baseball game in Tampa Bay history, jumping out to a commanding 11–0 lead and holding on for an 11–6 victory. Hall of Famers Ted Williams and Stan Musial, who were in attendance, must have felt the urge to suit up and take the field to help the Rays notch their first win. The Tigers jumped all over Rays starter Wilson Alvarez and reliever Dan Carlson the first five innings, scoring four in the second, two in the third, and five in the fourth, capped off by a two-run homer by Luis Gonzalez, a two-run double by Brian Hunter, and an RBI single by Bip Roberts. With the game well in hand, Wade Boggs connected for the first Rays home run in franchise history during the bottom of the sixth.

AUGUST 7, 1999: BOGGS HOMERS FOR HIT NUMBER 3,000

Known predominantly as a singles hitter for the majority of his career, Wade Boggs reached 3,000 hits in style, shocking the Tropicana Field crowd with a long ball. After collecting two hits earlier in the game, he drove a 2–2 pitch 372 feet into the right-field seats off Indians left-hander Chris Haney during the seventh inning, becoming the first player to hit a home run for a 3,000th hit, while accomplishing the feat in front of his wife and father. As Boggs circled the bases in a joyous dance, he exchanged a double high-five with first-base coach Billy Hatcher, pointed to the roof of Tropicana Field between first and second, pointed in the same direction one more time, and then saw a security guard tackle a rambunctious fan. Cleveland ended up winning the slugfest-like contest, 15–10 on the strength of 19 hits.

JULY 30, 2005: ROOKIE HITS THREE HOME RUNS

In an otherwise lackluster contest featuring two of the worst teams in baseball at the time, the Rays defeated the Kansas City Royals, 7–3, on the strength of the franchise's first three-home run performance from one of their players. Rookie outfielder Jonny Gomes accomplished the feat, hitting a solo shot in the third, another solo blast in the fourth, and then promptly welcomed in Royals reliever Mike MacDougal by going deep for the third and final time to become the first rookie since Jose Ortiz of the Rockies on August 17, 2001, to notch the hat trick.

> "That was cool, against the Royals being a rookie—everything you do as a rookie positive, negative, in-between—is kind of building your stock up as a player. That kind of put me on the map and the Rays at that time did not have too much success . . . but still do this day—one of my high memories from my Tampa days."
> —*Jonny Gomes*

OCTOBER 19, 2008: THE AL PENNANT COMES TO ST. PETERSBURG

The magic continued for the Rays, who continued their remarkable turn-around season as they defeated the Red Sox 3–1 in Game 7 of the ALCS, clinching their first berth into the World Series. Boston jumped out to an early 1–0 lead when Dustin Predroia connected for a first inning home run off Rays starter Matt Garza, and little did they realize that would account for their only run of the game. Evan Longoria stroked an RBI double in the fourth to tie it, and Rocco Baldelli slashed an RBI single in the fifth, giving the Rays a 2–1 lead. The final blow came in the seventh, when Willy Aybar hit a solo home run, which ultimately sent the Red Sox packing for the winter. Despite allowing a leadoff walk to Jason Bay in the ninth, Tampa Bay pitcher David Price buckled down to retire the next three batters to preserve the win.

OCTOBER 22, 2008: FIRST WORLD SERIES GAME IN TAMPA BAY

In a scene that many thought was never possible considering the franchise's first 10 years (90-plus losses in those seasons), the Rays hosted Game 1 of the 104th World Series, but the Phillies played the spoiler, winning a tight one, 3–2. The first two runs were registered by the National League

Champions, when Chase Utley took aim and blasted a two-run home run off Rays starter Scott Kazmir in the first inning. They added another run in the top of the fourth, when Carlos Ruiz drove in Shane Victorino, extending the lead to 3–0. Tampa Bay answered back in the bottom half, when Carl Crawford gave the Rays their first Fall Classic run with a home run off Phillies starter Cole Hammels, closing the gap to 3–1. An RBI double by Aki Iwamura made it 3–2, and that's as close as it would get for the upstart Rays, who went scoreless over the final four frames.

JUNE 25, 2010: AN OLD FRIEND NO-HITS THE RAYS

Former Tampa Bay pitcher Edwin Jackson strolled onto the pitching mound as a member of the Arizona Diamondbacks and promptly allowed no hits, helping the Diamondbacks defeat the Rays, 1–0, in front of 18,918 at Tropicana Field. Jackson didn't hold anything back, throwing 149 pitches, allowing eight walks, and striking out six in holding the division-leading Rays hitless once again, the third time it had happened since July 2009. Adam LaRoche provided all the offense the Diamondbacks would need, striking for a solo home run in the top of the second that traveled 372 feet. With two outs, he tossed his final pitch to Jason Bartlett, who hit a chopper to short that Stephen Drew collected and tossed to first for the game's final out.

JULY 26, 2010: FIRST RAYS NO-HITTER

A little more than a month after being the victim of a no-hitter, Matt Garza took to the mound for the Rays and pitched himself right into the history books. The 2008 American League championship MVP faced the minimum 27 batters—a second-inning walk to Brennan Boesch was erased via a double play—as the Rays defeated Detroit, 5–0. Garza, who struck out six, threw 120 pitches and was aided by an incredible catch made by right fielder Ben Zobrist, who made a leaping catch above his head to rob Danny Worth to preserve the no-hitter. The offense was led by Matt Joyce, who connected for a sixth inning grand slam off Tigers starter Max Scherzer, which proved to be all the offense they would need. Carl Crawford added a home run in the eighth, and in the ninth, pinch hitter Ramon Santiago hit a lazy fly ball to Joyce for the final out.

SEPTEMBER 28, 2011: RAYS CAP INCREDIBLE COMEBACK TO WIN WILD CARD

Tampa Bay rallied from a 7–0 deficit against New York and won on a twelfth-inning home run by Evan Longoria, capping an incredible month that saw them capture the American League wild card after trailing Boston by nine

SOUTH-CENTRAL REGION « 291

games on September 3. Mark Teixeira hit a grand slam in the second and a solo blast in the fourth, while Andruw Jones added a solo homer in the fifth to give the Yankees a comfortable 7–0 lead. But Tampa Bay wouldn't be denied, scoring six in the eighth, highlighted by a three-run shot from Longoria that pulled the Rays to within 7–6.

As if there wasn't enough drama, Tampa Bay was down to their final out when they called upon pinch hitter Dan Johnson—who had hit one home run all season—to save the game. With two strikes, he launched a pitch down the right-field line, tying the contest at seven and sending it into extra innings. In the twelfth, notification came across that the Red Sox had just lost to the Orioles and all it did was pump new life into Tropicana Field and the Rays. Not more than three minutes later, Longoria saved his best for last when he connected for a wild card–winning 327-foot home run to left, setting off a raucous celebration at Tropicana Field.

OCTOBER 4, 2011: RANGERS MOVE ON BEHIND BIG GAME FROM BELTRE

Adrian Beltre became the first player in Division Series history—and seventh overall in the playoffs—to hit three home runs in one postseason game, powering the Rangers to a 4–3 series-clinching victory. His power display began in the second, when he hit the first of three consecutive solo home runs, the other two coming in the fourth and seventh innings. Ian Kinsler provided the only other run recorded by Texas, a solo shot of his own in the first inning. Meanwhile, the Rays were coming off an exhausting stretch that enabled them to capture the wild card on the season's final day and put up a fight until the end, coming up short in the ninth, when Desmond Jennings grounded out with the tying run on base to end the ballgame.

WHAT THEY'RE SAYING ABOUT TROPICANA FIELD

CARL CRAWFORD: "I like that it is inside and you know the game is going to start on time every day. . . . It is just one of those things where you never have to worry about a rain delay or stuff like that and the weather is always going to be perfect."

JOHNNY DAMON: "I do not mind Tropicana Field just because you know you are always going to play a game. . . . It is 72 degrees in there and when it is pouring outside, you know there is always going to be a game."

RON GARDENHIRE: "Not big on domes—we lived in one for a long time [Metrodome], but there is an aura in there that gets it ripping like the Metrodome used to . . . but as far as all the catwalks and balls bouncing off of things, I have never been a big fan of that."

JOSH HAMILTON: "That is a tough one. It is what it is. . . . [There is] nothing great, historic, or anything like that. It is [just] a ballpark and the team I signed with. It is good to go in and see the fan base grow the last few years, but [there is] nothing really unique about it [Tropicana Field]."

TOM HAMILTON, BROADCASTER: "It would not be that bad of a ballpark if it were not for the catwalks, but because of those catwalks, it looks like a giant erector set."

KEN "HAWK" HARRELSON, BROAD-CASTER: "I would have loved to have played [at Tropicana Field]. . . . A lot of players think it stinks, but I love that and it would have been just a fabulous ballpark to hit in."

PAUL KONERKO: "From a player's perspective, it is probably not the nicest clubhouse in the league—it is not the worst. The place itself, when you play in front of 10,000 people, . . . is not the greatest, but when there are 30,000 people there, it is a whole different atmosphere."

EVAN LONGORIA: "I love it. . . . It plays fair, you hit the ball hard, and you are not going to hit it off the Green Monster when you think it is going to be a home run, [and] if you hit the ball hard and think it is going to be a home run, it is going to be a home run at Tropicana Field. The infield plays good and overall it is a good place for us to play [at]."

MATT MOORE: "As far as pitching at Tropicana Field, the dimensions seem to be pretty fair for everybody and I like the deep gaps being a pitcher. . . . Another great thing is when we fill this thing to capacity. It is one of the loudest places I have ever been in for sure."

TROY PERCIVAL: "[It] needs to be started all over again. . . . They have done a fantastic job on the inside as far as the clubhouse and stuff like that, but you should not have things that are in play that affect play and there is a lot of that there."

TROPICANA FIELD FACTS AND FIGURES

TROPICANA FIELD ADDRESS
One Tropicana Drive, St. Petersburg, FL 33705

TAMPA BAY RAYS TEAM WEB SITE
www.raysbaseball.com

FIELD DIMENSIONS (IN FEET)
Left Field: 315', Left-Center: 370', Center: 404',
Right-Center: 370', Right Field: 322'

SEATING CAPACITY (AS OF 2015)
34,078

ALL-STAR GAMES AT TROPICANA FIELD
None

TROPICANA FIELD FIRSTS
Game: March 31, 1998—Detroit 11, Tampa Bay 6
Single: Tony Clark, Detroit (March 31, 1998)*
Double: Joe Randa, Detroit (March 31, 1998)
Triple: Kevin Stocker, Tampa Bay (April 1, 1998)
Home Run: Luis Gonzalez, Detroit (March 31, 1998)

*Denotes first hit in the stadium.

TURNER FIELD
HOME OF THE ATLANTA BRAVES

Turner Field, Atlanta Braves (Photographed by Mark Whitt/Flickr)

U pon its completion for the 1996 Summer Olympic Games, Turner Field, which was formerly known as Centennial Olympic Park, debuted in the baseball world in 1997 and quickly saw its fair share of division titles, National League Championship Series, and World Series action. When it opened, it quickly became a recognizable structure within the Atlanta area and is a fan favorite because of its old-time baseball feel combined with all the amenities and top-notch technology, which most have come to expect at Major League ballparks today. The ballpark is named for owner Ted Turner, the man responsible for founding CNN, TNT, and WTBS, among others.

When the world's best athletes rolled into town during the summer of 1996, the stadium boasted a capacity of 85,000 seats along with a world-class track-and-field setup. When the games ended, a multi-million-dollar renovation project began that involved the removal of much of the north section of the stadium to create a functional Major League ballpark. Stands that were constructed especially for the Olympic Games were eliminated to make room for the current outfield stands and other attractions that soon followed.

When talks began about how to fund the stadium, both NBC and other sponsors stepped up to the plate, agreeing to pay approximately $170 million of the total $209 million tab. The Atlanta Committee for the Olympic Games then announced they would pay to have the entire stadium transformed for baseball, and this move was widely viewed as a great deal considering it would enable the Braves to replace the deteriorating Atlanta-Fulton County Stadium, which had hosted baseball since April 12, 1966.

In November 2013, Braves management shocked the baseball world by announcing that by 2017, they would be leaving Turner Field for a new $672 million, 42,000-seat ballpark in Cobb County to be known as SunTrust Park, located approximately 12 miles northwest of downtown Atlanta. As of this writing, the plans have called for the Braves to pay $372 million, while Cobb County would contribute the remaining $300 million via public funding. The Braves' decision to leave comes after the club elected not to sign a new 20-year deal with Turner Field, which is owned by the City of Atlanta and the Atlanta-Fulton County Recreation Authority and expires following the 2016 season. They cited traffic issues as one of the main reasons for the move.

In addition, Turner Field needed $150 million worth of infrastructure work including, but not limited to, replacing seats, upgrading lighting, etc., none of which would enhance the overall fan experience, according to a press release issued by the club. In order to make the ballpark more fan friendly, those costs would have exceeded $200 million.

The location for the new Braves ballpark, which calls for it to be owned by the Cobb-Marietta Coliseum and the Exhibit Hall Authority, will have easy access to I-75, I-285, and the U.S. 41/Cobb Parkway, enabling fans to get into the area easily. Construction began in the second half of the 2014 season and will be completed by Opening Day 2017. The remaining area will be developed by the Braves, and according to the official press release, is set to include "a world-class entertainment district featuring retail, restaurants, and hotel options."

As a result of their move to Cobb County, tentative plans call for Turner Field to be torn down once the Braves leave and the site developed to create a lively middle-class neighborhood.

SPECIAL FEATURES OF TURNER FIELD

755 CLUB

For members only, the 755 Club offers luxurious fine dining and is appropriately named for Hank Aaron, the man who once held baseball's all-time home run record. Renovations took place following the 2010 season. A new menu, access to a nearby lounge, and televisions that keep patrons abreast of all the action make this a true VIP experience.

ARTWORK

There is assorted artwork in Turner Field, including an exhibit by Michael Kalish, entitled *Legends in License Plate,* which is on the Terrace Level and pays tribute to the three homes of the Braves (Massachusetts, Wisconsin, and Georgia). It is a set of four statues of an umpire, batter, pitcher, and fielder, all constructed of license plates from those states. Other artwork in the surrounding area includes *Grand Slam,* a collection of seven different pieces of artwork located around Turner Field; *Three Pennants* by William Alexander, which pays tribute to the three World Series titles won by the Braves; and artist Bart Forbes has 15 oil paintings at the Braves Hall of Fame and Museum.

BRAVES CHOPHOUSE

With room for up to 500, this 8,000-square-foot venue overlooks right field and sits directly above the Braves bullpen. Consisting of a two-story design with indoor and outdoor areas, fans can dine in at the restaurant or opt to sip on a drink on the outside deck while viewing the action.

BRAVESVISION

Measuring nearly seven stories tall, the huge video board, dubbed Braves-Vision, is the world's largest high-definition video board, and was installed to give fans an excellent view regardless of their location in the ballpark. Live video, scoring information, and other relevant in-game statistics are in vibrant color. The overall dimensions of this behemoth structure measure 72 feet by 80 feet, and it weighs 49 tons.

CHAMPIONS ROOM

The Champions Room, an addition of the 755 Club, can be rented for meetings and will impress prospective clients and coworkers. Remodeled in 2004 and constructed for a capacity of 300, the Champions Room offers high-speed Internet, audio/video capabilities, a drop-down screen for projector use, and a sound system. If it gets too sunny in there, blinds can be activated with the push of a button. Now that's service at its best!

CHICK-FIL-A COW

Added in 2008 to complement the Neon Tomahawk is the signature animal of the Chick-Fil-A franchise, a 40-foot-tall, 15,000-pound cow wearing a Braves cap and holding a sign that reads, "DU THE CHOP, EAT THE CHIKIN." Based on its tremendous weight, it appears as though that cow has ingested plenty of chicken sandwiches in its lifetime!

DIVISION TITLES

Flags hang proudly in the left-center field second deck and boast of the Braves division, league championship, and World Series titles. A red flag with the year 1995 in blue and the words "WORLD CHAMPIONS" in white highlights the franchise's only Fall Classic win to date. All the other flags are yellow with numbers inscribed in blue for division crowns, red for league titles, and white for making the playoffs via the wild card. Of course, the Braves are best known for having won an incredible 14 straight division titles from 1991 to 2005, not counting the 1994 strike season.

FULTON COUNTY STADIUM TRIBUTE

A time line that pays tribute to the Braves' previous place of residence at Atlanta-Fulton County Stadium from 1965 to 1997 depicts the stadium's history in photographs, showing highlights along with the year and a brief description. The rounded, cookie-cutter ballpark saw plenty of memorable moments, including Hank Aaron's record-breaking 715th home run on April 8, 1974, which broke Babe Ruth's mark; a no-hitter by Phil Niekro on August 5, 1973; and the pinnacle of Atlanta baseball, a World Series–clinching victory over the Cleveland Indians in Game 6 on October 28, 1995.

GIANT COKE BOTTLE

Looking to imitate the gigantic Coke bottle at San Francisco's AT&T Park, the Braves installed their own version in 2009 behind left field. The bottle is 38 feet tall and is uniquely constructed solely of baseball equipment. The bottle is merely a small part of the Coca-Cola sky field, a 22,000-square-foot gathering location on top of the outfield roof that has picnic tables and benches available for use by fans during all home games.

GRAND ENTRY PLAZA

The Grand Entry Plaza is an extravaganza that has become a hot spot for fans ever since the ballpark opened. A photograph of Hank Aaron's 715th home run ball is front and center and measures 100 feet in diameter, dominating the landscape. Food pavilions, along with fun and games, are available for fans before, during, and after Braves contests.

HANK AARON DRIVE

When approaching Turner Field, take a close look at the street signs, and you'll notice that one of them has been named for one of the most prolific home run hitters of all-time, "Hammerin'" Hank Aaron. When the team was deciding what to name the ballpark, according to a poll conducted by

In the parking lot, a fence and wall mark the exact spot of Hank Aaron's historic 715th career home run. (Photographed by Alicia Barnhart/Flickr)

the *Atlanta Journal-Constitution,* many Atlanta residents had picked Hank Aaron Stadium as their favorite. While that didn't quite make the cut, the Braves have done an adequate job of paying homage to their former slugger.

IVAN ALLEN JR. BRAVES HALL OF FAME AND MUSEUM
Named for the fifty-second mayor of Atlanta, the Hall of Fame and Museum opened its doors to the public in 1999 and exhibits more than 600 artifacts and photographs that chronicle the history of the franchise, including Hall of Fame members, players in the National Baseball Hall of Fame, and other exhibits that highlight the long tradition of "Team Tomahawk." The Hall of Fame and Museum is located on the northwest side at Aisle 134.

MONUMENT GROVE
Monument Grove in Atlanta is free of charge to the public and honors great legends in Braves history. Located across from the Grand Entry Plaza, the park-like setting has picnic tables, benches, and bronze statues immortalizing Hank Aaron, Phil Niekro, Ty Cobb, which were all moved from Atlanta Fulton-County Stadium. A statue of Warren Spahn was added in 2003. There are also retired-number statues of players who have excelled for the Braves. A ticket is not necessary to gain entrance.

NEON TOMAHAWK
If you're a true baseball junkie, the first thing you associate with the franchise is the world-famous tomahawk. At the ballpark, fans are prompted

to do the "chopping" tomahawk when the 27-foot-long neon tomahawk perched atop the video board comes to life.

OVERSIZED DRUM

The center-field pavilion at Turner Field is home to one of the more exceptional pieces in Major League Baseball—a gigantic drum. A man beats on it throughout the course of the game. How awesome would it be if a player launched a home run, it bounced off the drum, and catapulted outside the ballpark? Now come on, am I the only one who thinks about these things?

RETIRED NUMBERS

The Atlanta Braves have retired 10 numbers, which are on the upper deck façade in left field. They include: Dale Murphy (3), Bobby Cox (6), Chipper Jones (10), Warren Spahn (21), John Smoltz (29), Greg Maddux (31), Phil Niekro (35), Eddie Mathews (41), Hank Aaron (44), and Tom Glavine (47).

SCOUTS ALLEY

Scouts Alley, which is mostly for kids but is available to anyone, offers the opportunity to demonstrate your talents both at the plate and on the mound. Tokens can be purchased nearby and used for two-speed pitch games and two hitting games. Who knows? If you're good enough, maybe the Braves will sign you to a contract! Highly unlikely, you say? Well, at least you can pretend you are a Major Leaguer!

SUNTRUST CLUB

This members-only accommodation opened in 2008 and has 150 field-level luxury seats right behind the plate, offering members true VIP treatment. Excellent food, an extensive list of cocktails, a full bar, and flat-screen televisions keep guests updated on all the action around the Majors. Valet parking is included.

TOONER FIELD

Tooner Field, which has two outdoor baseball fields, interactive games, and a climate-controlled environment, is a hands-on exhibit that will have the kids talking about the great time they had long after they leave the ballpark. Whether it's testing their skills on the baseball field or on the microphone, this section is sponsored by the Cartoon Network and will, without a doubt, be the highlight of any child's visit to Turner Field.

TOP OF THE CHOP

Top of the Chop, an extension of the existing Braves Chophouse, is a party deck in right field with seating for up to 300. One of the signature attractions is a full-service cabana bar, where you can order your favorite cocktail. Picnic tables, along with bar barrel tables, make this a hotspot for fun with friends and family.

TURF

A total of 110,000 square feet of sod—419 Hybrid Bermuda grass—covers the entire playing field and is watered on a daily basis by 60 sprinkler heads embedded in the field. In case of a flood, an extensive drainage system can remove 120,000 gallons of water per hour. Grass for repair is grown just behind the center-field wall underneath the main scoreboard.

WALK OF FAME

The Walk of Fame, an extension of the Braves Hall of Fame and Museum at Monument Grove, commemorates all the members of the Braves Hall of Fame with bronze plaques. From Greg Maddux to Hank Aaron to Dale Murphy, they are all here, and going through the names is sure to evoke memories of when these men starred on the field in a Braves uniform.

MEMORABLE GAMES AT TURNER FIELD

APRIL 4, 1997: FIRST GAME AT TURNER FIELD

The Braves wasted no time notching their first win at the transformed Olympic stadium, defeating the Chicago Cubs 5–4 in front of 45,044 behind a game-winning RBI from Chipper Jones. Jones, who finished the contest 3-for-4, registered the first hit in stadium history during the bottom of the first with a single to left field. In the bottom of second, Braves catcher Javier Lopez led off the frame with a double to center for the first extra-base hit, but was ultimately left stranded. Atlanta starter Denny Neagle went six innings, allowing five hits and two runs, but the win went to reliever Brad Klontz with Mark Wohlers registering the save. With Chicago ahead 4–3 in the bottom of the eighth, Atlanta's Kenny Lofton reached base thanks to an error, allowing Jeff Blauser to score the tying run, and two batters later, Jones connected for what would turn out to be the game-winning RBI single.

JUNE 13, 1999: BALTIMORE OUTSCORES ATLANTA BY THREE TOUCHDOWNS

In an Interleague contest that Atlanta would like to forget, the Orioles strutted into town and embarrassed the Braves, 22–1, behind a career day from Cal Ripken Jr. Baltimore tallied five runs in the first inning, which was only a prelude of things to come. Ripken Jr. dissected an otherwise-solid Braves pitching staff, finishing the game 6-for-6 at the plate with two home runs, a double, and three singles to complement six RBI. Baltimore first baseman Will Clark also turned in a stellar game, finishing 4-for-4 with three doubles, a home run, and five RBI. Braves starter John Smoltz allowed seven runs in 2⅓ innings while his immediate replacement, Justin Speier, didn't fare any better in giving up six runs in 2⅔ innings. In all, Baltimore tallied 25 hits to Atlanta's six, and scored in every inning but the second and eighth.

OCTOBER 19, 1999: ATLANTA TAKES DOWN METS TO CAPTURE PENNANT

The Braves wrapped up their first World Series berth in the Turner Field era with a wild 10–9 victory over the New York Mets in a game that went 11 innings. It looked as though it would be a cakewalk for Atlanta, scoring five runs in the bottom of the first, highlighted by run-scoring singles from Brian Jordan and Eddie Perez. But the Mets wouldn't go down easily, scoring three in the sixth, four in the seventh, and one in the eighth, tying it at eight heading into extra innings. The Mets struck first in the top half of the tenth with a sacrifice fly by Todd Pratt, giving the Metropolitans a brief 9–8 advantage.

Not to be outdone, Ozzie Guillen stroked an RBI single to right in the bottom half of the inning, which scored Chipper Jones and tied the contest at nine. Finally, in the bottom of the tenth with one out, Andruw Jones's patience at the plate helped send the Braves to the Fall Classic for the first time since 1996, after a bases-loaded walk scored Gerald Williams, finishing off the Mets and bringing the National League Championship back to Atlanta after a three-year absence.

OCTOBER 23, 1999: FIRST WORLD SERIES GAME AT TURNER FIELD

In a rematch of the 1996 World Series won by the New York Yankees in six games, the Fall Classic returned to Atlanta—this time at Turner Field—and the Yankees would take Game 1, thanks to a dominant pitching performance, 4–1. Hernandez would pitch a gem, striking out 10 and allowing one run on one hit—a solo home run to right field by Chipper Jones—in his seven innings on the mound. Maddux was just as good, but the Yankees struck for four runs in the top of the eighth when Derek Jeter punched a single into left field with the bases loaded, driving in Scott Brosius and tying the game at one. Braves reliever John Rocker was summoned and promptly gave up a two-run single to Paul O'Neill, pushing the New York lead to 3–1. Later, Jim Leyritz was walked with the bases loaded, extending the lead to 4–1, more than enough run support for closer Mariano Rivera. Four days later, New York would go on to sweep the Braves, clinching their second straight title.

MAY 17, 2004: JOHNSON RECORDS PERFECT GAME

Who says age matters when it comes to the game of baseball? At 40 years old, Randy Johnson became the oldest player in Major League history at the time to toss a perfect game—eclipsing the mark set by Cy Young at age 37—setting down the Braves in order in leading the Diamondbacks to a 2–0 win in Atlanta. It was the seventeenth perfect game in modern history and the first since David Cone did so against Montreal on July 18, 1999, at Yankee Stadium. Putting together a seamless performance, Johnson struck out 13 and went to three balls on just one hitter, Johnny Estrada, in the second frame. The closest thing to a hit came when pitcher Mike Hampton hit a slow roller that was fielded cleanly by Alex Cintron, who proceeded to throw out Hampton by a half-step in the sixth inning. Additionally, it also marked the first time Atlanta was no-hit since Ken Forsch of Houston did so on April 7, 1979. Alex Cintron connected for an RBI double in the second, and Chad Tracy added an RBI single in the seventh to account for the only runs Johnson would require.

APRIL 22, 2008: SMOLTZ RECORDS 3,000TH STRIKEOUT

In his twentieth Major League season with the Braves, pitcher John Smoltz added another accomplishment to his résumé by becoming the sixteenth player in Major League history to strike out 3,000, victimizing Felipe Lopez in the third inning of a 6–0 loss to the Washington Nationals. Smoltz, who returned to the rotation following a stint as Atlanta closer from 2002 to 2004, became just the fourth player to reach 3,000 with one team adding his name to an elite class that includes Walter Johnson (Washington), Bob Gibson (St. Louis), and Steve Carlton (Philadelphia). The Nationals, who led 1–0 going to the ninth, put the game out of reach with a five-run frame, keyed by a two-run double off the bat of Ryan Zimmerman.

APRIL 17, 2010: A COLORADO ROCKIES FIRST

Colorado starter Ubaldo Jimenez waltzed into Turner Field and hurled the first no-hitter in the 18-year history of the Rockies, shutting out the Braves, 4–0. Although Jimenez was wild, having allowed six walks in the contest, he worked out of the jams and retired the final 15 batters he faced. The Braves' best threat for a hit came in seventh, when Troy Glaus put a shot into the ball only to have center fielder Dexter Fowler swoop in to temporarily steal the show with a remarkable catch. With the no-hitter, the Rockies were able to eliminate themselves from the list of teams that had never experienced the thrill of a no-no, leaving the Padres, Mets, and Rays at the time as the only three to never experience the thrill of holding an opposing team without a hit. The Rockies offense, which tallied nine hits, was led by Brad Hawpe (3-for-4, RBI) and Carlos Gonzalez (2-for-5, 2 RBI). Jimenez helped out his own cause by connecting for an RBI single in the fourth inning, pushing Colorado's lead at the time to 2–0, a lead that would turn out to be more than enough for the hard-throwing right hander.

OCTOBER 5, 2012: FIRST WILD CARD PLAY-IN GAME

In a controversial one-game playoff to see who would move on to the Division Series, the St. Louis Cardinals capitalized on three throwing errors by the Braves and rallied from an early deficit to defeat Atlanta, 6–2. In the debut of the wild card play-in game, it lived up to its hype as a "do or die" after a 19-minute delay in the eighth when fans threw garbage onto the field after a play was disputed. Trailing 6–3 in the eighth, Andrelton Simmons lofted a fly ball that dropped between two fielders, making it seem as though the Braves would have the bases loaded. The umpire called for the infield fly rule, giving the Braves two outs, and all hell broke loose once the fans realized what occurred. When play resumed, Atlanta could not scratch across a run, and the Cardinals went in the history books as the first team to stand victorious in a one-game play-in to determine who would head to the Division Series.

SEPTEMBER 1, 2014: PHILLIES COMBINE TO NO-HIT BRAVES

Philadelphia starter Cole Hamels, along with three relievers, teamed up for the 11th combined no-hitter in Major League history, pulling off the feat on Labor Day during a dominating 7–0 victory over the Atlanta Braves. Offensively, the Phillies were led by leadoff hitter Ben Revere, who went 2-for-3 at the place and accounted for 5 runs batted in, and Jimmy Rollins, who had himself a day by finishing 3-for-5. But the story was the pitching; Hamels went six innings before giving way to reliever Jake Diekman, who promptly pitched a perfect seventh inning while striking out two. Ken Giles, who entered the game in the eighth for Philadelphia, proceeded to strike out the side, and closer Jonathan Papelbon sealed the deal in the bottom of the ninth by retiring the Braves in order.

WHAT THEY'RE SAYING ABOUT TURNER FIELD

CARLOS BELTRAN: "It is one of my favorites for me because the lighting is so good. The ballpark is big and fair and the outfield [is big too]. . . . Everything is great about that ballpark, and they keep it up very nicely."

BOB BRENLY: "I always felt Atlanta could have done a little more with their ballpark. It is beautiful and there is nothing wrong with it, but it is just kind of generic for me. . . . You could put it in any other city in the country and it would be just another ballpark."

R. A. DICKEY: "I do not know why, but it is not one of my favorites. . . . It is always really muggy there, but it is okay as far as fields go. It is just not one of my favorites."

STEPHEN DREW: "I grew up in Georgia, so I like to play in Atlanta at Turner Field. . . . They did a really good job with the new field and it is always fun to get there and play against some guys that I know."

DUANE KUIPER, BROADCASTER: "I think Turner Field is perfect because of where they came from [Atlanta Fulton-County Stadium] and moved 300 yards away. . . . [It is] built for pitching, yet you are still going to get some carry and I think it is a very fair ballpark. I have no problems with Turner Field."

ADAM LAROCHE: "That holds a special place in my career because that is where I came up playing and is where I made a lot of friends in the game. . . . As far as dimensions go, I think it is one of the more fair ballparks in the league."

JOSH LEWIN, BROADCASTER: "I was there for the opening game and I remember thinking at the time that they really did everything right. . . . Honestly, though, you look at the new ones that have opened since and you can kind of see how you get what you pay for. It is not like they did it on the cheap, but they did it on effectiveness."

BUSTER POSEY: "That is where I grew up, going to watch some games, and I see it differently now as a player than I did going there as a fan and seeing different ballparks. . . . It is good—it is not up on the top of my list, but I like it fine."

CHARLEY STEINER, BROADCASTER: "It is nice, [but] I think it is generic. . . . There is nothing about Turner Field [that makes me think] 'Gee, I cannot wait to see the nooks and crannies of Turner Field.' It is certainly no AT&T Park, no PNC Park, no Wrigley Field, no Yankee Stadium, no Dodger Stadium, [but] it is a nice ballpark."

DAVID WRIGHT: "When I think of Turner Field, I think of a fair ballpark. . . . To me, I really enjoy it there and growing up in Virginia with TBS, it seemed like every time you turned on the television, there was a Braves game on, so that brings me back to growing up in Virginia."

TURNER FIELD FACTS AND FIGURES

TURNER FIELD ADDRESS
755 Hank Aaron Drive, Atlanta, GA 30315

ATLANTA BRAVES TEAM WEB SITE
www.braves.com

FIELD DIMENSIONS (IN FEET)
Left Field: 335', Left-Center: 380', Center: 401',
Right-Center: 390', Right Field: 330'

SEATING CAPACITY (AS OF 2015)
49,586

ALL-STAR GAMES AT TURNER FIELD
July 11, 2000: American League 6, National League 3
MVP: Derek Jeter, New York Yankees (AL)

TURNER FIELD FIRSTS
Game: April 4, 1997—Atlanta 5, Chicago 4
Single: Chipper Jones, Atlanta (April 4, 1997)*
Double: Javy Lopez, Atlanta (April 4, 1997)
Triple: Brian McRae, Chicago (April 4, 1997)
Home Run: Michael Tucker, Atlanta (April 4, 1997)

Denotes first hit in the stadium.

WEST
REGION

ANGEL STADIUM OF ANAHEIM
HOME OF THE LOS ANGELES ANGELS

Angel Stadium, Los Angeles Angels *(Photographed by Russel Tiffin/Flickr)*

Angel Stadium of Anaheim was previously known as Anaheim Stadium (1964–97) and Edison International Field (1998–2003).

Since 1966, Angel Stadium of Anaheim has been the home of the Los Angeles Angels, and since 1997, it has undergone extensive renovations to create an improved baseball-only setting. Those alterations have made it a fan-friendly facility, while eliminating the impersonal, completely enclosed look that it once had.

Talks for what would eventually be known as Angel Stadium of Anaheim began on April 10, 1964, when members of the Anaheim City Council accepted a letter of intent during a special session of the Council of Orange County Board of Supervisors. However, the supervisors declined to join the City of Anaheim in backing and building the stadium. With the decision finalized, the City Council decided they would go it alone to do whatever it took to make the project a reality.

Contractor Del Webb pledged to complete Angel Stadium before the 1966 campaign. He proceeded, at his own risk, with the blueprints for the structure, pending the conclusive declaration of the Council. Feeling that it was a choice that had to be made, the Council finally approved the plan on August 8, 1964, and the City of Anaheim and the Angels signed a 35-year lease for the ballpark, thus making it official and overcoming a serious roadblock to having a Major League–ready facility constructed.

Ground was first broken on August 31, 1964, for "The Big A," and the Angels prepared to move from Dodger Stadium, a facility they had been renting while the new ballpark was being constructed. The ballpark, completed in time for the 1966 season at a cost of $24 million, was built on 160 acres. The land in the southeast portion of the area, near the intersection of three freeways, was formerly used for agriculture.

The renovating and tinkering this structure has undergone over the years have been nearly unprecedented. The most significant transformation, costing an estimated $100 million, occurred following the 1995 season and gave Angel Stadium of Anaheim its identity as a Major League Baseball–only ballpark. Seats that once were added to accommodate NFL football from straightaway center field were removed, and the outfield was restored to its original form, circa 1966.

SPECIAL FEATURES OF ANGEL STADIUM OF ANAHEIM

BIG A SCOREBOARD

Once the main showpiece of the outfield, and an imposing structure for every batter who strolled to the plate, the 23-story, 240-ton, halo-topped scoreboard now towers above the main parking lot. Relegated to its current location due to renovations, the main display—which at one time served as a primary information base for in-game statistics and a real-time box score—now offers passers-by promotional text as well as game times and other information.

BULLPENS

Looking to sneak a peek at the pitchers warming up in either the home or visitors' bullpen? Look no farther than in left field, where both are right behind the outfield wall. It is a two-tiered design, much like that of Oriole Park at Camden Yards in Baltimore. Los Angeles pitchers are stationed right behind the outfield wall, while the visiting team's location is closer to the Left Field Pavilion.

CALIFORNIA SPECTACULAR

One of the more notable recent changes was the addition of the California Spectacular, located just beyond the left-center-field fence. Complete with 90-foot-high geysers and a cascade of water flowing down among real trees and phony rocks, the attraction was designed to evoke the California coastline and offers a peaceful backdrop for fans. It comes to life with pyrotechnics whenever there is an Angels' home run or victory.

COURTYARD

The first- and third-base lines are home to outdoor courtyards. Attractive landscaping covers the grounds, and there are two large food courts. Other attractions nearby include a Music Garden at Gate 1, a statue of former owner Gene Autry at Gate 2, and the Michelle Carew statue at Gate 3.

FOLLOW THE FAN BRICK ROAD

The home plate gate is where the Angels have offered true die-hards the chance of a lifetime to become a part of the ballpark. For a fee, citizens were given the opportunity to purchase bricks and have personalized messages inscribed pertaining to the team or any special memories. They were later added to the home plate gate, and now serve as a special link between the fans and the team. Those who opted to take advantage received a replica brick to keep as a one-of-a-kind memento.

GENE AUTRY STATUE

While a statue of Michelle Carew is at the Gate 3 entrance, a likeness of Gene Autry guards Gate 2. Autry, the founder of the California Angels in 1961, was instrumental in the beginning stages of baseball in suburban Anaheim in 1966 and also took on the role of American League vice-president from 1983 until his death. He originally set out to be a part of the broadcast team, but after a meeting with baseball executives, they convinced him to be the owner of the Angels franchise, and he accepted. The bronze sculpture depicts a smiling Autry with his left hand on his right knee, while his right hand is extended, as if he were looking to shake hands with anyone nearby. Autry died of lymphoma on October 2, 1998, at the age of 91.

HIGHWAY 57

If your seat happens to be somewhere in the upper deck at Angel Stadium, you can see State Route 57—also known as Orange Freeway and Highway 57—as cars whiz by. It is the main thoroughfare into the ballpark and runs north and south, serving as a connection point between Interstate 5 and

State Route 22 to the Glendora Curve interchange with Interstate 210 and State Route 210 in Glendora. For the record, and according to Google Earth, a home run would have to travel over 1,300 feet to reach the highway.

HOME PLATE RESTAURANT

This full-service restaurant is positioned right behind home plate and offers ticket holders signature dishes and an all-you-can-eat buffet. An extensive wine selection and top-shelf liquor make this an experience that's difficult to top. A word to the wise: This restaurant is open to guests with tickets specifically for the Diamond Club seating areas an hour and a half before the first pitch, and while it's not a must, reservations are strongly suggested in order to ensure a table will be available for the game you will be attending.

KNOTHOLE CLUB

The Knothole Club, a restaurant that provides seating both inside and on the patio alongside the right-field pole, is on the club level. While reservations are not necessary, they can be made just to ensure seating will be available. One of their specialties is the Ultimate Gigantic Banana Split. A full-service bar, combined with exceptional views of the game, make this one of the better luxuries in all of baseball.

LOS ANGELES RAMS

When it was better known as Anaheim Stadium, the NFL's Rams moved from the gigantic, 100,000-seat Los Angeles Memorial Coliseum to the Angels' digs in 1980. To accommodate the masses for football, both the mezzanine and upper-deck sections were expanded, and the end result produced a totally enclosed stadium. In addition, elevated rows of bleachers were constructed in the right- and left-field areas, increasing the overall capacity to more than 70,000 for football and 64,593 for baseball. The Rams bid good-bye to the structure following the 1994 season, when they relocated to St. Louis.

MICHELLE CAREW STATUE

A bronze statue of Michelle Carew, the daughter of former Angels great and Hall of Famer Rod Carew, is prominently displayed at Gate 3. The sculpture, which depicts a smiling Carew with one arm around a dog, is encircled by flowers and honors a woman who exemplified compassion. Michelle lost her hard-fought battle with leukemia on April 17, 1996, at the age of 18, but was instrumental in encouraging others not to give up in their fight against the disease.

The grand entrance, featuring two baseball hats with a size of 649½, welcomes fans to Angel Stadium. (*Photographed by Russel Tiffin/Flickr*)

NAMING RIGHTS

When it first debuted, California's newest ballpark was called Anaheim Stadium, but over the years, there have been plenty of name changes. In 1998, the Angels reached a 20-year agreement with Edison International to rename the ballpark Edison International Field, but in 2003, the company exercised its rights to disassociate itself from the initial contract. It was then announced that the ballpark would simply be known as Angel Stadium of Anaheim, which is where things currently stand as of this writing.

OVERSIZED HELMETS

The main entrance to Angel Stadium of Anaheim is flanked by two gigantic Angels batting helmets with a hat size of 649½. During the "Disney Era" of 1997, they featured the Angels winged logo on blue paint, but once the colors and insignia changed for the 2002 season, they were repainted to reflect the current color scheme of red, complete with the identifiable halo emblem.

PRESS BOX

Prior to the 2013 campaign, the press box was moved from its original location behind home plate to its current location down the first-base side. This created a ticketed area called the Terrace Club, which has a total of 80 seats in three rows. The Angels joined the White Sox as the only Major League team not to have its press box situated right behind home plate.

The radio and television broadcast booths remained in the same place, one level above the old press box. It cost $1 million to convert the club level, near section 343, into the new press box and dining room.

RALLY MONKEY

What began innocently during the 2002 postseason as a way to rile up fans and get the Angels prepped to come back from any deficit has now become a mainstay at Angel Stadium. The free-swinging monkey first appeared when the Angels marched through the playoffs to capture their first World Series championship by defeating the San Francisco Giants. When run-scoring is needed, the Rally Monkey appears, urging the fans to start clapping, make noise, and do whatever they can to get behind the Los Angeles nine that day.

RETIRED NUMBERS

The Angels have retired five numbers over the course of their history, and they are beneath the big scoreboard in right field. They include: Jim Fregosi (11), Gene Autry (26), Rod Carew (29), Nolan Ryan (30), and Jimmy Reese (50).

TERRACE CLUB

As a result of relocating the press box for the 2013 season, the Terrace Club took over the space that once housed writers and broadcasters. This premium-style area, which offers incredible views of the action, can be accessed through several different 10-game packages offered by the club or through an 81-game season-ticket plan. The seating section, equaling three rows, features around 80 seats.

MEMORABLE GAMES AT ANGEL STADIUM OF ANAHEIM

APRIL 19, 1966: FIRST GAME AT ANGEL STADIUM OF ANAHEIM

A crowd of 31,660 packed Angel Stadium of Anaheim for the inaugural game, but watched the Chicago White Sox come into town and capture a 3–1 victory. Tommy John started for Chicago, allowing only one run—a home run by Rick Reichardt in the bottom of the second—in going seven effective innings while scattering only three hits. The White Sox went to work on the offensive end in the sixth, when a solo home run by Tommy Agee tied the game at one. Two more runs crossed the plate in the top of the eighth after back-to-back RBI singles by Don Buford and Floyd Robinson proved to be the difference. Angels shortstop Jim Fregosi registered the ballpark's first official hit, when he hit a double to right field in the first, perhaps offering some sort of consolation prize for the fans who went home disappointed.

SEPTEMBER 17, 1984: MR. OCTOBER'S 500TH HOMER

On the seventeenth anniversary of his first Major League home run, Reggie Jackson was at it again, this time connecting for his 500th career blast, but Kansas City spoiled the festivities and routed the Angels, 10–1. In a career that saw him become a legend during the 1977 World Series after he hit three home runs in three first-pitch at-bats, he added another accomplishment to his Hall of Fame credentials. The historic shot came in the bottom of the seventh, when Jackson led off and hit the first pitch he saw off Royals starter Bud Black. It accounted for the only run and unfortunately for fans in attendance, Kansas City was operating on all cylinders and ended the game outhitting the Angels, 12–3.

AUGUST 4, 1985: CAREW NOTCHES HIT NUMBER 3,000

Batting against his former team, the Minnesota Twins, Rod Carew lined a third-inning single off starter Frank Viola, becoming the sixteenth member of the 3,000th-hit club during the Angels' 6–5 victory. After grounding out in his first at-bat during the bottom of the first inning, Carew would not be denied in the third, lacing the historic hit and receiving a curtain call from fans as he stood on first base. The actual game proved to be high in drama. With the score tied at five-all in the eighth, Brian Downing came to the plate and connected for an RBI single, plating Gary Pettis for what turned out to be the decisive run. As for Carew, he became the first player since Boston's Carl Yastrzemski accomplished the feat on September 12, 1979, to achieve the 3,000th-hit mark.

OCTOBER 12, 1986: HENDERSON SAVES RED SOX

With a 5–2 lead in the game and a commanding 3–1 American League Championship Series advantage over Boston, it appeared as though the Angels were well on their way to punching their first ticket to the Fall Classic. All that changed in the ninth, when Don Baylor smoked a two-out, two-run home run, pulling the Red Sox to within 5–4. After a walk was issued to Rich Gedman, Angels reliever Donnie Moore was called upon to stop the bleeding and was saddled with the inevitable task of facing Dave Henderson.

With two strikes, Henderson guessed forkball all the way and was right, squarely putting bat on ball and depositing it over the left-field fence to give the Red Sox an improbable 6–5 lead. Although the Angels overcame that adversity and tied it in the bottom half on an RBI single by Rob Wilfong, which sent the game to extra innings, the Red Sox would not be denied. In the eleventh, they officially began their quest toward winning the AL pennant when Henderson was at it again, this time hitting a sacrifice fly, which proved to be the game-winner and sealed the demoralizing loss for the Angels.

SEPTEMBER 30, 1992: BRETT JOINS EXCLUSIVE CLUB

George Brett went 4-for-5 and led the Royals to a 4–0 win over the Angels, but the bigger story was that he became the latest member to join the 3,000th-hit club with a seventh-inning single. Having already doubled and singled twice, he stepped in against Angels reliever Tim Fortugno and promptly lined the first pitch he saw past second base, capping a remarkable night. Ironically, his historic hit came exactly 20 years to the day that Pittsburgh Pirates great Roberto Clemente collected his 3,000th and final hit, a double off the Mets Jon Matlack at Three Rivers Stadium in Pittsburgh.

OCTOBER 13, 2002: KENNEDY SLAMS THREE HOME RUNS TO MOVE ANGELS ON

Doing his best Babe Ruth impression, Adam Kennedy slammed three home runs and helped the Angels clinch the American League pennant and head to their first World Series in franchise history with a 13–5 rout of Minnesota. All seemed well for Minnesota after the Twins took a 5–3 lead into the seventh inning, but that's when things changed dramatically. In the bottom half, the Halos erupted for 10 runs, including the decisive three-run blast by Kennedy, his third, which sent the stadium into raucous celebration mode. Kennedy, who also singled, finished the game with five runs batted in.

> "[It happened] 30 miles from where I grew up. A lot of family was there, a lot of high school buddies, my high school coach was there, and people flew out from Kansas City to see it and little did I know I would do it all in one night. I got four hits in my first four at-bats— there were five games to go in the season and I did not know if I was going to retire at the end of the season. . . . I was scared to death in the on-deck circle, and walking up to home plate I was nervous, but as soon as I got in the batter's box, I calmed down, swung at the first pitch, and hit a rocket to right field."
> —George Brett

OCTOBER 27, 2002: FIRST WORLD CHAMPIONSHIP CLINCHED

In a Fall Classic that saw two wild-card teams competing for all the marbles for the first time in baseball history, the Angels stood victorious at the end and won their first World Series title with a 4–1, Game 7 victory over San Francisco. With the score knotted at one after two innings, the Angels got all the run support they would need in the bottom of the third after three were registered on the scoreboard. With the bases loaded, beloved Angels slugger Garret Anderson sent a 1–1 pitch down the right-field line for a bases-clearing, three-run double off San Francisco starter Livan Hernandez, giving the Angels a lead they would not relinquish. The Giants would come up dry the rest of the way, and Troy Percival recorded the final out on a fly ball to deep center hit by Kenny Lofton, sealing the first championship in franchise history.

"Hard to explain—just an exciting time for all of us and the fun Series with the Giants. . . . When you are going through it, you do not have time to think about what is going on, you are just in the grind of trying to win that game and when it is done, you just take a deep breath and it was really fun to be a part of."
—*Adam Kennedy*

"I had gone through it as a player and I was fortunate to win two World Series [with the Dodgers in 1981 and 1988]. . . . You cannot imagine the grind of not only getting through a full season, but getting through a second season that is a month's worth of playoff games. It was a great feeling of relief and accomplishment, and [I] was very happy for our players who experienced it for the first time."
—*Mike Scioscia, manager*

AUGUST 21, 2007: ANDERSON HAS MONSTER DAY VERSUS YANKEES

Garret Anderson went 4-for-6 and drove home 10 during an 18–9 win over New York, becoming the thirteenth player in baseball history to accumulate 10 or more RBIs in a game and the first player since Alex Rodriguez did so on April 26, 2005. Anderson connected for a two-run double in the first, while an RBI double the next inning upped his total to three, but that was just the beginning. In the bottom of the third, he blasted a three-run bomb off Edwar Ramirez, and the fans in attendance knew they were witnessing something special. Anderson further drove home that message when he connected for a sixth-inning grand slam off Sean Henn, giving him 10 RBI for the game with the Angels leading 18–5. In the bottom of the eighth, Anderson grounded out with two on missing his chance at a Major League record 13 RBI, had he homered again.

MAY 2, 2012: WEAVER DOMINATES TWINS, TOSSES NO-NO

Jered Weaver tossed the tenth no-hitter in Angels history—and the first since Ervin Santana pitched one at Cleveland on July 27, 2011—shutting down the overmatched Minnesota Twins, 9–0. The visitors really had no threats of breaking up the masterpiece outside of an innocent fly ball hit on the button by Trevor Plouffe, which was snagged with ease on the warning track by Torii Hunter in the fifth. The Angels offense provided plenty of run support for Weaver, scoring all nine of their runs through four innings headlined by Howie Kendrick, who went 4-for-4 with three runs batted in, and designated hitter Kendrys Morales, who went 3-for-5 with a single, double, home run, and three runs batted in. Weaver finished the 121-pitch outing with nine strikeouts.

WHAT THEY'RE SAYING ABOUT ANGEL STADIUM OF ANAHEIM

VINCE COTRONEO, BROADCASTER: "They spent a lot of money to make it a baseball-only facility and that works. . . . It is a little bit tricked up with the rock garden in left-center [and] it is kind of [like a] Disney-like-type field—a sea of red—and if I see the rally monkey one more time, it will be one more time too many."

RON GARDENHIRE: "Just a gorgeous ballpark [with] the big rocks—I guess the California Disney look—and [with] the background, it turned into just a gorgeous baseball field. . . . [It has] huge dugouts, [and] everything has been updated there and [is] very laid-back, just like you would expect. Baseball at night there is as good as it gets."

JASON GIAMBI: "It was really good hitting [at] when it was the 'Old A' and really closed and the ball was jumping out of that place really good. . . . The new one is nice and beautiful, [but] can be tough in day games, but it is fun to go play there."

CURTIS GRANDERSON: "Anaheim is my favorite ballpark. . . . [The] playing surface, the weather, [the] energy is always good there. [They] always have a good crowd, and I like the things that they do to keep the fans interacted throughout the course of the game."

JOSH HAMILTON: "Good environment as far as the setup of the ballpark, [and] you think about how it used to be a football stadium and they cut half the stadium out and reconstructed it, built the rocks in center, and the waterfall. . . . [It is] just a unique environment and fun to play at."

TORII HUNTER: "It is a nice stadium. When I was there as a visitor with Minnesota, we would go there and play and it [was] just a great atmosphere . . . the sun out there, the fans are great, [and] the stadium seems like Disneyland with the rocks out there in the outfield."

ADAM JONES: "[It is my] favorite ballpark to play in on the road away from home. . . . [I have] family there, it is always sunny, and you cannot go wrong with that."

EVAN LONGORIA: "I have been going there since I was young, watching ballgames there. . . . The Angels fans are good, they love their team, and it is always a fun place to play. I remember I got an autograph from Damion Easley once when I was younger when he was with the Angels and I was really excited about that."

ERIC NADEL, BROADCASTER: "I think it has been renovated marvelously. They did a spectacular job taking an all-purpose stadium [and] converting it into a baseball stadium. . . . I think it is one of the most underrated gems among the baseball ballparks."

MIKE SCIOSCIA: "It is really just a great baseball environment, relaxing, [and] a great family atmosphere. . . . The weather is always great and it is probably the best playing surface in baseball. The players enjoy coming [to Angel Stadium]."

ANGEL STADIUM OF ANAHEIM FACTS AND FIGURES

ANGEL STADIUM OF ANAHEIM ADDRESS
2000 Gene Autry Way, Anaheim, CA 92806

LOS ANGELES ANGELS TEAM WEB SITE
www.angels.com

FIELD DIMENSIONS (IN FEET)
Left Field: 330', Left-Center: 387', Center: 400', Right-Center: 370', Right Field: 330'

SEATING CAPACITY (AS OF 2015)
45,483

ALL-STAR GAMES AT ANGEL STADIUM OF ANAHEIM
July 11, 1967: National League 2, American League 1 (15 innings)
MVP: Tony Perez, Cincinnati Reds (NL)
July 11, 1989: American League 5, National League 3
MVP: Bo Jackson, Kansas City Royals (AL)
July 13, 2010: National League 3, American League 1
MVP: Brian McCann, Atlanta Braves (NL)

ANGEL STADIUM OF ANAHEIM FIRSTS

Game: April 19, 1966—Chicago 3, Los Angeles 1
Single: Buck Rodgers, Los Angeles (April 19, 1966)
Double: Jim Fregosi, Los Angeles (April 19, 1966)*
Triple: Paul Schaal, Los Angeles (April 20, 1966)
Home Run: Rick Reichardt, Los Angeles (April 19, 1966)

Denotes first hit in the stadium.

AT&T PARK
HOME OF THE SAN FRANCISCO GIANTS

AT&T Park, San Francisco Giants (*Photographed by Matthew D. Britt/Flickr*)

[*AT&T Park was previously known as Pacific Bell Park (2000–03) and SBC Park (2004–05).*]

If anyone in professional sports in the San Francisco area was a hero, it would have to be Giants owner Peter Magowan. He ensured that the Giants remained in San Francisco and had a state-of-the-art structure built that, no doubt, will be admired for many years, but it wasn't easy.

With the Giants on the verge of winning a referendum for public financing in 1989, the infamous and untimely earthquake changed a lot of minds, and the vote was narrowly lost because of the natural disaster, which cast a dark shadow over the whole situation. Bob Lurie, the Giants owner until Magowan bought the club from him, tried desperately to relocate the team to St. Petersburg, but Magowan saved the franchise, vowing to have a new stadium built. This action, in many people's opinion in the San Francisco area, was one of the greatest moments in Giants baseball history as he successfully saved the franchise from leaving town.

In December 1995, Magowan unveiled a plan to build a new 41,000-seat ballpark that would replace Candlestick Park, a wind-stricken, non-fan-friendly stadium that had long worn out its welcome. The new ballpark cost $306 million, but he was determined not to ask for any public taxpayer assistance, announcing that the stadium would be privately financed, and with that, it became the first Major League ballpark to be paid for in that way since Dodger Stadium in 1962. The Giants broke ground on December 11, 1997, and the stadium would be ready for baseball in April 2000.

Put simply, the Giants moved from Candlestick Park to a smaller structure and gained a picturesque waterfront location similar to that of the PNC Park in Pittsburgh and Great American Ball Park in Cincinnati. The brick-faced, open-air facility is situated on a 13-acre site at China Basin, just north of the Lefty O'Doul Bridge. The façade was made to resemble other buildings in the neighborhood. The designers used multicolored bricks to make the stadium look as if it had been there for many years. From downtown, the ballpark can be reached on foot in around 20 minutes, and public transportation makes it easy to get to and from AT&T Park.

Like many of the new ballparks, AT&T Park is the crown jewel in a city that once had little prospect of keeping a baseball team. Magowan accomplished his goal of creating an upbeat atmosphere around the city while at the same time building a stadium that has fast become a popular destination for fans.

SPECIAL FEATURES OF AT&T PARK

A MALL THAT WASN'T MEANT TO BE

Initially, plans for a mall to be constructed inside of the ballpark were discussed, which would have pushed the final bill to around $500 million. This idea, which was later scrapped, would have been similar to that at Rangers Ballpark in Texas, but it was probably best that it didn't pan out. After all, aren't ballparks for baseball games and shopping malls for shopping?

ARTWORK IN THE PARK

If you love paintings and sculptures, then you will be pleased to know that there is plenty of artwork around AT&T Park. On the club level are murals of larger-than-life players and memorabilia photos. Also, be sure to check out home plate–themed murals on the field club level, where you can also find photos of old-time catchers' masks.

BOB STEVENS PRESS BOX

The press box is on the upper deck of AT&T Park directly behind home plate and is named for a man who was a longtime sportswriter for the *San Francisco Chronicle*. Bob Stevens, who covered the San Francisco Seals and Giants from their West Coast inception, also attended and covered every All-Star and World Series game from 1958 to 1978. He later received the game's highest accolade after he was inducted into the sportswriting wing of the National Baseball Hall of Fame in 1999.

BULLPENS

Both the home and visitors' bullpens are positioned on the field of play down each line, creating a sense of nostalgia whenever a pitcher warms up. Fans have close-up views, allowing for a comparison with Wrigley Field, which is a true ballpark from an early era in baseball history.

BUSINESS CENTER

Situated on the suite level, the Business Center provides a range of services for suite holders and field club members by providing access to a fax machine, copier, and modem connections. It also has two conference rooms available for private meetings.

CHINA BASIN PARK AT MCCOVEY POINT

This is a beautiful mini-park that has generated a lot of attention. Featuring a grassy knoll, a T-ball field, and a walkway along the shoreline, the park also has a water promenade complete with a 1,500-foot wall inlaid with markers commemorating every San Francisco team from 1958 to 1999. The markers display all the players who wore a San Francisco uniform, along with their key achievements during those seasons. A 14-foot-tall bronze statue of Giants slugger and Hall of Famer Willie McCovey is in the northeast corner.

COCA-COLA BOTTLE

As impressive as the giant baseball glove next to it is an 80-foot, 130,000-pound wooden Coca-Cola bottle 465 feet away from batters sitting in left field. Kids can head to the top and make their way to the bottom by using one of the two 56-foot-long curving slides or one of the two 20-foot-long twisting slides. To celebrate a San Francisco long ball, bubbles spout out from the top of the bottle and dissolve in the air.

DIMENSIONS

Distances at AT&T Park are both unique and frustrating for hitters, and the layout presents some pretty interesting challenges. While the wall is a short distance of 307 feet down the right-field line, when it reaches center, it is 420 feet from home plate. The jagged fence offers plenty of nooks and crannies, which can induce a player to pop an acetaminophen or two by game's end.

EDIBLE GARDEN

AT&T Park became the second Major League ballpark to integrate a garden. The Giants opened the 3,000-square-foot organic patch to fans during the 2014 season, and it has been a big hit ever since. Utilizing space directly beyond the center-field wall, it features strawberries, avocados, and herbs, which fans can use as toppings for certain ballpark foods. Plant beds for peas, tomatoes, and greens, along with flowers, were later added.

GOTHAM CLUB

This debuted in time for the 2014 season and was named in honor of the franchise's first name in 1883, the New York Gothams Baseball Club. This members-only club is complete with pool tables and bowling alleys, as well as other amenities. There are various seating areas and an oversized bar to kick back and relax at. Membership requires an annual fee.

GIANTS WALL OF FAME

Located on the King Street side of AT&T Park and created in 2008 to celebrate the fiftieth anniversary of the Giants' move to San Francisco, the Wall of Fame, according to the Giants Media Guide, is a living tribute to the greatest players in franchise history. On September 23, 2008, the Giants inducted 43 players who have contributed to the legacy of the San Francisco Giants. To qualify, players must have played a minimum of nine seasons in a San Francisco uniform, or five seasons with one All-Star selection as a representative of the club.

HODGES-SIMMONS BROADCAST CENTER

The Broadcast Center is named for two men who starred as the inaugural announcers for the Giants upon their arrival in San Francisco. Russ Hodges, who covered the Giants while in New York, reeled off one of baseball's most memorable calls on October 3, 1951, when Bobby Thomson hit the "shot heard round the world," which prompted Hodges to exclaim, "The Giants win the pennant! The Giants win the pennant! The Giants win the pennant!" Lon Simmons, who covered the Giants in their first 16 seasons by the Bay,

skipped town to cover the Oakland Athletics from 1981 to 1995 before returning to call Giants games on a part-time basis from 1996 to 2002. Both
men were inducted into the National Baseball Hall of Fame.

KING STREET WINDOW DISPLAYS
Six window displays are located inside the ballpark at street level along
King Street and feature informative exhibits about the franchise. The Gi-
ants Wall of Fame, added in 2008, is also in this location.

LEFTY O'DOUL PLAZA AND BRIDGE
This historic bridge, constructed and built in 1933, is a working drawbridge
and at one time carried streetcar and train traffic, as well as automobiles
and pedestrians. The bridge is named for Francis Joseph O'Doul, a popular pitcher, outfielder, and manager, whose career spanned five decades.

LORI GARDINER FAMILY ROOM
Named for former Giants pitcher Mark Gardner's wife Lori, the family
playroom across from the Giants Clubhouse was rededicated in her name
after her courageous battle with liver cancer. Lori was very active within
the community and was always willing to do whatever it took to help. On
May 27, 2004, the Giants celebrated her life on Organ Donor Awareness Day.

LUXURY BOXES
Sixty-eight private luxury boxes can accommodate between 12 to 30 people.
The Giants have installed everything a fan could ever want: LCD flat-screen
televisions, radio/CD players, dual-line telephones, and a wet bar complete
with a refrigerator.

MCCOVEY COVE
At AT&T Park, fans anxiously gather in their canoes and swim gear, waiting
for a ball to travel into McCovey Cove, the water area renamed for Giants
legend Willie McCovey and conveniently positioned down the right-field
line, directly outside the ballpark. If people aren't in the right place at the
right time to retrieve the baseball, dogs have been trained to become "official ball retrievers," a first in Major League Baseball history.

MINIATURE AT&T PARK
Designed to give kids the opportunity to live out their dreams of becom-
ing a Major League Baseball player, there is a 50-foot by 50-foot replica of
AT&T Park with bases, an infield and outfield, and a chance to make plenty

of memories. Softballs or Wiffle balls can be hit via a batting tee or pitching machine, while kids can watch others playing at the park through open arches that mimic the stadium's portholes.

NEW ANGLE = LESS WIND RESISTANCE

At Candlestick Park, fans used to freeze their butts off on chilly nights because of the strong winds that swept around the ballpark. At the 1961 All-Star Game, pitcher Stu Miller was allegedly blown off balance by a stiff wind, causing a balk, which Miller vehemently denies. The constructors of AT&T Park took that factor into consideration and changed the overall positioning of the ballpark, so that the winds are now less of a threat than they were before. The wind is still there, but is not as strong as it once was.

NICK PETERS INTERVIEW ROOM

Nick Peters, a Major League Baseball writer for 47 years, had attended 50 Giants home openers and was a beat writer for the *Oakland Tribune* and *Sacramento Bee*. To show their appreciation for his dedication, the interview room in which he logged many hours gathering player quotes for stories was officially named after him. In 2014, the room was relocated to its current position, next to the main entrance of the Giants' clubhouse.

NUMBER ONE GIANTS FAN

Marjorie Wallace, a die-hard San Francisco Giants fan whose love affair with the team began in 1960, was widely known as "Ballpark Marge" and rarely missed games while the team played at Candlestick Park and later at AT&T Park. In appreciation for her support, the Giants provided Wallace with a chair in front of the clubhouse where at each home game, she would greet the players, giving them high-fives for good luck. Sadly, Ms. Wallace passed away on June 21, 2003. To celebrate her forever, the Giants placed her picture and a dedication plaque right outside the clubhouse.

OVERSIZED GLOVE IN LEFT

A 26-foot, four-fingered replica of a 1927 Rawlings baseball mitt weighing 20,000 pounds sits large and in charge in left field, next door to the Coca-Cola bottle. Designed by Gerald Howland and constructed of fiberglass over a steel frame, the glove sits exactly 501 feet from home plate and is approximately 36 times larger than actual gloves used by fielders. To date, no player has reached the glove with a home run ball.

PEOPLE-FRIENDLY

To make AT&T Park a people-friendly ballpark, the Giants have provided special services. Meeting rooms, restaurants, Giants team shops, and a public health center are all available during game days and non-game days. In addition, there are many concession stands, reducing the time it takes to grab a bite to eat or a beverage to quench one's thirst.

PERFECT GAME PLAQUE

In honor of pitcher Matt Cain's perfect game against the Houston Astros on June 13, 2012, the Giants unveiled a plaque on a walkway right outside the right-field wall on August 10, 2012. The word "Perfect" in oversized letters highlights the bronze piece, which displays Cain's portrait, and was laid into the ground much like a star on the Hollywood Walk of Fame. Cain, owner of Major League Baseball's twenty-second perfect game, struck out 14 batters in the dominating performance.

PORTHOLE

AT&T Park offers fans the chance to view the game for free through brick arches with Plexiglas portholes, a throwback to the old "Knot Hole" gang in the early days. A walkway along right-center field allows passers-by to take in the action. Depending on attendance size, the limit for viewing the contest is three innings to allow as many fans as possible to have the opportunity to participate in the excitement.

RETIRED NUMBERS

The San Francisco Giants have paid tribute to 11 of their greatest players, and those numbers are on the façade of the upper deck along the left-field line. They include: Christy Mathewson (the letters "NY"), John McGraw (the letters "SF"), Bill Terry (3), Mel Ott (4), Carl Hubbell (11), Monte Irvin (20), Willie Mays (24), Juan Marichal (27), Orlando Cepeda (30), Gaylord Perry (36), and Willie McCovey (44).

RETRO-STYLE CLOCK TOWERS

Two of the most prominent features of AT&T Park are the clock towers on King Street, which are 122 feet tall. Their pyramid-shaped roofs are topped by 45-foot flagpoles. There are two smaller clocks that highlight Seals Plaza and the Lefty O'Doul Plaza and are only 47 feet tall.

This is an exceptional view of the oversized Coca-Cola bottle in left field and the main scoreboard in center field. (*Photographed by Alicia Barnhart/Flickr*)

SAM SKINNER MEDIA LOUNGE

The media lounge, which is where announcers gather and get their notes together, is named for Sam Skinner, who was a longtime Bay Area sports journalist, writer, and radio reporter. He is the first man in Major League Baseball history to have two press areas named for him—the other one is at the O.co Coliseum press box in Oakland.

SCOREBOARD IN CENTER

The massive scoreboard, which is easily seen from any seat, measures 122 feet from the field to the top, and 179 feet to the top of the light standards. The main matrix board is 24 feet by 73 feet and requires 846,000 watts of power to generate its electricity. The video replay board, which is produced by Panasonic, is 32 feet by 24 feet and provides sharp images of the action on the field. Just for good measure, the top features an old-fashioned clock, whose face measures 17 feet in diameter.

SEALS PLAZA AT MARINA GATE

Beyond center field is the Seals Plaza at Marina Gate, named for San Francisco's first professional Major League Baseball team. There is a statue of the team's first logo, which features a seal performing a balancing act with a baseball on its nose. All the plazas create a snapshot of the San Francisco area and give fans a place to stop and smell the roses.

SEATING

There really is no bad seat in the house at AT&T Park, and all have great sight lines. If your hunter-green seat is in the club section, you'll have the advantage of watching the players take their cuts inside two batting cages. If you're looking for a view of Oakland and the Bay, purchase upper-reserve seats from which you will also have beautiful views of San Francisco's Bay Bridge and Oakland.

SPLASH LANDING

This right-field area offers fans the chance to witness history whenever a ball plops down in San Francisco Bay. A "Splash Hits" sign to the right, in foul territory, tallies the number of home runs hit into the aqua every year. As of this writing, to the left, a sign that says "HIT WATER WIN $500 FOR GIANTS COMMUNITY FUND" sits along the brick wall in the right-field area.

WILLIE MAYS TRIBUTES

The entrance at Willie Mays Plaza pays tribute to one of the greatest baseball players of all time. This tranquil setting features 24 palm trees (Mays's number was 24) and a nine-foot bronze statue depicting his famous swing, which earned him 660 career home runs.

MEMORABLE GAMES AT AT&T PARK

APRIL 11, 2000: FIRST GAME AT AT&T PARK

A capacity crowd of 40,930 witnessed a three-home-run performance in the first game ever at the brand-new, state-of-the-art San Francisco ballpark. The only problem for Giants fans was that it wasn't Barry Bonds who accomplished the feat but rather Kevin Elster of the Dodgers who turned in the rare hat trick. Elster, who connected in the third, fifth, and eighth innings for the first time in his career, became the first Major Leaguer to do so since Juan Gonzalez did it for the Texas Rangers on September 24, 1999. Bonds did homer in his second at-bat, taking Chan Ho Park deep in the third inning, but it wasn't enough firepower to stop the momentum of the Dodgers, who spoiled the fun and won the game, 6–5.

OCTOBER 5, 2001: BONDS ESTABLISHES NEW SINGLE-SEASON HOME RUN RECORD

With Mark McGwire in full view, Barry Bonds wasted little time establishing the single-season home run mark, connecting in his first two at-bats versus the Dodgers, becoming the first player to hit 71 and 72 home runs in a single season. In the first inning, he took a 1–0 pitch off Chan Ho Park and promptly deposited it over the right-center-field wall. His second blast—and seventy-second of the season—again came off Park, this time a solo shot to right field. Although the record had been set, the Giants were officially eliminated from the playoffs as the Dodgers went on to win the game, 11–10. The game took four hours and 27 minutes to play, establishing the record for the longest nine-inning game in baseball history.

> "It was such an odd year. It was 9/11 [and] he was totally going off and he hit 756 at home [as well]. . . . Everybody was kind of wrapped up into that and the problem was, they were also involved in a pennant race and they probably should have been more involved in that than the home run thing."
> —*Duane Kuiper, Giants broadcaster*

OCTOBER 7, 2001: HOME RUN NUMBER 73 ENDS INCREDIBLE YEAR

With two outs in the first inning of the final game of the year, Barry Bonds worked the count full before connecting for his seventy-third and final home run of a historic season as the Giants closed out the 2001 season with a 2–1 victory. After registering a 1-for-7 line in his career against Los Angeles knuckleballer Dennis Springer, Bonds adjusted accordingly and ended the season with a bang, hitting one deep into the right-field stands. Bonds also capped off a record-breaking year by establishing the single-season mark for slugging percentage at .863, eclipsing the previous mark held by Babe Ruth of .847, set all the way back in 1920.

OCTOBER 14, 2002: THE GIANTS WIN THE PENNANT! THE GIANTS WIN THE PENNANT!

The Giants wrapped up their first National League pennant since 1989, winning a pitcher's duel, 2–1 in Game 5 of the National League Championship Series, which ended dramatically. Seeking to avenge a 1987 NLCS matchup that saw the Cardinals defeat the Giants, Matt Morris took the hill for St. Louis and went 8⅔ innings, while Kirk Rueter lasted six innings for San Francisco. St. Louis struck first in the seventh, when Fernando Vina hit a sacrifice fly that scored Mike Matheny, who earlier doubled, giving the Cardinals a 1–0 lead. The game was evened in the eighth, when back-to-back one-out singles by Kenny Lofton and Rich Aurilla set the stage for Barry Bonds, who lofted a sacrifice fly of his own, bringing home Lofton and knotting the contest at one. It remained that way until the ninth, when back-to-back singles by David Bell and Shawon Dunston with two outs set the stage for Lofton, who, on the first pitch, lined a single to right field that enabled Bell to score the pennant-clinching run.

MAY 28, 2006: BONDS SLIPS PAST RUTH

Barry Bonds continued his assault on one of baseball's most hallowed records by blasting career home run number 715, passing Babe Ruth and moving ever so closer to Hank Aaron's all-time record during San Francisco's 6–3 loss to Colorado. The Rockies had tallied six runs in the top of the fourth to lead 6–0, but in the bottom half, Bonds strolled to the plate after Steve Finley got aboard via a walk. Facing Byung-Hyun Kim, he showed plenty of patience in working the count full before unloading on a 90 mph fastball, sending it 445 feet to center field. As Bonds began his trek around the base paths, streamers fell from the upper regions of the ballpark to celebrate the latest milestone for the San Francisco slugger.

AUGUST 7, 2007: BONDS PASSES HANK AARON

With the score tied 4–4 against Washington, Barry Bonds stepped in and promptly hit a 435-foot two-run home run to center field off Nationals starter Mike Bacsik. This wasn't just *any* home run—it was a date with destiny. With the blast, Bonds officially overtook Hank Aaron as baseball's all-time home run king by hitting the 756th home run of his career, but the Giants couldn't capitalize on the moment as they dropped the game to Washington, 8–6. In one of baseball's most anticipated events, Bonds doubled to right in his first at-bat and then connected for the history-making shot in the fourth. The Nationals seemed to be unfazed by the moment, and put the game away in the eighth after scoring four runs highlighted by back-to-back RBI singles from Nook Logan and pinch hitter Tony Batista.

JULY 10, 2009: SANCHEZ NO-HITS PADRES

As of this writing, the San Diego Padres have never had one of their own pitchers toss a no-hitter. The same can't be said for opposing teams, as Jonathan Sanchez was nearly perfect in no-hitting the Padres during an 8–0 Giants rout. With the exception of an eighth-inning error, Sanchez was unstoppable, mowing down San Diego with 11 strikeouts while not issuing any free passes. Pablo Sandoval fueled the Giants' offensive attack, hitting a three-run blast in the fifth inning, but the headline was Sanchez, who became the first pitcher to toss a no-no in a San Francisco uniform since John Montefusco did so in 1976. Things got dicey in the ninth, when pinch hitter Edgar Gonzalez sent a drive to deep center field, but Aaron Rowand tracked it down for the out, simultaneously crashing into the center-field gate in the process.

OCTOBER 27, 2010: FALL CLASSIC RETURNS, GIANTS VICTORIOUS

Looking to avenge their World Series loss to the Angels in 2002, San Francisco started off on the right foot by outslugging Texas in Game 1, 11–7. In a battle of outstanding aces, San Francisco's Tim Lincecum toed the mound and faced off against Rangers starter Cliff Lee, and anyone expecting a pitcher's duel got more than they bargained for. Texas scratched across two runs over the first two innings, but the Giants answered in the third with two of their own on an RBI double by Freddie Sanchez and an RBI single by rookie sensation Buster Posey. What helped put the Giants over the top was the six-run inning they would experience in the bottom of the fifth. Back-to-back RBI singles by Cody Ross and Aubrey Huff plated two, and Juan Uribe cracked a three-run homer later in the inning, increasing the lead to 8–2 and emphatically swinging the momentum in their favor. Three more runs in the bottom of the eighth served as the icing on the cake, sealing Game 1 and eventually leading the Giants to their first World Series championship since making the move from New York to the Bay Area in 1958.

JUNE 13, 2012: A GAME 130 YEARS IN THE MAKING

San Francisco pitcher Matt Cain recorded 14 strikeouts, dominating the Astros in becoming the first player in 130 years of Giants baseball to record a perfect game during a 10–0 thrashing of Houston. Having pitched a one-hitter earlier in the year against Pittsburgh, Cain was as dominating as they come but also got significant help in the outfield. In the seventh, Astros outfielder Jordan Schafer led off and on a 3–2 count, sent a drive to the right-center field gap that had "hit" written all over it. Instead, it was Giants outfielder Gregor Blanco who made an incredible catch, diving in front of the wall on the warning track to preserve history. The Giants offense hit three home runs and was led by Pablo Sandoval, who finished 3-for-4 with two RBI.

> "I am not exactly sure what to think about it. . . . I think it will all set in toward the end of the season when you get to settle down and not have to worry about pitching and stuff."
> —*Matt Cain*

OCTOBER 22, 2012: SAN FRANCISCO HEADS BACK TO WORLD SERIES

Facing yet another elimination game in the 2012 postseason, Hunter Pence smacked a broken-bat, bases-clearing double with no outs in the third inning as part of a five-run frame, and the Giants cruised to their second pennant in three years with a 9–0 shellacking of the St. Louis Cardinals in Game 7.

After accomplishing the unthinkable by rallying from a 2–0 series deficit against Cincinnati in the Division Series, the train—or trolley, if you will—kept rolling for San Francisco, who showed no signs of letting up during their rout of the defending World Series champions. The Giants were led by a stellar pitching performance by Matt Cain, who tossed five-hit, shutout baseball for 5⅔ innings. From there, the bullpen took over and eliminated any thoughts of a back-to-back pennant for St. Louis. In the eighth, Brandon Belt put it away for San Francisco, smacking a 388-foot home run into seats, subsequently starting the party among those in attendance at AT&T Park.

OCTOBER 24, 2012: SANDOVAL MAKES WORLD SERIES HISTORY

San Francisco third baseman Pablo Sandoval went 4-for-4 and joined Babe Ruth, Reggie Jackson, and Albert Pujols as the only players to homer three times in a World Series game, leading the Giants to an 8–3 Game 1 win against Detroit. Facing reigning American League Cy Young Award–winner Justin Verlander, Sandoval connected for a 421-foot blast to center field in the first, added a 379-foot shot to left field in the third, and finished off the power display with a titanic 435-foot clubbing to center field in the fifth for the first three-homer game at AT&T Park since Kevin Elster of the Dodgers did so in the very first game in the ballpark on April 11, 2000. The game seemed to set the tone for the entire series, as the Giants would go on to complete the four-game sweep, capturing their second title in three seasons.

SEPTEMBER 6, 2013: PERFECT GAME MISSED BY INCHES

Over the decades, the game of baseball has proven that it truly is a game of inches. That notion was no more evident than on this night, when Giants starter Yusmeiro Petit discovered it firsthand against the Diamondbacks during a dominating 3–0 victory. With 41,190 at AT&T Park on their feet, 26 batters retired in a row by Petit, and two outs in the ninth, Arizona pinch hitter Eric Chavez worked the count full before lining a ball to right field. San Francisco outfielder Hunter Pence rushed at it hard and dove, but the ball bounced just in front of his glove, ending Petit's bid for the second perfect game in franchise history. The next batter, A. J. Pollock, grounded to third for the final out, giving Petit the one-hit shutout. With the near-miss, it marked the first time in Major League Baseball history that two perfect games were broken up in the ninth inning with two outs in the same season, with Rangers pitcher Yu Darvish accounting for the other, on April 2 at Minute Maid Park versus Houston.

JUNE 25, 2014: LINCECUM CONTINUES DOMINANCE OF SAN DIEGO

For the second time in two seasons and less than a year apart, San Francisco right-hander Tim Lincecum dominated the San Diego Padres, tossing a no-hitter during an easy 4–0 victory. He became the second pitcher in Major League history to no-hit the same team twice, joining Hall of Famer Addie Joss, who did it while a member of the Cleveland Indians against the Chicago White Sox in 1908 and 1910.

Buster Posey led the offensive charge, collecting four hits, including a double, while driving in two runs and Lincecum notched two hits as well, becoming the first pitcher with a no-hitter and multiple hits at the plate since Rick Wise did so against Cincinnati on June 23, 1971. In addition, Pablo Sandoval got into the act with an RBI double in the third inning that would prove to be more than enough offense on this day.

OCTOBER 16, 2014: DRAMATIC HOME RUN GIVES GIANTS THE PENNANT

San Francisco's Travis Ishikawa blasted a dramatic three-run home run in the bottom of the ninth inning to end the National League Championship Series and simultaneously became the first National League player to accomplish the feat during a 6–3 victory over St. Louis. Ishikawa, who joined New York's Chris Chambliss (1976), Aaron Boone (2003), and Detroit's Magglio Ordonez (2006) of the American League as the only players to ever end an LCS on a home run, was given the opportunity to win the game thanks to Michael Morse, who in the eighth inning homered off of Cardinals reliever Pat Neshek, tying the score at 3. With the win, the Giants made it back to the World Series after standing victorious in both 2010 and 2012.

WHAT THEY'RE SAYING ABOUT AT&T PARK

BOB BRENLY: "It is a great ballpark. Having played most of my career at old Candlestick Park, I am jealous because I would have loved the opportunity to play in that ballpark. . . . The fact the fans come out and support the team the way they do—sold-out just about every game, full house—it is a fun place to go watch a ballgame."

MATT CAIN: "I like it. The overall view of it from the outside to the inside has just got a good feel. . . . You have got the ocean in the background, and it has got a lot of cool little things—the big glove, Coke bottle—I just enjoy being at home with that."

JACK CORRIGAN, BROADCASTER: "From a broadcaster's perspective, [it is] not as much fun, believe it or not, because the fans are too close to you. . . . They are right there below you, and at times [you] hear more [than you want to], and you want to go down and throttle somebody. The view is great and they did a really nice job with [AT&T Park]."

DUANE KUIPER, BROADCASTER: "I am very biased, so I happen to think it is the best of the newer ballparks and for a lot of reasons. . . . One is where we are located to do our broadcasts. We get a view of the water and bay and the Oakland hills, and we can see the tip of Mount Diablo, so it is defining for us."

JOSH LEWIN, BROADCASTER: "In terms of weather and sight lines, it stands in such a stark contrast to what is across the bay [O.co Coliseum in Oakland], and maybe that is why one is a cement bowl and the other one is so aesthetically pleasing."

DON MATTINGLY: "I like San Francisco. It is pretty and I like San Francisco from a standpoint that there is a lot of good energy in that ballpark, the crazy fans, and it is along the water there—I like that—and it is just a good-looking ballpark."

BUSTER POSEY: "For me, it is my favorite ballpark to play in. . . . It has got a lot of character and really is just a beautiful ballpark."

GIANCARLO STANTON: "San Francisco is really fun. . . . The atmosphere and the weather—it is usually a little cool—but when we go there in the deep summer, there is usually a little relief on the weather. The history there and how the seagulls collect in the eighth inning—it is just a cool tradition-type place."

MATT WILLIAMS: "It is one of the most beautiful, I think. Of course, I played 10 years in San Francisco and I have a special place for San Francisco. I actually think Candlestick Park was a better place to hit, [and] more forgiving from a hitting standpoint. . . . AT&T Park is probably a better hitter's ballpark, but nonetheless, on the Bay you cannot beat it."

BARRY ZITO: "I think it is probably the best ballpark in baseball aesthetically. . . . We have got all kinds of great food there—garlic fries are famous—kettle corn down low, [and] sometimes the boys will go down and get some kettle corn from the Diamond Club and bring it back [to] the clubhouse."

AT&T PARK FACTS AND FIGURES

AT&T PARK ADDRESS
24 Willie Mays Plaza, San Francisco, CA 94107

SAN FRANCISCO GIANTS TEAM WEB SITE
www.sfgiants.com

FIELD DIMENSIONS (IN FEET)
Left Field: 339', Left-Center: 384', Center: 399',
Right-Center: 421', Right Field: 309'

SEATING CAPACITY (AS OF 2015)
41,915

ALL-STAR GAMES AT AT&T PARK
July 10, 2007: American League 5, National League 4
MVP: Ichiro Suzuki, Seattle Mariners (AL)

AT&T PARK FIRSTS
Game: April 11, 2000—Los Angeles 6, San Francisco 5
Single: Devon White, Los Angeles (April 11, 2000)*
Double: Barry Bonds, San Francisco (April 11, 2000)
Triple: Doug Mirabelli, San Francisco (April 11, 2000)
Home Run: Kevin Elster, Los Angeles (April 11, 2000)

*Denotes first hit in the stadium.

CHASE FIELD
HOME OF THE ARIZONA DIAMONDBACKS

Chase Field, Arizona Diamondbacks (*Photographed by Mark Whitt/Flickr*)

[Chase Field was previously known as Bank One Ballpark (1998–2005).]

When the City of Phoenix was awarded a Major League Baseball franchise to begin play in 1998, it had signaled a new era for an area that was used to being only the home of spring training baseball throughout the years. Unlike the Tampa Bay Rays, who were also debuting for the 1998 season and had to use an existing structure that had undergone an extensive renovation, the Diamondbacks were fortunate to have a brand-new, baseball-only facility built, but not before funding difficulties took center stage.

In the spring of 1994, the Maricopa County Board of Supervisors approved a quarter-cent increase for the county sales tax to help finance a portion of the stadium's overall price tag. This was met with profound indifference because the city was in the midst of budget deficits and more times than not lacked the means to fund other services in and around the county. Making it more difficult, a referendum passed in 1989 prohibited the use of public subsidies for stadium projects, so citizens were unable to vote on the issue, which seemed to touch a nerve with the majority.

The projected costs for Chase Field were estimated at $279 million in 1995, but because of overruns attributed to the soaring prices of steel and various other materials, the final total checked in at $364 million. The additional $85 million put the franchise between a rock and a hard place right off the bat because it was established as part of the original stadium deal that both the Diamondbacks and Rays were prohibited from using the national Major League Baseball revenue for their first five seasons. Any extra costs totaling above $253 million due to construction overruns or additional expenses would have to be paid for by the Diamondbacks organization.

Construction finally began in 1996 and was completed on time for the 1998 season, which saw a total of 3.6 million fans stream through the gates to view a baseball game. It was only the third stadium in all of baseball at the time to have a retractable roof, and it was the first one of its kind in the United States. (Rogers Centre in Toronto and Olympic Stadium, the former home of the Washington Nationals when they were in Montreal as the Expos, were the other two.) Since then, a number of Major League ballparks have installed retractable roofs in their stadiums, but as for Arizona, such a roof made sense because of the intense, dry heat over the course of an entire season.

SPECIAL FEATURES OF CHASE FIELD

2001 REMINDERS

Most of the championship trophies won by teams around baseball seem to be hidden away in fancy clubs or lounges that cost a small fortune to enter. In Arizona, their hardware from winning the 2001 Fall Classic is displayed on the west concourse, along with artifacts from that magical season in which they defeated the mighty Yankees in an epic seven-game series. A three-sectioned display case, clad in hunter green with the Diamondbacks logo on top, features the American flag as a tribute to those lost in the September 11 tragedy, jerseys worn by Randy Johnson and Luis Gonzalez, and other assorted game-used memorabilia.

ARIZONA BASEBALL CLUB

This all-you-can-eat restaurant and bar, positioned above right field, gives fans an incredible, bird's-eye view of the action on the field from an outdoor patio. Traditional ballpark favorites such as hot dogs, salads, nachos, and wings are a given, but with specialties such as quesadillas and various kinds of sausages, this is a must-visit for those with a huge appetite. For parties of less than six, reservations at the Arizona Baseball Club are not necessary.

BASEBALL HISTORY

Surrounding the baseball field and situated throughout the main concourse are several video information boards that retrace baseball's roots. Divided into 10 different sections, each one shows a section of a timeline on how the game of baseball has evolved over the years. There are also display cases of memorabilia from various players throughout the years.

DIRT STRIP

Buck Showalter, the first manager in Diamondbacks history, came up with this idea, which was once a common sight at ballparks back in the day when Ebbets Field and the Polo Grounds were all the rage. The dirt strip from home plate to the pitcher's mound at Chase Field is a throwback to simpler times, and only one other current ballpark in the Major Leagues—Comerica Park in Detroit—incorporates what has since been phased out of the infield.

FAMILY FUN

Positioned just beneath the out-of-town scoreboards in the upper section of left field (in the northwest corner past section 332) is an area called The Sandlot, a family-friendly spot that offers a wide array of activities for every fan. There is a playground with two clubhouses, a batting cage, and the granddaddy of them all, a miniature replica of Chase Field for Wiffle ball batting practice. It's too bad they don't have a 1:32 version of the famous swimming pool!

GAME SEVEN GRILL

The Game Seven Grill, formerly known as Sliders, is a 20,000-square-foot eatery that honors the World Championship club of 2001. It has a family-friendly atmosphere, a barbecue-style menu, and can seat up to 300. The Game Seven Grill opens its doors three hours before the first pitch and stays open one-and-a-half hours once the final out is recorded. The restaurant has unique memorabilia from that historic Game 7 win over the New York Yankees such as World Series tickets, game balls, and pennants along with other championship furnishings.

GONZO SUITE #20

Situated inside the Diamond Level suites is this luxury suite named for one of the most beloved Diamondbacks of all-time, Luis Gonzalez. It celebrates the career he had with the club from 1999 to 2006 and the game-winning hit during Game 7 of the 2001 World Series that took down the New York Yankees, bringing the franchise its first World Series. Plush seating, a mahogany wet bar, and a balcony, complete with extra-wide padded seats, are available.

The high-definition scoreboard in center field is hard to miss at Chase Field.
(*Photographed by Alicia Barnhart/Flickr*)

HD CENTER-FIELD SCOREBOARD

Upgraded in 2008 for $12 million, the remodeled center-field scoreboard is eight times larger than the previous version and offers unparalleled, crystal-clear quality. Measuring 136 feet by 46 feet, it produces two high-definition 16:9 images at the same time. A clock, flanked by the United States flag on the left and the State of Arizona flag on the right, sits at the very top.

JOE GARAGIOLA BROADCAST BOOTH

On September 20, 2009, the Arizona Diamondbacks dedicated the broadcast wing of the press box to Joe Garagiola, who had been with the team since their inception in 1998. Following a nine-year career that included stints in St. Louis, Pittsburgh, Chicago, and New York, Garagiola began broadcasting Cardinals games on KMOX with Harry Caray and Jack Buck from 1955 to 1962. In 1961, he became associated with NBC, working nearly 30 years for the network before eventually coming to the Diamondbacks and serving as a color analyst before retiring in 2013. A 50-foot photo timeline detailing Garagiola's career was also installed inside the broadcasting section.

LEFT FIELD SPORTS GRILL

This sports grill in left field gives fans front-row views and combines excellent food with an upbeat atmosphere. This venue, open year-round from 11 A.M. to 9 P.M., is equipped with a private suite that can accommodate up to 50 individuals. Game-day table seating is limited and available on a first-come, first-served basis but can be purchased or reserved by calling the Diamondbacks ticket office directly. On non-game days, there is a happy hour from 4 P.M. to 7 P.M. with exceptional offers on libations.

NAMING RIGHTS

In 1998, the ballpark formerly known as Bank One Ballpark burst onto the scene, earning the nickname "The Bob." That all changed in 2005, when Bank One merged with JPMorgan Chase, bringing an end to the first ballpark name. The change was made official on September 23, 2005, and within the structure of the deal, Chase agreed to pay $2.2 million per year for the exclusive naming rights all the way through the year 2028, which, at that time, would make the home of the Diamondbacks 30 years old.

OUT-OF-TOWN SCOREBOARD

Above the left-field area near the Sandlot attraction are two long boards—one for the National League and one for the American League—that give updates of games from around the league. Primitive by today's standards, this particular model displays the current pitchers, a three-letter abbreviation for each team, runs scored, and the current inning of action.

PICTURE PERFECT

In his pursuit of Roger Maris's single-season home run record of 61 in 1998, St. Louis slugger Mark McGwire put on a show during one of the Cardinals' stops at Chase Field. During batting practice one hot summer night, McGwire took aim and launched a baseball that flew through the sweltering desert air and ended up going right through one of the windows in the outermost wall of the ballpark. One thing is for sure: the man could really hit a baseball.

RETIRED NUMBERS

The Diamondbacks have retired one number to this point, and it belongs to a man who helped lead the club to their first championship in 2001: Luis Gonzalez (11). It is on the façade above the party suites in right field.

SEDONA CLUB

If you love hamburgers and have some extra money, the Sedona Club offers fans the opportunity to construct their own ultimate burger featuring a wide array of cheeses, toppings, and condiments. And if that isn't enough, a build-your-own-sundae gives you an excellent reason to save room for dessert!

SOLAR PAVILION

Installed just in time for the 2011 season, the solar pavilion covers 17,280 square feet above the plaza, near the western entrance and ticket booth. Designed to have a 20-year lifespan, it not only provides shade for fans seeking cover from the hot desert sun, but it has also enabled Chase Field to become more environmentally friendly by producing up to 75 kilowatts of solar power for the ballpark.

STRIKEOUT METER

A strikeout meter, positioned on the second deck façade in right field, tallies the number of strikeouts recorded by Arizona pitchers throughout the course of a contest for quick reference. It must have been a real pain in the you-know-what to figure out a way to fit all those punchouts in there after Randy Johnson had the Cincinnati Reds reeling to the tune of 20 strikeouts during a game in 2001.

SWIMMING POOL

When it opened in 1998, Chase Field became the first Major League ballpark to feature a swimming pool in the outfield, which quickly became one of baseball's most enticing quirks. Located in right-center field and measuring 385 square feet with a depth of five feet, the pool is 415 feet from home plate and is an attractive target for batters. On May 12, 1998, as a member of the Chicago Cubs, Mark Grace became the first player to homer into it when he connected for a solo shot off Diamondbacks starter Andy Benes. Jarry Park Stadium, the former outdoor home of the Montreal Expos from 1969 to 1976, featured a preexisting swimming pool in a city park beyond the right-field fence, and San Francisco's Willie McCovey smacked a home run into it on August 24, 1969.

THE ROOF

Truly a trendsetter when it debuted in 1998, Chase Field became the first Major League ballpark built in the United States to boast a fully retractable roof. The structure is made up of 9 million pounds of structural steel and can open and close in approximately four-and-a-half minutes, thanks to a pair of 200-horsepower motors. More than four miles of cable, intertwined through a pulley system, enables the roof to be opened in any position to maximize sun exposure on the field, while at the same time minimizing it in the walkways.

THIRD BASE CLUB

While it's hard to top the lounge behind home plate, this club off the main entrance and overlooking third base offers luxury while providing great views of the action. A patio with floor-to-ceiling windows lets fans enjoy the game "outside." There is a private bar, complete with flat-screen televisions.

TOP-NOTCH LOUNGE

An extravagant lounge behind home plate has breathtaking views and luxurious amenities. Be prepared to shell out big bucks in a place where martinis are right at your fingertips and ordering only the finest cuisine is the standard. Options like sesame-crusted salmon or barbecue pulled-pork sandwiches are sure to make your mouth water. A full-service bar offers any spirit one can imagine. This area is accessible only to those with tickets to the clubhouse box or first- or third-base box.

MEMORABLE GAMES AT CHASE FIELD

MARCH 31, 1998: FIRST GAME AT CHASE FIELD

The Arizona Diamondbacks began as a Major League Baseball franchise by faltering to Colorado, 9–2, in front of a standing-room-only crowd at Chase Field. Darryl Kile started for the Rockies and completely shut down the Diamondbacks, allowing four hits and one run over seven innings amidst all the hoopla surrounding the debut of America's pastime in the desert. Already ahead 3–1, the Rockies put the game out of reach with a five-run seventh inning, which saw Ellis Burks connect for an RBI double, an RBI single by Larry Walker, and the biggest blow of the night, a three-run blast by Vinny Castilla. Although the home fans had little to cheer about, first baseman Travis Lee finished the night 3-for-4, which included recording Arizona's first hit—a single in the bottom of the first—and in the sixth, the franchise's first home run. In the bottom of the ninth, Karim Garcia connected for a solo home run to left field off Rockies reliever Jerry DiPoto.

JUNE 25, 1999: JIMENEZ OUT-DUALS JOHNSON, TOSSES NO-HITTER

If you were to conduct a brief survey of fans entering Chase Field on this particular day and ask, "Who do you think would toss a no-hitter today, Randy Johnson or Cardinals rookie Jose Jimenez?" it's a safe bet that the majority would have said Johnson. That wasn't the case as the rookie Jimenez shone and received gutsy defense from the outfield as part of a 1–0 win over the Diamondbacks. Eric Davis preserved the no-hitter on multiple occasions, making diving catches in right field, and the final out—a groundout by Tony Womack to second baseman Joe McEwing—touched off a scene of celebration with Jimenez, while Diamondbacks fans commended the young pitcher for his efforts with light applause. Johnson, who allowed only five hits while striking out 14, went the distance as well, allowing only Thomas Howard's RBI single in the ninth to account for the final margin of victory for the Cardinals.

OCTOBER 5, 1999: FIRST PLAYOFF GAME EVER AT CHASE FIELD

Coming off a historic 100-win season in which they captured the National League West title in only their second year of existence, the Diamondbacks participated in their first postseason game but fell to the wild card–winning Mets, 8–4 in Game 1 of the Division Series. With fireballer Randy Johnson on the mound for Arizona, Edgardo Alfonso got the ball rolling early for New York by hitting a solo home run in the first inning and later a two-run blast in the third by John Olerud increased the advantage to 3–0. The Diamondbacks got on the board in the bottom of the third when Jay Bell's sacrifice fly made it 3–1, but the Mets did a little sacrificing of their own in the next half-inning courtesy of Rey Ordonez's bunt, extending the lead to three again at 4–1. Two long balls, including a two-run shot by Luis Gonzalez in the bottom of the sixth, deadlocked the game at four before New York erupted for four runs in the top of the ninth, when Alfonso capped off his incredible day by launching a grand slam, putting the game out of reach.

MAY 8, 2001: JOHNSON STRIKES OUT 20

With a game-time temperature of 101, Randy Johnson turned up the heat on the mound, becoming the third pitcher in modern history to strike out 20 as Arizona went on to defeat Cincinnati 4–3 in 11 innings. Johnson had the Reds reeling right from the opening pitch, striking out two batters apiece through the first three innings and turning up the gas in the fourth, retiring Donnie Sadler, Juan Castro, and Barry Larkin with ease via the strikeout. Incredibly, the Reds got on the board in the top of the fifth when a single and stolen base by Aaron Boone paved the way for an RBI single by Ruben Rivera, giving Cincinnati a 1–0 lead. The Diamondbacks answered in the bottom of the sixth, when an RBI single by Reggie Sanders tied the game at one.

But the story continued to be Johnson, who, in the seventh and eighth, again struck out the side, bringing his strikeout total to 18 heading into the ninth. Looking for a spark, Deion Sanders was summoned from the bench to pinch hit for the Reds in the top of the ninth but promptly returned to the pine after striking out on three pitches. A groundout by Sadler for the second out, and another strikeout by Castro gave Johnson 20 strikeouts, and subsequently ended his day. In the eleventh, the Reds broke through for two on a sacrifice fly by Alex Ochoa that allowed Jason LaRue to tag up and score, and a throwing error allowed Sadler to scamper home.

Undeterred, the Diamondbacks weren't about to spoil Johnson's record day. They scored three in the bottom of the eleventh on the strength of a two-run double by Mark Grace and a bases-loaded walk to Matt Williams, which brought home Grace in the form of the game-winning run. In all, Johnson threw 124 pitches—92 for strikes—walked none, and became the first left-hander in baseball history to strike out 20 in a game.

NOVEMBER 4, 2001: DIAMONDBACKS WIN FIRST WORLD SERIES

A bloop single to center field by Luis Gonzalez off Yankees closer Mariano Rivera in the bottom of the ninth gave Arizona their first World championship in franchise history and wrapped up a winner-take-all Game 7, 3–2. The Yankees went ahead 2–1 in the eighth, prompting manager Joe Torre to summon Rivera from the bullpen for a potential two-inning save. The move paid immediate dividends, as baseball's all-time postseason ERA leader struck out the side, and it appeared as though New York would be headed for a fourth straight championship.

That changed in the ninth, when Mark Grace led off with a single, and Damian Miller put down a bunt that Rivera fielded and threw errantly to second, putting two men on. Jay Bell, pinch hitting for Randy Johnson, laid down a bunt, but pinch runner David Dellucci (for Grace) was thrown out at third. Tony Womack stepped in and laced a double down the right-field line, enabling Miller and Dellucci to score, knotting the game at two. After a pinch hit from Craig Counsel, Gonzalez stepped in and delivered the final blow, taking a 0–1 pitch and lining it over the drawn-in infield for the World Series winner and a spot in baseball lore.

"It is the pinnacle of what you play for. [I] had the chance to go two other times and lost—one time got swept and one time lost in extra innings in Game 7. I will tell you, being on the winning end is a lot better than being on the losing end."
—Matt Williams

"I am still kissing him [Luis Gonzalez] to the day. . . . That was probably the highlight of my Major League career because when we play this game, it is all about winning that World Series. When 'Gonzo' hit that ball and the team that we had—we had an older team—no one expected us to do what we did, but we shut up a lot of mouths and were able to win it."

—*Reggie Sanders*

JUNE 29, 2004: JOHNSON REACHES STRIKEOUT MILESTONE

Randy Johnson added another accomplishment to his already-impressive résumé by striking out his 4,000th career batter, becoming only the fourth player to do so during Arizona's 3–2 loss to San Diego. In the eighth, amidst the flashbulbs popping all around Chase Field, Padres third baseman Jeff Cirillo struck out on a pitch in the dirt, and with it, Johnson joined Nolan Ryan, Roger Clemens, and Steve Carlton as the only men to experience that milestone. As was the case when he notched number 3,000 on September 10, 2000, the Diamondbacks failed to win the game, and a solo home run by Khalil Greene in the top of the eighth ahead of the big moment proved to make the difference in the final margin of victory for the visiting Padres.

APRIL 3, 2013: MARATHON SLUGFEST ENDS IN ARIZONA'S FAVOR

In a game that ended in the early morning hours, the Diamondbacks outlasted St. Louis in a five-hour, 32-minute marathon after Cliff Pennington singled home Jason Kubel from second to seal the 10–9 victory in 16 innings. With the score tied at eight in the twelfth, it appeared as though the Cardinals had gained the upper hand after Pete Kozma stroked an RBI single to left field, scoring Yadier Molina, giving them a 9–8 advantage. Not to be outdone, Arizona put the first two batters on in the bottom of the twelfth, thanks to a single by Pennington and Eric Chavez, who took a pitch from St. Louis reliever Mitchell Boggs right to the ribs. A sacrifice bunt by Gerardo Parra moved them over, and Martin Prado promptly delivered with a sacrifice fly, tying the contest at 9-all. The next three innings proved to be a stalemate for each team before Arizona capitalized in the bottom of the sixteenth, ending the longest game as of this writing—by time—in the history of Chase Field.

WHAT THEY ARE SAYING ABOUT CHASE FIELD

STEVE BERTHIAUME, BROADCASTER: "Chase Field, I think, is a very, very comfortable ballpark. It is very cozy for its size and that is one thing that struck me the first time I went there. . . . I immediately noticed the proximity of the seats to the field and for its size, I think it is a very intimate ballpark."

BOB BRENLY: "Functional is the best way to put it. From the outside it looks like a big old airplane hanger and it is not the most aesthetically pleasing ballpark . . . given the fact we play in the Sonoran Desert and the temperatures are over triple digits just about every day in the summertime. It is very comforting [inside] and it is as nice as any ballpark in baseball."

R. A. DICKEY: "I do not really care for Chase Field all that much. . . . The ball flies a ton and the grass is real thin. They have trouble growing grass there and they are always having to paint the grass green to make it look nice."

MATT KEMP: "I actually love [Chase Field]. . . . It is a good hitter's ballpark and you see the ball really well. The backdrop with the black wall—you definitely see the ball really, really [well]—and they have got that jumbotron right in center field. It is definitely one of my favorite ballparks."

STEVE LYONS, BROADCASTER: "I like the fact that it is the first retractable roof, domed stadium that they built because it was too hot. . . . I always feel like I am watching the game sideways because the roof does not open from dead center field to home plate."

MARK MCGWIRE: "Great hitter's ballpark—I loved it—great backdrop and the ball jumps out of there. . . . That is a ballpark that you just lick your chops in because it is just gigantic gaps and [it is] just a nice place to play [at]."

JOSE REYES: "I love to play there. [Chase Field] is one ballpark that I love to hit at only because the ball's flying there and when you hit it in the ground, it is going to go through too. . . . [That is one ballpark that] I cannot wait to go there and play [at], plus it is beautiful too."

CHARLEY STEINER, BROADCASTER: "As retractable domes go, it is pretty darn good, especially when it is 119 degrees outside. . . . [When we did] our first Sunday night game there when I was at ESPN, I thought it was quite remarkable how a rectangle could work itself out and become a functional baseball ballpark, and of all the ballparks in the National League, [it is] the fairest one for hitters."

MATT WILLIAMS: "I think it is a perfect ballpark for where we play. The roof can close and 30 minutes later, it is 75 degrees and it can be 120 outside and we are able to maintain an environment. . . . It is difficult for our grounds crew to keep the grass growing because growing grass indoors is difficult, but I think it is one of the nicest ballparks in our league."

BARRY ZITO: "Chase Field is all right, but the grass is so finicky. . . . I understand they have got a hot sun and a roof, [but] the grass there is bad. It is a great field, but from a player's standpoint if you throw three throws in the same patch of grass, it is dirt and it goes to nothing."

CHASE FIELD FACTS AND FIGURES

CHASE FIELD ADDRESS
401 East Jefferson Street, Phoenix, AZ 85004

ARIZONA DIAMONDBACKS TEAM WEB SITE
www.dbacks.com

FIELD DIMENSIONS (IN FEET)
Left Field: 330', Left-Center: 376', Center: 407', Right-Center: 376', Right Field: 335'

SEATING CAPACITY (AS OF 2015)
48,633

ALL-STAR GAMES AT CHASE FIELD
July 12, 2011: National League 5, American League 1
MVP: Prince Fielder, Milwaukee Brewers (NL)

CHASE FIELD FIRSTS
Game: March 31, 1998—Colorado 9, Arizona 2
Single: Mike Lansing, Colorado (March 31, 1998)*
Double: Todd Helton, Colorado (March 31, 1998)
Triple: Neifi Perez, Colorado (April 2, 1998)
Home Run: Vinny Castilla, Colorado (March 31, 1998)

Denotes first hit in the stadium.

COORS FIELD
HOME OF THE COLORADO ROCKIES

Coors Field, Colorado Rockies (*Photographed by Brian Skversky/Flickr*)

When the Colorado Rockies franchise began play as an official Major League Baseball franchise in 1993, their home games were played at the 76,123-seat Mile High Stadium, the one-time dwelling of the NFL's Denver Broncos. All the Rockies did in their inaugural campaign (besides finish 67–95) was establish the all-time single season attendance record when 4,483,350 made their way through the turnstiles at the football-turned-baseball stadium. It also set a precedent for the construction of Coors Field, and it became critical for the stadium to be a structure that accommodated the masses while providing a beautiful facility for the Rockies to call their own.

The $300 million Coors Field occupies 76 acres in the downtown district and conveniently sits near Interstate 25. It was the first new complex to be constructed as part of a six-year sports venue upgrade that also included new buildings for the NFL's Broncos, the NBA's Nuggets, and the NHL's Avalanche, who share the same arena. The opening of the ballpark worked wonders for the city, helping to revive the business district and making it a popular destination during the baseball season.

Initial plans had the capacity at 43,800, but after attendance records were shattered at Mile High Stadium, ownership made a few alterations. When it opened in 1995, the final seat count was 50,200. At Mile High Stadium the famous "Rockpile" section was positioned in dead center field and what literally seemed like 5,280 feet away from the action. At Coors Field, the same concept was replicated, but it is positioned a little closer, albeit in the upper part of deep center field.

When the construction phase was well under way, workers may have gotten a little more than they bargained for when they came across a number of dinosaur fossils scattered throughout the area. They stumbled across something they most likely thought they'd never find: a seven-foot-long, 1,000-pound triceratops skull, which was normally one-third the length of the animal's entire body. It was one of the last creatures of its kind to survive more than 65 million years ago. Due to the findings, an early name considered for the ballpark was Jurassic Park, but when those plans were scrapped, the team opted to select a dinosaur as its mascot.

Coors Field, the first National League baseball-only ballpark to be built since Dodger Stadium in 1962, sits 5,277 feet above sea level and as a result, the ball travels 9 percent farther than at any other stadium in the Major Leagues. It is a striking brick-and-steel retro design that followed in the footsteps of Oriole Park at Camden Yards in Baltimore (1992) and Progressive Field in Cleveland (1994) and quickly established itself as one of the best in the league.

SPECIAL FEATURES OF COORS FIELD

ALTITUDE EXPLANATION

Long before it hosted a game, it was often speculated that Coors Field would be a home run haven because of one simple equation: low air density plus a high level of elevation equals a baseball cutting through the air like a hot knife through butter. It turns out the experts were right and as a result, the long ball was being hit at a record pace. As the years went on, research confirmed that a ball carries 9 percent farther at Coors Field than it does at a ballpark at sea level. The translation? A home run hit 400 feet at PNC Park in Pittsburgh (sea level) would equal a 440-foot shot in Colorado (one mile above sea level). Following the conclusion of the 2001 season, a humidifier was installed at the ballpark, which made baseballs more elastic when hitters made contact. It worked and since then, the number of home runs hit has been on pace with the other ballparks in baseball.

BLEACHER SECTION

While the center-field bleachers are nicknamed the "Rockpile," the bleachers in left field positioned in front of the scoreboard are not only a popular spot for home run seekers, but also for those looking to get an excellent view of the action. They stretch all the way from the left-field foul pole to the bullpens in center field, making them an affordable bargain.

BLUE MOON BREWERY

Outstanding food and microbrews are only some of what you can expect to find at the Blue Moon Brewery, located on the main concourse level behind section 112. When the weather is excellent, an outdoor patio is an option for those wishing to soak in the rays. Blue Moon beer, produced by Coors Brewing Company, is a Belgian-type brewski invented in Denver and is, not surprisingly, a fan favorite.

CHILDREN'S FREE-FOR-ALL

Positioned by the main concourse at Gate A and right behind the bullpens in center field is an interactive area for kids. The little ones will be so excited when they see what awaits them: a video batting cage (for adults, too), a speed pitch to clock the mph on your fastball, a T-ball cage, and a broadcast booth that allows fans to broadcast a live half-inning and receive a copy of it as a keepsake.

CONFERENCE CENTER

A conference center on the right-field suite level can be rented out for full or half days, and can accommodate between 50 to 400 individuals at a time. It is available for business meetings, birthday parties, anniversaries, wedding showers, baby showers, or other events. On days when the Rockies are playing a game at home, suites across the hall feature retractable glass walls, enabling fans to take in the action and adding yet another perk to an already exceptional experience.

COORS CLUBHOUSE

The Coors Clubhouse, situated directly behind the dish, provides a close view of the field and takes luxury to a whole new level. A wait-in service is available in the seating areas. Fans can celebrate a Rockies victory with a cocktail at the lounge, which is also a benefit limited to ticket holders.

FIRST IMPRESSIONS

The main entrance at Coors Field features a brick exterior, glass windows, and a clock tower. The Bulova clock is sandwiched between the words "COORS FIELD." Fourteen windows make this one of the finest entrances in the game. Nearby, a bronze statue of Branch Rickey stands at the forefront, unofficially monitoring the traffic passing by on Blake Street.

JUST LIKE HOME

The VIP Cabana Terrace, added for the 2014 season, is in the upper-deck section and offers fans a hearth, rooftop illumination, and comfortable furnishings. Fans are now treated to a breathtaking view of not only the downtown area, but also the Front Range, a mountain range of the Southern Rocky Mountains in the central portion of Colorado.

NAMING RIGHTS

In the first open-ended naming rights deal in Major League Baseball history, the Coors Brewing Company purchased the exclusive title rights to the Rockies' ballpark in 1995 after paying $15 million *total* in a deal that spans an indefinite amount of time. By comparison, other companies that bought naming rights for a ballpark pay for it on an annual basis.

OUT-OF-TOWN SCOREBOARD

A throwback to the good old days, the 14-foot-high manual scoreboard is part of the wall in right field and displays scores from other games going on around baseball. In the ground rules and according to the Colorado Rockies Media Guide, a provision was made to include a rule just in case a ball went through it. It states that if a ball goes through the scoreboard whether it is on the fly or bounce, that player is awarded two bases.

PARKING LOT DANGERS

Located just behind the big scoreboard in left field is a parking lot, a dangerous spot for vehicles considering that the chance of a home run flying out of Coors Field is a possibility. Although a ball would have to travel close to 515 feet to do some car damage (distance courtesy of Google Earth), it is not totally out of the question considering the rarified air in Colorado. San Francisco outfielder Hunter Pence came close in 2013 after he connected for a 476-foot moonshot that hit a brick wall, just behind the bleacher section. And in 1998 during the home run derby, a couple of players came close to depositing a baseball in the area.

PICNIC AREAS

Two picnic sites—the Coors outfield picnic area across from gate A and the Platte River Rendezvous inside Coors Field under cover of the Rockpile—offer fans the opportunity to chill out and enjoy their stay inside the ballpark. Equipped with picnic tables and chairs, these two spots can also be used for parties and other fancy shindigs. Consider it the next best thing to actually having a picnic in the Rocky Mountains.

PREMIUM CLUB

The Wells Fargo Club, a premier seating option, encompasses sections 214–27 down the first-base line and 234–47 down the third-base line. Outdoor seating includes wait service for each seat. Inside is a roomy, glassed-in area, complete with two full-service bars near sections 221 and 236 along with a number of specialty stations that feature a rotating menu. This is accessible only to those members holding Wells Fargo Club or Suite-Level tickets.

PURPLE SEATS

Marking the significance of being 5,280 feet above sea level and providing some of the most breathtaking views of the Denver skyline, a ring of purple seats encircles the twentieth row of the upper deck and dares to be different in a ballpark full of dark green chairs. A batted ball has never found its way into this location during a game, but during the 1998 home run derby, Jim Thome came pretty darn close to the purple chairs in the right-field upper tank.

RETIRED NUMBERS

On August 17, 2014, the Rockies organization retired their first number in franchise history, the number 17, which was worn by first baseman Todd Helton. As of this writing, Helton, the eighth pick in the 1995 amateur draft and the former backup quarterback at Tennessee behind Peyton Manning, is currently the all-time Rockies leader in games played (2,247), doubles (592), home runs (369), runs batted in (1,406), hits (2,519), and walks (1,335), among other categories. The only other retired number is that of Jackie Robinson's 42, which was preserved league-wide in 1997.

RIGHT FIELD BAR & GRILLE

The right-field corner is home to a fabulous Bar and Grille, which is available to all ticketed fans and has a two-level outdoor patio with fine-dining options. A large glass window can be opened on days when Mother Nature isn't busy flexing her muscles. An à la carte menu offers quick snacks or more substantial selections. The Rockies have displayed memorabilia (game-used bases, baseballs, and bats among the items) from the 2007 World Series to remind fans of their greatest success to date as a big-league franchise.

ROCKIES HALL OF HISTORY

Available to those with game-day tickets in the club or suite levels, along with anyone taking a tour of Coors Field, the Hall of History is behind home plate on the club level and chronicles the history of the franchise. In 2013, the Rockies celebrated their twentieth season as a Major League club. The Hall of History has historical artifacts celebrating moments such as the expansion draft, the first game at Coors Field in 1995, the 1998 All-Star Game, and the club's first trip to the World Series in 2007, plus photos.

ROCKPILE

The Rockpile, a popular seating section that can seat 2,300 at Mile High Stadium, was carried over to Coors Field and is in center field, just above the batter's eye. These bleacher seats have great views and are popular because of their affordable pricing, with tickets ranging from $1 to $4. The $1 tickets can be purchased only at the Coors Field box office and are good for children 12 and under, and those 55 and over.

SCOREBOARD

The primary scoreboard, located in left field just beyond the steel-backed bleachers, serves as the main information base and displays other pertinent information related to the game at hand. Upgraded to LED standards in 2006, the top video display showcases player photos and measures 27 feet high by 47 feet wide. Just below it, a 33-foot-tall by 73-foot-wide screen provides lineups, in-game player statistics, and the box score. On the very top, the Rockies logo featuring the signature Rocky Mountains, a baseball soaring through it, and the distinctive "ROCKIES" insignia illuminates in purple when the sun sets. The same logo is also on the back and lights up as well.

SOLAR PANELS

Coors Field was one of the first Major League ballparks to incorporate solar panels. Forty-six energy-saving panels were installed on the Rockpile in 2007 in conjunction with their agreement with Xcel Energy. The panels generate around 14,000 kilowatt hours of energy per year and through a monitoring system nearby, fans can check out the real-time usage of both the Rockpile LED scoreboard and overall energy production of the solar panels. Since the Rockies instituted this, many other teams have followed suit at their respective ballparks.

The scoreboard in left field rises high above the bleacher seats. (*Photographed by Brian Skversky/Flickr*)

SPECTATOR LAW

Enacted in 1993 as part of the Colorado Baseball Safety Act, this Colorado law states that an individual attending a game at Coors Field is responsible for his or her own safety while at the ballpark. Management, the owner of the baseball team, or the stadium are not liable for any injuries incurred during the game, which can include, but aren't limited to: baseballs hit into the stands, bats that fly out of the hands of players, or any other situation that may arise throughout the course of a game. In other words, always be on the lookout!

STADIUM SIGHTINGS

One of the best-kept secrets in all of sports is that you can see the other two stadiums from each of the three major stadiums in Denver (Rockies of Major League Baseball, Broncos of the National Football League, and the Nuggets of the National Basketball Association). That is, if you determine that a Rockies game is out of hand, head to the upper deck and look at the two other facilities in downtown Denver.

THE PLAYER STATUE

Commissioned by the Denver Rotary Club and unveiled on June 2, 2005, a bronze statue dubbed "The Player" stands outside the main entrance, paying tribute to one of baseball's most legendary scouts, Branch Rickey. The nine-foot six-inch-tall statue on top of a four-foot granite base depicts him holding a baseball in his left hand with a baseball bat slung over his right shoulder. The Branch Rickey Award is given each year to one Major League player who goes above and beyond the call of duty within the community. On the statue is a list of every award winner since 1992, along with a quote from Rickey: "It is not the honor that you take with you but the heritage you leave behind."

UNDERGROUND HEATING

When Coors Field opened in 1995, it became the first Major League ballpark to use an underground heating system. Since the chance of snow is a real possibility in early April and the postseason if the Rockies qualify, the installation of such a unit makes perfect sense. In the event the flakes fly, the underground heating melts the snow and prevents the walkways from becoming a huge ice skating rink. Target Field in Minnesota later installed an underground heating system when it debuted in 2010.

UPPER-DECK BAR

Seeking to utilize otherwise unused space during games, management authorized a complete overhaul to the right-field upper deck following the 2013 season. The end result was the largest rooftop deck in the Major Leagues, complete with two levels, clocking in at more than 38,000 square feet. The 5280 Craft Bar measures 52 feet, 80 inches long, and has 52 beer taps.

WATERFALL DISPLAY

The Rockies have done an unbelievable job in creating the essence of Denver in the center-field backdrop. There are seven fountains, three 10-foot waterfalls, and seven different types of trees native to Colorado. A pumping system, which distributes 3,200 gallons of water per minute, enables the fountains to shoot water 40 feet in the air following a Rockies home run, victory, and during the seventh-inning stretch. A grand total of 700,000 pounds of rock, along with a Kentucky blue grass base, makes a gorgeous display.

MEMORABLE GAMES AT COORS FIELD

APRIL 26, 1995: FIRST GAME AT COORS FIELD

In a sign of offense to come, the Rockies dramatically outslugged the New York Mets, winning on a three-run home run by Dante Bichette in the bottom of the fourteenth during an 11–9 victory. With a charged-up crowd of 47,228 in attendance, Colorado didn't waste any time making sure the scoreboard worked properly after Larry Walker hit an RBI double, scoring Walt Weiss. Two batters later, Bichette hit a sacrifice fly to drive home Walker, giving the Rockies a 2–0 lead.

It then turned into a game of "Can you top this?" when each Rockies score was countered by the Mets all the way into the ninth inning, when the road team took a 7–6 lead on an RBI single by Bobby Bonilla. Not to be outdone, Weiss walked, and Walker followed with another RBI double, tying the game at six and sending it into extras. After four innings of scoreless ball, New York momentarily took a 7–6 advantage on an RBI double by Joe Orsulak in the top of the fourteenth, but it was Bichette who had the last laugh and made the debut of baseball's newest ballpark a smashing success with the three-run bomb, sending the fans clad in purple home happy.

AUGUST 18, 1995: CUBS DESTROY ROCKIES

With the first season of baseball at Coors Field well under way, it was only a matter of time before a contest featured a team scoring a remarkable amount of runs. It happened when the Cubs erupted for 26, handing Colorado one of its most lopsided losses in franchise history, 26–7. The festivities began when Chicago greeted Rockies starter Bret Saberhagen by putting a seven-spot, highlighted by a three-run homer off the bat of Luis Gonzalez in the inning.

After tallying two in the third, the offensive assault continued in the top of the fifth, when six runs crossed the plate. With Gonzalez again in the middle of it, he stroked a two-run double and one batter later, Todd Zeile brought him home with a two-run blast, breaking it open at 15–1. In the top of the sixth, three consecutive RBI singles increased the lead to 18–2, and four more in the seventh, capped off by a three-run shot from Sammy Sosa, stretched the advantage to 22–4. In the eighth, and perhaps feeling the need to add a few more insurance runs, the bases were loaded for Scott Bullett, who promptly deposited a triple to left field, clearing the bases. The final dagger was an RBI single courtesy of Jose Hernandez, finishing off the scoring spree. In all, 27 hits were recorded and Gonzalez, who ended the game 3-for-6 with six runs batted in, led the offense.

OCTOBER 3, 1995: FIRST PLAYOFF GAME AT COORS FIELD

In baseball, very few teams have had the opportunity to christen their brand-new ballpark with a trip to the postseason. Thanks to the wild card, the Rockies got the chance and hosted the Atlanta Braves in Game 1 of the Division Series, but dropped a close one, 5–4. Scoreless until the third, Marquis Grissom stepped in and hit a solo home run off Kevin Ritz, giving the

Braves a 1–0 lead. Ellis Burks got things rolling for Colorado in the bottom of the fourth with a sacrifice fly that scored Larry Walker, and Vinny Castilla followed with a two-run blast, giving the Rockies their first playoff lead, 3–1.

Atlanta tied it at three in the sixth on a home run by Chipper Jones and a fielder's choice off the bat of Luis Polonia, and later went ahead 4–3 in the eighth on an RBI single by Dwight Smith. Not to be outdone, Burks doubled to deep left in the bottom of the frame, scoring Dante Bichette and deadlocking the contest at four. In the end, Jones lofted his second home run of the game in the top of the ninth, and despite a shaky outing, Mark Wohlers closed out the game for Atlanta, who eventually went on to win the series, three games to one.

MAY 18, 1996: MABRY HITS FOR CYCLE BUT CARDS SQUANDER LEAD
The Colorado Rockies overcame a four-run deficit in the bottom of the ninth, scoring five runs and overshadowing the first cycle at Coors Field during a 9–8 comeback victory. In what seemed like just another day at the ballpark, Cardinals first baseman John Mabry turned it into something special when he singled in the second, doubled in the fourth, hit an RBI triple in the fifth, and finished off the cycle by hitting a two-run home run in the seventh. With closer extraordinaire Dennis Eckersley on the mound for St. Louis in the bottom of the ninth, Colorado refused to be intimidated and proved it when Ellis Burks hit a two-run blast, and John Vander Wal later followed in the inning with a game-ending three-run bomb, finishing off the incredible come-from-behind victory.

SEPTEMBER 18, 1996: NOMO DOES THE COORS FIELD IMPOSSIBLE
In what seemed like an unlikely possibility for any pitcher taking the mound in the rare air, Hideo Nomo beat the odds, tossing the first no-hitter in the short history of Coors Field as his Dodgers defeated the National League's top-hitting team, 9–0. Unfazed by the offensive production possible, Nomo settled in after a two-hour rain delay and mowed down Colorado batters with ease, striking out eight while issuing free passes to only four batters. With the Dodgers leading 5–0 in the eighth, Nomo helped out his own cause, hitting an RBI single that plated Raul Mondesi, and Los Angeles pushed across three more runs in the top of the ninth that proved to be more than enough for the Japanese sensation. In the bottom of the ninth, the Rockies went down 1–2–3 with Ellis Burks striking out to end the game.

JUNE 19–20, 2002: YANKS AND ROX SLUG IT OUT
In their first trip to Coors Field, the New York Yankees took two out of three, scored in double digits each game, and made themselves right at home in the hitter-friendly ballpark. After winning the first game by a score of

10–5, the high-scoring Bronx Bombers took aim in the second game, doubling up the Rockies, 20–10. With the teams deadlocked at one going into the fourth, New York struck for three, which included an RBI double by starter Andy Pettite, his first career extra base hit. The Rockies answered right back, scoring seven runs in the bottom of the fourth, highlighted by a 2-for-2 performance off the bat of Larry Walker in which he hit a solo home run and two-run single in the inning. New York answered with 13 runs over the next three innings powered by Alfonso Soriano and Jason Giambi, who both hit home runs, ultimately putting the game out of reach.

On June 20, it appeared as though both teams saved the best for last, with the Rockies pulling off a dramatic 14–11 win behind a walk-off, three-run home run by Todd Zeile in the bottom of the tenth. Trailing 8–2 after 5½ innings, RBI singles by Terry Shumpert, Juan Pierre, Brett Butler, and Larry Walker made it 8–6, setting the stage for Todd Hollandsworth, who, with one swing of the bat, gave Colorado a 10–8 lead after his grand slam landed in the right-center-field seats. The Yankees got one run back in the seventh, when Rondell White delivered an RBI single, but Larry Walker answered in the bottom of the frame with an RBI single of his own, extending the Colorado lead to 11–9 heading into the ninth.

Colorado closer Jose Jimenez was summoned from the bullpen and couldn't hold it, as Ron Coomer and Jorge Posada hit back-to-back RBI singles tying it at 11, ultimately sending it into extra innings. That's when Zeile came up and put an end to the three-game series, which saw both teams combine for an incredible 70 runs, 95 hits, and 15 home runs.

JULY 9, 2005: FIRST 1–0 GAME IN COORS FIELD HISTORY

Up until this contest, a record-setting 847 regular season contests were played without a 1–0 decision at Coors Field. On this date, the Rockies made history by becoming the first team to win a 1–0 game after defeating the San Diego Padres. Behind the stellar pitching of Jason Jennings, who allowed only seven hits during seven innings of work, the lone run of the game was tallied when Colorado's Luis Gonzalez doubled in Aaron Miles during the bottom part of the sixth inning. The Rockies and Coors Field broke the previous record held by the Philadelphia Athletics of the American Association at Jefferson Street Grounds, who went 635 straight games without a 1–0 outcome.

OCTOBER 1, 2007: TIEBREAKER ENDS IN CONTROVERSY

With a 163rd game necessary to determine who would be heading to the National League Division Series, the Colorado Rockies defeated the San Diego Padres 9–8 in 13 innings. The Rockies jumped out to an early 3–0 lead, but in the third, Adrian Gonzalez gave the Padres their first lead with a grand slam, and another run courtesy of a groundout made it 5–3. Trailing 6–5 in the eighth, San Diego tied the contest when Brian Giles laced an RBI double off Colorado closer Brian Fuentes that scored Geoff Blum, tying the game at six and sending it to extra innings.

Scoreless until the thirteenth, San Diego's Scott Hairston connected for a two-run shot, which prompted the call to closer Trevor Hoffman to come in for the bottom half of the inning to help secure the playoff berth. It failed, as back-to-back doubles by Kaz Matsui and Troy Tulowitzki paved the way for Matt Holliday, who laced a game-tying triple. Jamey Carroll then sent a drive to deep right and on the catch, Holliday tagged up and arrived at home head-first just about the same time the ball did, scoring the winning run. Although numerous replays showed inconclusively that his hand touched the plate, the Rockies would ride the momentum of that game all the way to the World Series.

OCTOBER 15, 2007: ROCKIES CLINCH FIRST PENNANT

The Rockies captured their first National League pennant with a 6–4 series-ending sweep against the Arizona Diamondbacks, their astonishing twenty-first win in their last 22 games. Using a remarkable stretch of baseball to punch their ticket to the Fall Classic for the first time in franchise history, Matt Holliday—who was later named the NLCS MVP—hit the decisive blow in the fourth as part of a six-run inning, when he nailed a three-run home run to give Colorado a 6–1 lead. The Diamondbacks would never recover, and with their second consecutive sweep in the playoffs, the Rockies joined the legendary 1976 Cincinnati Reds "Big Red Machine" as the only Major League teams to date to begin a postseason 7–0.

OCTOBER 27, 2007: THE FALL CLASSIC COMES TO THE MILE-HIGH CITY

Already facing a 2–0 deficit in the World Series, Colorado fans were more than happy to welcome the Fall Classic to the Denver area for the first time ever. Turns out, that's the only excitement that would occur in the stands as Boston flexed their muscles during a 10–5 victory. The Red Sox pushed across six runs in the top of the third with rookie Jacoby Ellsbury hitting two doubles in the inning, and pitcher Daisuke Matsuzaka helped out his own cause by lacing a two-run single as part of the offensive attack. Colorado pulled to within one at 6–5 after a two-run sixth and three-run seventh in which Matt Holliday smacked a three-run blast. Boston would not falter, adding three more in the top of the eighth on the strength of back-to-back RBI doubles by Julio Lugo and Coco Crisp, increasing the lead to 9–5. A sacrifice fly by Jason Varitek in the ninth made it 10–5 and gave the Red Sox a commanding 3–0 series advantage, and they would wrap up the title the next day with a 4–3 win.

WHAT THEY'RE SAYING ABOUT COORS FIELD

CLINT BARMES: "I love Coors Field.... The outfield is bigger, there is a lot more area to cover for outfielders, a lot more holes for baseballs you may not square up, and that plays a factor. It is a hitter's ballpark, and having that big outfield and all that ground, it has an advantage toward a hitter."

JASON BAY: "For people [who] have not been there, it is an absolutely gorgeous ballpark [and] it is wide open in the back.... Everything inside is first-rate and the surface and everything about it is just a great ballpark."

HEATH BELL: "It is probably the best-looking ballpark to its environment.... You feel like you are in the Rockies in the stadium. It is pretty sweet and I think it is one of the best bullpens around. It is just a beautiful ballpark to look at."

GREG BROWN, BROADCASTER: "I like the looks of it, but I hate the baseball that is played there because that is not baseball, it is ping-pong.... It is [like a] video game and it is definitely not baseball."

JACK CORRIGAN, BROADCASTER: "I love Coors Field. . . . To sit on the right-field side—the first-base side—in the summer and [when you] get one of those unbelievable Colorado sunsets that you will see in the left-field corner, there is nothing like it."

JASON GIAMBI: "It is incredible there. You got play there every day and it was way ahead of its time when they built it because the amenities they have there are just like the new ballparks. . . . Everything is so green, it looks brand new."

MATT KEMP: "It is a little different, the grass is pretty thick, and it is hard to [have] fun out there sometimes as far as being an outfielder, and it gets kind of squishy and hard on your legs. . . . I have had some success [at Coors Field], so I really cannot complain."

ADAM LAROCHE: "Coors [Field] is probably my favorite just because of the city, the mountains, [and] the field. . . . [It is just] the whole package there."

JAMIE MOYER: "[It is a] beautiful ballpark in a beautiful city. . . . As a visitor in the bullpen, you almost feel like you have gone out in the woods because you are facing that backdrop of center field with a bunch of pine trees."

TROY TULOWITZKI: "If you go behind the scenes, it is not run down at all. . . . The people [who] work there really care about the field and how it appears to the outside."

COORS FIELD FACTS AND FIGURES

COORS FIELD ADDRESS
2001 Blake Street, Denver, CO 80205

COLORADO ROCKIES TEAM WEB SITE
www.coloradorockies.com

FIELD DIMENSIONS (IN FEET)
Left Field: 347', Left-Center: 390', Center: 415',
Right-Center: 375', Right Field: 350'

SEATING CAPACITY (AS OF 2015)
50,480

ALL-STAR GAMES AT COORS FIELD
July 7, 1998: National League 13, American League 8
MVP: Roberto Alomar, Baltimore Orioles (AL)

COORS FIELD FIRSTS
Game: April 26, 1995—Colorado 11, New York 9 (14 innings)
Single: Brett Butler, New York (April 26, 1995)*
Double: Larry Walker, Colorado (April 26, 1995)
Triple: Andres Galaragga, Colorado (April 27, 1995)
Home Run: Rico Brogna, New York (April 27, 1995)

Denotes first hit in the stadium.

DODGER STADIUM
HOME OF THE LOS ANGELES DODGERS

Dodger Stadium, Los Angeles Dodgers (*Photographed by Mark Whitt/Flickr*)

A s many famous stories have begun, once upon a time, former Dodgers President Walter O'Malley had a vision that would revolutionize the baseball scene in the Los Angeles district. He made sure to see it all the way through and, as a result, not only has Dodger Stadium become a crown jewel in California and all of baseball, but it also became a major landmark on the West Coast when Major League Baseball officially welcomed the Dodgers and the city of Los Angeles with open arms in 1962.

When it debuted, Dodger Stadium became the first Major League ballpark since the construction of Yankee Stadium in 1923, the first to be built solely with private financing.

Dodger Stadium was one of the few ballparks built in the 1960s that was not one of the rounded, multipurpose stadiums that swept the nation later that decade and into the 1970s. While those cookie-cutter-like structures were popping up in cities like Philadelphia and St. Louis, replacing older, more character-friendly ballparks, the home of the Dodgers seemed to be a trendsetter in its own right, almost as if it were the Oriole Park at Camden Yards of the 1960s. It bucked the usual tendency to have a fully enclosed outfield, opting instead for an open look. This afforded fans views of the city while enjoying America's pastime.

Dodger Stadium's parking lot is distinctive in its terraced-earthworks-style design, which allows ticket holders to park near their seats, thus minimizing the time it takes to get to their destination. The parking lot is also said to be earthquake-resistant, which is certainly an important feature to have considering what happened when the 1989 earthquake occurred during Game 3 of the World Series at Candlestick Park in San Francisco.

In the 1950s there was controversy when residents in the area were told that the land for Dodger Stadium would be used to construct low-income housing and that in return, residents would have their choice of new homes that were scheduled to be built. In the end, the city turned its back on the population, instead using the land to persuade the owner of the Brooklyn Dodgers to move the team to the Los Angeles area. The top of a local hill was removed, and soil was added to provide a level surface for both a parking lot and the ballpark. A few seasons after the ballpark opened, a nearby landowner claimed that a corner of his property had been paved over to make room for part of the parking lot.

Many renovations have taken place over the course of Dodger Stadium's history, most recently just in time for the 2013 season. At that time, the Dodgers put $100 million into the ballpark, adding new clubhouses, weight rooms, batting cages, concession stands, scoreboards, sound systems, and other improvements. In the outfield, seats were removed to widen concourses, and expanded bullpens were reconfigured. In addition, a high-definition LED video board was added above the left- and right-field pavilion seating areas, giving fans clearer views of replays and statistical information.

And just before the start of the 2014 campaign, there were additional upgrades: entrances at the field level were expanded, allowing fans to enter the ballpark on the north side of the stadium; the addition of team stores and memorabilia; moving the visiting teams' clubhouse closer to the visitors' dugout; and upgrading the electrical parts in Dodger Stadium, improving safety and giving fans the chance to experience the latest and greatest in technological advancements.

SPECIAL FEATURES OF DODGER STADIUM

ADVANTAGE = PITCHERS

Expansive foul territory was the norm during the early days at Dodger Stadium, and it appears as though the more things change, the more they stay the same. For pitchers, even those who tend to give up a lot of runs, Dodger Stadium is a dream come true. For starters, the baseball does not carry well here, and secondly, this is a very spacious field, to say the least. By combining these two elements, a pitcher can compile some pretty solid statistics. From 1962, when Dodger Stadium opened, to 1966, Los Angeles pitchers won five Cy Young Awards: Sandy Koufax (unanimous selection three times), and Don Drysdale and Dean Chance of the Los Angeles Angels (once each).

BEER RULES

To monitor fans and their intake of alcohol, Dodger Stadium has several rules to ensure a fan-friendly atmosphere. Each fan is limited to only two beers per contest, and sales are cut off following the conclusion of the seventh inning. There are no beer attendants who prowl the aisles looking for alcohol-thirsty patrons. What this means is that you have to take a hike and get it yourself from a nearby concession area.

DODGER DOGS

The most famous hot dog of all (sorry, Oscar Meyer Wieners), the Dodger Dog is one food you can't miss on your visit to Dodger Stadium. A fan favorite since the early 1970s, it is just one of the many foods available at the ballpark. In 2004, the Travel Channel named Dodger Stadium the world's best stadium for fine dining.

DODGER WAY

Dodger Way, part of a $500 million project to make Dodger Stadium even more fan friendly, is a tree-lined entrance that leads to an expertly manicured grand plaza just beyond the center-field area. This walkway leads to shops and other interactive exhibits for fans to enjoy before or after a game. Management is always seeking ways to improve an already-gorgeous ballpark.

DUGOUT CLUB

The Dugout Club, another fine option for entertaining, is the most exclusive at Dodger Stadium and has incredible views coupled with great beverage and food services. There is an adjacent club complete with a martini lounge, full bar, and restaurant-style seating for an unlimited complimentary high-end buffet. However, there's one catch: in order to take full advantage of this option, you must be a Dugout Club season-ticket holder.

FLOWER DISPLAYS

Dodger Stadium is surrounded by 15 different tree species, over 300 Olympic rose bushes, and more than 3,000 trees, all of which give the ballpark a natural-looking landscape. Colorful murals of current players and banners expressing Dodger pride welcome fans.

HISTORICAL REMINDERS

As part of upgrades completed in time for the 2013 season, the Dodgers incorporated many things around the ballpark to remind fans of the great tradition of Los Angeles baseball. The concourses have painted murals commemorating great moments and players, along with exhibits that honor Cy Young Award winners, Most Valuable Players, and those whose numbers have been retired.

JAPANESE GARDEN

In 1965, Japanese Hall of Famer Sotaro Suzuki presented the Dodgers organization with a 10-foot Japanese stone lantern, marking the long-standing relationship between Japan and the Los Angeles Dodgers. The lantern is in the Japanese garden, which is on a hill above parking lot 6 and a short distance from the right-field pavilion. Former owner Walter O'Malley would often frequent this area to clear his mind from the daily activities of the world. In 2003 the lantern was rededicated, and if you have the chance, take a peek out of right field once the sun sets to catch a glimpse of the light.

MIKE BRITO

A mainstay for many years, Mike Brito was the man who held the radar gun behind home plate, tracking speeds generated by Dodger pitchers. However, when management reconfigured the Dugout Club seats, the team had no choice but to put the radar gun on a mount. Brito is still with the organization serving as a scout in Mexico and is credited with discovering Fernando Valenzuela, a one-time rookie sensation who captured the hearts of Dodgers fans. All Valenzuela did in his first season in the big leagues was take home the National League Rookie of the Year and the Cy Young Award.

ONGOING RENOVATIONS

In addition to the latest and greatest facelift Dodger Stadium received just before the 2013 season, management has remained committed to keeping the ballpark in tip-top shape. Here is a brief history of the most recent upgrades.

Unveiled on April 14, 2000, were the following: an upgraded press box, 13 additional new luxury suites, and enhanced seating behind the dugouts. The new section also incorporated a restaurant and bar-style service, complete with a buffet area and monitors for fans to enjoy the game.

In 2004, there was another wave of enhancements. As part of a $15 million project, the dugouts were moved 23 feet closer to the field and equipped with modern amenities. Approximately 1,600 seats were added in various parts of the ballpark. The addition of an LED scoreboard was installed from foul pole to foul pole, alongside the base of the loge level.

In 2006, changes included replacing every seat in the primary seating bowl, repairs to the concrete and structure within the seating area, and construction of traditional box seats along each baseline. Finally, in 2008, a multimillion-dollar field-level restoration doubled the number of concession stands and restrooms, added two new clubs for baseline box seat holders, expanded walkways, and added energy-efficient equipment throughout the stadium. Ownership has remained committed to the fan experience, and each season, fans continue to flock to Dodger Stadium to enjoy all that it has to offer.

OUTSIDE FAÇADE
The Dodger Stadium experience begins long before you pass through the turnstiles. Much like that of the Rogers Centre in Toronto, oversized banners featuring action shots of players past and present welcome fans to the show.

PALM TREES
If you ever attended a contest at Qualcomm Stadium, the one-time multipurpose home of the San Diego Padres, this feature should bring back a couple of memories for you. The Padres planted palm trees beyond the outfield wall, accentuating the "California look." The Dodgers later followed suit, planting them down both the left- and right-field lines.

PAVILION ROOF
One target for home run hitters lies directly down the left-field line. Curvy roofs hang over the bleacher areas and tempt power hitters. This same design is used around the entire upper deck, most notably in the pavilion areas. While a member of the Dodgers in 1997, Mike Piazza hit a massive shot on the roof, and slugger Mark McGwire duplicated the feat during the 1999 season as a member of the St. Louis Cardinals.

PAVILION SEATS
Although they might be considered one of the best bargains in the game today, stern rules take away from the overall experience in this section. Once fans are in that section, strict rules prohibit them from leaving it to explore other parts of the ballpark. A word to the wise: Explore everything beforehand, so you're not caught between a rock and a hard place once you enter the section.

PLAYING FIELD
Dodger Stadium currently employs Prescription Athletic Turf (PAT) as its main surface, which includes a state-of-the-art drainage system. Using the latest in technology, 100,000 square feet of Bermuda grass is grown on pure

sand, beneath which is a vacuum chamber covered with a watertight plastic barrier that aggressively extracts water during heavy rains. A computer controller has the ability to reverse the process when the sand's moisture reading drops below its optimum level.

RETIRED NUMBERS

The Dodgers have 10 retired numbers, which are underneath the pavilion roof in right field. The men honored are: Pee Wee Reese (1), Tommy Lasorda (2), Duke Snider (4), Jim Gilliam (19), Don Sutton (20), Walter Alston (24), Sandy Koufax (32), Roy Campanella (39), Jackie Robinson (42), and Don Drysdale (53).

SCOREBOARDS

Upgraded and installed just before the 2013 season, the scoreboards above the left- and right-field seats now provide crystal-clear video and informational content. Tapping into their history, the Dodgers recreated the distinctive vintage hexagonal shape for both boards while becoming the first team to sport a sophisticated 10mm 1080p LED display in Major League Baseball. A high-definition broadcast control room runs the scoreboards.

The scoreboards were restored to their original hexagonal shapes for 2013. (*Photographed by Carol Ohler*)

SEAT COLORS

The seating bowls underwent a major overhaul following the conclusion of the 2005 season, and nearly all the seats were replaced with the original 1962 color scheme of yellow, light orange, turquoise, and sky blue. The rainbow-colored pattern of chairs once consisted of 1970 "Pirates yellow" on the first level, 1980 "Astros orange" on the second deck, and "Dodger blue" on the third level. Lastly, 1980 "California Angel red" was on the upper-deck sections. Seating is expandable to 85,000, which would easily make it the largest in all of baseball now that the Cleveland Municipal Stadium has been long gone!

STADIUM CLUB

The Stadium Club, one of the finer ways to take in a game at Dodger Stadium, opens its doors two hours before the start of each game and is on the club level. This first-class, full-service restaurant and bar offers members the opportunity to wine and dine in luxury. All of the dishes are complemented by a comprehensive wine list.

THE NEXT 50

In 2011, management unveiled a plan to ensure Dodger Stadium would be around for another 50-plus years and would be more attractive than ever. Several changes were made to encourage the public to see the stadium as a year-round destination. Stadium officials are hoping fans will arrive early and stay late in an effort to alleviate the traffic situation in and around the stadium.

VIN SCULLY PRESS BOX

On April 21, 2001, the main press box was dedicated to Vin Scully, who has been calling Dodgers baseball since 1949, the longest tenure of any broadcaster in sports history. Scully, one of baseball's all-time greats, has seen his share of unbelievable moments in his career. Here is a look at some of the events Scully has called in his colorful career as of this writing, courtesy of the Dodgers Media Guide:

- Three perfect games (Don Larsen in 1956, Sandy Koufax in 1965, and Dennis Martinez in 1991) and 18 no-hitters
- Game 7 of the 1955 World Series that saw Johnny Podres shut out the New York Yankees for the franchise's first championship
- Not only Don Drysdale's 58.2 scoreless innings streak in 1968, but Orel Hershiser's 59-inning scoreless streak that broke Drysdale's record in 1988
- Hank Aaron's 715th career home run that broke Babe Ruth's Major League record at Atlanta's Fulton County Stadium
- Barry Bonds and his record-breaking seventy-first, seventy-second, and seventy-third home runs in 2001 as he furthered his own Major League mark

MEMORABLE GAMES AT DODGER STADIUM

APRIL 10, 1962: FIRST GAME AT DODGER STADIUM

The Cincinnati Reds may have rolled into town and scored a 6–3 victory over the hometown Dodgers in the first game at Dodger Stadium, but the capacity crowd of 52,564 walked away awed by the beautiful ballpark that would fast become a fan favorite. Wally Post led the Reds' charge, collecting three hits, including a home run to go along with three runs batted in to spoil the party. Despite the hiccup of the inaugural contest, the Dodgers would go on to post a 102-win season, good enough for second place in the National League.

OCTOBER 6, 1963: DODGERS SWEEP MIGHTY YANKEES FOR TITLE

The Yankees were the favorites to win another title, after going back to back in 1961 and 1962, but it was the upstart Dodgers that played cool, calm, and collected, upsetting New York 2–1 in Game 4 to take home the crown. Playing in front of a raucous crowd at Dodger Stadium, it was a pitching rematch of Game 1 when Whitey Ford took to the hill against hometown hero, Sandy Koufax. It was a pitcher's duel until Frank Howard launched a home run in the fifth to give Los Angeles a 1–0 advantage. It wouldn't last, as two innings later in the seventh, Mickey Mantle exacted some revenge with a blast of his own, tying the score at one. The Dodgers would respond in the bottom half of the inning, scoring a run on a sacrifice fly by Willie Davis, and that's all they would need as Koufax would go on to close out both the game and the series.

SEPTEMBER 9, 1965: KOUFAX ETCHES HIS NAME IN THE RECORD BOOKS

In front of 29,139, Dodgers great Sandy Koufax made his mark on the game by tossing the sixth perfect game in Major League history against the Chicago Cubs during a 1–0 victory. In what was truly a dramatic sequence of events, the left-handed hurler struck out the final six Cubs batters he faced, finishing the contest with 14 overall. The Dodgers didn't have much luck at the plate either, mustering up only one hit on Lou Johnson's bloop double in the fifth, and Johnson ultimately accounted for the only run of the game when Chicago catcher Chris Krug airmailed a throw to third. The 113-pitch effort was completed in a brisk one hour, 43 minutes.

OCTOBER 15, 1988: GIBSON LEADS DODGERS TO GAME 1 WIN

In what is arguably the most dramatic pinch-hitting appearance in World Series history, Kirk Gibson came to the plate in the bottom of the ninth, much to the amazement of all in attendance at Dodger Stadium, and helped propel Los Angeles to an emotional 5–4 win. Sidelined for the start, Gibson was battling serious pain and the fact he could even walk was a shocker. With the adrenaline flowing, Gibson was the last chance for the Dodgers, who trailed 4–3 with one on in the bottom of the ninth inning versus the Oakland Athletics and closer Dennis Eckersley, who was lights out all season long. After falling behind 0–2, Gibson launched a home run into the right-field bleachers that is still talked about today. With the long ball, it marked the first time in history that a World Series game had been won on a come-from-behind bomb in the final inning (as Bill Mazeroski's shot versus New York in Game 7 of the 1960 World Series came in the bottom of the ninth with the score tied at 9 and in 1993, Toronto's Joe Carter would match Gibson's accomplishment in Game 6 against Philadelphia with a three-run blast to win the title, 8–6).

JULY 28, 1991: MARTINEZ HAS DATE WITH PERFECTION
Dennis Martinez took to the Dodger Stadium mound and pulled off one of the toughest feats in all of baseball, tossing the eleventh perfect game in baseball history against Los Angeles during a 2–0 win. With two outs and nobody on, Dodgers pinch hitter Chris Gwynn strode to the plate in search of the first heartbreaking hit. It didn't work, as Gwynn hit a fly ball out to center fielder Marquis Grissom, and with that, Martinez became the first Latin American pitcher in Major League history to record a perfect game. A two-run seventh, courtesy of two Dodger errors, enabled the Expos to net the only two runs of the contest.

APRIL 23, 1999: TATIS DOES THE UNTHINKABLE
Hitting two grand slams over the course of one game is tough enough, but Fernando Tatis took it one step further by hitting two in *one inning* as part of an 11-run Cardinal third inning at Los Angeles during a 12–5 victory. Tatis, who had never hit a grand slam to that point, also set a new record by tallying eight RBIs in the inning, breaking the mark of six set by many. The magic began when he sent a 2–0 fastball from Chan Ho Park sailing 450 feet into the left-field bullpen with no outs in the third. After McGwire blew his chance for a grand salami, Tatis stood in and lined Park's 3–2 slider into the lower seats in the left-field pavilion, etching his name into the record books. Park joined Pittsburgh's Bill Phillips—who also had the misfortune of accomplishing the feat in 1890—as the only players in Major League history to give up two grand slams in one inning.

OCTOBER 2, 2004: DRAMATIC HOMER CAPTURES WEST TITLE

Trailing 3–0 in the bottom of the ninth, and with the National League West Division championship hanging in the balance, Steve Finley pulled out some Hollywood magic in the most opportune of times. Finley's grand slam to the right-field seats capped a seven-run inning, and the Dodgers captured their first division title since 1995 with a 7–3 win over rival San Francisco. Things looked bleak for Los Angeles after San Francisco's Marquis Grissom stole the show by connecting for a two-run single in the fourth and a solo home run in the seventh. But the Dodgers never gave in, and the spectacular win gave Los Angeles their fifty-third comeback victory of the season, helping establish a new franchise mark that once was held by the 1953 Brooklyn Dodgers.

SEPTEMBER 18, 2006: INCREDIBLE FINISH FOR DODGERS

If there's one wonderful fact about the game of baseball, it's that it really is never over until it's over. On this night heading into the bottom of the ninth, the Dodgers trailed 9–5 against San Diego and unbeknownst to them, were about to make history. Consecutive home runs by Jeff Kent, J. D. Drew, Russell Martin, and Marlon Anderson tied the game at nine, equaling a franchise record for most long balls in a row. After surrendering a run in the top of the tenth, Nomar Garciaparra jacked a two-run tater that gave the men in blue and white an unfathomable 11–10 victory.

JUNE 28, 2008: NO HITS? NO PROBLEM!

For just the fifth time in Major League history, the Dodgers defeated the Los Angeles Angels, 1–0, despite accumulating no hits for the entire game during their Freeway Series matchup in front of a packed house of 55,784. The last time this occurred was on April 12, 1992, when Matt Young of the Boston Red Sox shut down Cleveland—and still lost—2–1 at Cleveland Municipal Stadium. In the Los Angeles victory, Blake DeWitt was responsible for the only run, driving in Matt Kemp courtesy of a sacrifice fly in the fifth inning.

JUNE 18, 2014: KERSHAW DOMINATES ROCKIES

In what is considered one of the greatest pitching performances in modern history, Los Angeles firethrower Clayton Kershaw tossed a no-hitter, struck out a career-high 15, and came within one error of a perfect game during an 8–0 victory. Facing the Major League's leader in batting average, hits, total bases, on-base percentage, and slugging percentage did not faze Kershaw at all as he mowed through the lineup on his way to the twenty-second no-hitter in Los Angeles Dodgers history.

The offense was led by Matt Kemp, who connected for an RBI single in the first and RBI double in the third, and Adrian Gonzalez, who finished the contest 2-for-4 with two runs batted in. After retiring the first 18 batters consecutively, Corey Dickerson led off for Colorado in the seventh and chopped a slow bounce to third baseman Hanley Ramirez whose throw went just wide of first for a two-base error. Kershaw recovered without a problem, becoming the first Major League player ever with 15 strikeouts without allowing a single hit or walk.

WHAT THEY'RE SAYING ABOUT DODGER STADIUM

STEVE BERTHIAUME, BROADCASTER: "I think Dodger Stadium needs to go. It is great when you are out there. Having watched it as a kid—growing up in Boston all those years and you see the blue outfield wall and the blue sky and the palm trees—you get this history . . . but when you go there now, it is by no means run down, but I think it is past its prime."

STEVE BLASS: "When I first got to the big leagues, I had my first Major League start at Dodger Stadium, which I consider a shrine, especially from a pitching standpoint. . . . It has stayed the same, it has a traditional look, and [it is so clean that] you can eat off the floors."

JASON GIAMBI: "The one that was always fun for me [as a kid] was Dodger Stadium because my dad worked in Los Angeles and we would always go watch the Dodgers play. . . . Instead of driving home in the traffic, we would always go down there and have dinner. That [Dodger Stadium] always had a special place in my heart."

KIRK GIBSON: "It is pretty cool. To this day we walk in there and it is still nice and for being built in the late 1960s, it is very clean. . . . It is Hollywood and there is a lot of history there, and they continue to make improvements on it. It was one of my favorite places to play a ballgame [at]."

MATT KEMP: "I think by far it is one of the best . . . the atmosphere, 56,000 fans can fill up the stadium, and for me, Dodgers fans are great and the atmosphere is just unbelievable and the surface is one of the best in baseball."

STEVE LYONS, BROADCASTER: "It does not really show its age, certainly on the field and in the stands—maybe a little bit in the clubhouses and areas they cannot really do a whole lot with. . . . Overall, it is a pretty sweet place still, especially given the fact that there are only two other places [Fenway Park and Wrigley Field] older than that."

DON MATTINGLY: "Dodger Stadium grows on me. It seems like you start to get used to the beauty of the stadium and be able to look out and get attached to the feel like it is perfect every time. . . . Seeing it from the inside, you know it needs a little work, but it is still just as pretty as ever."

MIKE PIAZZA: "It is very pleasant to play in as far as sight lines and weather. The field is very nice and it still is a nice baseball field even though it is one of the older stadiums in baseball, . . . but it [has] got a nice feel to it and it is a nice area."

MIKE SCIOSCIA: "I think it is still a classic stadium in Major League Baseball and it brought a lot of innovation to what stadiums are—it was probably the first generation of a different look of a stadium as opposed to some of the ballparks that were built—[but] it is still going strong, and it is just an incredible place to play baseball and watch a game."

CHARLEY STEINER, BROADCASTER: "It is as iconic a ballpark as there is in the game. The view from the press box is as gorgeous as there is in the game, and you have got the San Gabriel mountains—especially when the sun is setting—[that] just glisten off in the distance. . . . The grass seems to be just a little greener there than every place else."

DODGER STADIUM FACTS AND FIGURES

DODGER STADIUM ADDRESS
1000 Elysian Park Avenue, Los Angeles, CA 90012

LOS ANGELES DODGERS TEAM WEB SITE
www.dodgers.com

FIELD DIMENSIONS (IN FEET)
Left Field: 330', Left-Center: 375', Center: 395',
Right-Center: 375', Right Field: 330'

SEATING CAPACITY (AS OF 2015)
56,000

ALL-STAR GAMES AT DODGER STADIUM
July 8, 1980: National League 4, American League 2
MVP: Ken Griffey Sr., Cincinnati Reds (NL)

DODGER STADIUM FIRSTS

Game: April 10, 1962—Cincinnati 6, Los Angeles 3
Single: Vada Pinson, Cincinnati (April 10, 1962)
Double: Eddie Kasko, Cincinnati (April 10, 1962)*
Triple: Daryl Spencer, Los Angeles (April 10, 1962)
Home Run: Wally Post, Cincinnati (April 10, 1962)

Denotes first hit in the stadium.

O.CO COLISEUM
HOME OF THE OAKLAND ATHLETICS

O.co Coliseum, Oakland Athletics (*Photographed by Russel Tiffin/Flickr*)

[*O.co Coliseum was previously known as Oakland-Alameda County Coliseum (1966–98, 2008–11), Network Associates Coliseum (1998–2004), and McAfee Coliseum (2004–08).*]

The huge O.co Coliseum, known as the home of the Oakland Athletics, is intimidating when you first see it. It can handle up to 70,000 people and is a popular baseball venue for its exceptional sight lines and consistent weather.

In the 1950s and 1960s, Oakland wanted to construct a Major League–caliber ballpark so it could have a professional baseball team and create its own legacy distinct from the San Francisco Giants. In 1960 a nonprofit corporation was put together to ensure that the financing and development of the plans would proceed without any technical difficulties. Preliminary plans for the new ballpark were first unveiled in November 1960, and soon after, the Port of Oakland stepped in, ultimately becoming a major player in the development of the plans.

Following approval from the City of Oakland and Alameda County, by 1962, the first $25 million for financing the project was arranged without any snags. Construction of the ballpark began in 1962 but was delayed for two years due to a variety of legal issues and expenditure overruns. As a result, the stadium had to be altered slightly to stay within the overall budget guidelines.

Around this time, it was rumored that the Cleveland Indians might be heading west, instantly becoming a prime candidate to be the ballpark's first Major League tenant. As time wore on, any hopes of that becoming a reality were dashed when the Indians opted to stay put in Cleveland. Next in line was Charlie Finley's Kansas City Athletics, and after some difficulty in his efforts to turn the team into the Oakland Athletics, his wish was granted and the rest, as they say, is history.

With the Miami Marlins moving into their new ballpark just in time for the 2012 season, the Coliseum is the last ballpark in the United States to have a configuration that can accommodate both football and baseball.

SPECIAL FEATURES OF O.CO. COLISEUM

1995 RENOVATION PROJECT

In conjunction with the NFL's Raiders move from Los Angeles to Oakland, the Coliseum underwent extensive renovations to make it more suitable for football. At a final cost of $120 million, the renovations consisted of removing outfield bleachers and adding two clubs (the East Side Club is 40,000 square feet, and the West Side club is 15,000 square feet), 100 luxury suites, approximately 20,000 seats, and two new color video boards and scoreboards. When the Raiders are at home, the football field is configured on a line from first to third base, rather than the standard home plate to center field as arranged in previous years at other multipurpose facilities.

BART

The Bay Area Rapid Transit (BART), which gives fans easy access to and from the Coliseum, is a safe way to travel to avoid traffic. This rapid-rail system connects San Francisco with other cities located in the East Bay. By using the BART, fans can gain entrance directly into the ballpark via the BART station/Coliseum ramp. With a weekly average of around 357,000 passengers (according to the American Public Transportation Association), the BART is the fifth busiest rapid-rail system in the United States.

BILL KING BROADCAST BOOTH

Home to legendary Athletics play-by-play radio broadcaster Bill King from 1981 to 2005, King's catchphrase "Holy Toledo!" won over fans all around the Bay Area. The booth, located just beneath the third deck behind home plate, honors a man who began his career broadcasting high school football and basketball games in Illinois. In 1958, King got his big break when he was hired by the San Francisco Giants as an announcer.

In 1981, he was teamed with Lon Simmons for Oakland Athletics baseball, and his passion for America's pastime was evident right from the start. On October 25, 2005, King died of a pulmonary embolus, and on April 2, 2006, the Athletics officially dedicated the broadcast booth in his honor. A sign with the name "BILL KING," with a microphone in the middle and another sign with his famous "Holy Toledo!" line mark the location of the booth.

BILL RIGNEY PRESS LOUNGE

The press lounge, where members of the media can enjoy a buffet before the game, is named for a former front office staffer, Bill Rigney. He began as a player with the New York Giants from 1946 to 1953 before taking over the managerial reins from 1956 to 1976, compiling a career mark in the dugout of 1,239–1,321 with the Giants, Angels, and Twins. His best season at the helm came in 1970, when he guided the Minnesota Twins to a 98–64 mark and an American League West title before getting swept by the Baltimore Orioles in the ALCS. As a player, Rigney played second, third, and short, turning in his best overall season in 1949 with the Giants when he batted .278, hit six home runs, and drove in 47.

CAPITOL CORRIDOR TRAIN

If the BART is a bit too chaotic for your liking, an alternative method is to hop on the Capitol Corridor Train. This train, which has a 168-mile route from San Francisco to Sacramento that runs parallel to Interstate 80, has a safe, convenient, and fan-friendly atmosphere. Passengers avoid all traffic because the train deposits them right at the station at the O.co Coliseum. On average, nearly 1.5 million citizens annually use this to get in and around the Bay Area.

CHAMPIONSHIP BANNERS

The Oakland Athletics' history is celebrated on the third deck, which is festooned with tarps to create a more baseball-like atmosphere. The years that the Athletics captured the World Series are recorded on them, along with the names of former players who have been inducted into the National Baseball Hall of Fame. (For more, see "Tarps" later in this section.)

EAST SIDE CLUB

The 40,000-square-foot East Side Club can accommodate up to 3,000 people. Exclusive to NFL games, the Athletics utilize the area only a few times a year for special events. The East Side Club was also one of the main features added during the major renovation in 1995 and is officially part of the upper east deck. Inside, 90 luxury suites, along with meeting rooms, make this a very useful part of the Coliseum, even on non-game days.

FOUL TERRITORY

It's no coincidence that pitchers in both the American League and National Leagues love throwing at the Coliseum. That's because the amount of foul territory dwarfs that of any other ballpark currently being used in the big leagues. Deep down the first- and third-base lines are the best places to catch a baseball for an out that normally would be out of play in every other ballpark, and as a result, batting averages of hitters take a nosedive by approximately 5–7 points.

HOME PLATE SEATING

Home plate seating is available for a full or half-season and puts you close to the field. For $14,000 per seat for 81 games (the price as of this writing), fans have exclusive access to all-you-can-eat food options, vouchers for two alcoholic beverages, and private parking.

OUT-OF-TOWN SCOREBOARDS

As a subtle nod to the days of yesteryear, there are two out-of-town scoreboards in both the left- and right-field walls that are changed by hand, providing an update of other games happening in the world of Major League Baseball. A quick glimpse provides curious and inquiring fans with the basics: the number of the pitcher on the mound, a three-letter abbreviation of the teams playing, the inning in which the game is in, and the current score.

PRESS BOX

The press box, divided into two sections—the first-base side reserved for print media, the third-base side for electronic media—is located on the loge level, with access only by the press elevator. Game notes, statistics, and other significant information from both teams are distributed on the first-base side to members of the media and scouts. Nearby, the Bill Rigney press lounge is behind section 117 and offers members of the media the opportunity to grab a bite to eat from the buffet before the game begins. As is the case with all press boxes in the Major Leagues, cheering for a team is strictly prohibited and the press box is a working area only.

RETIRED NUMBERS

The Oakland Athletics have honored six men in their storied history, and the numbers are on tarps in the upper-deck portions. The men are: Reggie

Jackson (9), Rickey Henderson (24), Jim "Catfish" Hunter (27), Rollie Fingers (34), Dennis Eckersley (43), and William A. Haas Jr. (former owner).

SAM SKINNER PRESS BOX

Much like AT&T Park in San Francisco, the press box at the Coliseum is named for Sam Skinner, an African American writer who was widely recognized and liked among professional athletes. Skinner, arguably one of the nation's best sportswriters, broke into writing as a copy clerk during the 1960s before working part-time as a sportswriter for *The Examiner,* also during the 1960s. He then became sports editor in the 1970s for the *California Voice* and later covered events such as the 1972, 1984, and 1988 Olympic Games. Skinner died at the age of 56 following complications from a series of massive strokes.

TARPS

Green tarps are hung across the entire outfield upper deck. Various designs, including the years the Athletics captured the World Series championship along with the names and numbers of those players retired by the organization, are printed on top. In center field, the tarp displays the name "Athletics," while the tarp that covers the area behind home plate showcases the words "HOME OF THE OAKLAND ATHLETICS" sandwiched between two A's logos.

Sections in the upper deck are covered with tarps, creating a more intimate setting for baseball games. (*Photographed by Russel Tiffin/Flickr*)

UPPER EAST DECK

Prior to the construction of the center-field bleacher seats, views of the Oakland skyline and the East Bay Hills were available from pretty much any seat in the house. That changed dramatically in 1995, when a four-tier grandstand, capable of accommodating the masses for an NFL game, was installed, necessitating the removal of the outfield bleachers to make room for 22,000 seats and two 40,000-square-foot club levels.

WEST SIDE CLUB

The West Side Club—on the second level of the Coliseum and overlooking the playing field—is a fully furnished facility and one of the more premium dining options. It has a casual dining atmosphere hung with Oakland sports photos. It also holds the unique distinction of having the longest sports bar in northern California, offering some of the finest spirits.

MEMORABLE GAMES AT O.CO COLISEUM

APRIL 17, 1968: FIRST GAME AT THE COLISEUM

Behind the strength of a complete game, two-hitter turned in by Baltimore pitcher Dave McNally, the Orioles spoiled the party for 50,104 in attendance by taking the first contest, 4–1. Baltimore made themselves right at home, tallying the first two runs of the game on solo home runs courtesy of Boog Powell in the second and Mark Belanger in the third to take a 2–0 lead. It was more of the same in the fourth, when Davey Johnson's RBI single made it 3–0, and in the sixth, when Brooks Robinson flexed his muscles and blasted a homer off Athletics starter Lew Krausse, increasing the advantage to 4–0. In the bottom of the sixth, Rick Monday did his best to bring the Athletics back with a solo shot of his own, but it proved to be too little, too late. The only other Oakland hit was off the bat of pinch hitter Tony LaRussa in the bottom of the ninth but was later erased on a double play.

MAY 8, 1968: CATFISH HUNTER TOSSES A PERFECTO

In the first regular season perfect game in 46 years, Catfish Hunter domi-nated the Minnesota Twins, striking out 11 and helping his cause at the plate by driving in three runs en route to a 4–0 victory in front of 6,298 fans. In complete control the entire game, Hunter held big boppers Rod Carew (0-for-3) and Harmon Killebrew (0-for-3, three strikeouts) in check while the Oakland defense stood tall and refused to falter throughout the course of the contest. At the plate, Hunter finished 3-for-4 with two singles and a double. The only other Athletics run was courtesy of pinch hitter Danny Cater, who worked a bases-loaded walk against Twins starter Dave Boswell to drive in Ramon Webster.

OCTOBER 18, 1972: WORLD SERIES COMES TO OAKLAND

With Oakland already sporting an impressive 2–0 series lead, the scene shifted to the Bay Area for the first time in the Coliseum's history, and a crowd of 49,410 saw an impressive pitching duel won by Cincinnati, 1–0. Blue Moon Odom went for Oakland, Jack Billingham for the Reds, and they matched each other pitch for pitch through five scoreless frames. Oakland loaded the bases in the bottom of the sixth with one out, but the threat was snuffed out when Sal Bando bounced into a double play. In the seventh, the Reds broke through after Cesar Geronimo singled in Tony Perez, registering the only form of offense in the contest. In all, the two teams combined for one run, seven hits (Cincinnati: 4; Oakland: 3), and 21 strikeouts. Although Oakland struggled in this one, they would go on to wrap up the championship in seven games four days later at Riverfront Stadium in Cincinnati.

OCTOBER 21, 1973: ATHLETICS GO BACK TO BACK

For the second straight season, Oakland was back in the Fall Classic and for a second straight time, it went seven games. Behind two-run home runs from Bert Campaneris and World Series MVP Reggie Jackson, the Athletics collected their second straight crown en route to a 5–2 victory. Facing Mets starting pitcher Jon Matlack, the fourth inning proved to be New York's demise when Campaneris and Jackson both struck for long balls, and the Mets never recovered. Ken Holtzman took to the mound for Oakland and pitched brilliantly, going 5⅓ innings, allowing one run on five hits before giving way to Rollie Fingers. In the fifth, Joe Rudi put the icing on the cake after he delivered an RBI single, helping to give Oakland an insurmountable 5–0 lead. In the bottom of the ninth, reliever Darold Knowles—who faced one batter—induced Wayne Garrett into a pop-up to short, ending the game, series, and season.

OCTOBER 17, 1974: OAKLAND CAPTURES THIRD STRAIGHT TITLE

The Oakland Athletics were back at it again in 1974, returning to the World Series for the third straight year, this time against the Los Angeles Dodgers and capturing the trifecta with a 3–2 win. Oakland jumped out to an early 2–0 lead, but the Dodgers came back in the sixth after Jimmy Wynn hit a sacrifice fly to score Davey Lopes, and Steve Garvey followed with an RBI single, knotting it at two. But as they had all season long, the Athletics proved their resilience and came right back in the bottom of the seventh, when Joe Rudi sent the Coliseum crowd into a frenzy by hitting what turned out to be the decisive home run, giving Oakland a 3–2 lead they would not relinquish. Rollie Fingers would take the mound and proceed to hurl two scoreless frames and for the third straight season, the World Series championship remained in the Bay Area.

APRIL 20, 1990: HOLMAN FLIRTS WITH PERFECTION

With two outs in the ninth inning and one batter away from becoming the fifteenth pitcher in baseball history to register a perfect game, Seattle pitcher Brian Holman allowed a first pitch, pinch-hit home run to ex-Mariner Ken Phelps, ending his bid for history. Holman would retire Rickey Henderson for the final out as part of a 6–1 victory, but his brilliant 104-pitch effort was one of the more dominant efforts in baseball history. Before giving up the home run, Holman faced few threats: a McGwire fly ball to the warning track in the fifth and a three-ball count to Lance Blankenship in the sixth, before retiring the third baseman via a ground ball out. The Mariners tallied two runs in the fifth and four in the ninth, highlighted by RBI singles from Harold Reynolds and Jeffrey Leonard.

OCTOBER 20, 1990: REDS FINISH OFF IMPROBABLE SWEEP

Despite punching their ticket to the World Series as a huge underdog, the Cincinnati Reds avenged their Fall Classic loss from 1972 and waltzed into the Coliseum, winning Game 4, sweeping the Athletics, and wrapping up one of the biggest upsets in series history with a 2–1 victory. With flamethrowers Dave Stewart (Oakland) and Jose Rijo (Cincinnati) on the mound, it was evident right from the start that a pitchers' duel would be in the works, but Oakland had other plans. They got on the board first when Carney Lansford singled in Wille McGee to give Oakland an early 1–0 lead. The game stayed that way until the eighth, when the Reds broke through for two runs in the top of the eighth. With the bases loaded, Glenn Braggs hit an RBI groundout and Hal Morris added a sacrifice fly to put Cincinnati up for good at 2–1. The real story was Rijo, who at one point retired 20 straight batters before giving way to Randy Myers, who recorded the save.

MAY 1, 1991: HENDERSON STEALS HIS WAY INTO HISTORY

Throughout his colorful career, Rickey Henderson was a menace on the base paths, stealing an incredible amount year in and year out. He reached the top of the mountain on this date against the Yankees after he swiped stolen base number 939, eclipsing the record previously held by Cardinals great, Lou Brock. After sliding headfirst into third, he pulled the base from its moorings and lifted it high above his head, much to the delight of the

Coliseum crowd. He later addressed the crowd: "Lou Brock was a symbol of great base stealing, but today I am the greatest of all time." The celebrated Hall of Famer swiped a total of 1,406 bases over his 25 seasons in the big leagues. For the record, Oakland took advantage of the momentous occasion, defeating the Yankees, 7–4. Henderson finished 1-for-4 with a double and the record-breaking stolen base but was also caught stealing twice.

SEPTEMBER 1, 2002: DRAMATIC WIN KEEPS STREAK ALIVE

Having squandered a two-run lead in the top of the ninth inning, it looked bleak that the Athletics would continue a winning streak after reaching 17 in a row. However, it appeared as though there were not just angels in the outfield, but at the plate as well. After Minnesota had taken a dramatic lead in the top of the ninth, thanks to three solo home runs, Oakland went to work in the bottom half. Ramon Hernandez drew a walk against Twins reliever Eddie Guardado, and Ray Durham promptly singled to right, putting two on and nobody out. After pinch hitter Olmedo Saenz struck out, it set up Miguel Tejada's improbable three-run home run on a 1–2 pitch that not only gave the Athletics a 7–5 win over Minnesota, but extended a winning streak that also set a new franchise record.

SEPTEMBER 4, 2002: AMAZING STREAK HITS 20

Right from the start, it appeared as though the Oakland Athletics would be well on their way to a twentieth straight victory after taking an 11–0 advantage on the Kansas City Royals after three innings. Not so. Over the course of the next six frames, the visiting Royals would chip away, eventually tying the game at 11, giving the Athletics the dubious distinction of being the first team in 26 years to blow a lead of that caliber. After an innocent fly ball by Jermaine Dye in the bottom of the ninth, manager Art Howe summoned Scott Hatteberg off the bench to pinch hit for Eric Byrnes. After taking a ball, he capped an astonishing night by launching a home run into the right-center-field seats that not only won the game 12–11, but extended the longest winning streak in baseball over the last 67 years.

MAY 20, 2006: BONDS TIES THE BAMBINO

On his march to becoming the eventual all-time home run leader, Barry Bonds passed baseball's arguably greatest player with a second-inning smash off Athletics starter Brad Halsey for career home run number 714, tying Babe Ruth's career total during a 4–2, extra-inning victory. The blast, which landed in the right-field first deck, snapped a 29 at-bat homerless streak, placing him one step closer to one of baseball's most hallowed records. Although he didn't reach the mark in San Francisco, the Coliseum's close proximity made it possible for Giants fans to make the trek and witness history in the making. With the score tied in the tenth, San Francisco's Ray Durham singled home Omar Vizquel, and Steve Finley added a sacrifice fly to cap the scoring, propelling the Giants to the win.

JUNE 7, 2007: SCHILLING'S EFFORT: CLOSE, BUT NO CIGAR

With two outs in the ninth inning of a 1–0 Red Sox lead, it looked as though Curt Schilling would add a no-hitter to his brilliant résumé. Oakland's Shannon Stewart had other plans. Stewart lined a no-doubt single into right field, ending the no-hitter, but Schilling kept his composure and held on for the complete game, one-hit shutout in front of a pro-Red Sox crowd. Boston's David Ortiz hit a solo home run in the first, and that's all they would need in a game that was played in a brisk two hours, 10 minutes. In the sixth, Oakland nearly registered their first hit when Mark Kotsay led off and sent outfielder Coco Crisp to the center-field wall, but Crisp tracked down the 400-foot drive, thanks in part to the roominess of the outfield. During the 100-pitch effort, Schilling struck out four and walked none. It would have been an opportunity for a perfect game, but an error by Julio Lugo on a grounder by Dan Johnson in the fifth inning consequently put an end to that.

MAY 9, 2010: RAYS THE VICTIM OF PERFECT GAME

On Mother's Day, Athletics pitcher Dallas Braden was brilliant, firing the nineteenth perfect game—and the first Oakland pitcher to accomplish it since Catfish Hunter 42 years prior—in baseball history during a 4–0 victory over Tampa Bay. It marked the second time in two seasons that the Rays were the unfortunate victims of a perfect game, with the previous coming July 23, 2009, at U.S. Cellular Field after Mark Buehrle etched his name onto one of baseball's most elite list. With 12,228 in attendance, Braden registered his first career complete game, striking out six and atoning for Mother's Day 2009, after he was hit by a line drive off the bat of Vernon Wells. The Athletics offense did their job when RBI singles by Landon Powell in the second, Kevin Kouzmanoff in the third, and Daric Barton and Ryan Sweeney in the fourth accounted for all the support Braden would require.

"It was a lot of fun to be a part of that. . . . The ground ball to Cliff Pennington after the fact—the count was three balls and one strike, Gabe Kapler was up—and Braden still, to this day, says that he believed the count was two and two. The pitch really was not a strike and I think it spoke to the character of a guy like Gabe Kapler—a 3–1 pitch—he was not going to be walked on a borderline pitch. He believed in trying to earn his way on and he swung on a 3–1 pitch, hit a ground ball to short, and the Athletics won it."

—*Vince Cotroneo, Athletics broadcaster*

OCTOBER 3, 2012: ATHLETICS COMPLETE REMARKABLE TURNAROUND

Many prognosticators had predicted the Oakland Athletics would not even compete for a playoff spot, but they rebounded from being 13 games out on June 30, capturing the American League West crown in Game 162 with a stirring 12–5 win over two-time American League champion Texas. The Rangers jumped on the Athletics, pitching to the tune of five runs in the top of the third, but Oakland countered with a six-run fourth, highlighted by a misplayed ball hit to center fielder Josh Hamilton, who appeared to lose it in the hot California sun. Things were sealed in the bottom of the eighth, when Derek Norris homered and Brandon Moss singled, ultimately plating three runs after a throwing error by outfielder Nelson Cruz. Not since the 1995 Seattle Mariners overcame a 13-game deficit has a team stormed back to capture the division on the final day of the season.

WHAT THEY'RE SAYING ABOUT O.CO COLISEUM

VINCE COTRONEO, BROADCASTER: "It is a place where, historically, the Athletics have had an advantage because it is a pitcher's ballpark with a lot of foul territory. . . . It certainly has lost the charm that it had years ago before they erected the edifice in center field, which is referred to as Mount Davis back when you could see the Oakland Hills."

RAY FOSSE: "It is the last multipurpose stadium in all of baseball, so I think it is time [for a new stadium]. . . . It was nice as a baseball-only stadium before they put the Mount Davis in center field, but I think it is time they get a new one."

JASON GIAMBI: "I really liked it. It was great when we would play the Giants and sell it all out, or Fourth of July games. . . . The infield was always really manicured. I know there was a lot of foul ground, but it was fun to play there."

RENE LACHEMANN: "It is a shame what has happened since the Raiders came in because it used to be, to me, a beautiful stadium and you could go ahead and look out onto the mounds out there. . . . Now, with the addition of the center-field seats there, it has changed the ballpark entirely and as far as a baseball field, it is nothing that it was before in the past."

MARK MCGWIRE: "It was a great ballpark, a pitcher's ballpark, and a difficult ballpark to hit home runs in, especially at night, and then Al Davis decided to put a big structure behind the outfield. . . . I enjoyed playing there, [but] lost a lot of at-bats because of the huge foul grounds, but it was great days because we had some really great teams."

DAVID MURPHY: "With all the foul territory, and you are up there [at the plate], it is not that enclosed feeling [that gets you], but the wide open and it is almost like you are playing in a wide-open field as a kid. . . . I think the key in Oakland—and obviously it is not the mindset you are going up there with—you definitely do not want to hit a foul ball."

MIKE PIAZZA: "The monstrosity for the Raiders in the outfield make it not the most pleasant sight, but the fans are great and the vibe is pretty good. . . . It is a nice ballpark [and] as far as history, there have been a lot of great World Champion teams [that] played there, so I think as a player, you look at things a little more [nostalgically]."

NICK SWISHER: "It is where I started, so I have got good memories of that place. . . . It is different than everywhere else, it has a niche, and I like the fact that each ballpark has its own thing."

JUSTIN VERLANDER: "I like pitching in Oakland. There is a lot of foul territory and extra outs there."

BARRY ZITO: "I really enjoyed the Coliseum. I think a lot of guys do not like it because it is a little outdated, but it is so wide open and, of course, there is tons of foul territory, so pitchers love it."

O.CO COLISEUM FACTS AND FIGURES

O.CO COLISEUM ADDRESS
7000 Coliseum Way, Oakland, CA 94621

OAKLAND ATHLETICS TEAM WEB SITE
www.oaklandathletics.com

FIELD DIMENSIONS (IN FEET)
Left Field: 330', Left-Center: 362', Center: 400', Right-Center: 362', Right Field: 330'

SEATING CAPACITY (AS OF 2015)
35,067 (baseball capacity)

ALL-STAR GAMES AT O.CO COLISEUM

July 14, 1987: National League 2, American League 0 (13 innings)
MVP: Tim Raines, Montreal Expos (NL)

O.CO COLISEUM FIRSTS

Game: April 17, 1968—Baltimore 4, Oakland 1
Single: Davey Johnson, Baltimore (April 17, 1968)
Double: Curt Blefary, Baltimore (April 17, 1968)
Triple: Frank Coggins, Washington (April 19, 1968)
Home Run: Boog Powell, Baltimore (April 17, 1968)*

Denotes first hit in the stadium.

PETCO PARK
HOME OF THE SAN DIEGO PADRES

Petco Park, San Diego Padres (*Photographed by Mark Whitt/Flickr*)

In 2004, Petco Park, in the Gaslamp district, was another addition to the long list of new ballparks constructed over the past 15 seasons. Everyone else, with the exception of the Dodgers, who had the ageless wonder known as Dodger Stadium in Los Angeles, had relatively new facilities. San Diego was the only team at the time from the National League West Division looking for a baseball-only stadium as an alternative to their problem of sharing the once-loved multipurpose facility with the NFL's Chargers.

The ball got rolling in the right direction in 1998, after San Diego voters approved legislation on Proposition C, with 60 percent of the ballots cast in favor of a new ballpark. Passage of the resolution signaled the beginning of the Petco Park era. While there are loyalists who wish the old cereal bowl was still being used, the consensus is that Petco Park is a winner and that it could be one of the top three in all of baseball.

The cost of construction was $298 million; the total ended up being $474 million, which included both land acquisition and infrastructure work. Of the final amount, the City of San Diego was responsible for $205.9 million, while the Padres paid $173.2 million of the tab, including all construction cost overruns and other development costs.

A snag occurred in October 2000, when construction of Petco Park came to an abrupt stop after the money ran out. This problem was the result of two factors: the city was not selling bonds approved in the election, and there were numerous lawsuits instigated by tax protestors of the project. After a delay of 13 months, the City of San Diego took the necessary steps to continue the work, approving a $166 million bond to ensure the completion of the stadium.

The final outcome was a ballpark that captures the essence of San Diego. The exterior is Indian sandstone and stucco, a design meant to reflect the beautiful beaches, the crystal-clear blue ocean, and the white sails of boats in the bay nearby. Inside are native desert gardens and water displays.

The seating areas were also upgraded. The seats are a Pacific blue, and the total capacity is around 46,000, 42,000 of which are fixed seats spread out over three decks and feature more width and legroom than those at the old digs.

The goal was to create a distinctive, intimate seating-bowl design. All seats are strategically angled toward the home plate. A distinctive home run porch extends out in right field, creating quirky angles but plenty of fun for the fans in that section.

SPECIAL FEATURES OF PETCO PARK

19 PALM TREES
San Diego and its baseball franchise have been blessed to be associated with two of the greatest names in America's pastime: Ted Williams and Tony Gwynn. In the Park at the Park, 19 palm trees were planted as a tribute to the San Diego-born Williams and Gwynn, the last player to wear the number.

19 TONY GWYNN DRIVE
What better way to honor one of the greatest hitters in baseball—and argu-ably the best in Padres history—than to rename the street that Petco Park is on after "Mr. Padre" himself. This is a fitting tribute to the eight-time Na-tional League batting champion who wore the number 19 his entire career with the team. The decision to rename the street was formally announced on October 7, 2001, the final game of his illustrious 21-year career.

BATTER'S EYE PORCH
Fans can relax with friends pregame, postgame, or for special events at the batter's eye porch, located in center field. The hitter's background is painted Pacific blue, except for the side facing the Park at the Park, which is green. Nearby, a security command post and a 10-foot rotating sign provide a solid background when batters step in.

BULLPENS

The San Diego bullpen is in left field, and the visitors' bullpen—relocated before the 2013 season—is now in a tiered position behind the Padres' bullpen. The previous spot for the visiting team was in foul territory, in front of the stands and down the right-field line. Each team has a separate entrance to the field.

CHAMPIONSHIP REMINDERS

Pennants fly high on flagpoles behind the picnic terrace section to commemorate division crowns and pennants won by the franchise. The red-and-white flags symbolize the National League pennants won by the team, and navy-and-white ones represent the division titles captured by the club.

CLUB LOUNGES

The Field Club Lounge is off the main concourse and positioned right behind home plate. This is used exclusively by field-box ticket holders and has an open-air terrace dining area with an exceptional view. The Founders Club Lounge is similar but adjacent to the Padres Clubhouse. Exclusive to Founders Club members and their guests, the dining experience in this club is second to none and also provides a one-of-a-kind view into the Padres' batting tunnels.

FENCES MOVED IN FOR 2013

Following the 2012 season, Padres officials made Petco Park slightly more hitter-friendly. The fences were moved forward 11 feet in right field and about 12 feet in the gaps. The right-field fence was lowered to slightly less than eight feet, which matches the height in both left and center fields. Historically a pitcher's park, the changes still allow for the pitcher to reign supreme, but for hitters to be rewarded with a big swing instead of a long out.

FRIAR VISION

The 30-foot by 53-foot LED video board, commonly known as Friar Vision, is a permanent fixture in left field and offers high-resolution replays and graphics. Direct sunlight has no effect on the clarity of the picture. Atop Friar Vision, a 34-foot by 80-foot Matrix scoreboard displays animations, lineups, in-game statistics, and plenty of information to keep fans informed and up-to-date.

GOLD STAR

Jerry Coleman, San Diego's legendary announcer who began his tenure in 1972 as their lead radio announcer, had a trademark line: "You can hang a star on that one!" As a tribute to him, the Padres organization hung a gold star on the front of the press box, featuring Coleman's name in white.

HALL OF FAME PORCH

Unveiled just before the start of the 2005 season and located just to the left of the batter's eye, the Hall of Fame porch honors former Padres players who have received baseball's highest honor. As of this writing, the players elected to the National Baseball Hall of Fame who donned a San Diego uniform at one time include Roberto Alomar, Rollie Fingers, Goose Gossage, Tony Gwynn, Rickey Henderson, Willie McCovey, Gaylord Perry, Ozzie Smith, Dave Winfield, and announcer Jerry Coleman.

HOME PLATE PLAZA

This entrance at Park Boulevard and Tony Gwynn Drive is complete with cascading water, a coral tree, jacaranda trees, and other plants, lending a unique California charm. Be careful though; if your mind wanders too much you might actually mistake Petco Park for Sea World of San Diego!

HOME RUN HORN

If you are a visitor at San Diego's beautiful ballpark, be sure to listen closely whenever a Padres player goes deep. A recording of the Navy's USS *Ronald Reagan* horn is played whenever the ball clears the fence. The distinct horn is accompanied by fireworks during night games, providing quite a thrill whenever the home team connects for a home run.

JERRY COLEMAN STATUE

Near the east entrance to Petco Park and behind the right-field seats is a seven-foot five-inch, 650-pound statue of broadcaster Jerry Coleman, who not only was instrumental in Padres history, but American history as well. The bronze likeness of Coleman in his Marines pilot uniform sits on a granite base, and three four-foot by eight-foot panels behind the statue display photographs from his days in broadcasting, baseball, and the military. Coleman flew 120 combat missions in World War II and the Korean War, and is the only Major League player to have fought in two wars. Sadly, Coleman passed away on January 5, 2014.

LITTLE LEAGUE FIELD

A little league baseball infield, complete with 60-foot base paths and a full-size pitcher's mound is another attraction of the Park at the Park. Kids will daydream about putting on a Padres uniform and taking the field, and it will no doubt be a highlight of their day.

The Park at the Park, just beyond center field, is a popular hot spot for fans. (*Photographed by Scott Wachter/San Diego Padres*)

PALM COURT PLAZA

Dedicated in 2014 for the former commissioner of Major League Baseball Bud Selig, this plaza greets fans as they make their way to the ballpark and features 13 palm trees and 13,588 bricks, 10,842 of which are personalized and commemorative. As of this writing, plans are in the works to incorporate plaques honoring Hall of Famers into the area, including one that honors Selig. The setting itself creates an experience that makes fans feel as if they are in a beautiful garden and not a Major League ballpark.

PARK AT THE PARK

This park, beyond the outfield wall, has been a big hit for fans since it first opened in 2004. Petco Park became the first ballpark since Forbes Field in Pittsburgh closed in 1970 to have a park bordering the outfield. The 2.7-acre grassland is gently sloped for lawn seating and can accommodate up to 3,500 fans. An area called Picnic Hill in the park gives fans the opportunity to pack a lunch and enjoy the outdoors.

PRESS BOX TRIBUTE

The initials of former owner Ray Kroc are displayed in gold along with his name in white on the front of the press box. Kroc, who owned the San Diego Padres from 1974 to 1984, is best known for establishing and expanding the immensely popular corporation known around the world as McDonald's.

RETIRED NUMBERS

The San Diego Padres have honored four men who have made their mark on the franchise's history. Their numbers are above the batter's eye in center field: Steve Garvey (6), Tony Gwynn (19), Dave Winfield (31), and Randy Jones (55).

TECHNOLOGY GALORE

Fans who enjoy wandering around during a game won't miss any of the action, thanks to high-definition TV monitors. More than 500 computer-controlled speakers deliver the sound as a distributed signal, eliminating the audio delay from a central bank of speakers. Four stationary cameras, one roving camera, and Cox-TV cameras provide the images for video screens at Petco Park.

THE BEACH

The Beach, a sand-filled hotspot in front of the center-field bleachers, is where kids can let out all their energy and play. Or maybe you're in the mood to build a majestic sand castle?

TONY GWYNN STATUE

In another salute to San Diego legend Tony Gwynn (and rightfully deserved), the Padres unveiled a nine-foot, 1,200-pound bronze statue of the Hall of Famer on July 21, 2007, in Park at the Park. Created by sculptor William Behrends, the statue depicts Gwynn following through on his famous swing, which racked up 3,000-plus hits over the course of his career. It is surrounded by personalized bricks with messages from fans.

VEGETABLE GARDEN

The vegetable garden was started by Luke Yoder, Padres director of field and landscape maintenance. San Diego became the first team since the Mets at Shea Stadium to grow vegetables in their bullpen. There is a selection of 12 different types of peppers of varying degrees of spiciness. Some of the selections include Bhut Jolokia, which packs quite a punch. The vegetables were eventually used as condiments for fans at the ballpark.

WESTERN METAL SUPPLY COMPANY BUILDING

The historic red-brick Western Metal Supply Company Building, built in 1909 and down the left-field line, has ties to the Old West and is an attractive target for right-handed batters. Measuring just 334 feet from home plate, the four-story structure itself serves as the actual left-field foul pole. In its day, it originally provided horseshoes, wagon wheels, and metal supplies to blacksmiths. Each floor is renovated and provides a variety of services to fans.

The Padres Team Store is on the first floor and features a door that opens onto a standing room–only section in left field. The second and third floors have party suites for those who want to entertain. The fourth floor features a restaurant that offers terrace dining with incredible views of the field. The roof of the building, which sits 80 feet above the playing surface, has a bleacher section that evokes memories of Wrigley Field and standing room–only areas.

MEMORABLE GAMES AT PETCO PARK

APRIL 8, 2004: FIRST GAME AT PETCO PARK

It may have taken 10 innings, but the San Diego Padres made their first game at Petco Park a successful one, defeating the San Francisco Giants, 4–3. The offense centered squarely on Sean Burroughs, who came up big when the Padres needed him most. He kicked off the scoring in the third, lacing a ground-rule double, enabling Khalil Greene to trot home for an early 1–0 lead. It stayed that way until the top of the ninth when—against one of baseball's premier closers, Trevor Hoffman—Pedro Feliz and Michael Tucker started the inning with consecutive singles.

With two outs, Ray Durham came up big, giving the Giants a 2–1 lead after a double to deep left scored two. In the bottom half, Burroughs came through again, hitting an RBI single with one out, tying the contest at two and ultimately sending the game to extra innings. In the tenth, Marquis Grissom didn't waste any time, connecting for a leadoff home run off San Diego reliever Antonio Osuna, helping to swing the lead back in San Francisco's favor, 3–2. Not to be outdone, pinch hitter Miguel Ojeda cashed in on a ground-rule double to tie the game, and Burroughs once again was the difference, putting an end to the back-and-forth contest with an RBI single that sent the sellout crowd of 41,400 home satisfied.

OCTOBER 8, 2005: FIRST PLAYOFF GAME AT PETCO PARK

In 2005, the Padres finished the season at 82–80, and in most divisions that would put them around second or third place. With the National League West, it was good enough to capture a division title and a date with the St. Louis Cardinals in the Division Series. Having lost their first two games in the Gateway City, the Padres were hoping that a little home cooking would do the trick, but it wasn't meant to be. St. Louis shortstop David Eckstein kicked things off right away with a lead off single, and he would come around to score a few minutes later on an RBI double by Albert Pujols. Cardinals outfielder Reggie Sanders continued his white-hot pace by connecting for a two-run double in the second, which gave him 10 runs batted in for the series—a National League Division Series record—all but putting away the Padres. Although San Diego fell behind 7–0, they mounted a comeback but ended up falling just short by a final count of 7–4.

SEPTEMBER 22, 2006: YOUNG CLOSE TO PADRES HISTORY

Looking to become the first Padres pitcher in franchise history to record a no-hitter, starter Chris Young was cruising before allowing a two-run blast to pinch hitter Joe Randa with one out in the ninth inning during a 6–2 San Diego victory. Staked to a 6–0 lead highlighted by home runs off the bats of Adrian Gonzalez and Todd Walker, along with an RBI triple by Brad Johnson, Young was cruising before Randa connected for a 421-foot blast to center field. It marked the second time in 30 years that a San Diego pitcher flirted with history in the final inning, the other being Andy Ashby on September 5, 1997, against Atlanta, when the first hit allowed in that game was a line drive single by Kenny Lofton with nobody out in the ninth. After two outs were recorded, Young was replaced and Cla Meredith finished off the one-hitter.

SEPTEMBER 25, 2006: HOFFMAN BECOMES ALL-TIME LEADER IN SAVES

His tenure with San Diego began all the way back in June 1993, when he was dealt by the Marlins to the Padres as part of the Gary Sheffield trade. More than 13 years later, he cemented his place in the Hall of Fame. With a sellout crowd of 41,932 standing in anticipation during the ninth inning of the Padres' final home game of the season, Trevor Hoffman retired the Pirates in order, surpassing the previous saves mark of 478 in the process once held by legendary closer Lee Smith. While Hoffman was being mobbed by his teammates in the middle of the diamond, the Pirates showed their respect by applauding from the visitor's dugout. Russell Branyan and Josh Bard each connected for home runs, leading the San Diego offense during a tight 2–1 victory.

AUGUST 4, 2007: BONDS TIES HAMMERIN' HANK

Taking another step in his quest to become baseball's all-time home run leader, Barry Bonds uncorked a second-inning, opposite-field blast off Padres starter Clay Hensley that traveled 382 feet, giving him 755 for his career during a 3–2, 12-inning loss. His historic blast came a half-inning after Scott Hairston put San Diego in front with a solo homer of his own. In the second, Bonds stepped in amidst boos echoing all around Petco Park, and connected on a 2–1 fastball shortly thereafter. Bengie Molina put San Francisco ahead after his groundout scored Bonds in the fourth, but the Padres answered an inning later when Mike Cameron tripled home the game-tying run. It stayed knotted until the bottom of the twelfth, when Khalil Greene struck for a bases-loaded single, scoring Marcus Giles in the form of the winning run.

APRIL 17, 2008: 22-INNING AFFAIR ENDS WAY OF THE ROCKIES

In a game that lasted six hours, 16 minutes and didn't conclude until 4:21 A.M. on the East Coast, Colorado outlasted San Diego when Troy Tulowitzki doubled in Willy Taveras during the top of the twenty-second, helping lead the Rockies to a 2–1 energy-sapping win. It was scoreless when, in the top of the fourteenth, the Rockies took a 1–0 lead after Brad Hawpe walked with the bases loaded. Not to be denied, the Padres answered in the bottom half when Josh Bard singled to center field, scoring Kevin Kouzmanoff, tying it at one. Eight innings later, Tulowitzki put the Rockies ahead to stay. In all, it was the longest game since Minnesota beat Cleveland on August 31, 1993, at the Hubert H. Humphrey Metrodome—a game that also went 22 innings—and established new marks for longevity as of this writing in both Colorado Rockies history and the history of Petco Park.

JULY 13, 2013: LINCECUM DOMINANT, NO-HITS PADRES

Giants pitcher Tim Lincecum, who was the opposing pitcher only 11 days earlier when Homer Bailey of the Cincinnati Reds no-hit San Francisco at Great American Ball Park, turned in a no-hitter of his own, baffling the Padres during a spectacular 9–0 victory. Lincecum, who struck out 13 and walked four during a 148-pitch performance, received help from right fielder Hunter Pence in the eighth to preserve the gem. With two outs, San Diego outfielder Alexi Amarista connected for a shot that was sinking quickly, but it was Pence who saved the day by recording the out after going into a full dive. Pence also assisted offensively, finishing 2-for-4 and hitting a three-run triple in the top of the fifth, which put San Francisco comfortably ahead at the time, 7–0. It was a 1–2–3 ninth inning as Lincecum retired Chase Headley (strike out), Carlos Quentin (line out), and Yonder Alonso (fly out) with ease.

WHAT THEY'RE SAYING ABOUT PETCO PARK

STEVE BERTHIAUME, BROAD-CASTER: "I really like the area around it, which I think is important. They did a wonderful job with the Park at the Park beyond right field. . . . It is a pretty ballpark. You very much do get the sense of the heavy salt air around you all the time and you could see how that would stifle home run balls."

BOB BRENLY: "As the city has built up and the skyscrapers have been built up, you have a nice view now out over the outfield fence. When they initially built it, there was nothing out there and I often thought that you have the water behind you, the beautiful bridge going over the Coronado, why did they not turn it the other way? . . . But as the city has built up, it is starting to take on its own charm."

MATT CAIN: "Petco [Park] is beautiful. There is not really anything about that ballpark that is bad. . . . Everything is nice, it is a big field—the field is perfect—it is in a great location, and that is always a nice place to go to."

DICK ENBERG, BROADCASTER: "I think it is one of the charming ballparks . . . the little touches, including the Western Metal Supply Company as part of the left-field corner, the view of downtown San Diego being open through center field, and having a Park at the Park, where fans can come and actually picnic [are nice]. It is a delight to sit there and look out at the great city."

MATT KEMP: "That ballpark is good for us to play at because a lot of Dodgers fans come to the stadium in support since it is right down the street. . . . At night, it is tough to hit home runs because the air is pretty thick and the ballpark is pretty thick. It is not a ballpark I would like to play at every day."

DUANE KUIPER, BROADCASTER: "Petco Park's another really good one. . . . I do not think it is ever going to get a lot of credit for how good it is because the front of the ballpark really is not in an area where people are ever going to see the front because they all come in from the sides and back."

STEVE LYONS, BROADCASTER: "It does not get any play when people talk about the best ballparks in the game, and I think it probably gets a bad rap. . . . It is not a good offensive ballpark, so I think people may get tired of seeing 2–1 games."

DON MATTINGLY: "Petco [Park] is all right. I may be judging it from a different standpoint, but the dugouts are really small on the visitor's side. . . . It is such a big ballpark, but it is pretty and a little too big for me, kind of like it is unfair to right-center field in there. I would like to see it a little more reachable."

BUSTER POSEY: "Not a good hitter's ballpark, but for me, it has a good feel and I think it is a good atmosphere for fans to watch a game at."

BARRY ZITO: "I grew up in San Diego, so I am a big advocate of that ballpark. . . . They do not fill it up too often, but it is quite a yard."

PETCO PARK FACTS AND FIGURES

PETCO PARK ADDRESS
100 Park Boulevard, San Diego, CA 92101

SAN DIEGO PADRES TEAM WEB SITE
www.padres.com

FIELD DIMENSIONS (IN FEET)
Left Field: 336', Left-Center: 390', Center: 396', Right-Center: 391', Right Field: 322'

SEATING CAPACITY (AS OF 2015)
42,524

ALL-STAR GAMES AT PETCO PARK
None

PETCO PARK FIRSTS
Game: April 8, 2004—San Diego 4, San Francisco 3
Single: Brian Giles, San Diego (April 8, 2004)*
Double: Sean Burroughs, San Diego (April 8, 2004)
Triple: Brian Giles, San Diego (April 11, 2004)
Home Run: Marquis Grissom, San Francisco (April 8, 2004)

Denotes first hit in the stadium.

SAFECO FIELD
HOME OF THE SEATTLE MARINERS

Safeco Field, Seattle Mariners (*Photographed by Brian Skversky/Flickr*)

The year was 1995 and what transpired was an unbelievable comeback story for the Seattle Mariners. Having stood victorious in a one-game tiebreaker over California to determine who would be heading to the playoffs, they completed a remarkable turnaround that saw them come back and win the division after sitting 13 games out of first at the beginning of August.

But for one moment, let's change the course of history and pretend that it never happened. Let's say the Mariners continued at the pace they were on prior to their frantic finish and completed the season 10 games out of first. If that were the case, there might be no Safeco Field, no section in this book about it, and, more devastating, no Major League Baseball franchise in Seattle.

That one season made all the difference between funding a new ballpark and leaving town. The renewed sense of energy and excitement catapulted the franchise to new heights, and plans for a new stadium soon followed.

It wasn't an easy road, but the Mariners remained committed and pushed through, finally receiving the funds necessary to accomplish what they were hoping to do with Safeco Field.

On March 30, 1994, King County executive Gary Locke got things rolling in the right direction by appointing a 28-member task force to research the cost, need, and potential location for a new ballpark. A vote by the public on September 9, 1995, narrowly defeated a proposal to increase the sales tax by .01 percent in King County, which would have helped pay for the construction of Safeco Field. However, the Mariners franchise was not to be denied, so it was on to Plan B.

On October 14, 1995, there was a special session among Washington state legislators, and they outlined an alternate means of funding the ballpark. A King County food and beverage tax in restaurants and bars, along with a car rental surcharge, were among the sources of funding. Nine days later, the proposal was accepted by the King County Council, ending all doubts about the Mariners franchise bolting for a new city.

The ballpark location was later selected on September 9, 1996, and on March 8, 1997, a crowd of 30,000 turned out to watch fan-favorite and Mariners legend Ken Griffey Jr. officially break ground.

For the Mariners, securing the new ballpark and staying in Seattle were perhaps the biggest victories in franchise history. The success of the 1995 team catapulted the Mariners into the spotlight, providing the necessary attention it needed to stay put in the Emerald City for many years to come.

A slight alteration was made following the 2012 season, when the Mariners went to work to make Safeco Field a more hitter-friendly venue. The hand-operated scoreboard was moved, allowing for the outfield wall to to be raised to eight feet. The wall was also moved forward four feet from the left-field corner to the left-field power alley, the distance of the left-field power alley decreased from 390 to 378, left-center to straightaway center was moved in, and the distance from the right-field power alley was altered from 385 feet to 381 feet. The Mariners followed a trend that Detroit used at Comerica Park in 2005 and that the Mets employed at Citi Field in 2010 in the hopes of increasing offensive numbers in otherwise offense-lacking ballparks.

SPECIAL FEATURES OF SAFECO FIELD

ALL-STAR CLUB

A private cash bar and all-inclusive buffet are available in the attractive All-Star Club, a premium seating option on the suite deck alongside the first-base line. This lavish lounge can accommodate up to 140 and is available in package increments of 10, 20, 40, or for an entire 81-game season. Other perks included are parking in the Safeco Field garage and assigned seating.

ARTWORK

Different kinds of artwork have been integrated into the overall landscape of the ballpark and nearby parking garages, celebrating America's pastime. Some of the items include an oversized bronze mitt outside the left-field gate and an awe-inspiring chandelier of 1,000 transparent, regulation-size baseball bats hung high above the majestic staircase by the home plate gate.

BASEBALL MUSEUM OF THE PACIFIC NORTHWEST

Located on the main concourse along the third-base line is the Baseball Museum of the Pacific Northwest, which is open to all fans free of charge and offers a unique look at the history of the franchise. The museum, which opened in 2007, delves into the annals of the game in the Pacific Northwest, while covering America's pastime from the 1880s to the current era. This area is also the official home of the Seattle Mariners Hall of Fame, which honors great players, broadcasters, and moments in franchise history.

CHAMPIONSHIP BANNERS

In the right field are championship banners commemorating the American League Western Division, along with a special one that pays tribute to the 2001 ballclub, which won a Major League–record 116 games. That one-of-a-kind team stormed through the regular season with a final mark of 116–46, but faltered against the Yankees in the American League Championship Series, four games to one.

CHILDREN'S PLAYFIELD

A baseball-themed playground on the main concourse level situated in center field gives the little ones the opportunity to run around and use up their pent-up energy before the first pitch is thrown. Once they finish, a kid-friendly concession stand awaits, complete with peanut-butter-and-jelly sandwiches, small hot dogs, and other ballpark munchies.

DAVE NIEHAUS BROADCAST CENTER

The press box, on the club level behind home plate, was renamed after Dave Niehaus, who had broadcast a total of 5,284 Mariners games spanning 34 seasons. Prior to their home opener against the Cleveland Indians on April 8, 2011, the Mariners rededicated the structure to Niehaus and placed his headset and microphone by the seat he once occupied in the booth. Niehaus died of a heart attack prior to the 2011 season.

DAVE NIEHAUS STATUE

One of the most detailed bronze statues to ever be erected at a Major League ballpark is the statue of the Mariners' legendary announcer, Dave Niehaus. It was unveiled on the main concourse level in right-center field on September 16, 2011, and features Niehaus with his favorite blazer and tie, seated behind the broadcast desk with his microphone. Look closely: The actual scorecard from Game 5 of the 1995 Division Series on October 8, 1995, against the Yankees is there, and it looks as though he's all ready to score that famous hit by Edgar Martinez, which drove in the winning runs. An open seat next to the always-smiling Niehaus allows fans the opportunity to hop in for a photo-op with the Mariners' most lovable broadcaster. Nearby, railings at the back of the statue are hung with placards featuring some of his famous lines, including, "My oh my!" and "Fly away!"

FAN WALK

To raise funds for the Seattle Mariners Hall of Fame, the Washington State Major League Baseball Stadium Public Facilities District sold personalized bricks to fans. In total, 12,500 bricks were purchased and line the way to a fan attraction in left and center field, which has a bonfire pit.

LOOKOUT LANDING

Searching for an incredible view of the game along with picturesque views? Be sure to visit Lookout Landing at the end of the left-field line in the upper-deck section, where you can take breathtaking photos. In the distance are the popular Space Needle and Puget Sound.

This stunning picture of Safeco Field and the home of the NFL's Seahawks was taken from Dr. Jose Rizal Park on the west side of Beacon Hill. (*Photographed by Mark Whitt/Flickr*)

MAIN SCOREBOARD

Prior to the 2013 season, the Mariners installed a brand-new, 3,840-foot by 1,080-foot surface-mounted LED display in right-center field, replacing the previous 14-year-old version. With a surface area of 11,425 square feet, it qualifies, as of this writing, as the third largest in the United States behind Charlotte Motor Speedway (16,000) and Cowboys Stadium (11,520). In addition, 1,200 individual panels make up the screen display, outputting an incredible 4,147,200 pixels that give fans unprecedented video quality.

MEET THE MOOSE

For kids seeking a photo-op with the Mariners' official mascot, the Mariner Moose, they are in luck. The Moose Den is on the main concourse level at section 191 near the ever-popular Children's Hospital Playfield. At the den, kids can pose for pictures, meet the moose, exchange pleasantries, and ask him what it's like to be the official mascot of a Major League Baseball team.

NAMING RIGHTS

On June 4, 1998, the Mariners sold naming rights for their new ballpark when Seattle-based Safeco Corporation signed an agreement to become the sole sponsor for the ballpark's name at a price tag of $40 million. Safeco is an insurance company founded in Seattle that offers coverage on home, auto, and other insurance products.

OLD-FASHIONED SCOREBOARD

A manually operated scoreboard in left field, a throwback to the olden days and a subtle salute to Fenway Park, is part of the outfield fence and displays the box score of the current game on the field. Measuring six feet high, five feet wide, and 100 feet long, both the Mariners and visiting team logos are on each side of the display, with room for innings 1–9, and a blank spot at the end for any runs tallied in the extra innings. A yellow line on top shows whether a ball hit is a home run or not. After the 2012 season, the scoreboard was moved back to allow for the outfield wall to maintain an eight-foot height.

OUT-OF-TOWN SCOREBOARD

New in 2010, a colorful out-of-town scoreboard located over both bullpens in left-center field showcases other games around the league, giving the current score, runners on base, and what the count is. It also displays information for pitchers warming up, a condensed box score for a selected game, and other information pertinent to the game. NBA, NFL, and NHL scores are also shown when any of those seasons happen to overlap the baseball campaign.

PLAYING FIELD

Designed with the Northwest climate and stadium roof in mind, a blend of Kentucky bluegrass and perennial ryegrass provides a durable playing surface. One advantage of the grass is that the roof can be closed for up to six consecutive days without the grass dying or turning brown.

RETIRED NUMBERS

Other than Jackie Robinson's number 42, which was retired by baseball universally on April 15, 1997, as of this writing the Seattle Mariners have no retired uniform numbers.

RETRACTABLE ROOF

In baseball and as of this writing, Houston, Milwaukee, Seattle, and Miami are the only franchises that have retractable-roof ballparks in the Major Leagues. At Safeco Field, the roof covers but does not enclose the field and seating area completely, in order to preserve the overall feel of the great outdoors. The roof weighs an incredible 22 million pounds, which, according to the Mariners Media Guide, is enough steel to build a 55-story skyscraper.

In all, 128 steel wheels, powered by 96 10-horsepower electric motors, glide along, opening and closing the roof in 10–20 minutes. Rain may be a constant in Seattle, but fans purchasing a ticket can rest assured that no matter what happens with Mother Nature, a baseball game will always be played. On April 18, 2001, Ryan Raburn of the Detroit Tigers became the first batter to hit any part of the roof with a batted ball when he struck one of the trusses with a foul pop-up.

RIGHT-FIELD CAFÉ

There are three levels of tiered seating in this right-field section, better known as the Hit It Here Café, which is located on the same level as the terrace club. With the exception of season-ticket holders who can make reservations well before game time, tickets are sold on a first-come, first-served basis. Full-service dining, including sandwiches, salads, and other concession favorites, can be purchased, while televisions keep fans updated on all the action.

SEATTLE MARINERS HALL OF FAME

The Seattle Mariners Hall of Fame opened in 2007 and is in the Baseball Museum of the Pacific Northwest. Artifacts, pictures, and other baseball memorabilia pay tribute to teams of the past, including the Seattle Pilots and their previous home, the Kingdome.

THE 'PEN

Described by the Mariners as an "event within an event," The 'Pen (formerly known as The Bullpen Market) offers fans the chance to enjoy their time at Safeco Field both before and after a Mariners game. Situated behind left and center field are a cozy fire pit and premium concessions.

TRAIN IN THE DISTANCE

Throughout the course of a contest, five trains pass by Safeco Field behind the right-field area. Fans are notified of the trains' presence courtesy of the conductor, who sounds two long whistles, followed by a short whistle and then another extended whistle as it passes through the intersection. All aboard!

WISHING WELL

A wishing well, a small-scale version of the General Motors fountain at Comerica Park in Detroit, is a water display that comes to life following a Mariners home run. When a blast off the bat becomes official, a column of water spurts up to honor the long ball. Fans can toss in loose change, and all of the proceeds fished out of the bottom are donated to the Seattle Children's Hospital to support patient care.

MEMORABLE GAMES AT SAFECO FIELD

JULY 15, 1999: FIRST GAME AT SAFECO FIELD

With 47,000 on hand to view the first outdoor game in Seattle, the San Diego Padres spoiled the fun with a 3–2 victory behind a bases-loaded walk and sacrifice fly at the top of the ninth inning. With San Diego ahead 1–0 going into the bottom of the eighth, the Mariners' bats came to life as David Bell and David Segui promptly hit back-to-back RBI doubles to give the Mariners a 2–1 advantage heading to the ninth. Closer extraordinaire Jose Mesa on the mound issued three straight walks, loading the bases with nobody out but came back to strike out Dave Magadan. He then walked his fourth batter of the inning, Quilvio Veras, and the tying run was forced home. One batter later, Eric Owens hit a sacrifice fly that proved to be the difference as the Mariners went down 1–2–3 in the bottom of the ninth.

AUGUST 1, 2000: LONGEST GAME IN MARINERS HISTORY

It took five hours, 34 minutes, and 19 innings to play, but in the end, the Mariners were the last team standing in a 5–4 win over the Boston Red Sox. The scoring kicked off in the top of the third, when Boston took an early

4–0 lead on a two-run homer by Darren Lewis and RBI singles by Jason Varitek and Troy O'Leary. Seattle struck for two runs off Red Sox starter Tim Wakefield in the bottom of the fifth, fueled by a solo blast by Stan Javier and a sacrifice fly by Dan Wilson that cut the lead in half at 4–2. In the bottom of the sixth, the Mariners offense picked up where they left off, adding two and tying the game at four, thanks to an RBI groundout by John Olerud and RBI single by Javier. Little would anyone realize the next scoring play would occur 13 innings later when, in the bottom of the nineteenth, Mike Cameron would lead off the inning and hit a 2–2 pitch over the fence, ending the marathon affair, which concluded well after 3 A.M. on the East Coast.

OCTOBER 14, 2000: CLEMENS DOMINATES MARINERS IN CHAMPIONSHIP SERIES

New York starting pitcher Roger Clemens overwhelmed the Seattle Mariners, striking out 15 and allowing one hit during a complete game shutout as the Yankees stood victorious, 5–0, in Game 4 of the American League Championship Series. Clemens took a no-hitter into the seventh inning before allowing a leadoff double to Al Martin, whose hard hit bounced off the glove of first baseman Tino Martinez. The Yankees offense was powered by Derek Jeter's three-run blast off Seattle starter Paul Abbott, and a two-run home run by David Justice off relief pitcher Jose Mesa. New York would go on to win the American League pennant in six games, and eventually win the World Series for the third time in a row and twenty-sixth overall when they beat the crosstown rival Mets, four games to one.

OCTOBER 5, 2001: MARINERS SET AMERICAN LEAGUE WIN MARK

In a season filled with memorable moments and career years for most players on the team, the Mariners added another accomplishment by defeating the Texas Rangers, 6–2. But it wasn't just any win; it was victory number 115, breaking the American League mark of 114 set by the Yankees in their championship-winning season of 1998. In the contest, Jamie Moyer became the oldest pitcher to record 20 wins in a season, and Mark McLemore tripled twice and scored three times to help lead Seattle. McLemore became the first Mariners player to hit two triples in a contest since Joey Cora did so on June 28, 1996. Needing two wins to set the Major League record for victories, they recorded a victory in one of their last two games, which was good enough to tie the 1906 Chicago Cubs, who finished with 116 victories that season.

OCTOBER 1, 2004: ICHIRO AT IT AGAIN

A model of consistency at the plate since he broke into the Major Leagues in 2001, Ichiro Suzuki established a new single-season hits record when he collected his 258th hit, breaking the record once held by George Sisler, who did so in 1920, during Seattle's 8–3 win over Texas. Needing two hits to establish the new mark, Suzuki wasted no time leading off the first with a single over a drawn-in infield. He returned in the third inning and, with the crowd on their feet and a full count, he singled up the middle, setting off a wild celebration at Safeco Field, which included fireworks and congratulations from members of Sisler's family, who were in attendance. The Mariners' offense was powered by a seven-hit, six-run third, which ultimately put the game out of reach.

JULY 15, 2005: PALMEIRO NOTCHES HIT NUMBER 3,000

With a double in the fifth inning against Mariners starting pitcher Joel Pineiro, Rafael Palmeiro etched his name in the record books by becoming the fourth player in Major League Baseball history to notch 500 home runs and 3,000 hits, joining Hank Aaron, Willie Mays, and former Oriole Eddie Murray. Following the milestone, Safeco Field fans gave him a standing ovation for joining one of baseball's most elite clubs. He later singled, passing Roberto Clemente on the all-time list, and ultimately finished 2-for-4 in the game as the Orioles defeated the Mariners, 6–3. He became the first player to notch his 3,000th hit since Rickey Henderson did so for the San Diego Padres on October 7, 2001.

SEPTEMBER 13, 2011: RIVERA NOTCHES 600TH SAVE

It was business as usual for a man who has made it look easy throughout the course of his career as a closer. Mariano Rivera clinched his 600th save when he took the mound to close out a 3–2 New York win over the Seattle Mariners in front of a pro-Yankees crowd of 18,306. In a season that also saw Derek Jeter collect his 3,000th hit, Rivera joined Trevor Hoffman as the only two men to eclipse the 600-save plateau in Major League Baseball history. In the bottom of the ninth, Willy Mo Pena led off and did his best to get something started for the Mariners, falling victim to the strikeout. Ichiro singled, and the Yankees turned in a strike 'em out of Kyle Seager and throw 'em out of Ichiro, who attempted to steal second for a game-ending double play.

APRIL 21, 2012: HUMBER PERFECT AGAINST MARINERS

White Sox pitcher Philip Humber, who was relatively unknown until this game, completed the twenty-first perfect game in baseball history, striking out nine and keeping Seattle off-balance all day during a 4–0 Chicago victory. In the ninth, Humber looked as though he might lose his bid for perfection after throwing three straight balls to Michael Saunders leading off the frame, but came back with a vengeance to strike him out. John Jaso hit a fly ball out for the second out, and pinch hitter Brendan Ryan took a check swing on a full-count pitch that was low—the umpire ruled it a strikeout—but when the ball got away from catcher A. J. Pierzynski, he made a throw down to first just in case.

Paul Konerko supplied the early offense for Chicago, blasting a solo home run in the second and an RBI single in the third; Pierzynski added an RBI single in the third, and Alejandro De Aza gave the White Sox insurance with an RBI single of his own in the ninth. Humber, who came into the contest having started only 29 games and 11 wins under his belt, became the third White Sox pitcher to register a perfect game, joining Mark Buehrle (July 23, 2009, versus Tampa Bay), and Charles Robertson (April 30, 1922, versus Detroit).

> "Once it got to the ninth inning, [I] was just really trying to appreciate the moment and hoping that it would happen. . . . When it did, [I] was just blown away—just an awesome time—and I will never forget Safeco Field because of that."
> —*Philip Humber*

> "When he struck out Brendan Ryan on that 3–2 breaking ball, I was just ecstatic for him."
> —*Ken "Hawk" Harrelson, White Sox broadcaster*

JUNE 8, 2012: A SIX-PACK OF MARINERS NO-HITS DODGERS

It might have taken six Seattle Mariners pitchers, but the end result was a combined no-hitter during a 1–0 Interleague victory over the visiting Los Angeles Dodgers. Kevin Millwood started for Seattle and went six innings before departing due to a strained right groin. From there, the Mariners paraded out Charlie Furbush, Stephen Pryor, Lucas Luetge, Brandon League, and Tom Wilhelmsen, who finished off the third no-hitter in Mariners history, and the first in baseball history to feature six pitchers since Houston defeated the Yankees on June 11, 2003. The only run of the game came courtesy of Kyle Seager, who laced an RBI single in the bottom of the seventh, bringing home Ichiro Suzuki. In all, the pitchers combined for six strikeouts, three walks, and 114 pitches.

AUGUST 15, 2012: KING FELIX STANDS TALL

Seattle ace Felix Hernandez continued Tampa Bay's misery with no-hitters, facing 27 batters and striking out 12 en route to the twenty-third perfect game in baseball history and a 1–0 victory. The 2010 American League Cy Young Award winner was never really in any trouble of giving up a hit and got better as the game went on, proving that notion by striking out the side emphatically in the eighth inning. The only offense necessary was an RBI single by Jesus Montero in the bottom of the third inning, plating Brendan Ryan for the only run of the game. For Tampa Bay, it was the fourth no-hitter pitched against them in franchise history—and the third perfect game.

JUNE 5, 2013: WILD 16-INNING AFFAIR GOES WAY OF THE WHITE SOX

After 13 scoreless innings, a wild fourteenth inning, and five hours, 42 minutes of baseball totaling 16 innings, the White Sox finally outlasted the pesky Mariners, 7–5. It looked as though Chicago would take the victory after scoring five runs in the top of the fourteenth, highlighted by an RBI double that scored two runs off the bat of Hector Gimenez; but it's what the Mariners did in the bottom half that proves baseball is unpredictable.

After an RBI single by Endy Chavez cut the deficit to 5–1, the bases were loaded with two outs for Kyle Seager. Down to his last strike, Seager connected for a 406-foot grand slam, tying the game and becoming the first player in Major League history to hit a game-tying, four-run blast in extra innings. In the sixteenth, Chicago plated two—courtesy of RBI singles from Alejandro De Aza and Alex Rios—and White Sox reliever Addison Reed struck out the side in the bottom half, ending the marathon. It became the first game in big league history in which both teams scored five runs or more after going scoreless through nine.

WHAT THEY'RE SAYING ABOUT SAFECO FIELD

JASON GIAMBI: "It is a beautiful ballpark. They do a nice job, but the only tough part is [that] sometimes you get those cold games.... [The retractable roof] keeps the rain off of you, but not the cold."

RAUL IBANEZ: "I think I am biased to some of the ballparks I have played in, but I really like playing at Safeco Field.... It has got a great feel—just the whole vibe of the city, the ballpark, the colors of the stadium, good atmosphere. The fans get fired up, and it is just a beautiful ballpark."

DUANE KUIPER, BROADCASTER: "I think of the potential out of the ballparks you can close the roof [at], I think Seattle is the very best one mainly because you are never, ever totally inside. . . . When they pull the roof over top of the stadium, it is still open around the sides so you get the fresh air and I think that is really, really important."

JOSH LEWIN, BROADCASTER: "Safeco Field is fantastic. You can see the mountain off in the distance, which is really cool, [and] it is very easy to walk around."

JAMIE MOYER: "As far as clubhouses go, [it is] very accommodating. The mound is one of my favorite mounds to throw off of, and I like the retractable roof."

BRANDON PHILLIPS: "I think [Safeco Field] is the best field. . . . The retractable roof, the atmosphere itself—there is just something about that field that is just amazing and the way it is set up."

A. J. PIERZYNSKI: "You know, I have always loved Seattle. . . . [It] just has a good feel, good sight lines, it has a good atmosphere to go to whether the roof is open or closed, and it just feels like you are in a good spot."

RICK RIZZS, BROADCASTER: "I think they really got it right when they built Safeco Field. Before they put a shovel in the ground, they went to every ballpark in Major League Baseball—the new ones, the old ones, and all the ballparks in between—to find out what was right for the fans and players. . . . On so many levels, it is so functional and great for the fans and players."

JOHN STERLING, BROADCASTER: "The best overall for every reason is Safeco [Field] in Seattle. . . . First of all, it is a retractable dome and the late [Mariners broadcaster] Dave Niehaus said, 'We have spent an enormous amount of money and it is worth it.' It is almost in many ways a perfect ballpark."

BARRY ZITO: "Early in my career, we would just have so many great battles and wild-card runs and American League West runs with Seattle. . . . They always had a packed house and had incredible teams back then, so just the whole vibe, [plus] Seattle itself is a great town. That ballpark is pretty special."

SAFECO FIELD FACTS AND FIGURES

SAFECO FIELD ADDRESS
1250 First Avenue South, Seattle, WA 98104

SEATTLE MARINERS TEAM WEB SITE
www.seattlemariners.com

FIELD DIMENSIONS (IN FEET)
Left Field: 331', Left-Center: 378', Center: 401',
Right-Center: 381', Right Field: 326'

SEATING CAPACITY (AS OF 2015)
47,476

ALL-STAR GAMES AT SAFECO FIELD
July 10, 2001: American League 4, National League 1
MVP: Cal Ripken Jr., Baltimore Orioles (AL)

SAFECO FIELD FIRSTS
Game: July 15, 1999—San Diego 3, Seattle 2
Single: Eric Owens, San Diego (July 15, 1999)*
Double: David Bell, Seattle (July 15, 1999)
Triple: Tom Lampkin, Seattle (July 17, 1999)
Home Run: Russ Davis, Seattle (July 17, 1999)

*Denotes first hit in the stadium.

CONCLUSION

I hope you gained a wealth of knowledge about each ballpark that you might not have known before. If you have the time—and the money—I encourage you to take a road trip and explore these stunning ballparks.

While at the game, buy yourself some peanuts and Cracker Jacks and be sure to take in all the sights and sounds that only a Major League ballpark can provide. Above all, make lasting memories with family, friends, and loved ones at the greatest game in the world: America's pastime, baseball.

BIBLIOGRAPHY

ONLINE ARTICLES

Albanese, Laura. "Home Run Apple a Core Value for Mets Fans." *Newsday—the Long Island and New York City Source News,* March 26, 2010.

"Angel Stadium History—Information." *The Official Site of the Los Angeles Angels,* June 6, 2011. http://losangeles.angels.mlb.com.

"AT&T Park Information—A-to-Z Guide." *The Official Site of the San Francisco Giants,* June 6, 2011. http://sanfrancisco.giants.mlb.com.

Bagli, Charles V. "Bloomberg Says Details on Stadiums Were Omitted." *The New York Times—Breaking News, World News & Multimedia,* January 16, 2002.

———. "Yankees Propose New Stadium, and Would Pay." *The New York Times—Breaking News, World News & Multimedia,* July 30, 2004.

"Ballpark Information—A-to-Z Guide." *The Official Site of the Cincinnati Reds,* June 6, 2011. http://cincinnati.reds.mlb.com.

Barry, Dan. "Mayor Making Case for Yanks on West Side." *The New York Times—Breaking News, World News & Multimedia,* April 20, 1998.

Belko, Mark. "Bud-Branded Lounge Set for PNC Park." *Pittsburgh Post-Gazette,* January 31, 2012.

Boatwright, Josh. "Rays Unveil Tropicana Field Upgrades, Vow Better Fan Experience." *The Tampa Tribune,* December 4, 2013.

"Bonus Season for Baseball." *New York Times,* January 17, 2002.

"Brewers Unveil Plaque to Memorialize the Final Home Run of Hank Aaron's Career, #755." *The Official Site of the Milwaukee Brewers,* June 7, 2007.

Brown, David. "Albert Breaks Busch's 'Big Mac' Sign with Mammoth Home Run." *Big League Stew,* May 21, 2009.

———. "Knuckleballer R. A. Dickey Throws Second Straight One-Hitter, Strikes Out 13." *Big League Stew,* June 19, 2012.

"Busch Stadium Information—A-to-Z Guide." *The Official Site of the St. Louis Cardinals,* June 6, 2011. http://stlouis.cardinals.mlb.com.

"Cards to Celebrate Stan Musial Day on Sunday." *The Cardinal Nation.com,* May 17, 2008. http://stlcardinals.scout.com/2/755519.html.

"Chase Field Information—Chase Field History." *The Official Site of the Arizona Diamondbacks,* June 6, 2011. http://arizona.diamondbacks.mlb.com.

"Citizens Bank Park, Home of the Phillies, Goes High Definition!" *The Official Site of the Philadelphia Phillies,* January 19, 2011.

"Citizens Bank Park Information—Fun Features." *The Official Site of the Philadelphia Phillies,* June 6, 2011. http://philadelphia.phillies.mlb.com.

"Clemens Fans a Record 20." *The Boston Globe,* April 30, 1986.

Coffey, Wayne. "Babe Ruth, Other Monuments Settle in New Yankee Stadium Home." *New York Daily News,* February 25, 2009.

"Coliseum Information—A-to-Z Guide." *The Official Site of the Oakland Athletics,* June 6, 2011. http://oakland.athletics.mlb.com.

Collins, Glenn. "For Mets Fans, a Menu Beyond Peanuts and Cracker Jack." *The New York Times,* March 24, 2009.

"Comerica Park Information—Ballpark Attractions." *The Official Site of the Detroit Tigers,* June 6, 2011. http://detroit.tigers.mlb.com.

Cook, Mike. "Target Field Gets LEED Certification." *The Official Site of the Minnesota Twins,* April 8, 2010.

"Coors Field Information—A-to-Z Guide." *The Official Site of the Colorado Rockies,* June 6, 2011. http://colorado.rockies.mlb.com.

"Fenway Park Information—Milestones." *The Official Site of the Boston Red Sox,* June 6, 2011. http://boston.redsox.mlb.com.

Fernandez, Yolanda. "St. Petersburg's Tropicana Field Will Get $1.3 Million in Improvements." *Wfla.com,* November 25, 2013. www.wfla.com.

Finch, Justin. "Marlins Sod New Ballpark with Bermuda Grass." *NBC 6 Miami,* February 2, 2012.

Flynn, Julie. "Little Tribe Fans Have a New Place to Play at Progressive Field." *Newsnet5 Cleveland,* May 2, 2012.

Gagne, Matt. "Padres' Jody Gerut Opens Citi Field with a Bang, Homering on Third Pitch." *New York Daily News,* April 14, 2009.

Gonzalez, Alden. "Halos Move Press Box for New Fan Seating Opportunity." *Angels Baseball,* January 16, 2013.

Greenberg, Chris. "Mets Pitcher Throws First No-Hit Game in Franchise History." *The Huffington Post,* June 1, 2012.

Herrmann, Mark. "A Tale of Two New Ballparks." *Newsday,* July 13, 2009.

"High-Performance Celebration Bermuda Grass." *Bethel Farms,* n.d.

Hoffarth, Tom. "A Southern California Guide to Fenway Park." *Los Angeles Daily News,* August 5, 2008.

Johns, Greg. "New Dimensions Make Safeco More Hitter Friendly." *MLB.com,* October 2, 2012.

"Kauffman Stadium—More Kauffman Stadium Information." *The Official Site of the Kansas City Royals,* June 6, 2011. http://kansascity.royals.mlb.com.

Klemish, Dawn, and MLB.com. "Gonzalez Homers, but Dodgers Sink." *The Official Site of the Los Angeles Dodgers,* June 24, 2007.

Lay, Travis. "Other Fun Things to Do at Coors Field." *Examiner.com,* March 31, 2009.

Levy, Paul. "No Vikings Stadium Bill Now, but Next Year, Maybe?" *Star Tribune,* August 22, 2011.

"Mariners Combine for Six-Man No-Hitter." *Fox News,* June 9, 2012.

"Marlins New Ballpark Highlights." *The Official Site of the Florida Marlins,* June 6, 2011. http://florida.marlins.mlb.com.

"Marlins Park Will Be Ready If TS Isaac Visits." *Sports Business News,* August 24, 2012.

"Miller Park Information—A-to-Z Guide." *The Official Site of the Milwaukee Brewers,* June 6, 2011. http://milwaukee.brewers.mlb.com.

"Minute Maid Park Information—A-to-Z Guide." *The Official Site of the Houston Astros,* June 6, 2011. http://houston.astros.mlb.com.

"Nationals Park Information—Facts & Figures." *The Official Site of the Washington Nationals,* June 6, 2011. http://washington.nationals.mlb.com.

"NetSuite Diamond Level Seats." *The Official Site of the Oakland Athletics,* June 6, 2011. http://oakland.athletics.mlb.com.

"The New Stadium." *New York Daily News,* March 2009.

"ORACLE Arena & O.co Coliseum." *Special Event Rental.* http://coliseum.com/info.

"Oriole Park at Camden Yards Information—History." *The Official Site of the Baltimore Orioles,* June 6, 2011. http://baltimore.orioles.mlb.com.

"Orioles Legends Celebration Series." *Orioles Press Release,* April 26, 2012.

Palermo, Philip. "Visualized: Seattle Mariners Unveil 'Largest Screen in Major League Baseball.'" *Engadget,* April 3, 2013.

"Phillies Wall of Fame." *The Official Site of the Philadelphia Phillies,* June 6, 2011.

"PNC Park Information—Overview." *The Official Site of the Pittsburgh Pirates,* June 6, 2011. http://pittsburgh.pirates.mlb.com.

Price, Bill. "Pepsi Porch Great for Mets Fans, but Maybe Not Ryan Church." *New York Daily News,* April 12, 2009.

"Rangers Ballpark in Arlington Information—A-to-Z Guide." *The Official Site of the Texas Rangers,* June 6, 2011. http://texas.rangers.mlb.com.

"Red Sox Break Record for Consecutive Sellouts." *Sports Top Stories—Z100—New York's Hit Music Station,* September 8, 2008. www.SportsNetwork.com.

Rogers, Phil. "Ballpark Village Rising into View at Busch Stadium." *Cardinals.com,* October 11, 2013. www.cardinals.com.

"Rogers Centre History." *The Official Site of the Toronto Blue Jays,* June 6, 2011. http://toronto.bluejays.mlb.com.

"Safeco Field Information—History." *The Official Site of the Seattle Mariners,* June 6, 2011. http://seattle.mariners.mlb.com.

Sandomir, Richard. "At Close of Games, Braves Will Move into Olympic Stadium." *New York Times,* July 30, 1996.

———. "A Distinctive Facade Is Recreated at New Yankee Stadium." *New York Times,* April 14, 2009.

Shaughnessy, Dan. "A Baseball Showcase in Football Land." *The Boston Globe,* October 25, 2005.

Shea, Bill. "Detroit Tigers Installing Scoreboard—4th Largest in Baseball—at Comerica Park." *Crain's Detroit Business,* February 17, 2012.

Sports Reference LLC. Baseball-Reference.com—Major League Statistics and Information. December 5, 2011. http://www.baseball-reference.com/.

"St. Louis Cardinals Energize Busch Stadium with Solar Power." *Microgrid Solar,* April 16, 2012.

"Target Field Information—A-to-Z Guide." *The Official Site of the Minnesota Twins,* June 6, 2011. http://minnesota.twins.mlb.com.

"Tropicana Field Information—Tropicana Field Facts." *The Official Site of the Tampa Bay Rays,* June 6, 2011. http://tampabay.rays.mlb.com.

Tucker, Heather. "Felix Hernandez Pitches Perfect Game." *USA Today,* August 15, 2012.

"Turner Field Information—History." *The Official Site of the Atlanta Braves,* June 6, 2011. http://atlanta.braves.mlb.com.

"Two MN Companies Keep Baseball Tradition Alive." *KEYC-TV News,* January 20, 2009.

Waldstein, David. "Mets Hopes Dashed in Blink of an Eye." *New York Times,* August 23, 2009.

"Worthy of a Post: the Miami Marlins' Bobblehead Museum." *Cards 'N Stuff,* April 6, 2012.

"Wrigley Field Information—History." *The Official Site of the Chicago Cubs,* June 6, 2011. http://chicago.cubs.mlb.com.

"Wrigley Field's $500 Million Facelift Approved." *USA Today,* April 15, 2013.

"Yankee Stadium Information—A-to-Z Guide." *The Official Site of the New York Yankees,* June 6, 2011. http://newyork.yankees.mlb.com.

TEAM MEDIA GUIDES

Angels Information Guide. Anaheim, CA: Los Angeles Angels Media Relations Department, 2013.

Chicago White Sox Media Guide. Chicago, IL: White Sox Media Relations Department, 2013.

Indians Information & Record Book. Cleveland, OH: Cleveland Indians Media Relations Department, 2013.

Los Angeles Dodgers Guide. Los Angeles, CA: Los Angeles Dodgers, Inc., 2013.

Mariners 2011 Information Guide. Seattle, WA: Seattle Mariners Media Relations Department, 2013.

Miami Marlins Media Guide. Miami, FL: Miami Marlins, LP, 2013.

New York Mets Media Guide. Flushing, NY: Mets Media Relations Department, 2013.

Oakland Athletics Media Guide. Oakland, CA: Oakland Athletics Media Relations Department, 2013.

Orioles Media Guide. Baltimore, MD: Baltimore Orioles, LP, 2013.

Pittsburgh Pirates Media Guide. Pittsburgh, PA: Pittsburgh Pirates Media Relations Department, 2013.

Record and Information Book. Minneapolis, MN: Minnesota Twins Media Relations Department, 2013.

San Diego Padres Media Guide. San Diego, CA: San Diego Padres Media Relations Department, 2013.

Tigers Information Guide. Detroit, MI: Detroit Tigers Baseball Media Relations Department, 2013.

Toronto Blue Jays Media Guide. Toronto, ON: Toronto Blue Jays Media Relations Department, 2013.

TEAM YEARBOOKS

Baltimore Orioles Yearbook. Baltimore, MD: Baltimore Orioles, 2011.

Chicago White Sox Yearbook. New York, NY: Professional Sports Publications, 2011.

Los Angeles Dodgers Yearbook. New York, NY: Professional Sports Publications, 2011.

New York Mets Yearbook. New York, NY: Professional Sports Publications, 2011.

Official Minnesota Twins Team Yearbook. New York, NY: Professional Sports Publications, 2011.

The Official Yearbook of the Washington Nationals. New York, NY: Professional Sports Publications, 2011.

San Diego Padres Yearbook. New York, NY: Professional Sports Publications, 2011.